THE PRINCETON GUIDE TO
HISTORICAL RESEARCH

Skills for Scholars

The Princeton Guide to Historical Research

Zachary M. Schrag

PRINCETON UNIVERSITY PRESS

PRINCETON & OXFORD

p56 start

Published by Princeton University Press
41 William Street, Princeton, New Jersey 08540
6 Oxford Street, Woodstock, Oxfordshire OX20 1TR

press.princeton.edu

Library of Congress Cataloging-in-Publication Data

Names: Schrag, Zachary M., author.
Title: The Princeton guide to historical research / Zachary M. Schrag.
Description: Princeton : Princeton University Press, 2021. | Series: Skills for scholars | Includes bibliographical references and index.
Identifiers: LCCN 2020049221 (print) | LCCN 2020049222 (ebook) | ISBN 9780691210964 (hardback) | ISBN 9780691198224 (paperback) | ISBN 9780691215488 (ebook)
Subjects: LCSH: History—Research.
Classification: LCC D16 .S345 2021 (print) | LCC D16 (ebook) | DDC 907.2—dc23
LC record available at https://lccn.loc.gov/2020049221
LC ebook record available at https://lccn.loc.gov/2020049222

British Library Cataloging-in-Publication Data is available

Editorial: Peter Dougherty and Alena Chekanov
Production Editorial: Natalie Baan
Cover Design: Matt Avery (Monograph LLC)
Production: Erin Suydam
Publicity: Kathryn Stevens
Copyeditor: Cathryn Slovensky

This book has been composed in Miller

Printed on acid-free paper. ∞

Printed in the United States of America

10 9 8 7 6 5 4 3 2 1

For my teachers and my students

CONTENTS

THE PRINCETON GUIDE TO
HISTORICAL RESEARCH

History Is for Everyone

Historical research has been for me an arena of joy and intellectual
passion. I always feel a shiver of anticipation when I enter an archive or a
rare book collection: what am I going to find?

—NATALIE ZEMON DAVIS, *A PASSION FOR HISTORY*

IN 2004, Afua Cooper walked the streets of Old Montreal, seeking the ghost of Marie-Joseph Angélique. Two hundred and seventy years earlier, Angélique—an enslaved woman—had been tortured and executed for setting a fire that burned much of the city. By telling Angélique's story, Cooper believed, she could tell a story about Atlantic slavery, about Canada's place in the Atlantic world, about "an experience of woe and sorrow." "Since much of the Black past has been deliberately buried, covered over, and demolished," Cooper writes, "it is our task to unearth, uncover, and piece it together again. This we are called to do because the dead speak to us."[1] Not all history has been so deliberately buried, covered over, and demolished. Not all historical figures are silent ghosts. But, like Cooper, all historians believe they are called to unearth, uncover, and piece together a lost past. We remember what must not be forgotten. We tell the stories that must be told.

These stories matter. Ten years before Cooper's walk, Roy Rosenzweig and David Thelen directed a telephone survey that

1. Afua Cooper, *The Hanging of Angélique: The Untold Story of Canadian Slavery and the Burning of Old Montréal* (Athens: University of Georgia Press, 2007), 9, 11.

asked fifteen hundred Americans how they engaged with the past. While a distressingly high proportion of respondents complained that their history classes in school had been boring, and that they rarely read history books, a majority reported some kind of enthusiastic exploration of history, through visits to museums, participation in hobbies, or, most of all, through the sharing of stories with family members. "Using the past is as natural a part of life as eating or breathing," Thelen concluded. "What we have in common as human beings is that we employ the past to make sense of the present and to influence the future."[2] "History-making," insists Gerda Lerner, "is not a dispensable intellectual luxury; history-making is a social necessity."[3]

At National History Day competitions, students as young as sixth grade pose questions and share their findings. As they weave sources into stories, they engage in the same basic project as my colleagues in a university history department. Moreover, many of the contestants are perfectly capable of reading, understanding, and imitating some of the same works that I would assign to graduate students. Likewise, adults who do not think of themselves as historians take part in the great task. Over the years, I have worked with lawyers, architects, planners, engineers, ethicists, military officers, and other professionals, whether in the classroom, at conferences, or in oral history interviews. None has had any trouble understanding the goals of the historian or the importance of the work, and many have made significant contributions to the study of the past. Conversely, when I have worked with journalists, curators, public officials, and advocates to share some of my own findings in the form of newspaper stories, television documentaries, museum exhibits, or recommendations for public policy, I feel I have done pretty well at grasping their needs and making myself useful.

I hope, then, that this book will reach historians from middle school through doctoral study and beyond, as well as those who identify not as historians—anthropologists, economists, geographers,

2. Roy Rosenzweig and David Thelen, *The Presence of the Past: Popular Uses of History in American Life* (New York: Columbia University Press, 1998), 190.

3. Gerda Lerner, "The Necessity of History and the Professional Historian," *Journal of American History* 69 (1982): 10.

political scientists, policy makers, sociologists, journalists, and non-fiction writers—but who want to answer questions about the past.

One peril of any guide to research is that it will suggest that the process is more linear than it really is. Ski jumpers must perform their tasks in a set order: in-run, take-off, flight, and landing. If they deviate from this order, they have violated not only the rules of the sport but the laws of physics as well. Figure skaters, by contrast, get to choose the order in which they will perform the various spins and jumps on which they will be judged. Writing history is more like figure skating in this regard; so long as you eventually perform all the tasks, the order is relatively unimportant. (In point of fact, figure skaters get bonuses for moves performed later in their program. Please ignore this complication for the purpose of simile.)

In this book I have tried to present the skills of the historian in what strikes me as a plausible order. In practice, you should expect to deploy these skills as needed, jumping back and forth, repeating some tasks and skipping others. As William McNeill once described his process, "I get curious about a problem and start reading up on it. What I read causes me to redefine the problem. Redefining the problem causes me to shift the direction of what I'm reading. That in turn further reshapes the problem, which further redirects the reading. I go back and forth like this until it feels right."[4]

Two researchers with similar goals may differ widely in the tools and methods that produce the best result. One may work for an hour each morning, write a first draft in longhand, and never pause to outline or count words until they have a substantial bit of work on paper. Another may set aside one day per week for intensive work, starting with an outline, typing every word, and obsessively tracking progress. Some historians do not begin to write until they have gathered all the sources they think they will need for a project, transcribed key passages, and composed a complete outline.[5] If that were the only way to write history, I would need to find another job.

---

4. Quoted in John Lewis Gaddis, *The Landscape of History: How Historians Map the Past* (New York: Oxford University Press, 2002), 48.

5. Hidetaka Hirota (@hidehirota), "How Are You Writing Your Dissertation? How Did You Write Yours? How Do You Write Your Books? This Is My Method (so Far). Note: I'm a Historian. #writing 1," Twitter, August 7, 2019, https://twitter.com/hidehirota/status/1159131324789116930.

Even the individual historian must use multiple methods at different stages in a project. Sometimes you need to read a source closely, teasing out each nuance. At other times, you need to use outside information to put the source in context, or assemble hundreds or thousands of sources in order to discern a pattern. And just because one method works for one project, it may not work for the next. A work based mostly on primary sources has a different rhythm from one based mostly on secondary sources, and perhaps it demands different tools as well. Similarly, some projects—and some researchers—can take advantage of the very latest in computer technology and digital resources, while others will do just fine using methods similar to those employed by scholars hundreds of years ago.

If a method works for you, it is not my place to challenge it. Rather, I hope in this book to document some of the methods that historians have used to pose and answer questions, to craft stories and arguments. Instead of telling you what to do, I hope to show you some options. Similarly, you should feel free to read the following chapters in whatever order makes the most sense to you. For example, reading the chapters on outlining and writing early may help you understand some of the chapters that precede them in the book. By learning the components of a finished work, you may have an easier time framing questions, identifying sources, and taking notes.

This book mixes recommendations (I hesitate to call them instructions) with model passages from historians, showing various techniques in practice. As both a learner and a teacher, I have found such combinations effective, and I hope my readers will as well. If nothing else, I hope the examples show that most of the guidance in this book is not a set of arbitrary rules that I have devised but rather a compilation of practices used by a wide range of historians across many genres and specialties. When judging the usefulness of my advice, do not take my word for it. Check the evidence I provide for its effectiveness.

In selecting examples, I have tried to suggest some of the range of topics studied by historians, but I have not done so systematically. Instead, I have started with works I know I like, most of them about the history of the United States. Of course, each field of history presents its own challenge, and a general-purpose guide like this is no substitute for mastering the existing scholarship on a particular topic and the tools that other scholars have developed to work with specific sources. But as I read the histories of other places and eras, I find most of the historian's tools to be familiar. I am therefore hopeful that the examples in this guide will prove useful far beyond the specific topics they address. I also hope that they will suggest some of the excitement of recent scholarship and inspire readers to track down the works from which they are drawn.

Most of the examples are drawn from single-authored books, which have not only been a standard form of historical scholarship for centuries but also give historians greater space to discuss research methods and sources than one is likely to find in articles, textbooks, museum exhibits, or other equally valuable forms of presenting historical knowledge. As argued in later chapters, the lessons of book writing apply to these other forms. A ten-page student paper or a five-hundred-page book manuscript both need questions, sources, characters, plots, and arguments, and this guide aims to help creators find them. Moreover, as discussed in greater detail below, books are composed of chapters, which themselves are often built from sections about the length of a ten- or fifteen-page research paper. Thus, if you want a sense of the scale of a topic that can be addressed in the length of a term paper, look for books with chapters explicitly divided into sections with their own headings. Then consider the questions and sources the historian used to write each section. Analyzing how successful historians built their stories will make you both a better writer and a better reader.

Researching history is like collecting stamps, sewing a quilt, solving a jigsaw puzzle, and reading a murder mystery at the same time. Like any human endeavor, it is at times difficult, boring, and frustrating. But when the research all comes together, it is deeply, deeply satisfying. Have fun.

PART I

Definitions

{⟨═══⟩}

THE TERM *HISTORY* threatens to mean everything and therefore nothing. If, as the wildest champions of "Big History" claim, *history* encompasses not only the study of everything that has happened in the past fourteen billion years but also the prospects for the next five billion, the term has lost some of its precision. At the very least, we need to distinguish between *history* as the events of the past themselves and *history* as the study of those events. (This distinction is analogous to the difference between plants and botany, money and economics.) Beyond that, it can be helpful to consider history as the study of people's choices. And, finally, we can present history as a set of values shared by historians.

CHAPTER ONE

Defining History

OVER THE CENTURIES, historians and philosophers have offered various competing definitions of history. Charles Beard, citing Benedetto Croce, called history "contemporary thought about the past."[1] Conyers Read described it as "the memory, recorded or unrecorded, of past human experience."[2] Marc Bloch called it "the science of men in time."[3] Most historians could likely agree to definitions along these lines, all of which suggest that history is the study of the past. And yet, at the risk of presumption, let me offer my own definition, one that argues that history is not about the past but rather about people: *history is the study of people and the choices they made.*

Tips

- Ask not what happened. Ask what choices people made.
- Answer questions by telling stories.
- Understand your work as part of an ongoing search for knowledge that began before you and will continue after you.

1. Charles A. Beard, "Written History as an Act of Faith," *American Historical Review* 39 (1934): 219.

2. Conyers Read, "The Social Responsibilities of the Historian," *American Historical Review* 55 (1950): 275.

3. Marc Bloch, *The Historian's Craft: Reflections on the Nature and Uses of History and the Techniques and Methods of Those Who Write It*, trans. Peter Putnam (1953; repr., Princeton, NJ: Vintage, 1964), 27.

History Is the Study of People and
the Choices They Made

History does not include every study of the past, for, as Bloch observed, a great many events of the past belong to scholarly disciplines other than history. He offers the example of the siltation of an inlet, centuries ago. Once there was water; now there is land. There is no question that this change took place over time, an event. Yet had natural forces alone caused that event, the best scholar to explain it would be a geologist. Bloch next tells us that the people of Flanders had both assisted the siltation by building dikes and channels, and that they reacted by moving the harbor of Bruges. With that information we are firmly in the territory of the historian, though presumably the geologist would still have valuable insights to offer.[4] To be sure, historians care about the power of nonhuman elements—natural forces, technologies, commodities— to shape and constrain human action.[5] But objects alone do not make history. According to its subtitle, Marcy Norton's *Sacred Gifts, Profane Pleasures* is *A History of Tobacco and Chocolate*, both inanimate substances. According to its introduction, however, it is the story of "determined and frightened soldiers, zealous missionaries, resourceful plantation slaves, defiant Mesoamerican nobles, adaptive Indian commoners, mestiza love sorceresses, unsubjugated Carib Indians, cosmopolitan European humanists, crypto-Jewish Portuguese traders, lofty Sevillan merchants, worldly clergyman, scrappy sailors, reforming financial ministers, the patrons of smoky taverns, and the guests of well-appointed noble mansions."[6] Now *that's* history.

It is perhaps more controversial to insist that history is the study of *choices*, but I would argue that the interest in choice distinguishes history from the purely descriptive work sometimes done by archaeologists, demographers, epidemiologists, and other

4. Bloch, *The Historian's Craft*, 24–26.

5. Linda Nash, "The Agency of Nature or the Nature of Agency?," *Environmental History* 10 (2005): 67–69; Sara B. Pritchard, *Confluence: The Nature of Technology and the Remaking of the Rhône* (Cambridge, MA: Harvard University Press, 2011), 14–15.

6. Marcy Norton, *Sacred Gifts, Profane Pleasures: A History of Tobacco and Chocolate in the Atlantic World* (Ithaca: Cornell University Press, 2010), 12.

students of the human past. (I am well aware that practitioners of these fields are often quite interested in the choices people made.) When historians read words, they want to understand why people chose those words. When historians examine artifacts, they want to understand why people chose to create, acquire, and perhaps discard those artifacts. When historians trace pathogens, they want to know how people understood disease and how they tried to prevent it, heal it, or infect others.[7] Norton wants to know why Europeans *chose* to adopt tobacco and chocolate in the forms they did.

Many historians focus on people's choices about what to do, that is, their actions. Thucydides sought to explain why Athenians and Peloponnesians went to war after a thirty-year truce, and for centuries historians focused on similar choices of statecraft. In the nineteenth and especially the twentieth centuries, historians broadened their view to include a great many humbler folk, but these people also had choices to make. At what age to marry? What job to pursue? Should they stay home or emigrate to a new town or a new land? Learn to read?[8] Other scholars study people's choices, not about what to do but about what to think and feel: their thoughts and emotions. These can be elite intellectual histories, such as questioning why Margaret Fuller embraced transcendentalism, or they can tell the stories of how large groups of ordinary people understood the world around them. Whether the subjects are near universal experiences (pregnancy, death) or new phenomena (electricity, nationalism), explaining why a person chose one path and not another is the work of history.

In studying choices, historians embrace *contingency*: the belief that had people made different choices, matters could have turned out differently. The concept is perhaps most easily grasped in military history; soldiers fight and die in war because they believe that their actions on the battlefield will determine the fate of nations. Historians believe this as well. Thus, in his epic history of the Civil War, *Battle Cry of Freedom*, James McPherson identifies "four major

---

7. Elizabeth A. Fenn, *Pox Americana: The Great Smallpox Epidemic of 1775–82* (New York: Hill and Wang, 2001).

8. Charles Tilly, "Retrieving European Lives," in *Reliving the Past*, ed. David William Cohen et al., *The Worlds of Social History* (Chapel Hill: University of North Carolina Press, 1985), 23–24, 30.

turning points" that could have led to the granting of Southern independence and a world unimaginably different from our own. "Northern victory and southern defeat in the war," he concludes, "cannot be understood apart from the contingency that hung over every campaign, every battle, every election, every decision during the war."[9]

Contingency appears in other genres of history as well. Historians describe as *contingent* the meanings that people ascribed to mirrors and to wilderness, and the decision by some societies to maximize profit rather than equality.[10] "Why did slavery expand in the early national United States?" asks Adam Rothman. The expansion, he argues, "emerged from contingent global forces, concrete policies pursued by governments, and countless small choices made by thousands of individuals in diverse stations of life."[11] Similarly, Allan Brandt does not believe that Americans were destined to take up cigarette smoking. "Without resorting to a set of fantastical counterfactuals," he writes, "it is clear that the history of tobacco might well have followed different routes and taken decidedly different turns. Following the cigarette through the century offers a fundamental opportunity to evaluate the contingent nature of historical change."[12]

The opposite of contingency is *determinism*: the belief that a particular outcome was inevitable—geography, technology, or some other nonhuman factor forced people to act as they did. Historians generally hate this; if a historian calls you determinist, you have been insulted.

Closely related to contingency is the concept of *agency*: the power of people to shape the world in which they live. Historians

9. James M. McPherson, *Battle Cry of Freedom: The Civil War Era* (New York: Oxford University Press, 1988), 858.

10. Paul S. Sutter, "'A Blank Spot on the Map': Aldo Leopold, Wilderness, and U.S. Forest Service Recreational Policy, 1909–1924," *Western Historical Quarterly* 29 (1998): 188; Rebecca K. Shrum, *In the Looking Glass: Mirrors and Identity in Early America* (Baltimore: Johns Hopkins University Press, 2017), 9; Joyce Appleby, "The Cultural Roots of Capitalism," *Historically Speaking* 12 (2011): 9–10.

11. Adam Rothman, *Slave Country: American Expansion and the Origins of the Deep South* (Cambridge, MA: Harvard University Press, 2009), xi.

12. Allan Brandt, *The Cigarette Century: The Rise, Fall, and Deadly Persistence of the Product That Defined America*, reprint ed. (New York: Basic Books, 2009), 13.

have long attributed such power to princes and generals, but only relatively recently have they attributed agency to humbler people: women, defeated industrial workers, slaves. Even when constrained by those with far more power, they argue, these people could engage in small acts of resistance.[13] As Naomi Lamoreaux explains, many historians hope "to show that ordinary people in some group (typically defined in terms of race, class, gender, or ethnicity) had agency—that their lives were not completely determined for them, that they had space to make their own choices."[14]

Historians do recognize that contingency and agency have their limits. No individual is powerful enough to snap their fingers and change the world. While Franklin Roosevelt could have done more or less than he actually did to better the conditions of African Americans in the 1930s, he could not have eliminated race prejudice by executive order. And he was an unusually powerful president; most people have less power, less agency.[15] "History encourages us to be more compassionate toward individuals navigating few choices," writes Marcia Chatelain, "and history cautions us to be far more critical of the institutions and structures that have the power to take choices away."[16]

"The task," argues Fredrik Logevall, "is to balance out the elements of human agency, on the one hand, with impersonal forces on the other, and to write history that strives to stitch together persuasively all the causative factors and to take into account their interaction."[17] Or, as Karl Marx memorably put it: "Men make their own history, but they do not make it just as they please; they do not

13. See, e.g., Robin D. G. Kelley, "'We Are Not What We Seem': Rethinking Black Working-Class Opposition in the Jim Crow South," *Journal of American History* 80 (1993): 75–112.

14. Naomi R. Lamoreaux, "Rethinking Microhistory: A Comment," *Journal of the Early Republic* 26 (2006): 559.

15. Peter A. Coclanis, review of *Generations of Captivity: A History of African-American Slaves*, by Ira Berlin, *William and Mary Quarterly* 61 (2004): 544–55; Peter Coclanis, "Slavery, African-American Agency, and the World We Have Lost," *Georgia Historical Quarterly* 79 (1995): 873–84; Walter Johnson, "On Agency," *Journal of Social History* 37 (2003): 113–24.

16. Marcia Chatelain, *Franchise: The Golden Arches in Black America* (New York: Liveright, 2020), 21.

17. Fredrik Logevall, "Presidential Address: Structure, Contingency, and the War in Vietnam," *Diplomatic History* 39 (2015): 5.

make it under circumstances chosen by themselves, but under circumstances directly encountered, given and transmitted from the past. The tradition of all the dead generations weighs like a nightmare on the brain of the living."[18]

History Is a Means to Understand Today's World

As Louis Gottschalk noted in 1953, historians have long debated whether it is more important "to understand the past in its own setting, to appreciate history for its own sake," or "to understand the past in order to throw light upon the present."[19] Some historians seek to expunge present concerns from their work. "Obsession with the events of the moment prevents the historian from exercising the faculty of empathy, the faculty of describing how people, like us, but different, felt and behaved as they did in times and places similar to, but different, from our own," Oscar Handlin argued. "The writer or teacher interested only in passing judgment on the good guys and the bad will never know what it meant to be an Irish peasant during a famine, or the landlord; an Alabama slave in the 1850s, or the master; a soldier at Antietam, or a general."[20] Perhaps. But— as Handlin surely knew—without interest in (if not obsession with) the events of their own moments, historians would not have begun to care about Irish peasants, Alabama slaves, and other people previously neglected by historians only interested in the powerful.[21] Other historians embrace the present. "The creative historian lives a double life," writes John Higham, "responsive on one side to the questions and issues of his own age, faithful on the other side to the integrity of an age gone by."[22]

18. Karl Marx, *The Eighteenth Brumaire of Louis Bonaparte*, 2nd ed. (1869; repr., New York: International, 1963), 15.

19. Louis Gottschalk, "A Professor of History in a Quandary," *American Historical Review* 59 (1954): 276.

20. Oscar Handlin, *Truth in History* (Cambridge, MA: Harvard University Press, 1979), 404.

21. David A. Gerber, "*The Uprooted* Would Never Have Been Written If Oscar Handlin Had Taken His Own, Latter-Day Advice," *Journal of American Ethnic History* 32 (2013): 68–77.

22. John Higham, "Beyond Consensus: The Historian as Moral Critic," *American Historical Review* 67 (1962): 609.

Today, some historians—including those who may not identify primarily as historians—work in that tradition, studying history specifically to extract perspective on the present. Historians of sexuality study the past in part to understand the range of human behavior and to suggest ways that sexual minorities might achieve liberation.[23] Historians of medicine explore ways that previous generations understood physical and psychiatric ailments, in part to remind current practitioners that today's diagnoses are not the only ones we could imagine, and that older conceptions of disease can help us, both doctors and patients.[24] Economic historians study wage gaps over history in part to explain why they persist today.[25] And knowing that some judges seek to interpret the Constitution based on what they believe to have been the conditions under which it was drafted, legal historians and legal scholars document those conditions.[26] Introducing a book about presidential impeachment, published during investigations of President Trump's conduct, Jeffrey Engel admits the obvious: "You are most likely reading this book because of impeachment's contemporary salience," he tells his reader, "and also because you realize history matters."[27]

"I don't see a bright line between past and present," notes Thomas Sugrue. "It's a fallacy to see the present as somehow uprooted from history. The opportunities and constraints that we experience in the here and now are the result of historical processes."[28] And the world in which the historian lives will inevitably shape their scholarship.

23. Samuel Clowes Huneke, "What's Wrong with Queer History?," *Boston Review*, June 28, 2019, https://bostonreview.net/gender-sexuality/samuel-clowes-huneke-anthony-appiah-queer-history.

24. Steven J. Peitzman, "From Dropsy to Bright's Disease to End-Stage Renal Disease," *Milbank Quarterly* 67 (January 1989): 16–32; Allan V. Horwitz and Jerome C. Wakefield, *The Loss of Sadness: How Psychiatry Transformed Normal Sorrow into Depressive Disorder*, reprint ed. (New York: Oxford University Press, 2012).

25. Tanya Devani, "Narrowing the Wage Gap: An Interview with Claudia Goldin," *Harvard International Review; Cambridge* 38 (2017): 68–70.

26. Richard Primus, "Segregation in the Galleries: A Reconsideration," *Michigan Law Review Online* 150 (2020), https://repository.law.umich.edu/mlr_online/vol118/iss1/3.

27. Jeffrey Engel, introduction to *Impeachment: An American History*, ed. Jon Meacham et al. (New York: Modern Library, 2018), xxiii.

28. Destin Jenkins, "Public Thinker: Thomas J. Sugrue on History's Hard Lessons," *Public Books* (blog), April 2, 2019, https://www.publicbooks.org/public-thinker-thomas-j-sugrue-on-historys-hard-lessons/.

For better or for worse, today's cutting-edge history becomes tomorrow's relic. In 1949, Conyers Read argued that "history has to be rewritten for every generation. We ask different questions of the past from those our fathers asked, emphasizing considerations which our fathers ignored, and ignoring considerations which our fathers held to be of paramount importance. The older historians move in never-ending march from our studies to our attics and from our attics to our dustbins."[29] For today's historians, Read's gendered language is further evidence of his point. By writing only of fathers and not mothers, he himself took a step up toward the attic.

Historians' debates are not simply *academic* in either sense of the word—they are neither confined to the university nor irrelevant to decision making. Stories of the past can comfort us or they can challenge us. They drive debates over museum exhibits, the naming of roads and buildings, the selection of school textbooks, and—most prominently in 2020—the pulling down of monuments to men who had expanded or defended slavery.[30] Historians challenge collective national narratives, expose wicked deeds by national heroes, and generally attack the notion of a "good old days" to which we might return.[31] Many historians cannot escape the political implications of their findings, even if they wished to. Nor can politicians escape history. As Seth Cotlar and Richard Ellis argue, US leaders spend so much time making historical claims and manipulating historical symbols that we should consider the president "the nation's historian in chief."[32]

With or without historical knowledge, decision makers are apt to reach for historical analogies.[33] Ideally, they will have a range

29. Read, "The Social Responsibilities of the Historian," 275.

30. Edward T. Linenthal and Tom Engelhardt, eds., *History Wars: The Enola Gay and Other Battles for the American Past* (New York: Holt Paperbacks, 1996); Tony Taylor, "Australia's 'History Wars' Reignite," *The Conversation* (blog), March 31, 2016, http://theconversation.com/australias-history-wars-reignite-57065; Susan Chira, "Korean Students Want One Homeland and No Americans," *New York Times*, June 12, 1988.

31. Anita Shapira, "Politics and Collective Memory: The Debate over the 'New Historians' in Israel," trans. Ora Wiskind-Elper, *History and Memory* 7 (1995): 9–40.

32. Seth Cotlar and Richard Ellis, *Historian in Chief: How Presidents Interpret the Past to Shape the Future* (Charlottesville: University of Virginia Press, 2019).

33. Yuen Foong Khong, *Analogies at War: Korea, Munich, Dien Bien Phu, and the Vietnam Decisions of 1965* (Princeton, NJ: Princeton University Press, 1992).

to draw from. "You always benefit . . . from knowing more history," notes political scientist Gary Bass, "than when you go through the world with only one historical example in mind, and everything looks like Munich, or everything looks like Vietnam."[34] Thinking with examples can include asking, What is the best outcome we can imagine, and what is the worst? How might this situation appear to other people involved? What did previous generations fail to anticipate, and what questions should we be asking to avoid the same mistakes?[35] "What human beings have done in the past, the enormous range in ways of living and possible actions," argues Natalie Zemon Davis, "is a source both of hope and despair . . . We can draw hope from it in the sense that if things have been different in the past, perhaps we're in a position to make them a little different today—at least a little bit different."[36]

The most explicit efforts to use history to shape today's world are variously called *applied history* or *public history*, which the National Council on Public History defines as "the many and diverse ways in which history is put to work in the world. In this sense, it is history that is applied to real-world issues." As "historical consultants, museum professionals, government historians, archivists, oral historians, cultural resource managers, curators, film and media producers, historical interpreters, historic preservationists, policy advisers, local historians, and community activists," the council explains, "all share an interest and commitment to making history relevant and useful in the public sphere."[37] Some public history projects—such as television documentaries or major museum exhibits—may be seen by millions, while others are created for a select few, perhaps even classified as government secrets. But all are designed to bring history outside of the purely scholarly debates among historians to people whose main concern is the world as we live in it today.

34. BBC *Newshour*, June 21, 2020.

35. James Gross, *Broken Promise: The Subversion of U.S. Labor Relations* (Philadelphia: Temple University Press, 2010), xiii.

36. Natalie Zemon Davis, *A Passion for History: Conversations with Denis Crouzet*, Early Modern Studies 4 (Kirksville, MO: Truman State University Press, 2010), 73.

37. "About the Field," National Council on Public History, https://ncph.org/what-is-public-history/about-the-field/.

History Combines Storytelling and Analysis

One of the more tedious, perpetual debates in history is the relationship between the thorough scholarship that populates specialized academic journals and the lively writing of the best-selling books sold at airport newsstands.[38] The former makes more explicit analytical claims, while the latter seeks to tell a good story. Some critics are splitters, seeing a wide gap between these two genres, or whining that "history professors have retreated from public debate into their own esoteric pursuits."[39] I am a lumper, believing that the more scholarly and more popular works contain the same basic elements, just in different proportions. However devoted to proving a thesis, great scholarly history tells stories about people—stories with characters and conflicts, plots and outcomes. And every work of popular history has a thesis, though it may be implicit rather than stated, and evident more in the assumptions than in the text itself.[40]

The genres of scholarly and popular history remain close enough that many titles succeed in both realms, but not just any work of history can become a best seller. In the United States, for instance, the market for popular history is dominated by stories about the United States, especially stories of war, murder, scientific discovery, disaster, and sports, with a heavy emphasis on stories about men.[41] Popular historians can slip a great variety of issues into those categories, and a few have broken out with stories of commodity exchange or slavery that would have seemed not the best topic for a beach read. But a great many topics will work only for scholarly monographs or journals.

38. Thomas Babington Macaulay, "History (May, 1828)," in *Miscellaneous Writings, Speeches and Poems* (London: Longmans, Green, 1880), 56; Robert B. Townsend, "From the Archives: Why Can't Historians Write?," *Perspectives on History*, March 25, 2008.

39. Max Boot, "Americans' Ignorance of History Is a National Scandal," *Washington Post*, February 20, 2019.

40. For some background to this debate, see Lawrence Stone, "The Revival of Narrative: Reflections on a New Old History," *Past & Present* 85 (1979): 3–24; David Greenberg, "Academics Historians vs. Popularizers," *Slate*, May 17, 2005 and "That Barnes & Noble Dream," *Slate*, May 18, 2005; Aaron Sachs and John Demos, eds., *Artful History: A Practical Anthology* (New Haven, CT: Yale University Press, 2020).

41. Andrew Kahn and Rebecca Onion, "Is History Written About Men, by Men?," *Slate*, January 6, 2016.

While even the ablest writer would struggle to interest the mass market in some topics that fascinate specialists, it is every historian's duty to tell every story as dramatically and clearly as possible to their intended readers. If the scholarship is strong enough, and the topic important enough, I require my graduate students to read some pretty awful storytelling. But I cannot do so without wishing that the author had learned a few lessons from more popular formats.

The English words *history* and *story* both derive from the Latin *historia*; only in recent centuries have the words gradually diverged to the point where we expect the former to narrate true events while the latter can refer to either fact (a newspaper story) or fiction (a short story).[42] And even with this divergence, history still contains story, and with it the storyteller's imperative. Some histories are single stories, told from beginning to end. Others are collections of stories, all taking place around the same time. Either way, historians must answer the journalist's basic factual questions—the who, what, where, and when. And, like other storytellers, historians bring these facts alive with character, setting, and plot. "The human need for storytelling is not likely ever to go away," William Cronon reminds us. "It is far too basic to the way people make sense of their lives—and among the most important stories they tell are those that seek to understand the past."[43]

But historical research is about more than telling a good story, and since the early twentieth century, some historians have termed their efforts *scientific*.[44] They do not claim that human events are as predictable as the orbits of the planets. Rather, they use methods comparable to those who study the natural world. This is especially true in matters of scholarly communication. Like chemists and physicists—as well as sociologists, literary critics, and epidemiologists—academic historians immerse themselves in previous scholarship, cite their evidence, and submit their work

42. Katy Steinmetz, "This Is Where the Word 'History' Comes From," *Time*, June 23, 2017, http://time.com/4824551/history-word-origins/.

43. William Cronon, "Storytelling," *American Historical Review* 118 (2013): 5.

44. Robert B. Townsend, *History's Babel: Scholarship, Professionalization, and the Historical Enterprise in the United States, 1880–1940* (Chicago: University of Chicago Press, 2013), chapter 1.

for peer review. Sometimes they even get grants to conduct their research. Like scholars in those other fields, they hope that by following standard procedures of research and writing, they can create a shared base of knowledge greater than any individual could achieve on their own.

And, like the sciences, history can even be predictive. I do not mean that in the sense that it predicts the choices people will make in the future—historians believe in contingency. Rather, it is predictive of future *findings*. Paleontologists do not predict what life-forms will emerge in the future; they predict what kinds of fossils will be found in various strata in different parts of the world. Similarly, historians can predict what ideas and events will be found in sources similar to the ones they have reviewed. For example, Hidetaka Hirota read the words of nineteenth-century opponents of Irish immigration in New York and Massachusetts, and found that they despised the Irish for being paupers.[45] This finding does not constitute a prediction that in the year 2045, opponents will condemn immigrants for being poor (though that is the way I would bet). Rather, it constitutes a prediction that if another historian does their own research using additional sources, one will find similar claims. And indeed, Hirota's analysis helped me understand the arguments of nativists in Pennsylvania, which was beyond the geographical scope of his study. Thus, he predicted what I would find.

Historical claims are rarely capable of objective proof, as might be the case in math or physics. Rather, the goal of the historian is to *persuade* readers that the argument set forth helps make sense of the choices people made in the past. Not every reader will find a given claim equally persuasive, and you do not need to persuade every reader in order to have achieved success. Success comes with enlightening the readers whom you care about the most.

"History has been called a science, an art, an illustration of theology, a phase of philosophy, a branch of literature," proclaimed Charles Beard in 1933. "It is none of these things, nor all of them

45. Hidetaka Hirota, *Expelling the Poor: Atlantic Seaboard States and the Nineteenth-Century Origins of American Immigration Policy* (New York: Oxford University Press, 2017).

combined."[46] True, some historians deny the variety of their discipline and insist that every history must be analytical, or narrative, or literary, or national, or transnational, or long-term, or popular, or public, or expert, or profitable, or open-access, or patriotic, or transgressive. In fact, however, historians as a group write in a range of voices, as do individual historians. Even a single historian working on a single research project may share their findings through articles in specialized journals, a book for fellow scholars and interested laypeople, and contributions to museum exhibits, documentaries, and journalism that reach far larger numbers.

Choices about topic, the scope of a project, the research methods used, and the means of presentation generally demand trade-offs, and it is not obvious whether it is more important to forever change the minds of the twelve leading experts in a subfield or satisfy the mild curiosity of five thousand readers outside the academy. As a reader, you should be able to identify a historian's own goals for their work, and to appreciate that work on those terms. As a creator, what is important is that you set goals for yourself and shape your work to achieve those goals, and that you periodically reassess what it is you are aiming to achieve.

History Is an Ongoing Debate

Like other scholars, historians reject the notion that a question can be settled forever, however brilliant and scrupulous the researcher. We are constantly discovering new sources, posing new questions, considering new contexts, and suggesting new ideas about the past. Historians routinely revisit events previously studied by others, believing that old versions of the past may no longer serve today's needs.

There can be something unsettling about seeing today's historians reject previous interpretations, since it implies that today's interpretations will soon lose their value. Why work so hard to produce a product so ephemeral? In practice, however, the best interpretive debates produce not stalemate but synthesis. In 1989,

46. Beard, "Written History as an Act of Faith," 219.

Lawrence Levine wrote of historians' "confidence that, although we might operate in cycles of historical interpretations, the general movement was upward toward an increasingly sophisticated understanding of the past."[47] And even when interpretations grow too stale to use, basic factual findings endure. I have relied on the work of historians who wrote decades ago, whose conclusions I may question, but whose research I trust. I would like to think that whatever they think of my own interpretations, future historians will learn something from my own factual discoveries.

Historians enjoy tracing the history of their own enterprise, retelling the clashes between conservatives and insurgents; the expansion of the discipline from a study of past politics to a wider exploration of human experience; the rise and fall of such approaches as psychohistory and cliometrics; the entry into the profession of women, ethnic and religious minorities, and people of color; and the waxing and waning of historians' influence on popular culture and public policy.[48] Even the definition of *historian* is fluid. At the start of the twentieth century, the term embraced people who today might use other titles—archivist, political scientist, or teacher—even as they pursue historical knowledge.[49]

Yet for all this, I am more struck by the continuities in the history of historical research than I am by the changes. Today's historians write of topics that might have baffled Edward Gibbon (1737–94) or Henry Adams (1838–1918), yet they tell their stories in ways that Gibbon, Adams, and even Thucydides and Tacitus— writing thousands of years ago—could recognize. And they do so in the same confidence that writing history is a core function of any civilization.

The most innovative tools work best when combined with more traditional approaches. For instance, a computer algorithm can help answer questions, but older methods of posing questions and searching archives still have great value.[50] The same continuities

47. Lawrence W. Levine, "The Unpredictable Past: Reflections on Recent American Historiography," *American Historical Review* 94 (1989): 671.

48. Sarah Maza, *Thinking About History* (Chicago: University of Chicago Press, 2017).

49. Townsend, *History's Babel*.

50. Kellen Funk and Lincoln A. Mullen, "The Spine of American Law: Digital Text Analysis and U.S. Legal Practice," *American Historical Review* 123 (2018): 144

appear when historians ask new questions; even those who wish to overturn existing histories can do so using established tools. Jean O'Brien (White Earth Ojibwe), for example, has shown how nineteenth-century New England historians misled readers about their region's Native past and denied the continued residence of Indians in their states. Yet she bases this critique on her own meticulous research into primary sources preserved in archives. Rather than rejecting the methods of previous generations of historians, she deploys them with a different perspective and greater skill than her predecessors.[51]

In the spring of 2009, I spent some time at the Library of Congress exploring notes taken by David Maydole Matteson, a historian born a century before me. Decades earlier, Matteson had started work on a never-completed history of riots in the United States, a subject that interested me as well. He had worked with steel pen, ink, and paper; I had a laptop computer and a digital camera. Yet despite the apparent revolution in technology, my task was not much different from his: reading through old newspapers, magazines, books, and official records, taking notes, and hoping to synthesize those notes into a coherent story. We can still learn from the age of the note card and the age of the microfilm reader. In this guide, I hope to highlight general practices that come to us from those earlier periods and—despite future changes in both scholarly focus and technological capacity—will endure.

51. Jean M. O'Brien, *Firsting and Lasting: Writing Indians Out of Existence in New England* (Minneapolis: University of Minnesota Press, 2010).

CHAPTER TWO

Historians' Ethics

IN ADDITION to being defined by its goals and methods, history is defined by the values held dear by its practitioners. The bespectacled scholar, carefully turning the pages of a yellowed newspaper or scowling at a peer reviewer's unkind comments, may not seem particularly fearsome, but the collective enterprise of history can sway jury verdicts, build or destroy reputations, and even send nations to war. And as members of a profession, historians shape the careers and lives of students and colleagues. Cognizant of this power, historians' associations have crafted codes of ethics. The American Historical Association's "Statement on Standards of Professional Conduct" is a particularly useful starting place, but historians should also seek more specialized codes, and ethics discussions, that are relevant to their work, such as those concerning oral history, public history, local history, archiving, and other such fields.[1] While all historians share some fundamental values, they work in a range of situations. The ethical freedom enjoyed by a tenured professor may be out of reach to a consulting historian on contract to a business firm, but the latter should still maintain some firm limits.[2]

---

1. American Historical Association, "Statement on Standards of Professional Conduct (updated 2019)," https://www.historians.org/jobs-and-professional-development/statements-standards-and-guidelines-of-the-discipline/statement-on-standards-of-professional-conduct.

2. Carl Ryant, "The Public Historian and Business History: A Question of Ethics," *Public Historian* 8 (1986): 31–38.

Ethics evolve in response to new situations and debates. For example, in the twenty-first century, historians, librarians, and archivists pay increasing attention to the respectful use of culturally sensitive Native American archival materials, to the provenance of rare material that had been displaced by purchase or war, and to the benefits and perils of making primary sources and new scholarship freely available on the internet.[3] Perhaps, then, historians' first ethical obligation is to understand that historians have ethical obligations, and to educate themselves appropriately.

Tips

- Ask honest questions, and be open to surprises.
- Avoid falsehoods by showing your work.
- Care about people, living and dead.

Curiosity

The first virtue of the research historian is curiosity. If you already know the answer when you begin a project, you are not doing research. As noted later in chapter 3, historians form questions in many ways, and they must keep their minds open as much as possible. Like researchers in other fields, historians must avoid *confirmation bias*: the tendency to ignore evidence that challenges one's beginning assumptions, and to highlight evidence that reinforces them. Confirmation bias can creep in at any stage of a project: framing the question, establishing a research design, taking notes, or writing up findings. It is the force that allowed generations of male historians to ignore the women in the stories they were researching, and generations of white historians to downplay the horrors of slavery. It has also tripped up individual scholars who have become so entranced by what appears to be a wonderful story that they ignore their doubts and twist evidence to fit their preferred narrative. We

3. Kritika Agarwal, "A Way Forward," *Perspectives on History*, October 2018; Kritika Agarwal, "Doing Right Online: Archivists Shape an Ethics for the Digital Age," *Perspectives on History*, November 2016; Mike Kelly, "Introduction," *RBM: A Journal of Rare Books, Manuscripts, and Cultural Heritage* 6 (2005): 10–13; Seth Denbo, "Academic Presses Explore Open Access for Monographs," *Perspectives on History*, March 10, 2017.

cannot identify all of our biases, and future generations of historians will delight in pointing out the limits of our imaginations. But we can attempt some self-awareness and look for evidence that complicates the narratives that we have inherited.

"Professional integrity in the practice of history requires awareness of one's own biases and a readiness to follow sound method and analysis wherever they may lead," insists the American Historical Association. "Historians should not misrepresent their sources. They should report their findings as accurately as possible and not omit evidence that runs counter to their own interpretation."[4]

Accuracy

"To praise a historian for his accuracy is like praising an architect for using well-seasoned timber or properly mixed concrete in his building," wrote E. H. Carr in 1961. "It is a necessary condition of his work, but not his essential function."[5] In reality, architects do gain praise for sensitive and innovative uses of materials, and a great deal of the historians' work consists of finding trustworthy materials for their projects.[6]

Moreover, accuracy is a matter of degree. A simple traffic accident can easily produce contradictory eyewitness accounts, and larger historical events generate even greater discrepancies. Thus, even writing a simple timeline of what happened when can become an exercise in weighing evidence, and thus in interpretation. "Historians aspire to tell 'the truth,'" writes Richard White, "but we usually settle for avoiding known falsehoods, trying not to make unsubstantiated claims, and providing evidence for what we say so others can check for themselves."[7] Historians who work with hundreds or thousands or tens of thousands of contradictory, fragmentary sources—some, perhaps, in a foreign language, or produced in

---

4. American Historical Association, "Statement on Standards of Professional Conduct (updated 2019)."

5. E. H. Carr, *What Is History?* (New York: Vintage, 1961), 8.

6. "2014 Pritzker Architecture Prize Jury Citation for Shigeru Ban," Pritzker Architecture Prize, https://www.pritzkerprize.com/laureates/2014; David Hackett Fischer, *Historians' Fallacies* (New York: Harper Torchbooks, 1970), 41.

7. Richard White, "New Yorker Nation," *Reviews in American History* 47 (2019): 162.

a time or place or profession that the historian has never directly experienced—do not expect to attain complete accuracy.

Instead, as White suggests, the real standard is not accuracy but *replicability*, meaning that, as in laboratory science, "a study can be repeated because a detailed study methods description is available."[8] For scholarly history, this takes the form of quotations and footnotes or endnotes with citations to additional sources. When the stakes are high enough, it may be worth laying out alternative possibilities to the reader, either in the main text or in a discursive note. In exceptional cases, a historian might be asked to produce their working notes for a project.[9] A commitment to accuracy also requires the admission of doubt, and sometimes the words, "I don't know."[10]

Factual accuracy alone does not guarantee good history. "Facts . . . do not select themselves or force themselves automatically into any fixed scheme of arrangement in the mind of the historian," argued Charles Beard in 1933. "They are selected and ordered by him as he thinks."[11] To select and order facts in a way that contributes to human understanding, the historian must embrace additional virtues.

Judgment

"My purpose is not to relate at length every motion, but only such as were conspicuous for excellence or notorious for infamy," wrote Tacitus, early in the second century. "This I regard as history's highest function, to let no worthy action be uncommemorated, and to hold out the reprobation of posterity as a terror to evil words and

8. Rik Peels and Lex Bouter, "The Possibility and Desirability of Replication in the Humanities," *Palgrave Communications* 4 (2018): 95.

9. Stanley N. Katz, Hannah H. Gray, and Laurel Ulrich, *Report of the Investigative Committee in the Matter of Professor Michael Bellesiles* (Atlanta, GA: Emory University, 2002), 18–19.

10. Marc Bloch, *The Historian's Craft: Reflections on the Nature and Uses of History and the Techniques and Methods of Those Who Write It*, trans. Peter Putnam (1953; repr., Princeton, NJ: Vintage, 1964), 60.

11. Charles A. Beard, "Written History as an Act of Faith," *American Historical Review* 39 (1934): 220.

deeds."[12] Two millennia later, Julia Laite tweeted a similar sentiment: "Being a historian is all about muttering 'you f**ker' to long-dead prime ministers whilst alone at one's desk."[13]

Less judgmental historians can still help readers form their own conclusions. "It is the function of the historian to keep before the people, with as much clarity as possible, the different lines of action that have been taken, the several, often complicated reasons for such action, and to point to the conflicts and inconsistencies, the contradictions and illogicalities, and the defects and deficiencies when they exist," argued John Hope Franklin. "One might argue that the historian is the conscience of his nation, if honesty and consistency are factors that nurture the conscience."[14] Others disagree. Bloch regarded passing judgment as a lazy alternative to explanation. "How much easier it is to write for or against Luther than to fathom his soul," he wrote, "to believe Pope Gregory VII about Emperor Henry IV, or Henry IV about Gregory VII, than to unravel the underlying causes of one of the greatest dramas of Western civilization!"[15]

Historians must decide which people should be held accountable for their words and deeds. In his history of white Southerners' reactions to the civil rights movement, Jason Sokol names the segregationists who wrote letters to New Orleans mayor deLesseps Morrison; as citizens they were taking part in a public debate and writing to a public official. But Sokol treats differently the essays written by University of Georgia students who were asked by their calculus instructor to record their views on integration. "These students did not write for public consumption, or to be published," Sokol explains. "For these reasons their names need not be disclosed." He does provide initials, allowing subsequent researchers to check his work.[16]

12. *The Annals* by Tacitus, trans. Alfred John Church and William Jackson Brodribb, Internet Classics Archive, http://classics.mit.edu.

13. Julia Laite (@julialaite), "Being a Historian Is All about Muttering 'You F**ker' to Long-Dead Prime Ministers Whilst Alone at One's Desk," *Twitter*, May 23, 2019, https://twitter.com/JuliaLaite/status/1131566942207250437.

14. John Hope Franklin, "The Historian and Public Policy," *History Teacher* 11 (1978): 390.

15. Bloch, *The Historian's Craft*, 141. For more on this debate, see Gordon Wright, "History as a Moral Science," *American Historical Review* 81 (1976): 1–11.

16. Jason Sokol, *There Goes My Everything: White Southerners in the Age of Civil Rights, 1945–1975* (2006; repr., New York: Vintage, 2007), 153, 372n27.

Oral historians may be the most tempted to pull their punches. "When you like and admire the people you are interviewing," notes Valerie Yow, "you are also subtly influenced in the direction of seeing things positively instead of realistically."[17] Other historians have advised a sterner approach. "To the historian all men are dead," insisted John Kaye in 1870. "If a writer of contemporary history is not prepared to treat the living and the dead alike—to speak as freely and as truthfully of the former as of the latter, with no more reservation in the one case than in the other—he has altogether mistaken his vocation, and should look for a subject in prehistoric times."[18]

Indeed, while the temptation to limit criticism might be greatest when you are writing about living individuals, similar pressures can face any historian whose findings might threaten cherished myths about families, institutions, or ethnic groups. Public historians may be tempted—even unconsciously—to write favorably about their employers. "Like all bureaucrats," writes Marin Reuss, at the time a historian for the US Army Corps of Engineers, "federal historians are expected to enhance the power of the agencies for which they work . . . Agencies, sometimes consciously, sometimes unknowingly, occasionally pressure history offices to use history selectively to further agency programs."[19]

In some cases, historians may shy away from making certain claims in order to avoid legal trouble. In 2018, for instance, Poland passed a law—later modified—criminalizing some claims "that the Polish Nation or the Republic of Poland is responsible or co-responsible for Nazi crimes committed by the Third Reich."[20] I could go on, but even as I write these words, I must weigh the consequences of the examples I could give against the chance of their tarnishing the reception of my research, interfering with my future travel, or increasing the likelihood of my being sued.

17. Valerie Raleigh Yow, *Recording Oral History: A Guide for the Humanities and Social Sciences*, 2nd ed. (Walnut Creek, CA: Altamira, 2005), 147.

18. John William Kaye, *Kaye's and Malleson's History of the Indian Mutiny of 1857–8*, ed. G. B. Malleson, vol. 2 (London: W. H. Allen, 1892), xiii.

19. Martin Reuss, "Government and Professional Ethics: The Case of Federal Historians," *Public Historian* 21 (1999): 136.

20. "AHA Condemns Polish Law Criminalizing Public Discussion of Polish Complicity in Nazi War Crimes," *Perspectives on History*, April 2, 2018.

Ideally, the historian acts without such fear, even knowing they may give offense. As a South Carolina caretaker in his nineties told Lonnie Bunch, "If you're a historian, your job is to help people understand not just what they want to remember, but what they need to remember."[21]

Empathy

Historians do their best to empathize with the people they write about, to understand their thoughts and deeds. Sometimes this is easy; you find a character whom you admire, whose arguments make sense to you. You still need to write about that person critically, but the task is pleasant. At other times, historical actors' decisions are baffling, at least at first glance.

Whenever possible, historians try not to dismiss such actions as irrational but instead keep working to find an explanation that makes sense to them. "Merely to talk of 'superstition' and 'delusion' explains nothing at all," writes J. B. Peires of the Xhosa people's destroying much of their own food supply in the 1850s. "We have to try and understand why beliefs which seem to us—and to all Xhosa now living—patently absurd and impossible seemed logical and plausible to the Xhosa of 1856."[22] He proceeds to explore the "internal logic" not only of Xhosa beliefs but also of British beliefs, which he finds equally absurd and impossible.

Obviously, historians write about some dreadful people: murderers, thieves, enslavers, war criminals. They are not bound to share the beliefs of the people they study, nor to forgive their crimes.[23] But even if historians come to despise some of the people they study, they are bound to attempt to see the world through their eyes, and to try to explain their motives. "Our goal is not to critically assess how Jefferson made his way through the world and determine what his life might or should mean for

21. K. K. Ottesen, "'You Can't Be a Historian of Black America without Being Hopeful,' Says Smithsonian Secretary Lonnie Bunch," *Washington Post*, June 23, 2020.

22. Jeffrey B. Peires, *The Dead Will Arise: Nongqawuse and the Great Xhosa Cattle-Killing Movement of 1856-7* (Bloomington: Indiana University Press, 1989), 123.

23. Christopher R. Browning, *Ordinary Men: Reserve Police Battalion 101 and the Final Solution in Poland* (New York: HarperPerennial, 1998), xx.

us, for better or for worse—what we think he ought to have been doing," write Annette Gordon-Reed and Peter Onuf. "We instead seek to understand what *Thomas Jefferson* thought he was doing in the world."[24]

The greatest storytellers are those who humanize their villains. Satan in *Paradise Lost* is still Satan, but through Milton's telling we get a sense of why he might have been so intent on defying God and corrupting humans. Historians, though working on a less cosmic scale, can learn from Milton's example. "While communicating his disagreement with people, he manages to avoid painting them as hateful caricatures," writes a reviewer, praising Timothy Lombardo's *Blue Collar Conservatism*. "He shows them as fully formed individuals with complex motivations, prone to errors in judgment, as we all are, but not deplorable or easily written off."[25] Even when writing about people who are, in fact, deplorable, the historian's goal is to understand everyone as fully formed.

This is not to say historians should limit their accounts to the actors' own understanding. "The empathy of the historian," explains Lincoln Mullen, "does not consist simply in retelling other people's stories for them. They can do that well enough for themselves. Rather, it consists in going beneath individual accounts to reveal deeper patterns of thought, word, and deed, in demonstrating to people that though they may have acted of their own will yet they have acted within historically conditioned constraints. The empathy lies in demonstrating what it was possible for people to say so that they can better understand what they have said."[26]

Gratitude

History is among the more solitary pursuits in the academy. Scientists have their labs, archaeologists their digs, musicians their ensembles. Ethnographers always find someone to talk to. And

24. Annette Gordon-Reed and Peter S. Onuf, *"Most Blessed of the Patriarchs": Thomas Jefferson and the Empire of the Imagination* (New York: W. W. Norton, 2016), xx.

25. "The Populist Politics of Philadelphia Mayor Frank Rizzo," *National Review* (blog), November 21, 2018.

26. Lincoln A. Mullen, *The Chance of Salvation* (Cambridge, MA: Harvard University Press, 2017), xii.

many disciplines that could, in theory, be pursued by single scholars have developed traditions of coauthorship, with multiple authors on most articles. History, by contrast, tends to value single authors, especially for scholarly books and articles. And there are good reasons for this, especially when it comes to authorial voice. That said, while a single name may be on the cover of a book or the heading of an article, historians work with other living people in a variety of settings. While some of the best interactions will be unexpected, it can be useful at the start of a project to think about who else will be involved.

Because they depend on others, historians accumulate debts. As members of institutions, they get help from colleagues, mentors, and students. As people, they get help from family members, friends, and neighbors. And as researchers, they depend on other scholars, coauthors, funders, librarians and archivists, editors and publishers, and, ultimately, readers.

Most obviously, historians—like all scholars—need to cite their sources and distinguish their contributions from the work of others. They must avoid plagiarism: copying others' words and presenting them as one's own, a topic discussed in greater detail in later chapters. But citing sources and attributing quotations are only the baseline. Good historians credit the aid they receive, with explicit thanks not only in citations but also in acknowledgments sections, public remarks, and mentions of other scholars' work in press interviews or even casual conversations; one has many opportunities to plug other scholars' work. And historians try to pay forward some of what they have received by helping other scholars and all those who are interested in history. For instance, they seek out the work of junior scholars and historians from underrepresented communities, citing their work to make it more visible to others.

Historians consume public resources. Whether we are fortunate enough to be paid directly for our work, through jobs and grants, or simply rely on publicly supported libraries and archives, or claim the time of experts and witnesses, we rely on our communities to help us with our work. In return, we have some duty to share our findings.

Sharing can mean many things. It can mean writing in a style that is understandable and appealing to as many potential readers as possible. It can mean formatting websites in ways that work for people with disabilities, limited bandwidth, or small screens. It can mean choosing journals and publishers that price their products reasonably, or making at least some version of your findings available without charge. It can mean depositing datasets, interviews, and other materials in repositories for other scholars and future generations. And it can mean sharing findings in public lectures, school classrooms, and other open venues. You do not have to work for free; history is hard work, and compensation is honorable. But historians should feel some duty to the society that supports them.

Truth

"We study history," wrote Lawrence Cremin, "not because in its absence there will not be any history, but rather because in its absence we shall have a corrupt history; we shall have the myths, distortions, and the ideologies that flourish in the absence of critical scholarship."[27] Some people openly invent characters and events, setting novels and movies in the past. These creations can inspire people to learn the truth, or at least they can suggest that truth, even at the expense of some details. In other cases, works of art propagate dangerous misunderstandings about the past. As Gary Gallagher laments, "it is likely that more people have formed perceptions about the Civil War from watching *Gone with the Wind* than from reading all the books written by historians since [David O.] Selznick's blockbuster debuted in 1939."[28] And those perceptions are not good; *Gone with the Wind*, and works like it, have led many Americans to believe that African Americans were content to be slaves, and that Southern enslavers began the war for some reason other than to defend their ability to keep enslaving.

27. Lawrence A. Cremin, "American Education: Some Notes Toward a New History," Monograph for American Educational Research Association—Phi Delta Kappa Award Lecture, Bloomington, Indiana, Phi Delta Kappa International, 17–18, 1969, quoted in James D. Anderson, "Lawrence A. Cremin," in *Routledge Encyclopaedia of Educational Thinkers*, ed. Joy A. Palmer Cooper (New York: Routledge, 2016).

28. Gary W. Gallagher, "Hollywood Has It Both Ways: The Rise, Fall, and Reappearance of the Lost Cause in American Film," in *Wars Within a War: Controversy and Conflict over the American Civil War*, ed. Joan Waugh and Gary W. Gallagher (Chapel Hill: University of North Carolina Press, 2009), 158.

Worse still are those who spread historical myth without even the pretense of fiction. Whether it is a book by a television pundit who has cherry-picked a few facts to support a deeply misleading thesis, a facile historical analogy offered by a politician who knows nothing of the events they are describing, or a full-scale irredentist land claim or genocide denial that becomes national policy, bad history imperils our ability to make wise choices. Thus, some historians explicitly define their work as demythologizing events.[29]

At other times, professional historians have added to the myth-making, letting their assumptions or politics cloud their judgment.[30] Much as we might like to blame myths about Reconstruction on *Gone with the Wind*, its author, Margaret Mitchell, drew upon the dominant white scholarship of the era, and the *William and Mary Quarterly* praised her novel's "historical accuracy."[31] At such times, it can take a layperson or activist—armed with better history—to challenge the mainstream interpretation. As Selznick was adapting *Gone with the Wind* for Hollywood, civil rights leader Walter White advised him to read African American historian W.E.B. Du Bois's *Black Reconstruction* as a corrective.[32]

In 1968, Thomas Bailey noted historians' culpability, and argued that "we historians have a special obligation to set the record straight and keep it straight. We cannot muzzle the poets, the play-wrights, the pedagogues, the 'patrioteers,' the press, the politicians, and other muddiers of historical waters; but we can, if we will, control ourselves." One of his proposals was a "centralized Myth

29. Joy Lisi Rankin, *A People's History of Computing in the United States* (Cambridge, MA: Harvard University Press, 2018), 10; Kristin L. Hoganson, *The Heartland: An American History* (New York: Penguin, 2019), xix; Ronald H. Fritze, "On the Perils and Pleasures of Confronting Pseudohistory," *Historically Speaking* 10 (2009): 2–5.

30. Thomas A. Bailey, "The Mythmakers of American History," *Journal of American History* 55 (1968): 11–15.

31. John Hope Franklin, "Mirror for Americans: A Century of Reconstruction History," *American Historical Review* 85 (1980): 1–14; Jennifer W. Dickey, *A Tough Little Patch of History: "Gone with the Wind" and the Politics of Memory* (Fayetteville: University of Arkansas Press, 2014), 12.

32. National Association for the Advancement of Colored People, letter from the National Association for the Advancement of Colored People to David O. Selznick, June 7, 1938. W.E.B. Du Bois Papers (MS 312), Special Collections and University Archives, University of Massachusetts Amherst Libraries, http://credo.library.umass.edu/view/full/mums312-b086-i157.

Registry, for both articles and books. . . . Then, with the marvelous data-recovery processes now being perfected, the requisite information can be made speedily available on request. Such an agency should be a gold mine for teachers, researchers, and especially textbooks writers, who have a heavy obligation to keep abreast of this verbal Niagara."[33]

Half a century later, in the age of the internet, we know that "marvelous data-recovery processes" are not the panacea that Bailey wished. Websites and social media disseminate falsehoods every bit as efficiently as they debunk them, and some of those falsehoods even make it into textbooks.[34] Maintaining the centralized Myth Registry turns out to be exhausting, unending work for the historians of Twitter.[35] As Melvin Kranzberg famously declared, "technology is neither good nor bad; nor is it neutral."[36] It is up to a technology's users to choose the good.

Historians will never control a monopoly on the past, nor can they hope that the good history they write and share will drive out the bad. But there is honor in the effort.

33. Bailey, "The Mythmakers of American History," 18.

34. Kevin Sieff, "Virginia 4th-Grade Textbook Criticized over Claims on Black Confederate Soldiers," *Washington Post*, October 20, 2010.

35. Emma Pettit, "How Kevin Kruse Became History's Attack Dog," *Chronicle of Higher Education*, December 16, 2018.

36. Melvin Kranzberg, "Technology and History: 'Kranzberg's Laws,'" *Technology and Culture* 27 (1986): 545.

PART II

Questions

{⚜︎}

THE STARTING POINT of research in history, as in any other field of research, is a question. There is nothing more miserable than slogging through material that does not rouse your curiosity—and nothing more joyous than pursuing a question that truly excites you. Take time to frame your question, since it will drive the rest of the project. Once you have done so, you can craft a research design with which you can answer your question in the time and space available to you, and that will make others care about the answer.

CHAPTER THREE

Asking Questions

"WHAT IS *THAT* DOING *HERE*?" asked an astonished Andrew Need-ham, spotting a vast coal-fired power plant as his family drove through the high desert of New Mexico. Years later, Needham would answer that question in his prize-winning book, *Power Lines: Phoenix and the Making of the Modern Southwest.*[1] Above all else, historians must learn to ask questions about how the world came to be, and stay curious for as long as it takes to get the answer.

Biologists write of "life cycles" of the species they study, tracing their progression from gametes to juvenile to adult forms, which in turn produce more gametes. History projects grow the same cyclical way, so historians can jump in at any point in the cycle. Start with the seed of an idea, nourish it through its delicate early stages, watch it bloom into full maturity, and, if you are really lucky, perhaps collect seeds for the next generation. Or, start with the adult, then collect its seeds. Or start with the juvenile, and nour-ish it into adult form. Questions lead to answers, but answers lead to questions as well. Secondary sources may steer you to primary sources, but those primary sources spark questions that you can answer most easily by consulting additional secondary sources. The research process resembles a climb up a spiral staircase, in which upward progress depends on your circling back to a spot near where

1. Andrew Needham, *Power Lines: Phoenix and the Making of the Modern Southwest* (Princeton, NJ: Princeton University Press, 2014), ix.

you were before. Still, since this section of this book must start somewhere, let us start with an early stage in any project: wonder.

Tips

- Choose topics that spark your sense of wonder.
- Start with a question, not a thesis.
- Frame your question using dialectics.

Wonder

How did you get interested in that topic? It is a question every historian hears, and it is often a good one to ask: not only does it frequently elicit an entertaining tale, but it can also reveal something important about the way the historian's mind works, and their aims in tackling a particular subject. It can also be a question historians ask of themselves, as they lift their tired eyes from the sources and try to recall how they got there. And while every answer is unique, a few basic patterns appear again and again.

AUTOBIOGRAPHY

Walter Prescott Webb once described his monumental book *The Great Plains* as "an autobiography with scholarly trimmings." He began it "at the age of four when my father left the humid East and set his family down in West Texas, in the very edge of the open, arid country which stretched north and west farther than a boy could imagine."[2] Webb was hardly the first or the last historian to draw inspiration from events and settings in his own life, and a great many works of history could be described as autobiography with scholarly trimmings.

Some historians write about events that they themselves witnessed or even shaped. Before he wrote his history of the Peloponnesian War, Thucydides commanded troops in that war. Before they wrote their ten-volume *Abraham Lincoln: A History*, John

2. Walter Prescott Webb, "History as High Adventure," *American Historical Review* 64 (1959): 273–74.

Hay and John Nicolay had served as Lincoln's secretaries. Ruth Rosen, a veteran of the women's movement of the 1960s, writes about that movement with scholarly rigor. Yet she also slips into the first person to give readers a glimpse of her own participation, such as engaging in an effort to take over a Berkeley radio station.[3]

Other historians write about their ancestors. John Hay's friend, Henry Adams, defended the reputation of his grandfather, John Quincy Adams.[4] Winston Churchill wrote biographies of his father, Lord Randolph Churchill, and his more remote ancestor, the first Duke of Marlborough. Winston's son, Randolph Churchill, in turn published two volumes of a biography of his father and was working on more at the time of his death. More recently, Catherine Mulholland has written a biography of her grandfather, engineer William Mulholland, and Stephen Carter has written of his grandmother, an influential lawyer at a time when few African American women practiced law.[5] As Catherine Mulholland acknowledges, the reader may doubt the objectivity of such accounts, but that same reader should read *all* historical accounts critically, regardless of their authors' ancestry.[6]

Even when an ancestor is not a major character, they can inspire and inform a work. "My father came home every morning from his graveyard shift at a plywood mill covered with industrial glue, his shirts stained purple," writes Eric Loomis. "Scars crisscross his arms from a lifetime of wood splinters cutting his skin." Those scars, as well as his father's love for the outdoors, influenced Loomis's *Empire of Timber: Labor Unions and the Pacific Northwest Forests*.[7] Alexander Aviña was inspired by his uncle's kidnapping and

3. Ruth Rosen, *The World Split Open: How the Modern Women's Movement Changed America*, rev. ed. (New York: Penguin Books, 2006), 207.

4. Edward Chalfant, *Better in Darkness: A Biography of Henry Adams; His Second Life, 1862–1891* (Hamden, CT: Archon Books, 1994), 358.

5. Catherine Mulholland, *William Mulholland and the Rise of Los Angeles* (Berkeley: University of California Press, 2002); Stephen L. Carter, *Invisible: The Forgotten Story of the Black Woman Lawyer Who Took Down America's Most Powerful Mobster* (New York: Henry Holt, 2018). See also Beryl Satter, *Family Properties: How the Struggle over Race and Real Estate Transformed Chicago and Urban America* (New York: Picador, 2010).

6. Mulholland, *William Mulholland*, xviii.

7. Erik Loomis, *Empire of Timber: Labor Unions and the Pacific Northwest Forests* (New York: Cambridge University Press, 2015), 1–2.

disappearance to study the history of Mexico's drug wars and other violence.[8] Years before she published her history of anti-Chinese violence, Beth Lew-Williams heard her grandfather's story of being detained, as a nine-year-old boy, on Angel Island.[9] Ned Blackhawk and Timothy Lombardo relate snippets of family history, in part to suggest their sympathy with the communities whose histories they tell.[10] Tera Hunter starts *Bound in Wedlock* with a photograph of her great-great-grandparents' marriage certificate and her family tree.[11]

Some historians write not about biological ancestors but ancestors in spirit: people who shared the historian's experiences or passions. In the nineteenth-century United States, for instance, historians working or studying at Catholic universities and publishing in Catholic journals wrote histories of the church and Catholic communities that remain superb resources today. In the twentieth century, they were joined by members of various racial, ethnic, and religious minorities, as well as by women, all of whom brought new perspectives about the communities that had produced them. As a child immigrant to the United States from Cuba, Lillian Guerra faced discrimination at school. "History was how I grasped for straws of cultural and racial dignity when fellow second-graders denigrated my slightly flatter, decidedly non-Anglo nose, relatively hairy limbs, and propensity to tan a dark brown rather than bake into a bright, bubbly red in the Kansas summer sun," she later reflected. "Why did they think being blond was better? I wondered." In her works on the history of the Caribbean, she has both answered questions and asserted her worth.[12] Paul Longmore survived polio

8. Alexander Aviña (@ Alexander_Avina), "12 years ago this week, masked gunmen kidnapped & disappeared my uncle Pablo Godinez Sandoval," Twitter, May 1, 2019, https://twitter.com/Alexander_Avina/status/1123695492729397248.

9. Beth Lew-Williams, *The Chinese Must Go: Violence, Exclusion, and the Making of the Alien in America* (Cambridge, MA: Harvard University Press, 2018), 339–40.

10. Ned Blackhawk, *Violence over the Land: Indians and Empires in the Early American West* (Cambridge, MA: Harvard University Press, 2006), 13–15, and Timothy J. Lombardo, *Blue-Collar Conservatism: Frank Rizzo's Philadelphia and Populist Politics* (Philadelphia: University of Pennsylvania Press, 2018), 313.

11. Tera W. Hunter, *Bound in Wedlock: Slave and Free Black Marriage in the Nineteenth Century* (Cambridge, MA: Harvard University Press, 2017), 2–3.

12. Lillian Guerra, "Why I Am a Historian," *Perspectives on History*, July 2, 2019.

as a child and advocated for disability rights as an adult, experiences that informed both his studies of the American Revolution and his histories of disability. "As both a professional historian and a person with a disability," he explained, "I have explored how cultural values, social and political ideologies, and social processes shaped individual and collective identities and how revolutions in ideas and institutions redefined those identities."[13]

Professional training in other fields, or even an intense hobby, can complement historical training. We have wonderful military histories by veterans, legal and medical histories by historians who also have degrees in law and medicine, and histories of technology by historians with engineering backgrounds. In other cases, formal degrees matter less than lived experience. Adrienne Hood spent years working as a weaver before enrolling in graduate school "to research and write about cloth rather than make it."[14] Though her book *The Weaver's Craft* tells the story of weavers who worked centuries before she did, her passion for textiles, and her knowledge of looms, no doubt helped her write their story. James Longhurst, a dedicated rider and restorer of bicycles, drew on those experiences when writing *Bike Battles: A History of Sharing the American Road.*[15] Other historians try to understand the places in which they grew up. Lizabeth Cohen's *A Consumers' Republic: The Politics of Mass Consumption in Postwar America* is a national narrative, but throughout Cohen returns to her home landscape of suburban New Jersey, even including a photograph of herself at age four.[16]

None of this is to say that the historian must have a family or personal connection to the people they write about. In the 1960s, Carl Bridenbaugh was appropriately denounced for suggesting that historians "of lower middle-class or foreign origins [i.e., Jews] find themselves in a very real sense outsiders on our past" and therefore

13. Paul K. Longmore, *Telethons: Spectacle, Disability, and the Business of Charity* (New York: Oxford University Press, 2015), xv.

14. Adrienne D. Hood, *The Weaver's Craft: Cloth, Commerce, and Industry in Early Pennsylvania* (Philadelphia: University of Pennsylvania Press, 2003), 3.

15. James Longhurst, *Bike Battles: A History of Sharing the American Road* (Seattle: University of Washington Press, 2015), ix.

16. Lizabeth Cohen, *A Consumers' Republic: The Politics of Mass Consumption in Post-war America* (New York: Vintage, 2003), 3.

lacked an understanding of the American past somehow common to those who grew up in rural America.[17] Sometimes an outsider's perspective is exactly what is needed to ask new questions and find new answers, and to correct the accounts by insiders who may have, however unintentionally, written history to glorify their own group at the expense of others.[18] And while personal experience may contribute to one's historical research, it is no substitute for the research itself.

EVERYTHING HAS A HISTORY

"We have been puzzled for a while about how salt and ground black pepper became the standard spices on the American dinner table," wrote two readers of Cecil Adams's column, *The Straight Dope*. "Why don't we use cinnamon or oregano or something else instead?" The learned Adams replied, "This is just the kind of thing that fascinates historians, gang, something you may want to consider next time a historian asks you out for a date."[19] Indeed, asking about the origins of things we see around us—from table condiments to institutions to persistent causes of conflict—is one of the most common inspirations for historical research. In 2015, James Grossman, executive director of the American Historical Association, coined a slogan for the truth underlying this approach: "Everything has a history."[20]

Tracing the histories of elements of today's world may be the most common form of historical research, simply because it is a necessary step in so many fields. As Grossman notes, politicians, economists, doctors, and journalists, if they have any sense, explore

17. Carl Bridenbaugh, "The Great Mutation," *American Historical Review* 68 (1963): 323; Peter Novick, *That Noble Dream: The "Objectivity Question" and the American Historical Profession* (New York: Cambridge University Press, 1988), 339.

18. Corinne Lathrop Gilb, "Should We Learn More About Ourselves?," *American Historical Review* 66 (1961): 989; Lawrence W. Levine, "The Unpredictable Past: Reflections on Recent American Historiography," *American Historical Review* 94 (1989): 675.

19. Cecil Adams, "How Did Salt and Pepper Become the Standard Table Spices?," The Straight Dope, November 14, 1986, https://www.straightdope.com/columns/read/393/how-did-salt-and-pepper-become-the-standard-table-spices/.

20. James Grossman, "Everything Has a History," *Perspectives on History*, December 2015.

the history of a problem before seeking to explain or solve it. When a company plans an initial public offering of shares, its prospectus likely offers a rosy history of the company's founding. When a commercial airplane catches fire, the National Transportation Safety Board explores the work history of the crew and the manufacture history of the defective part, as well as the events that took place once the fire began.[21]

Historians, too, get curious about things they see around them. Like Andrew Needham, environmental historians William Cronon and Timothy LeCain mention first encountering the sites of their later scholarship (Chicago, the Berkeley Pit) on family trips.[22] The Statue of Liberty has a history, as does the Grand Canyon.[23] Cynthia Kierner was inspired not by her first encounter with the Jersey Shore but rather that landscape's sudden devastation by Superstorm Sandy in 2012, which led her to investigate concepts of disaster in the past.[24]

We not only have histories of salt and pepper but whole series of *commodity histories* explaining how now-common foods and other products became objects of mass production and consumption. And we do not need to stop with places or physical objects. Ideas, too, have histories. When did people first conceive of the idea of the middle class, of pollution, of immigration as a problem?[25] Policies

21. National Transportation Safety Board, "Uncontained Engine Failure and Subsequent Fire, American Airlines Flight 383, Boeing 767–323, N345AN, Chicago, Illinois, October 28, 2016," January 30, 2018.

22. Timothy J. LeCain, *Mass Destruction: The Men and Giant Mines That Wired America and Scarred the Planet* (New Brunswick, NJ: Rutgers University Press, 2009), xi; William Cronon, *Nature's Metropolis: Chicago and the Great West*, reprint ed. (New York: W. W. Norton, 1992), 5.

23. Yasmin Sabina Khan, *Enlightening the World: The Creation of the Statue of Liberty* (Ithaca: Cornell University Press, 2010); Stephen J. Pyne, *How the Canyon Became Grand: A Short History* (New York: Penguin, 1999).

24. Cynthia A. Kierner, *Inventing Disaster: The Culture of Calamity from the Jamestown Colony to the Johnstown Flood* (Chapel Hill: University of North Carolina Press, 2019), xi.

25. Stuart Mack Blumin, *The Emergence of the Middle Class: Social Experience in the American City, 1760–1900* (New York: Cambridge University Press, 1989); Peter Thorsheim, *Inventing Pollution: Coal, Smoke, and Culture in Britain since 1800* (Athens: Ohio University Press, 2006); Katherine Benton-Cohen, *Inventing the Immigration Problem: The Dillingham Commission and Its Legacy* (Cambridge, MA: Harvard University Press, 2018).

have history. When did Americans start providing poverty relief, and why did they attach such a stigma to it?[26] Economic structures have a history. Thomas Piketty opens *Capital in the Twenty-First Century* by observing that "the distribution of wealth is one of today's most widely discussed and controversial issues. But what do we really know about its evolution over the long term?"[27]

Even common human behaviors have histories. As she lay on the delivery table, having given birth for the first time, Judith Walzer Leavitt imagined a history of women's experience of childbirth.[28] Further along in parenthood, Peter Stearns watched his slouching children and realized he had not chastised them the way his father had chastised him. When, he wondered, had Americans abandoned the stiff postures of their ancestors?[29] If your mind is prepared, every waking moment can inspire a research project.

NARRATIVE EXPANSION

What happened next? What happened before? What did events look like from another character's point of view? How might these events have played out in a different setting? These are questions that occur to many lovers of stories, some of whom make the effort to craft additional stories themselves. The questions are as old as literature. The *Aeneid* picks up where the *Iliad* leaves off. *A Connecticut Yankee in King Arthur's Court* repurposes Arthurian legend. Jean Rhys's 1966 novel, *Wide Sargasso Sea*, builds on Charlotte Brontë's *Jane Eyre* by telling the story of previous events in the world of *Jane Eyre* and through the perspective of characters downplayed by Brontë. More recently, Alice Randall's 2001 novel, *The Wind Done Gone*, tells the events of Margaret Mitchell's *Gone*

26. Michael B. Katz, *In the Shadow of the Poorhouse: A Social History of Welfare in America*, 2nd ed. (New York: Basic Books, 1996).

27. Thomas Piketty, *Capital in the Twenty-First Century*, trans. Arthur Goldhammer (Cambridge, MA: Harvard University Press, 2014), 1.

28. Judith Walzer Leavitt, "True Facts and Honest History: A Review of Certain Practices, a Mea Culpa, and Other Thoughts about the Writing of History," *Historically Speaking* 14 (2013): 11–13.

29. Peter Stearns, "Behavioral History: A Brief Introduction to a New Frontier," *Journal of Social History* 39 (2006): 946; David Yosifon and Peter N. Stearns, "The Rise and Fall of American Posture," *American Historical Review* 103 (1998): 1057–95.

with the Wind from the perspective of Scarlett O'Hara's enslaved half sister. Amateur creators do similar work, setting "fan fiction" stories in the worlds of *Star Trek*, *Harry Potter*, and pretty much any popular television program or film series you can name. Critic Armelle Parey gathers various such works—prequels, sequels, transfictions—under the inclusive label of *narrative expansions*.[30] Since historians, like novelists, write narratives, it is perhaps unsurprising that they too often read an existing narrative, then expand it.

"On the very first day of my very first class in my very first year of graduate school," writes Honor Sachs, she joined a seminar in discussing David Hackett Fischer's *Albion's Seed*. "One sentence jumped out at me. It stated that the only difference between the colonial backcountry and the American frontier was the direction that people faced." Unsettled by that image, Sachs wrote her own stories of the early national frontier, eventually producing her book, *Home Rule*.[31] Similarly, Sarah Jo Peterson was intrigued by Nelson Lichtenstein's two-paragraph account of a failed effort to build a "Defense City" adjacent to the Willow Run bomber plant outside of Detroit. Peterson eventually expanded Lichtenstein's narrative into a book about not only that failure but the broader challenge of housing defense workers at the plant, with significant implications for our understanding of the relationship between New Deal and home front planning during World War II.[32]

These kinds of narrative expansions deepen our historical knowledge. Some refocus our gaze on new characters in the story. The first histories of an event often emphasize the most powerful leaders, men whose names were recorded in chronicles and newspapers. Such histories do important work not only by telling the stories of those actors but also by establishing the sequence of events, which can help subsequent historians fill in the story with

30. Armelle Parey, "Introduction: Narrative Expansions—The Story So Far," in *Prequels, Coquels and Sequels in Contemporary Anglophone Fiction*, ed. Armelle Parey (New York: Routledge, 2018), 1–24.

31. Honor Sachs, *Home Rule: Households, Manhood, and National Expansion on the Eighteenth-Century Kentucky Frontier* (New Haven, CT: Yale University Press, 2015), ix.

32. Nelson Lichtenstein, *The Most Dangerous Man in Detroit: Walter Reuther and the Fate of American Labor* (New York: Basic Books, 1995), 172; Sarah Jo Peterson, *Planning the Home Front: Building Bombers and Communities at Willow Run* (Chicago: University of Chicago Press, 2013), and correspondence with the author.

a broader cast. For instance, generations of scholarship on Thomas Jefferson and George Washington helped prepare the way for Annette Gordon-Reed and Erica Armstrong Dunbar to tell the stories of two women enslaved by those founders: Sally Hemings and Ona Judge.[33] As he prepared to explore the civil rights era, Jason Sokol read biographies of prominent white Southerners, never denying their importance. "But overall," he explains, "an insistent focus on powerful citizens—such as political leaders and newspaper editors—renders barely visible the populace that buys the papers, and casts the votes."[34] By rendering that populace visible, Sokol complements earlier accounts.

Prequels and sequels do similar work of expanding a narrative. Consider book titles like *The Stamp Act Crisis: Prologue to Revolution*; *Prelude to the Dust Bowl: Drought in the Nineteenth-Century Southern Plains*; and *After Roe: The Lost History of the Abortion Debate*.[35] Whole subfields of history are dedicated to understanding how people remembered events in the past.

Other historians keep the time and change the place. In *Independence Lost: Lives on the Edge of the American Revolution*, Kathleen DuVal tells the story of the American Revolution in the familiar time frame of the 1770s but moves the action away from the Atlantic seaboard to the Gulf Coast, for whose peoples "the Revolution seemed to be just another imperial war, another war fought for territory and treasure." "The narrative of the Revolutionary era," DuVal argues, "is more true to its people and more fascinating in its complexity if it includes less familiar regions and peoples and if it encompasses the war's experiences and results in all their diversity."[36] One caveat is

33. Annette Gordon-Reed, *The Hemingses of Monticello: An American Family* (New York: W. W. Norton, 2008); Erica Armstrong Dunbar, *Never Caught: The Washingtons' Relentless Pursuit of Their Runaway Slave, Ona Judge* (New York: 37 Ink/Atria, 2017).

34. Jason Sokol, *There Goes My Everything: White Southerners in the Age of Civil Rights, 1945–1975* (2006; repr., New York: Vintage, 2007), 9.

35. Edmund S. Morgan and Helen M. Morgan, *The Stamp Act Crisis: Prologue to Revolution* (1953; repr., Chapel Hill: Omohundro Institute and University of North Carolina Press, 1995); Kevin Z. Sweeney, *Prelude to the Dust Bowl: Drought in the Nineteenth-Century Southern Plains* (Norman: University of Oklahoma Press, 2016); Mary Ziegler, *After Roe: The Lost History of the Abortion Debate* (Cambridge, MA: Harvard University Press, 2015).

36. Kathleen DuVal, *Independence Lost: Lives on the Edge of the American Revolution* (New York: Random House, 2015), xv.

that readers do want a somewhat new story. Determining that what happened in one town also happened in another town ten miles away is unlikely to win attention.

In fiction, readers and writers distinguish between "canon" (the version approved by the copyright owner) and fan versions. While canon may have some inconsistencies, it generally coheres. By contrast, any two fan creations, however consistent with canon, may diverge wildly from each other, since there is no controlling authority to keep them in line. Historical scholarship makes no such distinctions. If you do your work well, your account of an event will be every bit as accurate as anyone else's account of an adjoining event. While interpretations may differ, your facts should mesh with the existing canon.

The more widely you read, the more questions may occur to you. If all of your books are from white, male history professors at research universities in a single country, you are unlikely to get all of the perspectives possible, and will therefore miss some promising questions. Read works by women, scholars of color, scholars in other countries, scholars outside of academia, and scholars in other fields.

FROM THE SOURCE

Some historians start with a source, then devise a question. "Research at its most effective and delightful is a journey of unexpected discovery," writes ShawnaKim Lowey-Ball. "We don't really form our arguments—or even discover our true research subjects—until we've sat with our documents and found the interesting truths within them."[37] Bernard Bailyn began a thorough reading of pamphlets of the American Revolution as a largely bibliographic project, and only later realized the possibilities for analysis and interpretation. "More was called for in preparing this edition than simply reproducing accurately and annotating a selected group of texts," he later realized. That "more" evolved into his landmark book, *The Ideological Origins of the American Revolution.*[38] Martha Hodes and Cynthia Kierner

37. ShawnaKim Lowey-Ball, "History by Text and Thing," *Perspectives on History,* March 2020.

38. Bernard Bailyn, *The Ideological Origins of the American Revolution* (Cambridge, MA: Harvard University Press, 1967), v.

each came across bundles of women's letters and found stories they wanted to tell.[39] Jonathan Rees was in an engineering library, on his way to the bound volumes of the trade journal *Iron Age*, when he spotted another trade journal with an intriguing title: *Ice and Refrigeration*. That became the seed of his book *Refrigeration Nation: A History of Ice, Appliances, and Enterprise in America.*[40]

In each of these cases, the historians brought some latent questions—about the origins of the Revolution, about women's places in the country that Revolution produced, and about American industry—that made them see potential in the sources. Absent a curiosity about the history of business and technology, Rees would not have been prowling through the print journals section of an engineering library. And while Bailyn and Kierner could have come up with something to say about each other's sources, they would not have written with the same passion that they brought to the sources that sparked their interests. For this reason, it may be more useful to start with a question you care about and then see if sources are available, rather than starting with sources. On the other hand, you will need sources, so it is worth considering what is out there as you form your question. (See this book's chapters on sources for a great deal more detail on identifying and using primary sources.)

Quite frequently, historians begin exploring sources with one question in mind, only to stumble onto another topic. "When I set out to write a cultural history of [California's Central Valley]," writes Linda Nash, "I found ample evidence of settlers' market orientation and belief in environmental conquest. Clearly they looked upon the western landscape as a resource ripe for exploitation, and they eagerly set about to mine the region's gold, harvest its timber, and plow up its prairies. But I also stumbled across settlers' overwhelming concern with the region's effect on their health, and here I found a different way of thinking about the land. . . . The extent of this preoccupation surprised me, and I thought it might make

39. Martha Elizabeth Hodes, *The Sea Captain's Wife: A True Story of Love, Race, and War in the Nineteenth Century* (New York: W. W. Norton, 2006), 18; Cynthia A. Kierner, *Scandal at Bizarre: Rumor and Reputation in Jefferson's America* (Charlottesville: University of Virginia Press, 2006), vii.

40. Jonathan Rees, *Refrigeration Nation: A History of Ice, Appliances, and Enterprise in America* (Baltimore: Johns Hopkins University Press, 2013), 227.

for an interesting paragraph or two. Instead it reoriented my entire project, as I realized how important perceptions of health were to understanding the natural landscape in earlier eras."[41]

PUBLIC HISTORY

Public and applied historians may have less freedom to choose their topics. A client or supervisor who is not a historian may have a specific need in mind: to commemorate an anniversary, to win a lawsuit, to ensure that a building can be razed without objection, or perhaps to air dirty laundry. Even then, the historian may have some choices to make about how to define the scope of their work, or to explain to the client the advantages of a history more complex than they may have originally wanted. As Martin Reuss has argued, while public relations may draw on stories from the past, history is not public relations. Historians, he insists, must do more than "pick out facts that reinforce the agency self-image or policy." He continues, "Utilizing well-researched, analytical history to further agency goals and publicize its heritage should be encouraged. Publishing poor history, or selective nuggets of received truth, to do the same is shameful; the same may be said of museum exhibits that tell the story incompletely."[42] Thus, the historian may have an obligation to at least try to tell a more complete story than an institution originally wished.

RESEARCH AGENDA

Novice historians, such as undergraduates, should probably not have long-term research agendas. True, it is possible for a term paper to become the seed of a larger, long-term project.[43] As an undergraduate, Theodore Roosevelt began work on what would

41. Linda Nash, *Inescapable Ecologies: A History of Environment, Disease, and Knowledge* (Berkeley: University of California Press, 2007), 5.

42. Martin Reuss, "Government and Professional Ethics: The Case of Federal Historians," *Public Historian* 21 (1999): 138.

43. Elizabeth Fenn first learned of the smallpox epidemic of 1775–82 while writing an undergraduate essay. I first wrote about Metro for an undergraduate course taught by John Stilgoe; sixteen years later I published a book on the subject. Elizabeth A. Fenn, *Pox Americana: The Great Smallpox Epidemic of 1775–82* (New York: Hill and Wang, 2001), ix.

become his first book, *The Naval War of 1812*, which later shaped his service as assistant secretary of the navy and president of the United States. But that is not the pattern for most undergraduates, who can afford to play with a topic for a semester, then abandon it.

For a career historian, high stakes are more common. In order to write a graduate seminar paper that really advances scholarly knowledge, you may need to master specific languages or other skills, learn how to work with specific sources, and immerse yourself in particular scholarly debates. A dissertation may define you for decades or even for the rest of your life, if it establishes your reputation or leads to future, related projects.

Committing to a general area of interest brings strong efficiencies of scale. You get to know the institutions, sources, personalities, and language of a particular time and place. You also build human networks. If your interests stay focused enough for you to attend the same subdisciplinary conference every year, you will know and be known by others working on similar projects. Historians who teach may be able to shape their syllabi so that many of the books and articles they read inform both their teaching and their scholarship.[44] Public historians can likewise coordinate their research with the mission of the museum, site, or agency where they work, so that the research does double duty.

Ideally, these historians will find inspiration for new projects even as they research older ones. Carlo Ginzburg was writing about trials for witchcraft in sixteenth- and seventeenth-century Italy when he encountered the curious case of Menocchio, charged with arguing that the world had originated from putrefaction. He wrote down the number of the trial and, years later, told Menocchio's story in the now classic microhistory, *The Cheese and the Worms*.[45] Decades later, Erica Armstrong Dunbar was doing a last round of research for her first book, *A Fragile Freedom*, when she noticed something shocking. "I was doing the work, digging in the archives, and looking through 18th-century newspapers on microfilm," she recalls, "when up pops a fugitive

44. Kierner, *Inventing Disaster*, 215.

45. Carlo Ginzburg, *The Cheese and the Worms: The Cosmos of a Sixteenth-Century Miller*, trans. John Tedeschi and Anne C. Tedeschi, reprint ed. (Baltimore: Johns Hopkins University Press, 1992), xi.

slave ad from the nation's first president about a woman who had escaped his household." That ad became the seed of her second book, *Never Caught: The Washingtons' Relentless Pursuit of Their Runaway Slave, Ona Judge*. She credits her work on the first book not only for the encounter with the ad but also for giving her the background knowledge needed to understand Judge's life.[46] Alan Taylor has written multiple books on the borderlands of the early decades of the United States. Though each book tells a different story, each is related by theme and era.

As always, there are trade-offs. If you have completed one project so well that it answers the biggest questions you had about that topic, you may find a related topic uninspiring, and no topic is harder to research than one that does not interest you. "Supposedly, I was studying water management in French North Africa during the colonial and postcolonial eras, a project that flowed (sorry) from my previous research on the history of the transformation of France's Rhône River since World War II," writes Sara Pritchard, of a conversation with a new colleague, who had asked about her work. "I had done eight weeks of research during two archival stints in France, and written an article and a conference paper that could lead to another publication, but I just couldn't get excited about the project. I didn't feel that I had anything new or important to say. 'But I'm obsessed with light pollution,' I confessed to her. 'Perhaps I'll jump ship and work on that.'"[47] She did.[48] "It's not that I get bored staying in one place, rather I get attracted by another," explains Natalie Zemon Davis. "It's like a jewel, a diamond that one turns, and suddenly there's a whole other face. It's that new face of history that I want to examine."[49]

46. Jim Knable, "Talk of Souls in Slavery Studies," *Gilder Lehrman Institute of American History* (blog), February 26, 2019, https://medium.com/@gilderlehrman/talk-of-souls -in-slavery-studies-c41e6c893a4f.

47. Sara B. Pritchard, "On (Not) Seeing Artificial Light at Night: Light Pollution or Lighting Poverty?," *Discard Studies* (blog), June 12, 2017, https://discardstudies.com/2017 /06/12/on-not-seeing-artificial-light-at-night-light-pollution-or-lighting-poverty/.

48. "Sara B. Pritchard," Cornell University, July 10, 2020, http://sts.cornell.edu/sara-b -pritchard.

49. Natalie Zemon Davis, *A Passion for History: Conversations with Denis Crouzet*, Early Modern Studies 4 (Kirksville, MO: Truman State University Press, 2010), 8.

Questions

The worst paper I wrote in graduate school resulted when I quickly settled on a thesis and then went searching for evidence. My professor easily diagnosed the problem, and I can still remember the pained disappointment in her comments. A genuine research project will start with a question, not an answer.

If you begin your research with a firm idea of your intended argument, you are likely to find evidence. As Aileen Kraditor observes, "if one historian asks, 'Do the sources provide evidence of militant struggle among workers and slaves?' the sources will reply, 'Certainly.' And if another asks, 'Do the sources provide evidence of widespread acquiescence in the established order among the American population throughout the past two centuries?' the sources will reply, 'Of course.'"[50] Or, as my advisor Ken Jackson used to warn us, "You can find an example of anything." When writers cherry-pick examples to support their previous beliefs, they are doing the work of propaganda, not history.

To avoid such confirmation bias, try to frame questions that truly puzzle you, so that you are as ready to accept evidence for one explanation as for another. If you find yourself, in the course of a project, alternating back and forth between two explanations of the same event, you are likely doing valuable work, and you will be prepared to pick out the crucial evidence that will help you and your readers decide the case. (See chapter 13, "Organization," for a thesis-statement template that emphasizes the weighing of alternative explanations.)

FACTUAL QUESTIONS

Though historians shudder at the misconception that learning history is a matter of memorizing names and dates, all histories deploy facts, and some histories answer only or primarily factual questions. Sometimes historians seek factual information in the service of applied history. Knowing where chemicals were stored,

50. Aileen S. Kraditor, "American Radical Historians on Their Heritage," *Past & Present* (1972): 136–53.

what treaties were signed, and how old a building is can help institutions meet legal obligations, or, if that fails, hold them to justice. Historians help the producers of feature films and television programs, sometimes by addressing big themes, but also by offering details about what people wore and how they talked. And historians assemble facts for themselves and one another. Teams of historians have compiled and edited the papers of prominent individuals and families, mapped vanished landscapes, and built databases of slaving voyages. The Johns Hopkins University Press has an entire series called "How Things Worked," devoted to such topics as "How Banking Worked in the Early American Republic" and "How Americans Kept Warm in the Nineteenth Century."[51]

INTERPRETIVE QUESTIONS

Valuable as facts are, historians tend to gather facts in service of more interpretive questions. In 1953, Louis Gottschalk distinguished between the *"who, where, what,* and *when* of the original testimony and evidence" and the *"why,* the *how,* and the *with-what-consequences* of individual and social behavior in the past" that require some speculation, or interpretation.[52] It is the *why,* the *how,* and the *with-what-consequences* that drive historical research, that keep weary historians turning those pages, looking for answers. Even popular histories, which emphasize storytelling over analysis, depend on interpretive questions for some of their power. "Beneath the gore and smoke and loam," writes Erik Larson of his best seller *The Devil in the White City,* "this book is about the evanescence of life, and why some men choose to fill their brief allotment of time engaging the impossible, others in the manufacture of sorrow."[53] The more a story has such a *why* underneath it, the deeper it will draw the reader in. While the movie consultant may be asking how much lace was in an aristocrat's cuff, they are

51. How Things Worked series, Johns Hopkins University Press Books, https://jhupbooks.press.jhu.edu/series/how-things-worked.

52. Louis Gottschalk, "A Professor of History in a Quandary," *American Historical Review* 59 (1954): 279.

53. Erik Larson, *The Devil in the White City: Murder, Magic, and Madness at the Fair that Changed America* (New York: Vintage Books, 2004), xi.

also asking how much freedom of bodily movement the aristocrat had, how careful the lady had to be not to stain her dress. The legal consultant may need to answer factual questions about what the chemical company dumped and whether its executives had reason to think the waste was toxic, but they are helping to answer a broader, interpretive question about responsibility.

Academic historians also mix factual and interpretive questions. In 1708, Cotton Mather rattled off a series of mortality statistics in the middle of a funeral sermon. Three centuries later, Ted McCormick asked, "Where did these numbers come from, what did they mean to Mather, and what were they doing in his sermons?" "The first question is the easiest to answer," writes McCormick of the question of where Mather got his numbers. He quickly gets past this factual question, then devotes most of his article to what he considers the juicier second and third questions, which are more interpretive. McCormick cares greatly about the facts, but his goal is to understand meaning.[54]

Dialectics

The best interpretive questions concern the unexpected. As the old newspaper adage advises, "If a dog bites a man it isn't news. But, if a man bites a dog, it is."[55] Rather than trust their readers to know that it is surprising for a man to bite a dog, historians often lay out their reasons for believing they have come across a conundrum or, better still, a paradox.

A fact is not surprising simply because you did not know it before. "I did not know that the capital of South Carolina was Columbia" does not promise much. "I was surprised to learn that the capital of South Carolina is Columbia, when Charleston is a more prominent city," is much better, since you are getting toward

54. Ted McCormick, "Statistics in the Hands of an Angry God? John Graunt's Observations in Cotton Mather's New England," *William and Mary Quarterly* 72 (2015): 564.

55. Garson O'Toole, "'Dog Bites a Man' Is Not News. 'Man Bites a Dog' Is News," *Quote Investigator* (blog), November 23, 2013, https://quoteinvestigator.com/2013/11/22/dog-bites/. For a more realistic appraisal of what makes news, see Russell Baker, "Observer; Tooth and Man," *New York Times*, December 4, 1982.

a *why* question. Dig a little more, and you might learn that prior to the American Revolution, all British colonies in North America had Atlantic ports as their capitals. After the Revolution, eleven of the thirteen original states moved their capitals, mostly to inland locations. So why the change?[56]

The more puzzling the riddle, the greater the value in its solution. To demonstrate such value, historians often frame their theses as dialectics. *Dialectic* is a Greek term, literally meaning "conversation." In philosophy, the term describes the process by which thinkers seek the truth by exchanging opposing arguments. Historians use such comparisons of opposites to craft arguments about the past. Indeed, dialectics distinguish mere recitation of facts from interpretive claims about the past. A dialectic is more than a simple assertion that two ideas, events, or statements were *different*; the word *different* and its synonyms—diverse, varied, and so on—is too vague. Instead, historians present several distinct types of dialectics to explain debates and struggles of the past.

OPPOSING FORCES

One common type of comparison juxtaposes the words and deeds of two or more actors or groups of actors who disagreed about some point. Opposing forces often show up in studies of politics and policy. For example, Alan Taylor's *Liberty Men and the Great Proprietors* describes the conflict, in the decades after the American Revolution, between "gentlemen of property and standing" who expected to control large land grants and monopolize political power, and small farmers who believed in spreading land ownership and authority as widely and equitably as possible.[57] Another common use of the opposing-forces comparison is in the history of technology. Historians often list the pros and cons of two competing technologies or systems to explain why people chose one

56. Rosemarie Zagarri, "Representation and the Removal of State Capitals, 1776–1812," *Journal of American History* 74 (1988): 1239–56.

57. Alan Taylor, *Liberty Men and Great Proprietors: The Revolutionary Settlement on the Maine Frontier, 1760–1820* (Chapel Hill: University of North Carolina Press, 1990), 5.

over the other. Sacks of grain or grain elevators, wooden airplanes or metal airplanes, and septic tanks or sewer systems—all were debates demanding resolution.[58]

A thesis concerning two opposing forces should explain why people disagreed about an issue and, ideally, how they resolved their disagreement. Taylor, for example, argues that, faced with the conflict between agrarians and elites, "Jeffersonian politicians reframed political ideology in a manner that permitted compromise legislation and defused the confrontation."[59] Keep in mind that that resolution may have been amicable—compromise or persuasion—or coercive, with one side driven into bankruptcy, chased out of office, or defeated in the courts or on the battlefield.

INTERNAL CONTRADICTIONS

Not all debates take place between opposing forces. Just as psychologists portray people's minds as soups of conflicting impulses, historians have traced ways in which individuals and groups have found themselves torn between contradictory goals. Michael Katz, for example, identifies four purposes of American social welfare policy over the centuries: "relief of misery, preservation of social order and discipline, [the] regulation of the labor market [and] political mobilization." He then shows that these purposes "have always been inconsistent with each other, and the unresolved tensions between them have undercut virtually all attempts to formulate coherent welfare policy."[60]

Edmund Morgan begins his classic work, *American Slavery, American Freedom*, by noting that even as they demanded their liberty from British rule, George Washington and Thomas Jefferson deprived hundreds of enslaved Americans of even more basic liberties. "The rise of liberty and equality in America had been accompanied by the rise of slavery," Morgan writes. "That two such

58. Cronon, *Nature's Metropolis*, chapter 3; Eric Schatzberg, *Wings of Wood, Wings of Metal* (Princeton, NJ: Princeton University Press, 1998); Adam Ward Rome, *The Bulldozer in the Countryside: Suburban Sprawl and the Rise of American Environmentalism* (New York: Cambridge University Press, 2001), chapter 3.

59. Taylor, *Liberty Men*, 10.

60. Katz, *In the Shadow of the Poorhouse*, xi.

seemingly contradictory developments were taking place simultaneously over a long period of time, from the seventeenth century to the nineteenth, is the central paradox of American history."[61] Who would not want to read a book explaining the central paradox of American history?

Accounts stressing such contradictions must explain how people could hold clashing beliefs or why they seemed to act against their own interests. They should determine whether people were aware of their own inconsistencies, or whether they lived in denial.

COMPETING PRIORITIES

In some stories, the competition is subtler. In these cases, historical actors did not *have* to choose one outcome over another. It is enough to show that they *did* prioritize that outcome, and to explain why.

Sam Lebovic, for instance, begins his book with a 1938 speech by Franklin Roosevelt stressing that "freedom of the news" was as important as "freedom of the press." Lebovic continues:

> FDR never developed the idea of "freedom of the news," but he was neither the first nor the last American to try to articulate a concept of press freedom that went beyond a First Amendment right to free speech. Over the course of the twentieth century, a wide variety of lawyers, journalists, philosophers, and politicians grappled with the same problem: How could one guarantee that informative and accurate news would flow to the public through the press? The notion that First Amendment rights did not produce a truly free press may seem jarring to us, but in the quite recent past, Americans of diverse political inclinations were concerned that press freedom had to mean something more than freedom of expression.

Note the signals that Lebovic uses to establish his question and its significance. First, he shows that the question mattered to significant historical actors, from the president on down. Second, he phrases

61. Edmund S. Morgan, *American Slavery, American Freedom* (1975; repr., New York: W. W. Norton, 2003), 4.

the question as a question, complete with a question mark. Finally, he notes that a previously common idea "may seem jarring to us," promising the reader that he will surprise, and therefore teach.[62]

DETERMINING FACTORS

Any event may have multiple causes; the historian's job is to point out the most important ones. In what may be the most famous thesis statement in American historical writing, Frederick Jackson Turner argued that "up to our own day American history has been in a large degree the history of the colonization of the Great West. The existence of an area of free land, its continuous recession, and the advance of American settlement westward, explain American development." This emphasis on geography contrasted with what Turner called "the germ theory of politics," which emphasized the European political traditions of American settlers. Though Turner thought his readers would know the germ theory well enough that he did not have to elaborate it himself, the strength of his thesis comes from his implied comparison of two possible causes of American political development.[63]

A more recent example of this sort of comparison is the ongoing debate over the decision to use the atomic bomb against Japan. How much were President Truman and other policy makers influenced by the desire to hasten the end of fighting with Japan, compared to their hopes of limiting postwar Soviet power, or their assumption that any weapon, once developed, should be used? Without denying that Truman could have—and likely did—act in response to multiple concerns, scholars weigh these factors in various ways, producing a lively debate.[64]

Determining-factors questions do require full consideration of alternatives, and historians must avoid consulting only sources that would tend to confirm their initial beliefs. For example, Bernard

---

62. Sam Lebovic, *Free Speech and Unfree News: The Paradox of Press Freedom in America* (Cambridge, MA: Harvard University Press, 2016), 2.

63. Frederick J. Turner, "The Significance of the Frontier in American History," *Annual Report of the American Historical Association*, 1893, 199.

64. See, e.g., Martin J. Sherwin, *A World Destroyed: Hiroshima and Its Legacies* (Stanford, CA: Stanford University Press, 2003).

Bailyn's 1967 *Ideological Origins of the American Revolution* remains a key interpretation of that event. But Bailyn's claim that "the American Revolution was above all else an ideological, constitutional, political struggle and not primarily a controversy between social groups undertaken to force changes in the organization of the society or the economy" is weakened by its reliance on pamphlets produced by some of the wealthiest, best educated, most powerful actors in the story. As Thomas Slaughter has noted, "it smacks of circular reasoning to select a body of literature generated by an elite group, notice that these members of the highest stratum are content with the existing social structure, and then conclude that there was no meaningful controversy over the distribution of wealth. Other sources, generated by other groups, might be expected to tell a different story."[65]

HIDDEN OR CONTESTED MEANINGS

A subtle type of thesis compares what people *said* to what they *meant*, especially when that meaning was unspoken, deliberately hidden, or forgotten over the course of years. "World War Two meant many things to many people," writes John Dower. While acknowledging that some participants regarded the war as a struggle for ideology, an imperial contest, or meaningless suffering, he argues that "to scores of millions of participants, the war was also a race war."[66] His book seeks to discover this last meaning, often forgotten amid the others. Other works seek to document several meanings, rather than prioritize one. David Nye, for instance, indicates this in the subtitle of his book on electricity: *Social Meanings of a New Technology*. The plural form of *meanings* indicates his approach.[67]

Some meanings are hidden, perhaps even from their creators. Scientists may believe themselves to be searchers for an objective

65. Bailyn, *The Ideological Origins of the American Revolution*, vi; Thomas P. Slaughter, "The Historian's Quest for Early American Culture(s), c. 1750–1825," *American Studies International* 24 (1986): 32.

66. John W. Dower, *War without Mercy: Race and Power in the Pacific War* (New York: Pantheon Books, 1986), 4.

67. David E. Nye, *Electrifying America: Social Meanings of a New Technology, 1880–1940* (Cambridge, MA: MIT Press, 1992).

truth, but historians of science can tease out the contexts that shaped scientists' beliefs and messages. "Against the unpredictability of living in a fast-changing, pluralistic society, in which even the real itself seemed unstable, color scientists (largely middle class, white, male, and Christian) espoused a vision of society in which professionals such as themselves undertook to monitor and judge the sensations of their fellow citizens, for the good of all," argues Michael Rossi. Color science, he explains, "was not just a new way of thinking about color. It was a new way of understanding how human communities, especially the fractious communities of self-consciously modernizing nations like the United States of the late nineteenth and early twentieth centuries, ought to understand the good, the right, the just, the beautiful, and the real."[68]

Uncovering hidden or contested meanings demands careful, critical reading, and heavy research. Rossi supports his arguments with close readings of scientific texts, Dower collects hundreds of instances showing that Americans and Japanese used ideas of race to understand the Pacific War, while Nye compares descriptions of electricity in technical journals, popular newspapers and magazines, and novels and artworks. That is a lot of work, but if you find a significant, consistent pattern of hidden or contested meanings, you have almost certainly crafted a thesis.

BEFORE AND AFTER

All historical dialectics contribute to the central dialectic in historical scholarship: the comparison between the beginning and the end of an event. History has been defined as "the analysis of change over time," so it makes sense that many historians turn to before-and-after comparisons to provide tension in their work.[69]

Some change is surprising for its rapidity. In *Making a New Deal*, Lizabeth Cohen notes that industrial workers "sustained defeats in 1919 and . . . refrained from unionism and national politics during

---

68. Michael Rossi, *The Republic of Color: Science, Perception, and the Making of Modern America* (Chicago: University of Chicago Press, 2019), 243.

69. Social Science Research Council, Committee on Historiography, *The Social Sciences in Historical Study: A Report* (New York: Social Science Research Council, 1954), 24.

the 1920s. Why did workers suddenly succeed in the thirties as both CIO trade unionists and Democratic Party faithfuls?"[70] The key words here are *why* (which promises an interpretation) and *suddenly* (sudden change is surprising). Similarly, Jessica Martucci notes that in the years after World War II, "most physicians favored formula feeding and women regularly received lactation suppressants without their knowledge. Today, however, mothers endlessly hear about the benefits of breastfeeding and four out of five of them decide to give it a try." Hence her question: "How can we account for this rapid turnaround?"[71]

Other changes take generations but are notable for their magnitude. Jo Guldi begins *Roads to Power* with a particularly vivid before-and-after comparison.

> In 1726, the roads of Britain were mire and muck. A few cobblestoned streets in well-off villages punctuated long stretches of dirt track between towns. Rain-soaked wheel ruts and eroding banks made long-distance travel impossible for considerable periods of the year. Occasionally a peasant dug a hole in the middle of the road to obtain mud to make bricks. If the hole was disguised by rainwater, a traveler's horse could disappear into it. The courts had only recently declared this practice remediable.
>
> By 1848, the road system consisted of forty-foot-wide highways of level gravel that extended to every village and island in the nation. The tiniest pebble of the road had been measured by the hands of out-of-work women and children, watched by appointed surveyors who sent paper forms testifying about their repairs back to engineers in the nation's capital. Networks of strangers traded goods and intelligence by post, stagecoach, and rail, and working-class radicals, traveling on the same roads, plotted the possibility of equal voting rights for all. Houses had been torn down to make room for the roads, and officials in London combed through piles of reports about the regulation of distant surveyors.[72]

70. Lizabeth Cohen, *Making a New Deal: Industrial Workers in Chicago, 1919–1939* (New York: Cambridge University Press, 1990), 5.

71. Jessica Martucci, "From Living Rooms to Hospitals: The Breastfeeding Movement and the Limits of Success," *American Historian*, August 2017.

72. Jo Guldi, *Roads to Power: Britain Invents the Infrastructure State* (Cambridge, MA: Harvard University Press, 2012), 2.

That is an astonishing difference. If Guldi can explain all those changes, she has succeeded in her project.

DIALECTICS CREATE QUESTIONS, NOT ANSWERS

Dialectics allow you to shape your research without committing too early to a thesis. As you gather evidence, you may find yourself thinking first that one factor was determining, then shift to another. You might decide that one side in a dispute had the better argument, then, as you learn more, sympathize instead with their opponents. You get to change your mind as much as you like, all the while knowing what you are looking for in the sources. Only when each new source confirms what you think, rather than troubling it, will it be time to settle on a thesis.

CHAPTER FOUR

Research Design

ARISTOTLE ADVISES in his *Poetics* that narrative poetry "should have for its subject a single action, whole and complete, with a beginning, a middle, and an end. It will thus resemble a living organism in all its unity, and produce the pleasure proper to it. It will differ in structure from historical compositions, which of necessity present not a single action, but a single period, and all that happened within that period to one person or to many, little connected together as the events may be." While a historian might be doomed to record every event in a battle, Aristotle argued, Homer "never attempts to make the whole war of Troy the subject of his poem, though that war had a beginning and an end. It would have been too vast a theme, and not easily embraced in a single view." Instead, Homer "detaches a single portion": the wrath of Achilles.[1]

All honor to Aristotle, but the best histories do not try to narrate "all that happened within that period to one person or to many, little connected together as the events may be." Whether they write a narrative—with a beginning, a middle, and an end—or a more thematic study, they too must avoid choosing "too vast a theme." Instead, they must choose events with a connection in order to craft a coherent whole.

1. Aristotle, "Poetics," part 23, trans. S. H. Butcher, Internet Classics Archive, http://classics.mit.edu/Aristotle/poetics.3.3.html.

Tips

- Make your topic manageable by selecting a time, a place, and, most importantly, a set of characters.
- Read others' works as models, and to show that you are answering new questions.
- Write a prospectus to plan your work, knowing that you will change your plan as you proceed.

Scope

It can be hard to know in advance how big a topic is. Undergraduates in particular tend to announce their wish to study topics that would take a shelf of books to explore in any depth. Reading works published in undergraduate history journals—there are several—can provide a more realistic sense of what can be achieved.[2]

Dissertation writers have it the toughest. The perpetual, inconclusive debate about whether the PhD candidate should conceive of the dissertation as its own finished product or as the first draft of a book reflects the grim truth that there are some penalties for being too ambitious and others for not being ambitious enough. Carve out a question that is too big, and you will run out of time and money before you get your degree. Limit yourself to one that is too small, and you will struggle to compete for academic jobs (if that is your wish) against candidates whose dissertations make claims big enough to signal that they will soon become important books.

Some historians start books, only to realize that they can answer their questions in an article or two. Others start articles and find themselves with more material than they can handle. When I first started researching the history of the ethical regulation of social science research, I hoped to find enough material for a 10,000-word article. But my initial research led me to additional events and sources, so for a while I resigned myself to writing two articles. By the time I had written 20,000 words and still had much to cover, I decided I would need at least 50,000 words to tell my story. Since this was approaching book length, I raised the possibility with an

---

2. Society of Undergraduate Humanities Publications, https://www.suhp.org/.

acquisitions editor at a university press. By the time I submitted the manuscript for *Ethical Imperialism*, it ran eight chapters, about 70,000 words. (This is a wonderful way to start a book: start by writing an article or two, without committing to a book until you are 10- or 20,000 words in. By that point, you will know you care enough about the subject to keep going, yet you will also have the flexibility to respond to feedback from potential editors and other helpers.)

No historian can tell every story, yet any selection you make can open you up to criticism from readers who wished you had made different choices. "Most readers see only the finished form" of a book, writes Richard White, "but other historians recognize what has been cut away."[3] To head off criticism of your choices, clarify what questions you are asking, and how your chosen research design answers those questions.

Explore the benefits & pitfalls of using established models in shaping the trajectory of your research

COPY OTHER WORKS

The first step in research design may be to copy from someone else's research design. At the beginning of Robert Altman's 1992 movie, *The Player*, screenwriters pitch their ideas to skeptical studio executives, often offering mashups of previously successful films, such as "*Out of Africa* meets *Pretty Woman*."[4] Historians sometimes imagine their own works as movie mashups. Introducing *The Four Deaths of Acorn Whistler*, Joshua Piker explains, "I sometimes describe this book as *Rashomon* meets *Last of the Mohicans*, with a dash of *Who Framed Roger Rabbit?*"[5] More commonly, it may be helpful to think of your project as a mashup, not of Hollywood films but rather of previous scholarly works.

Identifying comparable works fulfills several functions. First, it increases the chances you will enjoy the work. The happiest historians write the kind of history they love to read. If you enjoy reading

3. Richard White, "New Yorker Nation," *Reviews in American History* 47 (2019): 159.

4. Katy Waldman, "It's *Out of Africa* Meets *Pretty Woman*! The Art and Science of Mixture Descriptions," *Slate*, November 23, 2015, https://slate.com/human-interest/2015/11/mixture-descriptions-why-researchers-are-suddenly-obsessed-with-elevator-pitches.html.

5. Joshua Piker, *The Four Deaths of Acorn Whistler: Telling Stories in Colonial America* (Cambridge, MA: Harvard University Press, 2013), 27.

books and articles that are richly illustrated with maps, look for research topics that will allow you to study maps yourself. If you like to read about the history of sports, why not write about the history of sports? If you were stirred by the way other historians recovered stories of the silenced and oppressed, try recovering some yourself.

Second, it is a good check on length. To estimate whether your idea is appropriate for its proposed length—student paper, journal article, book, and so on—is to see if anyone else has done a comparable project. (See chapter 13, "Organization," for typical word counts of projects of different scales, especially if you are preparing to write at greater length than your previous work.)

Third, the models can provide guidance on structure. Having enjoyed William Cronon's *Changes in the Land: Indians, Colonists, and the Ecology of New England*, Timothy Silver happily adopted it as the "structural and methodological model" and a "how-to manual" for his own study. That still left Silver plenty of room for new findings, since Cronon had written about New England, and Silver was writing about English colonies far to the south, with their distinct climate, vegetation, and economy. Silver thus used Cronon's tools to create something new.[6] Even if the fit is looser, models can help. For example, if you are planning a project that consists of four case studies, any history consisting of four case studies may be helpful, regardless of the topic. Nate Holdren used an article by Margot Canaday as a template, not because its content matched his but because its format would work for his story. "Where . . . Professor Canaday's article said there was a vignette, I wrote a vignette," he explains. "Where there was a summary of the historiography relevant to the article, I wrote a summary of the historiography relevant to my article. Where Canaday had a summary of her argument, I wrote '[paragraph summarizing argument goes here]' because I was still figuring out my argument."[7]

[handwritten margin note: what structure would be the best to perform your topic? findings]

6. Timothy Silver, *A New Face on the Countryside: Indians, Colonists, and Slaves in South Atlantic Forests, 1500–1800* (New York: Cambridge University Press, 1990), ix, xi.

7. Nate Holdren, "How I Went from Dissertation to Book: Escaping Blank Pages, Part 1," *Legal History Blog*, July 16, 2020, https://legalhistoryblog.blogspot.com/2020/07/how-i-went-from-dissertation-to-book.html.

Finally, identifying models is a step toward publication. If you model your work on articles in the *Journal of X*, you will increase your chances of writing a paper that the *Journal of X* will want to publish. If you model your dissertation or book manuscript on half a dozen successful books, you can list them in your book proposal, perhaps sending it to the publisher of your models.

As of 2020, members of the American Historical Association crafting their profiles could choose among seventy-four "Thematic Areas of Interest," ranging from Borderlands and Genocide to Print Culture and Sports. Each of these categories represents a filter that historians have used to make sense of the complex reality of events. For instance, one can read a legal history of the Civil War, a religious history of the Civil War, an environmental history of the Civil War, a sensory history of the Civil War, and even a military history of the Civil War.[8] Many historians blend two or more approaches. Both Thomas Andrews and Ellen Stroud identify as environmental historians, but Andrews mixes his environmental history with labor history, while Stroud mixes hers with urban history.[9] Intellectual filters can help you write a coherent story, but do not exclude evidence just because it does not fit your preferred approach. *[margin annotation: ways to help write a coherent story]*

Of course, sometimes historians do work so innovative that it demands, or at least rewards, new forms. The vast majority of history writing, however, draws on one or more established subgenres. In those cases, there is no shame in following conventions.

8. Laura F. Edwards, *A Legal History of the Civil War and Reconstruction: A Nation of Rights* (New York: Cambridge University Press, 2015); George C. Rable, *God's Almost Chosen Peoples: A Religious History of the American Civil War* (Chapel Hill: University of North Carolina Press, 2010); Judkin Browning and Timothy Silver, *An Environmental History of the Civil War* (Chapel Hill: University of North Carolina Press, 2020); Brian Allen Drake, ed., *The Blue, the Gray, and the Green: Toward an Environmental History of the Civil War* (Athens: University of Georgia Press, 2015); Mark M. Smith, *The Smell of Battle, the Taste of Siege: A Sensory History of the Civil War* (New York: Oxford University Press, 2014); Williamson Murray and Wayne Wei-siang Hsieh, *A Savage War: A Military History of the Civil War* (Princeton, NJ: Princeton University Press, 2016).

9. Thomas G. Andrews, *Killing for Coal: America's Deadliest Labor War* (Cambridge, MA: Harvard University Press, 2010), 16; Ellen Stroud, *Nature Next Door: Cities and Trees in the American Northeast* (Seattle: University of Washington Press, 2012), 163n6.

HISTORY BIG AND SMALL

Perhaps the greatest challenge for historians at any level is to define a topic of an appropriate breadth. One extreme of the scale is "microhistory," extremely detailed studies of events directly involving only a handful of people, such as a murder or other crime.[10] Microhistories do not lack ambition. In exploring four rival accounts of the 1752 death of an obscure Creek warrior, Piker seeks to tell "a tale about Indian country, the American colonies, the British empire, and the early modern world that encompassed them all."[11] Similarly, Linda Gordon writes about the seizure, in 1904, of forty Irish American orphans from the Mexican American families that sought to adopt them, arguing that the event reveals deep divisions over race, religion, and gender. Gordon acknowledges that her "protagonists are not renowned or heroic. The small town they lived in is rarely mentioned in history books." But, she continues, "the issues about which these people fought remain with us today, unresolved. And although their story is virtually unremembered outside the town itself, yet it is packed with timeless and placeless meaning. It offers simultaneously universal and local knowledge."[12]

At the other extreme, some historians seek that universal knowledge by telling stories beyond the perspective of any person or place, like the rise of capitalism or changes in global climate. For instance, in the late eighteenth century, a smallpox epidemic swept over North America, covering vastly greater distances than any human communications network. By combining dozens of accounts of local outbreaks, Elizabeth Fenn understood the epidemic more completely than did any individual alive at the time.[13]

A bigger story is neither better nor worse than a smaller one. As Julia Laite argues, "if it is the big-story historian's job to shake

10. Richard D. Brown, "Microhistory and the Post-Modern Challenge," *Journal of the Early Republic* 23 (2003): 1–20; Sigurður G. Magnússon, *What Is Microhistory? Theory and Practice* (New York: Routledge, 2013).

11. Piker, *The Four Deaths of Acorn Whistler*, 28.

12. Linda Gordon, *The Great Arizona Orphan Abduction* (Cambridge, MA: Harvard University Press, 1999), ix.

13. Elizabeth A. Fenn, *Pox Americana: The Great Smallpox Epidemic of 1775–82* (New York: Hill and Wang, 2001).

complacent policy makers, it is the small-story historian's job to convince people that the small stories from the past that have moved them are unfolding in myriad ways today as well; to encourage their sentiment to become conscience. Big history might 'shake' citizens, but small history makes them."[14] And many historians move comfortably from one scale to another, telling big stories in one project, smaller ones in the next.

Most histories are neither microhistory nor big history, but stories told somewhere in the vast middle between those poles. They are human in chronological scale, covering the months, years, or decades that could make up the human experience, rather than the century or ages visible only to the detached observer. Yet they concern events beyond those of daily life, whether the wars and revolutions that once dominated scholarship, or changes in economic, social, or cultural life that still made headlines (or the period equivalent).

PICK YOUR PEOPLE

Why are all perspectives important?

The historian's choice of characters shapes the narrative. A story of a handful of powerful men, for whom records are plentiful, will read differently from one about a large social group whose history must be compiled from fragments. The story of a scoundrel will read differently from the story of a hero. Just as importantly, the choice of characters shapes the argument, perhaps more than any other choice. For centuries, historians told the stories of kings, generals, and diplomats, assuming that those were the people whose words and deeds counted as history. Since the late nineteenth century, some historians have continued that tradition, while others have sought to tell the stories of people who have been left out of earlier accounts.

why should we focus on individual voices?

To tell someone's story is to assert that their life mattered. "Hawaiians can and should understand their world from their own Hawaiian perspectives, not those of their colonizers," writes David Chang. "Hawaiʻi is best understood as a land deeply rooted in the

14. Julia Laite, "The Emmet's Inch: Small History in a Digital Age," *Journal of Social History* 53 (2020): 982.

I know your limits

Pacific sea of islands, not merely a peripheral dependency of some other power (notably the United States)."[15] Mar Hicks wants to recover the story of women in computing, and not just the stories of exceptionally prominent women, such as Grace Hopper or Stephanie Shirley. Those stories make for compelling, inspiring stories, but that is not what Hicks is after. "A focus on individual voices tends to reproduce the narrative structures and historiographical methods that erased the impact of gender from the history of computing in the first place, positioning most women as too low level, peripheral, or anonymous to be a valid, formative part of computer history," Hicks explains. "The majority of these workers cannot speak through the archives as individuals, only as a group, and the explanatory power of their experiences lies in this realization."[16]

Playing up one set of actors requires the downplaying or outright exclusion of others. It is easy for critics to complain that a history leaves out one or more apparently important groups, and historians have learned to anticipate such complaints by explaining the absences. Perhaps relevant records simply did not exist.[17] Or the stories are more distinct than the reader might expect. Knowing that readers of a book titled *Gay New York* might expect stories of women as well as men, George Chauncey justifies his neglect of the former. "The book focuses on men because the differences between gay male and lesbian history and the complexity of each made it seem virtually impossible to write a book about both that did justice to each and avoided making one history an appendage to the other," he explains. "The differences between men's and women's power and the qualities ascribed to them in a male-dominated culture were so significant that the social and spatial organization of gay male and lesbian life inevitably took very different forms."[18] Like any historiographical claim, this is a matter of debate. But

15. David A. Chang, *The World and All the Things upon It: Native Hawaiian Geographies of Exploration* (Minneapolis: University of Minnesota Press, 2016), viii.

16. Mar Hicks, *Programmed Inequality: How Britain Discarded Women Technologists and Lost Its Edge in Computing* (Cambridge, MA: MIT Press, 2018), 233.

17. Mary P. Ryan, *Cradle of the Middle Class: The Family in Oneida County, New York, 1790–1865* (New York: Cambridge University Press, 1983), xiii.

18. George Chauncey, *Gay New York: Gender, Urban Culture, and the Making of the Gay Male World, 1890–1940* (New York: Basic Books, 1994), 27.

at the very least, Chauncey has shown respect for the lesbian New Yorkers of the past by stating his wish that their story be told, just not in this particular book.

ADD AND SUBTRACT

Once you have defined the basic scope of your project, you will be able to add and subtract words with relative ease. In her article, "From Service to Sales: Home Economics in Light and Power, 1920–1940," Carolyn Goldstein offers more detail about cooking lessons and lighting advice than about other work performed by home economists.[19] Had she been constrained by time or word limits, I imagine she could have shortened these sections. Conversely, writing a book gave Goldstein the opportunity to tell the story of home service departments at significantly greater length, which she used to add details and examples. The chapter version of "From Service to Sales" is about 75 percent longer than the article version.[20] And even in the longer versions, Goldstein stays focused on a set of protagonists, the sources that allow her to tell their story, and the main action of her narrative. If you can define these three elements— characters, sources, and action—you have control. At any scale, prioritizing the stories and evidence will most persuade your reader of your claims. If you end up with more time or more room, then you can include the elements that are still helpful but less essential.

What should be prioritize and when can we start adding non-essential info?

NARRATIVE VERSUS THEMATIC SCHEMES

As noted above, some histories tell single stories from beginning to end. It is rare to find a purely chronological account, since that would both baffle the reader and misrepresent the experience of the characters, who experienced each event in light of multiple threads in the past. For instance, Michael Flamm's *In the Heat of the Summer*, about the New York riots of 1964, organizes seven of its twelve

---

19. Carolyn M. Goldstein, "From Service to Sales: Home Economics in Light and Power, 1920–1940," *Technology and Culture* 38 (1997): 121–52.

20. Carolyn M. Goldstein, *Creating Consumers: Home Economists in Twentieth-Century America* (Chapel Hill: University of North Carolina Press, 2012), chapter 6.

chapters to the events of a single Friday-to-Thursday week, with one chapter for each day. Yet to make sense of those days, Flamm must expand his chronology. For instance, on Sunday, July 19, civil rights leader James Farmer appeared on live television to denounce the actions of the New York City police. To show how "out of character" these remarks were, Flamm must flash back to Farmer's childhood, pacifism, and career as a civil rights advocate, starting in 1942. To build this account, Flamm draws on an obituary written after Farmer's 1999 death. Thus, to explain the significance of a few minutes of televised commentary in 1964, the historian must reach back to the 1940s and forward to the 1990s.[21]

Most narrative histories are even more flexible with their chronologies than is *In the Heat of the Summer*. For instance, Ernesto Chávez tells the story of Los Angeles's Chicano movement as "a multiplicity of protest groups that differed sharply in their tactics and emphases during that eventful decade from the early 1960s into the 1970s."[22] Putting every event in the book in strict chronological order would be bewildering, since during several years, more than one group was operating, and the reader would be whipsawed from one scene to another. Instead, Chávez presents each major group's story in a single chapter, with the chapters placed in the order each group was founded. The effect is like a shingled roof, with each shingle overlaid on the next, but going a bit further, as one movement group eclipses its predecessors.

In other works, each story may have its own narrative arc, but they all take place more or less simultaneously and could be reordered within the work without changing the meaning too much. Such thematic histories are often more illustrative than comprehensive. In *The Chance of Salvation: A History of Conversion in America*, for example, Lincoln Mullen does not try to narrate every type of religious conversion but rather to "capture something of the varieties of religious conversions available to nineteenth-century Americans, the seemingly inexhaustible array of options from

---

21. Michael W. Flamm, *In the Heat of the Summer: The New York Riots of 1964 and the War on Crime* (Philadelphia: University of Pennsylvania Press, 2016), 105–10.

22. Ernesto Chávez, *"¡Mi Raza Primero!" (My People First!): Nationalism, Identity, and Insurgency in the Chicano Movement in Los Angeles, 1966–1978* (Berkeley: University of California Press, 2002), 117.

which converts had to select."[23] He does this with six chapters, each telling the story of one option in that array. Similarly, Daniel Rodgers, writing an intellectual history of the last quarter of the twentieth century, explains that he did not try to include every intellectual movement. "In a historical inquiry of this sort," he concedes, "it is impossible to deal with more than a fraction of the ideas in motion across an age. . . . In every modern society there is a surfeit of ideas and claimants for primacy. Any one history can draw out only some of these, hoping to make sense out of a major part (but never the whole) of the terrain."[24]

A hybrid form of history sandwiches thematic chapters between more chronological brackets. Lisa McGirr, for instance, organizes her history of Prohibition in eight chapters. Chapter 1 describes the events leading up to the imposition of Prohibition in 1920, and chapter 8 describes its repeal in 1933. The middle chapters all take place in between those dates and are organized by topic, not chronology.[25] Similarly, the central chapters of Mae Ngai's *Impossible Subjects* all take place around the same time, as she tells the stories of Filipinos, Braceros, Japanese Americans, and Chinese Americans before, during, and after World War II. She brackets these between opening chapters on the Johnson-Reed Act of 1924 and the Hart-Celler Act of 1965.[26]

The narrative and thematic approaches are not wholly distinct. Creators of beginning-to-end narratives must make decisions about which episodes in a story to include, and which to omit; that is why two biographies of the same person can pose different questions and produce different answers. And each section of a collection of stories can still be told start to finish. For instance, John Findlay's *Magic Lands* and Samuel Zipp's *Manhattan Projects* each tells four stories of postwar city-building projects. Each story in each

---

23. Lincoln A. Mullen, *The Chance of Salvation: A History of Conversion in America* (Cambridge, MA: Harvard University Press, 2017), 22.

24. Daniel T. Rodgers, *Age of Fracture* (Cambridge, MA: Harvard University Press, 2011), 13.

25. Lisa McGirr, *The War on Alcohol: Prohibition and the Rise of the American State* (New York: W. W. Norton, 2015).

26. Mae M. Ngai, *Impossible Subjects: Illegal Aliens and the Making of Modern America* (Princeton, NJ: Princeton University Press, 2014).

book stands alone as a useful narrative but gains value when juxtaposed against others in the book. Indeed, I would argue, each story becomes even more illuminating if you read the two books together and consider all the linkages among all eight episodes.[27]

Periodization

Periodization is one of those rare bits of professional jargon that historians need. Though the word itself is likely unfamiliar to most readers of history who have not attended graduate school, the concept is implicit in popular as well as scholarly history. Between 1935 and 1975, for instance, Will and Ariel Durant published an eleven-volume series, *The Story of Civilization*, five volumes of which included "Age" in their titles: the Age of Faith, the Age of Reason, the Age of Louis XIV, the Age of Voltaire, and the Age of Napoleon. Behind each of these titles is the argument that we can set apart a certain period of time and turn it into a story with a beginning, middle, and end. That is periodization.

Like the Durants, many historians have used wars and revolutions to divide time periods; historians of the United States, for instance, write of antebellum America, interwar America, and post-war America, among other periods. This is partly due to the fact that well into the twentieth century, war and revolution were among the central topics of elite historians. For other topics, different markers would be appropriate. Marc Bloch noted that it makes no more sense to periodize the history of science by political events than it would to write the "diplomatic history of Europe from Newton to Einstein."[28] On the other hand, even if you are not writing primarily about war or politics, military and political events may define your periods. For instance, John D'Emilio describes World War II as a "nationwide coming out experience" for gay Americans, while Bruce

27. John M. Findlay, *Magic Lands: Western Cityscapes and American Culture after 1940* (Berkeley: University of California Press, 1992); Samuel Zipp, *Manhattan Projects: The Rise and Fall of Urban Renewal in Cold War New York* (New York: Oxford University Press, 2010).

28. Marc Bloch, *The Historian's Craft: Reflections on the Nature and Uses of History and the Techniques and Methods of Those Who Write It.*, trans. Peter Putnam (1953; repr., Princeton, NJ: Vintage, 1964), 183.

Mazlish argues that the war represented a "rupture" in legal history as well as the start of what we now call globalization.[29] Thus, the war may be as appropriate a marker for the histories of sexuality, law, and culture as it is for military and diplomatic history. ✗ *confine history in an exact date range*

Conversely, a war's official start and end may not be the best dates with which to understand even a military topic. Rachel Herrmann rejects the idea of confining her story of the American Revolution to the years 1775–83, when American troops were actively fighting British regulars. As she explains, "the war's chronological boundaries were largely irrelevant to the Indians and enslaved peoples who participated in it," and those are the people whose story she wants to tell.[30] And Mary Dudziak notes that by some legal definitions, the United States remained at war with Germany and Japan into the 1950s, though that defies common-sense understanding that the war ended in 1945.[31]

Periodization can feel artificial, even silly. That is the joke behind Virginia Woolf's line, "On or around December 1910, human character changed." As Woolf immediately concedes, "I am not saying that one went out, as one might into a garden, and there saw that a rose had flowered, or that a hen had laid an egg." And yet, she continues, "in life one can see the change, if I may use a homely illustration, in the character of one's cook. The Victorian cook lived like a leviathan in the lower depths, formidable, silent, obscure, inscrutable; the Georgian cook is a creature of sunshine and fresh air; in and out of the drawing-room, now to borrow *The Daily Herald*, now to ask advice about a hat. Do you ask for more solemn instances of the power of the human race to change?"[32]

For people living in the moment, one day follows the next, and no one wakes up with the realization that the Age of Reason has begun. Yet they do notice change, whether because the cook has borrowed

29. John D'Emilio, *Sexual Politics, Sexual Communities*, 2nd ed. (Chicago: University of Chicago Press, 1998), 24; Bruce Mazlish, "Ruptures in History," *Historically Speaking* 12 (2011): 32–33.

30. Rachel B. Herrmann, *No Useless Mouth: Waging War and Fighting Hunger in the American Revolution* (Ithaca: Cornell University Press, 2019), 5.

31. Mary L. Dudziak, *War Time: An Idea, Its History, Its Consequences* (New York: Oxford University Press, 2012), chapter 2.

32. Virginia Woolf, *Mr. Bennett and Mrs. Brown* (London: Hogarth Press, 1924), 4–5.

the *Daily Herald*, or because the *Daily Herald* has announced the result of an election or the declaration of war. Periodization is the process by which the historian makes choices about which of these changes are significant enough to function as the start or the end to a story. Historians must make such choices, knowing all the time that different, equally justifiable choices would yield results that would be better for some purposes, worse than others.

In US history, perhaps the clearest example is the history of the civil rights movement. There is no single start date to the movement, nor a single end date, so each historian has to decide when to begin and end their account. In her influential Organization of American Historians presidential address, "The Long Civil Rights Movement and the Political Uses of the Past," Jacquelyn Dowd Hall argued that Americans focus too much on the period between the 1954 *Brown v. Board of Education* and the Voting Rights Act of 1965. "By confining the civil rights struggle to the South," Hall argued, "to bowdlerized heroes, to a single halcyon decade, and to limited, noneconomic objectives, the master narrative simultaneously elevates and diminishes the movement."[33] Subsequent historians have taken up the challenge, writing histories of civil rights that stretch back into the 1930s and forward into the 1990s. Collectively, these accounts force readers to rethink not only the significance of the events between 1956 and 1965, but also the very definition of civil rights.[34]

In some cases, periodization is the main argument of a work. "Conventional historiography generally concludes that the involvement of the federal government in U.S. airline industry regulation began with the Civil Aeronautics Act of 1938," writes Robert van der Linden in the opening line of his *Airlines & Air Mail*. "Although there is some validity to this argument," he continues, "a better argument to the contrary can be made. The airline industry was

33. Jacquelyn Dowd Hall, "The Long Civil Rights Movement and the Political Uses of the Past," *Journal of American History* 91 (2005): 1233–63.

34. For examples, see Tomiko Brown-Nagin, *Courage to Dissent: Atlanta and the Long History of the Civil Rights Movement* (New York: Oxford University Press, 2011); Risa Lauren Goluboff, *The Lost Promise of Civil Rights* (Cambridge, MA: Harvard University Press, 2007); Hasan Kwame Jeffries, *Bloody Lowndes: Civil Rights and Black Power in Alabama's Black Belt* (New York: New York University Press, 2009).

born in the mid-1920s and thrived under the watchful eye of the federal government, which fostered its creation and growth long before Roosevelt took office."[35] Judith Stein encapsulates both periodization and argument in the title of her book *Pivotal Decade: How the United States Traded Factories for Finance in the Seventies*.[36] By arguing for the significance of particular times, such works emphasize particular choices.

[handwritten: What beginning would best suit the structure of your story? What structure do you wanna use?]

BEGINNINGS

[handwritten: ↑ peaceful → climax]

Stories need to start at some moment: once upon a time. Many histories begin with a chapter establishing a relatively stable situation, a description of the world before the action starts. Thus, Edward Gibbon begins his *History of the Decline and Fall of the Roman Empire* by describing the empire in the Age of the Antonines.

[handwritten: How can I shape your story? How can beginnings, endings interact with your intended audience?]

> In the second century of the Christian era, the Empire of Rome comprehended the fairest part of the earth, and the most civilised portion of mankind. The frontiers of that extensive monarchy were guarded by ancient renown and disciplined valour. The gentle but powerful influence of laws and manners had gradually cemented the union of the provinces. Their peaceful inhabitants enjoyed and abused the advantages of wealth and luxury. The image of a free constitution was preserved with decent reverence: the Roman senate appeared to possess the sovereign authority, and devolved on the emperors all the executive powers of government.[37]

After expanding this description over the course of nine chapters, he has impressed us with the might of Rome, leading us to wonder how so great an empire could decay.

Today's historians use similar structures. Economist Robert J. Gordon not only evokes Gibbon's title in his *Rise and Fall of American Growth*, but he also borrows Gibbon's insight that a story of

---

35. F. Robert Van der Linden, *Airlines and Air Mail: The Post Office and the Birth of the Commercial Aviation Industry* (Lexington: University Press of Kentucky, 2002), vii.

36. Judith Stein, *Pivotal Decade: How the United States Traded Factories for Finance in the Seventies* (New Haven, CT: Yale University Press, 2011).

37. Edward Gibbon, *The Decline and Fall of the Roman Empire*, vol. 1 (1776; repr., New York: Modern Library, 1932), 1.

decline and fall, or rise and fall, needs to start on a plateau, which he calls "The Starting Point: Life and Work in 1870."[38] Cynthia Kierner's *Inventing Disaster* argues that only during the Enlightenment did Europeans develop the concept of "disaster" that Americans use today. To support this claim, she must show that at some earlier point, Europeans lacked this concept, which indeed is the argument of her first chapter.[39]

Your choice of starting points shapes the story. Will it be, like Gibbon's, a story of steady decline? Or, like Gordon's, one of rise and fall? Or, like Kierner's, one of creation or invention? Or perhaps something more nuanced? As he begins his history of the gentrification of Brooklyn, Suleiman Osman takes pains to include both the bad and the good in his starting point. "To describe Brownstone Brooklyn's unions and political machines as place-centric is not to romanticize an older working-class gemeinschaft," he writes, as he describes a Brooklyn that included racketeers, pilferers, extortionists, and street gangs along with its hardworking families with their authentic ethnic traditions.[40] Thanks to this complexity, the rest of his story is not a simplistic story of decline but instead a tale that challenges the reader to consider both the gains and the losses in Brooklyn's transformation. (See chapter 14, "Storytelling," for more discussion along these lines.)

ENDINGS

Historians have various methods to leave the reader feeling that the story has come to an end. Some of my favorite books take the story right up to the present. Michael Katz's magnificent *In the Shadow of the Poorhouse* traces debates about poverty relief from the early nineteenth century to the time of its writing in the 1980s. In 1996, he added a chapter to bring the book forward through the

---

38. Robert J. Gordon, *The Rise and Fall of American Growth: The U.S. Standard of Living since the Civil War* (Princeton, NJ: Princeton University Press, 2017), chapter 2.

39. Cynthia A. Kierner, *Inventing Disaster: The Culture of Calamity from the Jamestown Colony to the Johnstown Flood* (Chapel Hill: University of North Carolina Press, 2019), chapter 1.

40. Suleiman Osman, *The Invention of Brownstone Brooklyn: Gentrification and the Search for Authenticity in Postwar New York* (New York: Oxford University Press, 2012), 48.

Clinton-era debates.[41] Taking the story to the present emphasizes the continuities of debates about welfare, as Americans repeatedly, and futilely, seek to distinguish between the deserving and the undeserving poor. It tracks the problem of poverty for two centuries, shows all the failed efforts to solve it, and then, in the final chapter, dumps it in the reader's lap, making them an actor in the very history they have read.

[handwritten: involves the readers "we are making history"]

Another satisfying ending is the death of a main character, or perhaps an institution. Tammy Ingram's *Dixie Highway* ends with the distinctively named road network of her title being absorbed into the US highway system, its red and white "DH" markers replaced with a variety of numbers.[42] Lisa McGirr's *War on Alcohol* sensibly ends with the repeal of Prohibition in 1933.[43] Other stories are less easily framed. Cultural and social movements lack the crisp delineation of military or legal history, though they may borrow from them.

And even sharply defined events make ripples that last far into the future. The title of Greg Downs's *After Appomattox* suggests the argument: the Confederate "surrender marked a turning point, not an end point, for the state of war."[44] Most of the violence at New York's Attica Correctional Facility took place over the course of five days: September 9–13, 1971. But Heather Ann Thompson continues the story into the 2000s, detailing decades of lawsuits, cover-ups, and interpretations.[45]

The choice of an end point can shape the message of a narrative. "Most narratives of King Philip's War," writes Lisa Brooks, "whether written in 1676 or 2006, mark the late spring of 1676 as the moment when the 'tide turned' toward English victory." She disagrees, considering participants and places that get little attention in other narratives, as well as longer-term political and environmental

41. Michael B. Katz, *In the Shadow of the Poorhouse: A Social History of Welfare in America*, 2nd ed. (New York: Basic Books, 1996).

42. Tammy Ingram, *Dixie Highway: Road Building and the Making of the Modern South, 1900–1930*, reprint ed. (Chapel Hill: University of North Carolina Press, 2016), 175.

43. McGirr, *The War on Alcohol*.

44. Gregory P. Downs, *After Appomattox: Military Occupation and the Ends of War* (Cambridge, MA: Harvard University Press, 2015), 11.

45. Heather Ann Thompson, *Blood in the Water: The Attica Prison Uprising of 1971 and Its Legacy* (New York: Pantheon, 2016).

consequences of the fighting. "The conflict that began in Metacom's homeland continued long beyond his death, perhaps for another hundred years," she concludes. "Or, as some would say, perhaps that war has never ended at all."[46] For a historian sympathetic to the aims of the New Deal, a story of American politics that ends in 1939 or 1948 can appear to be a triumph, and even later setbacks can be dismissed as momentary in a larger trend. But, argue Jefferson Cowie and Nick Salvatore, as one continues to extend the timeline, it is the New Deal that appears exceptional. "From the standpoint of the twenty-first century," they write, "Roosevelt's version now seems less of a liberal triumph than it does a historical aberration."[47]

PACE

In between the beginning and end of a narrative, the historian has great control over the pace. If you had two weeks to get from New York to San Francisco, you could maintain an even pace of about 215 miles per day on I-80. Or you could do longer drives on some days in order to linger a bit in Chicago, Omaha, and Salt Lake City, or avoid the major cities in favor of small towns, or catch a nonstop flight on your first day and spend the rest of the time exploring the Bay Area. Historians can similarly choose to cover roughly the same amount of time in each chapter, or rush through less interesting segments in order to spend more time on critical junctures. In his history of the New York City subway, for instance, Clifton Hood takes only one chapter to narrate the 1913 creation of the "Dual System of Rapid Transit." Peter Derrick devotes an entire book to the same set of events, offering vastly more detail and a greater appreciation for the significance of the agreement. Each account serves its own purpose, and the most enthusiastic readers of transit history will welcome both.[48]

46. Lisa Brooks, *Our Beloved Kin: A New History of King Philip's War* (New Haven, CT: Yale University Press, 2018), 302.

47. Jefferson Cowie and Nick Salvatore, "The Long Exception: Rethinking the Place of the New Deal in American History," *International Labor and Working-Class History* 74 (2008): 5.

48. Clifton Hood, *722 Miles: The Building of the Subways and How They Transformed New York* (New York: Simon & Schuster, 1993), chapter 6; Peter Derrick, *Tunneling to the*

"Do you mind if we hurry through the early years?" George Packer asks in his biography of Richard Holbrooke. "There are no mysteries here that can be unlocked by nursery school."[49] Whether or not Packer is correct about the insignificance of Holbrooke's childhood experiences, he is certainly right that the historian controls the time machine's throttle, and with it the power to hover, linger, hurry through, or skip altogether.

THE BALKY TIME MACHINE

The historian cannot always control the span of the story. Sometimes you set your time machine for a particular year, only to have it deposit you a bit earlier or later, so you have to research your way on foot to your destination. In the early 1980s, John Dower began writing a book about the American occupation of Japan at the end of World War II. It struck him that to explain the surprising amity between the two nations during the occupation, he would need to first discuss the "burning passions and unbridled violence that preceded Japan's surrender in August 1945," so he included a mention of the mutual "race hates" during the war. "What occurred next may seem agonizingly familiar to many other historians," Dower later explained. "The passing comment was expanded to a paragraph, which grew into a section, then became a separate chapter, and finally emerged as a major research project in and of itself."[50] Only after he finished a book on the war years was Dower able to return to the occupation, his original destination.[51]

Similarly, Kevin Kruse planned to "explore the roots of the Religious Right in the 1960s and 1970s," and thought that a good year to begin would be 1962, when the Supreme Court ruled that school-sponsored prayer in public schools is unconstitutional. But as he

---

Future: The Story of the Great Subway Expansion That Saved New York (New York: New York University Press, 2001).

49. George Packer, *Our Man: Richard Holbrooke and the End of the American Century* (New York: Knopf, 2019), 11.

50. John Dower, *War without Mercy: Race and Power in the Pacific War* (New York: Pantheon, 1986), x.

51. John W. Dower, *Embracing Defeat: Japan in the Wake of World War II* (New York: W. W. Norton, 1999).

read the letters that Americans had written to the Supreme Court that year, he found that many of them referenced the phrases "one nation under God" and "in God we trust" that had been added to the Pledge of Allegiance and the paper currency in the 1950s. Researching that decade took him to the 1930s. "I could have gone further back," Kruse later explained. "Americans had fused faith and free enterprise in the decades before the Depression, and arguments that the United States was a 'Christian nation' had been made since the early eighteenth century." But he decided that the 1930s would be a good place to start his story. By the end of the book, he had arrived at his original starting place.[52]

If you want to be sure to get to the period that initially interested you, eat dessert first. Start your efforts in that period, then trust yourself to write a short background section when the time comes.

Geography

Along with a temporal scope, every historian must decide on the geographic scope of their project. While political boundaries, especially national boundaries, are an easy choice, historians should consider larger, smaller, and less fixed areas of the world as alternatives.

NATIONAL

For much of the nineteenth century, the default geographical unit of analysis was the nation, chronicled in such works as Leopold von Ranke's *History of the Reformation in Germany*, Thomas Macaulay's *History of England from the Accession of James the Second*, and Henry Adams's *History of the United States during the Administrations of Jefferson and Madison*. In the twenty-first century, many historians continue this tradition, and for good reason. Laws, language, and institutions shape people's lives, especially their interactions with others. Residents of Maine and Texas may have more in

52. Kevin Kruse, "Why I Wrote This Book: Kevin M. Kruse, *One Nation Under God*: How Corporate America Invented Christian America," *Hamilton and Griffin on Rights* (blog), June 2, 2015, http://www.hamilton-griffin.com/2015/06/02/why-i-wrote-this-book-kevin-m-kruse-one-nation-under-god-how-corporate-america-invented-christian-america/.

common with each other than with residents of neighboring New Brunswick or Coahuila. Institutions—government agencies, professional organizations, and sports leagues—operate at the national scale. Even multinational institutions, such as corporations and religious bodies, often have divisions organized to correspond to national boundaries. When historians write on the national scale, they are staying true to an important part of their characters' lived experience. That said, people do not experience life only on the national scale, and it is worth considering some alternatives.

LOCAL AND REGIONAL

Regions, states, cities, and even neighborhoods all have their own histories that deserve attention for the same reason that national-level stories do. Religious awakenings in eighteenth-century New England and the civil rights movement in Atlanta are as worthy of study as any national narrative.[53] Pekka Hämäläinen found that spaces defined in European terms, like New Mexico and Texas, did not reflect the world of the Comanches, who are the protagonists of his book. "A creation of itinerant nomadic bands," he writes, "the Comanche empire was not a rigid structure held together by a single central authority, nor was it an entity that could be displayed on a map as a solid block with clear-cut borders."[54] His geographical unit of analysis, the Comanchería, is therefore not a fixed location, but one that grows, shrinks, and moves with the narrative.

A smaller geographical scale allows for a more complete review of the evidence, while still allowing the historian to make big claims. "This study is based on a reading of almost every extant document written in or about Petersburg, Virginia, from 1784, when the town record books were begun, to 1860," writes Suzanne Lebsock in *The Free Women of Petersburg*. "It is only one community, but the records of a single community can change the way we understand women

53. Douglas L. Winiarski, *Darkness Falls on the Land of Light: Experiencing Religious Awakenings in Eighteenth-Century New England* (Chapel Hill: University of North Carolina Press, 2017); Brown-Nagin, *Courage to Dissent*.

54. Pekka Hämäläinen, *The Comanche Empire* (New Haven, CT: Yale University Press, 2008), 4.

in the past. In so doing, they can change the way we look at history itself."[55] Local history may be particularly good for student researchers. In 2015, for instance, a class of undergraduate students at the University of Oklahoma explored the New Deal by studying projects in their state. They had an easier time visiting both written sources and extant New Deal sites, and they were able to tell stories overlooked by historians writing about the New Deal as a national phenomenon.[56]

Local and regional history can illuminate broader geographies. As Kristin Hoganson explains, her study of Champaign County, Illinois—on its surface a local history—"led to Anglo-Saxonist pigs, Chinese miracle plants, celebrity bulls, polar explorers, African winds, World War I aces, racialized bees, Cuban radio chatter, and UFOs. One thread led to an 1873 cavalry invasion of Mexico; another to diarrhea-induced scandals on British ships. Still other threads connected Champaign to consular outposts in Germany, bioprospectors in Manchuria, congresses of the Inter-Parliamentary Union, and a fledgling agricultural college in Piracicaba, Brazil."[57] Andrew Sandoval-Strausz wanted to show how Latino immigrants helped revitalize cities across the United States, but he needed to work at a neighborhood scale to explain how that happened. So he chose two neighborhoods—one in Chicago, the other in Dallas—as exemplars of the larger trend.[58]

TRANSNATIONAL AND GLOBAL

While some stories take place on stages smaller than sovereign countries, others cross national frontiers, or de-emphasize them. Many countries control, or have controlled, colonial possessions; will they be part of the national narrative? What about citizens who travel or migrate, with or without changing their citizenship?

55. Suzanne Lebsock, *The Free Women of Petersburg: Status and Culture in a Southern Town, 1784–1860* (New York: W. W. Norton, 1985), xiv.

56. "Making Modern America," http://newdeal.oucreate.com/.

57. Kristin L. Hoganson, *The Heartland: An American History* (New York: Penguin, 2019), xxv.

58. A. K. Sandoval-Strausz, *Barrio America: How Latino Immigrants Saved the American City* (New York: Basic Books, 2019).

Some historians have achieved great insight simply by following their subjects ~~across borders~~. In *Liberty's Exiles: American Loyalists in the Revolutionary World*, for example, Maya Jasanoff tracks former residents of the Thirteen Colonies to their new homes in Nova Scotia, New Brunswick, Quebec, Jamaica, the Bahamas, Great Britain, India, Australia, and Sierra Leone.[59] In *Atlantic Crossings: Social Politics in a Progressive Age*, Daniel Rodgers follows a group of "cosmopolitan progressives," Americans who studied, and often traveled to, Britain, Germany, and other European countries in search of social policies that could be replicated at home. In a period when European models shaped American approaches to streetcar regulation, old-age pensions, and labor arbitration, Rodgers argues, a thorough narrative of American social policy must cross the ocean.[60]

In other cases, it is not so much the individuals as the events that cross national boundaries. Many victims of the twentieth-century atrocities documented by Timothy Snyder did not leave their homelands, but the perpetrators of those atrocities inflicted them across a wide swath of Eastern Europe. "Perfect knowledge of the Ukrainian past will not produce the causes of the famine," writes Snyder. "Following the history of Poland is not the best way to understand why so many Poles were killed in the Great Terror. No amount of knowledge of Belarusian history can make sense of the prisoner-of-war camps and the anti-partisan campaigns that killed so many Belarusians. A description of Jewish life can include the Holocaust, but not explain it. Often what happened to one group is intelligible only in light of what had happened to another."[61]

Such approaches may be termed *transnational history, world history*, or *global history*, each with its own traditions and connotations. Each label is useful to the degree that it reminds historians

---

59. Maya Jasanoff, *Liberty's Exiles: American Loyalists in the Revolutionary World* (New York: Knopf, 2011), 9–10.

60. Daniel T. Rodgers, *Atlantic Crossings: Social Politics in a Progressive Age* (Cambridge, MA: Harvard University Press, 1998), 3–5.

61. Timothy Snyder, *Bloodlands: Europe between Hitler and Stalin* (New York: Basic Books, 2012), xix.

that people, ideas, goods, and pathogens often ignore national lines on a map.[62]

However appealing intellectually, transnational or global approaches require significant trade-offs. They can require a heavy investment in time to master new languages and bodies of scholarship, and travel to archives in multiple countries is expensive, in both time and money.[63] The largest stories—covering multiple centuries and all parts of the globe—cannot possibly be told by consulting all the relevant archives and must instead rely on secondary sources. But while these may sacrifice some detail, they also reveal patterns of history that national histories, or even histories of continents, cannot.

COMPARATIVE

My dissertation advisor, Kenneth Jackson, liked to quote Kipling: "What should they know of England who only England know?" I'm not sure that Jackson was using the poem in the way that Kipling intended, but the line was an effective reminder that to understand your object of study, you need to step back and see it in a larger context. Some histories tell the stories of two or more similar places or institutions in order to highlight commonalities that might not be immediately apparent, and to explore the effects of different choices made by people in similar circumstances. For instance, while we might think of the Civil War–era North and South as drastically different places, Edward Ayers reminds us that the sky was the same color on both sides of the Mason-Dixon Line.[64] In her book *Plutopia*, Kate Brown does something similar with the Cold War rivals of the United States and the Soviet Union. While hardly diminishing

---

62. Sebastian Conrad, *What Is Global History?* (Princeton, NJ: Princeton University Press, 2016), 12, 47–48.

63. Lara Putnam, "The Transnational and the Text-Searchable: Digitized Sources and the Shadows They Cast," *American Historical Review* 121 (2016): 397; Benjamin R. Young, "Wealth, Access, and Archival Fetishism in the New Cold War History," *History News Network* (blog), June 23, 2019, http://historynewsnetwork.org/article/172318.

64. Edward L. Ayers, *In the Presence of Mine Enemies: War in the Heart of America, 1859–1863* (New York: W. W. Norton, 2003); Edward L. Ayers, *The Thin Light of Freedom: The Civil War and Emancipation in the Heart of America* (New York: W. W. Norton, 2017).

their differences, she shows that the shared imperative of producing nuclear weapons led the United States to adopt some of the secrecy and economic control it usually attributed to the Soviets, while the Soviets rewarded scientists and engineers with consumer luxuries they associated with the decadent West.[65]

In *Missions for Science*, David McBride tells stories of four legally distinct parts of the world: the southern United States, the Panama Canal Zone, Haiti, and Liberia. By showing important similarities among these places, he helps us see them as components of a twentieth-century black Atlantic.[66] By studying both Muslim and non-Muslim Asian societies, Cemil Aydin challenges interpretations that attribute anti-Westernism to just Islam or the experience of being colonized.[67] At a much smaller scale, Robin Bachin studies commercial venues (nightclub and stadium) along with nonprofit institutions in Chicago, detecting commonalities.[68]

For other works, comparisons emphasize the effects of differing choices. While a historian cannot run an experiment in the past, they can report the results of "natural experiments," cases in which similar entities chose different paths with different results. Historians, political scientists, economists, and other scholars have explored how people in different countries extracted labor, built railroads, and pensioned the old.[69] These studies can test hypotheses: if the same conditions in two countries led to different results, you can reject claims that those conditions necessarily led to those results. On the other hand, comparative studies can obscure both variation within

---

65. Kate Brown, *Plutopia: Nuclear Families, Atomic Cities, and the Great Soviet and American Plutonium Disasters* (New York: Oxford University Press, 2013).

66. David McBride, *Missions for Science: U.S. Technology and Medicine in America's African World* (New Brunswick, NJ: Rutgers University Press, 2002), 1–3.

67. Cemil Aydin, *The Politics of Anti-Westernism in Asia: Visions of World Order in Pan-Islamic and Pan-Asian Thought* (New York: Columbia University Press, 2007), 2.

68. Robin F. Bachin, *Building the South Side: Urban Space and Civic Culture in Chicago, 1890–1919* (Chicago: University of Chicago Press, 2008).

69. Peter Kolchin, *Unfree Labor: American Slavery and Russian Serfdom*, ACLS Humanities e-book (Cambridge, MA: Harvard University Press, 1987); Colleen A. Dunlavy, *Politics and Industrialization: Early Railroads in the United States and Prussia* (Princeton, NJ: Princeton University Press, 1994); Ann Shola Orloff, *The Politics of Pensions: A Comparative Analysis of Britain, Canada, and the United States, 1880–1940* (Madison: University of Wisconsin Press, 1993).

one country (or state, or city) and the importance of connections between places.[70] And one must compare like to like. As Kenneth Pomeranz notes, comparing eighteenth-century Britain to India or China—simply because India and China are now unified nations— is a bit silly, since "India and China are each more comparable in size, population, and internal diversity to Europe as a whole than to individual European countries." Instead, he suggests comparing Britain to an area of roughly the same size, such as the Yangzi Delta or Gujarat. "Unless state policy is the center of the story being told," he cautions, "the nation is not a unit that travels very well."[71]

In the long run, local, regional, national, and transnational histories complement one another. A national history can become part of a transnational history by being placed next to a comparable work on a bibliography, syllabus, or nightstand. Moreover, transnational and local histories often depend on more traditional national histories for context. If you are writing about the New Deal's impact on Chicago or on Latin America, you will probably be glad if someone else has written a relevant narrative of the New Deal in the United States as a whole. Since no one work will tell the complete story of any topic, you should consider whether yours is best written as a comparison or as part of a comparative conversation with other works.

Historiography

Historiography (literally, the writing of history) is the term that historians use for what other scholarly disciplines call a literature review: a summary of previous scholarship on a subject, explaining past debates and the current state of knowledge. Such reviews save time for both researchers and readers. If a new work adds nothing to our shared knowledge, a scholar may not want to invest the time to write it, or even read it. If, however, you have found something

---

70. Micol Seigel, "Beyond Compare: Comparative Method after the Transnational Turn," *Radical History Review* 91 (2005): 62–90; Micol Seigel, *Uneven Encounters: Making Race and Nation in Brazil and the United States* (Durham, NC: Duke University Press, 2009), xi–xvi.

71. Kenneth Pomeranz, *The Great Divergence: China, Europe, and the Making of the Modern World Economy*, Princeton Economic History of the Western World (Princeton, NJ: Princeton University Press, 2000), 7–8.

new to say, a historiography can help the reader appreciate how it breaks new ground. (The stakes are somewhat different for popular or public history. If a public historian retells a tale in a way that reaches new audiences, that is also a worthy contribution.)

WHAT IS NEW ABOUT YOUR APPROACH?

The goal of research is to expand human knowledge. While you will not know the precise scope of your contribution until you have completed the research, it can be useful to make some claim of novelty at the start, even if you change it later. Historians make such claims in several forms.   *be useful*

I am telling an untold or neglected story

While it is rare for a historian to tell a story that has *never* been told, historians can often show that they are emphasizing parts of the story that previous accounts have neglected. Introducing her history of nurses' relationship to technology, Margarete Sandelowski acknowledges that others have told part of the story, but argues that they have not given it the attention it deserves. "Technology can be seen in long-standing debates concerning the relative dominance of the hands, mind, and spirit of the nurse and whether nursing is an art, science, and/or (woman)craft, but it has rarely taken center stage," she writes. "The nursing/technology relation has been the subject largely of anecdotes and speculation rather than the focus of formal research or critique."[72] Similarly, Darren Dochuk writes that previous studies of modern conservatism "have cordoned off evangelicalism as an interest that nudged politicians and inflected politics only sporadically as a voice of protest from the periphery." Dochuk pledges to "challenge this notion and help fill these gaps by demonstrating how southern evangelicalism was, from the very beginning, aligned with the forces that created the Sunbelt and embedded in the political processes that upset this region's Democratic allegiances and constructed its Republican Right."[73]

72. Margarete Sandelowski, *Devices and Desires: Gender, Technology, and American Nursing* (Chapel Hill: University of North Carolina Press, 2000), 9.

73. Darren Dochuk, *From Bible Belt to Sunbelt: Plain-Folk Religion, Grassroots Politics, and the Rise of Evangelical Conservatism* (New York: W. W. Norton, 2010), xxii.

I am using new sources

Some historians bring new evidence to an ongoing debate. Robert Trent Vinson and Benedict Carton cite extensive scholarship that explores how Nobel Peace Prize winner Albert Luthuli regarded the justifiability of violence against South Africa's system of apartheid. But, they argue, previous work had not incorporated material held by the Schomburg Research Center for African American History and Culture, Yale, and Michigan State University. "These sources," they argue, "chart Luthuli's evolving definition of resistance, which blurred the line between conciliation and confrontation."[74]

I am presenting new voices or emphasizing new characters

Retelling a story from the point of view of different characters will yield new lessons. "Much of planning history remains focused on the planner as the primary shaper of urban growth, often ignoring the roles played by urban communities in challenging both the design and the use of city spaces," writes Robin Bachin. "Other studies emphasize the promotional and regulatory nature of the state in shaping urban growth. In addition, some recent scholars have demonstrated the strong connections between private interests and public policy in structuring city development. This book offers a more expansive view of planning history, examining how various urban residents sought to imprint their identities and interests on city spaces through the ways they both designed and used them."[75] For Sarah Milov, the new characters are country folk, not city dwellers. "Tobacco farmers have had a significant—and overlooked—amount of agency in constructing the global cigarette," she explains. "Producers ought to be central to the history of the cigarette specifically, and to consumption more generally.[76]

---

74. Robert Trent Vinson and Benedict Carton, "Albert Luthuli's Private Struggle: How an Icon of Peace Came to Accept Sabotage in South Africa," *Journal of African History* 59 (2018): 74.

75. Bachin, *Building the South Side*, 12.

76. Sarah Milov, "Smoking as Statecraft: Promoting American Tobacco Production and Global Cigarette Consumption, 1947–1970," *Journal of Policy History* 28 (2016): 710.

I am combining previously separate historiographies

Some historians braid two or more existing stories together to create something new. "We know a good deal about the business and culture of the mass market," writes Meg Jacobs. "We also know about the rise of the modern welfare state and postwar Keynesian tax-and-spend fiscal policies, which sought to smooth the rough edges of modern capitalism. But we know less about the intersection." Jacobs explains that her research "combines political and social history, drawing on government documents and presidential records as well as on grassroots sources and popular periodicals, in order to show the dynamic interplay between the state and its citizenry over marketplace issues during the twentieth century."[77]

I am redefining categories

Other histories add value by challenging existing conceptual frames. "While in most histories conservationism remains almost exclusively a Western, rural, and sylvan movement," notes David Stradling, "in actuality it entailed much more than the direction of Western watersheds through government management of forests and grasslands. It was a broad-based crusade designed to manage efficiently all of the nation's resources, both in public and in private hands. . . . Conservationism inhabited progressive cities as well as Western lands."[78]

ARE YOU WORKING IN A SPECIFIC THEORETICAL TRADITION?

Scholars can use the past to deploy, test, or develop specific theories of human thought and behavior, often borrowed from other disciplines in the humanities and social sciences. Theory can help historians make sense of sources and place specific events into a broad context. For example, scholars of American political development—a joint enterprise of historians and political scientists—seek

77. Meg Jacobs, *Pocketbook Politics: Economic Citizenship in Twentieth-Century America* (Princeton, NJ: Princeton University Press, 2007), 6.

78. David Stradling, *Smokestacks and Progressives: Environmentalists, Engineers, and Air Quality in America, 1881–1951* (Baltimore: Johns Hopkins University Press, 2002), 5.

to study "durable shifts in governing authority." Such a definition, argue Karen Orren and Stephen Skowronek, can help frame questions of significance: "Did the Supreme Court's holding in *Plessy v. Ferguson* (1896), that for constitutional purposes separate could be equal, shift authority in any way or did it merely confirm and justify the status quo? Did the Reagan administration mark a political about-face or a failed revolution?"[79] Similarly, social historians, cultural historians, economic historians, and others can draw on work in other disciplines to develop questions that will help explain not only the specific events one is researching but also a broader set of events.

Some historians reject theory altogether, insisting that they deal in facts, not abstractions. Others read theory deeply and carefully, making it central to their work.[80] Still others avoid reading theory directly but get it second- or thirdhand. For instance, even if you do not read the pioneering theoretical works by such scholars as Joan Wallach Scott and Benedict Anderson, you are likely to encounter their ideas about gender and nationalism in the work of the many scholars who have.[81] One approach to avoid is to invoke theory without reading it. If you are going to declare your approach as Foucauldian, make sure you have read Foucault.[82]

WHAT HAVE OTHERS WRITTEN?

To show that their findings are novel, scholars often contrast their work to previous scholarship. Occasionally this means disparaging that scholarship. "Previous studies," Cynthia Orozco writes, "have been flawed as they relate to class, identity, immigration, citizenship, social movements, biography, periodization, and

79. Karen Orren and Stephen Skowronek, *The Search for American Political Development* (New York: Cambridge University Press, 2004), 123.

80. Nigel Raab, *The Crisis from Within: Historians, Theory, and the Humanities* (Leiden: Brill, 2015), 13–14.

81. Joan W. Scott, "Gender: A Useful Category of Historical Analysis," *American Historical Review* 91 (1986): 1053–75; Benedict R. O'G. Anderson, *Imagined Communities: Reflections on the Origin and Spread of Nationalism* (London: Verso, 1983).

82. Helen Sword, *Stylish Academic Writing* (Cambridge, MA: Harvard University Press, 2012), 118.

methodology."[83] More commonly, historians can praise previous scholarship and explain how their findings build on it. For example, Kate Masur explains the significance of her study of Reconstruction in Washington, DC, by lauding previous scholarship for explaining contested meanings of freedom while noting that "the focus on freedom has left other important concepts relatively unexplored. Equality is one of them."[84]

In some cases, another scholar has covered pretty much the same events that you will explore, so it is best to lay out the previous understanding of events before presenting your correction or complication of that interpretation. "Historians have acknowledged that some southern women owned slaves," writes Stephanie Jones-Rogers, "but they usually focus on the wealthiest single or widowed women. When they do encounter married slave-owning women in nineteenth-century records, they generally assume that the women's legal status as wives prevented them from owning slaves in their own right." Only after explaining all of the mistaken assumptions corrupting previous accounts does she then offer her corrective.[85] Similarly, Bradford Hunt knows he must explain why anyone would read his account of public housing in Chicago if they have already read Arnold Hirsch's acclaimed work on that topic: *Making the Second Ghetto*. Hunt's introduction devotes three paragraphs to summarizing Hirsch's work, noting its contributions and limits, and then explains how his account differs.[86]

For recent events, you may be the first historian on the scene. If so, you can take the time to explain that while other scholars have addressed topics somewhat similar to yours, you are the first to explore a particular set of events. And you can still use other scholars' work for context. For instance, David Kieran's article about President Obama's honoring veterans first appeared while

83. Cynthia Orozco, *No Mexicans, Women, or Dogs Allowed: The Rise of the Mexican American Civil Rights Movement* (Austin: University of Texas Press, 2009), 6.

84. Kate Masur, *An Example for All the Land: Emancipation and the Struggle over Equality in Washington, D.C.* (Chapel Hill: University of North Carolina Press, 2010), 4.

85. Stephanie E. Jones-Rogers, *They Were Her Property: White Women as Slave Owners in the American South* (New Haven, CT: Yale University Press, 2019), xi–xii.

86. D. Bradford Hunt, *Blueprint for Disaster: The Unraveling of Chicago Public Housing* (Chicago: University of Chicago Press, 2009), 11.

Obama was still in office, when historians had yet to write much about the Obama administration. Instead, Kieran contextualized Obama's decisions by drawing on previous scholarship about the Reagan and Bush administrations' handling of the memory of the Vietnam War.[87]

ARE OTHERS WORKING ON IT?

Since historical research on a book or other major project can take years to complete, there is always a possibility that someone else will publish on the subject you are working on before you finish. Some historians shrug off this danger. Each work is different, so two books on what appear to be the same topic can remain distinct. For instance, in 2009, Oxford and Cambridge University Presses each published books titled *The G.I. Bill*. Despite the identical main title and publication date, reviewers quickly noted that each book had its own goals and strengths, and its own mission in the world.[88] That said, being scooped can be painful, especially if the rival work succeeds in gaining a great deal of attention. History professor Michael Socolow was working on a manuscript about the University of Washington crew team, which won the gold medal in the 1936 Olympics, when another author published a prominent book on the same subject, using—among other sources—interviews Socolow himself had conducted. Socolow eventually published his own book, but without the publicity and royalties his nonacademic rival secured.[89]

There is no sure way to avoid this from happening, no universal registry of works-in-progress that would allow you to find out who else is working on a given topic or to stake your own claim. And even if another writer knows you are working on a topic, there is nothing

87. David Kieran, "'Never Too Late to Do the Right Thing': Barack Obama, the Vietnam War's Legacy, and the Cultural Politics of Military Awards during the Afghanistan War," *Journal of American Studies* 51 (2017): 515–17.

88. Beth Bailey, "Losing the War," *Reviews in American History* 39 (2011): 196–204; Stephen R. Ortiz, "The GI Bill: A New Deal for Veterans/The GI Bill," *American Historical Review* 115 (2010): 1494–96.

89. Michael J. Socolow, "How I Got Scooped," *Inside Higher Ed*, October 20, 2016. See also Noah Berlatsky, "My Nemesis, Jill Lepore," *Chronicle of Higher Education*, November 26, 2014.

to stop that writer from pursuing it as well. Still, historians starting projects can take some steps to see if others are working on a given topic. Ask senior historians. Ask archivists. Browse conference programs. And advertise your own work. Use those same networks to tell people what you are up to. With luck, you will flush out those who are working on similar themes, and find ways that you can work together and produce distinct and valuable works, rather than competing.

WHAT MIGHT YOUR CRITICS SAY?

Writing the historiography of your topic can help you anticipate the kinds of criticism you may ultimately receive. Read not only articles and books but also responses to those articles and reviews of those books, and consider what kind of challenges they pose. Did critics complain of too little theory or too much? Of the absence of women or people of color among the people in the story or the scholars cited? Did they consider the chronological and geographical scope too small or too large? How would you respond if someone criticized your planned work in the same way? You likely will not satisfy all your critics, but you can ready answers that will satisfy you. Yes, you will want to be able to say, "I did consider that challenge, and here's why I thought this was the best plan." "Swedish, British, German, Japanese, and Soviet and Russian contributions, in particular, receive much less attention here than they deserve," concedes Paul Edwards in his history of climate modeling. "My defense is that no scholar and no book can do everything." Indeed, that is every historian's defense, and the best we can do is acknowledge our limits.[90]

Proposal

Before they commit to a research project, historians must often document their plans in the form of proposals for seminar papers, grant proposals, dissertation prospectuses, or book proposals.[91]

---

90. Paul N. Edwards, *A Vast Machine: Computer Models, Climate Data, and the Politics of Global Warming* (Cambridge, MA: MIT Press, 2010), xxiv.

91. Rachel Toor, "Why It's Important to Write a Proposal for an Academic Book," *Chronicle of Higher Education*, May 19, 2020.

And even if someone else is not forcing you to write down your assumptions, questions, and plans, it may be worth doing so for your own purposes. As you get into the research, you can then refer back to the plan. What exactly am I hoping to learn? Have I achieved my goals? Have those goals changed? Proposals are also great for sharing; without overwhelming your reader, they may offer enough detail to elicit valuable feedback. When Diane Miller Sommerville shared a grant proposal with her former adviser, Jan Lewis, Lewis asked why Sommerville had not included the African American experience. Lacking a good answer, Sommerville added two chapters about African American Southerners, which strength-ened the book.[92]

A proposal should describe the elements of research design cov-ered here and in chapter 3. It should state your question, describe the scope of the project (people, place, period), the ways your study could challenge or complicate existing scholarship, and the sources you will use—a topic covered in the following chapters. In many cases, you will be asked to propose a timeline for completion, though scholars know not to put too much reliance on aspirational deadlines.

No research plan should be so rigid as to prevent you from changing course in response to your research discoveries. As Sarah Jo Peterson put it to me, the historian who searches for a needle in a haystack must beware of missing the haystack. Good histori-ans are able to change plans as their sources dictate. David Chang started by asking how Native Hawaiians thought about history. "But as I delved into the sources—especially the nineteenth-century Hawaiian-language newspapers, which contain many serialized histories," he writes, "I was struck by the relationship between his-torical and geographical writing." The sources changed his ques-tions to focus more on geography.[93] Jeffrey Engel changed course particularly rapidly. "This is not the study I set out to write," he notes in the preface to *Cold War at 30,000 Feet*. He explains that he began with one set of assumptions, but "realized after two days in

---

92. Sarah Handley-Cousins, "Understanding Trauma in the Civil War South: A Con-versation with Diane Miller Sommerville," *Nursing Clio* (blog), March 20, 2019, https://nursingclio.org/2019/03/20/understanding-trauma-in-the-civil-war-south-a-conversation-with-diane-miller-sommerville/.

93. Chang, *The World and All the Things upon It*, xviii.

the archives that I had an entirely different story on my hands."[94] Not every archive will so disrupt the historian's expectations so quickly, but if you never find any surprises along the way, you are likely doing something wrong. Note, however, that both Chang and Engel entered the archive with questions. Those initial questions alerted them that the sources were not what they had expected, and thus prepared them for the surprises that led to their most important findings.

94. Jeffrey A. Engel, *Cold War at 30,000 Feet: The Anglo-American Fight for Aviation Supremacy* (Cambridge, MA: Harvard University Press, 2007), ix.

PART III

Sources

{⚜⚜⚜}

ONCE YOU HAVE SOME IDEA—however tentative—of the questions you wish to answer, the next step is to find the evidence to answer them. While other fields may speak of "data," historians emphasize "sources": those documents, images, artifacts, and other tangible remnants on which we rely to know what happened and what it meant. A research topic is therefore a marriage between questions and sources. No question, however worthy, can become a research topic unless you can identify sources with which to answer it. No sources, however rich, tell a story unless you can pose questions to them. Only when you have both framed your questions and found the sources that can answer them will you be able to commit to a project.

CHAPTER FIVE

Sources

HISTORIANS DESCRIBE scenes they have not witnessed, converse with people they have never met, and remember events that pre-dated their birth. They perform these wonders through encounters with evidence. "Sources from the past, primary or secondary, are not a prison," explains Natalie Zemon Davis. "They are a magic thread that links me to people long since dead and with situations that have crumbled to dust."[1]

The magic has its limits. "Most human affairs happen without leaving vestiges or records of any kind behind them," writes Louis Gottschalk.

> The past, having happened, has perished with only occasional traces. To begin with, although the absolute number of historical writings is staggering, only a small part of what happened in the past was ever observed. . . . Only a part of what was observed in the past was remembered by those who observed it; only a part of what was remembered was recorded; only a part of what was recorded has survived; only a part of what has survived has come to the historians' attention; only a part of what has come to their attention is credible; only a part of what is credible has been grasped; and only a part of what has been grasped

---

1. Natalie Zemon Davis, *A Passion for History: Conversations with Denis Crouzet*, Early Modern Studies 4 (Kirksville, MO: Truman State University Press, 2010), 22.

can be expounded or narrated by the historian. . . . Most of history-as-record is only the surviving part of the recorded part of the remembered part of the observed part of that whole.[2]

In Lin-Manuel Miranda's musical, *Hamilton*, Eliza Hamilton burns her letters right there onstage. "I'm erasing myself from the narrative," she sings to her absent, unfaithful husband. "Let future historians wonder / How Eliza reacted when you broke her heart." If historians are in the audience, it is their hearts that break.

Even when you can find sources, you must understand their limits. "So great was the tragedy," writes J. H. Powell of Philadelphia's 1793 yellow fever epidemic, "so astounding the scenes of suffering, that one after another of those who lived through the plague wrote down what they saw. They are responsible for all the facts recorded here; and if they sometimes saw things that could not happen, told stories beyond belief, that is because they were men, not cameras. The historian can never construct a record of events. All he can do is construct a record of records."[3] Humbling as such pronouncements are, they should not deter the historian, for a record of records of small parts of the human experience is still vastly better than no record at all. The historian pieces together clues until they form a coherent story of what happened.

Tips

- Accept the fact that the available sources represent only a tiny fragment of the human experience.
- Identify *sets* of sources: collections of material that will form the heart of your research.
- Understand that more powerful people created and preserved more records, but that skillful historians can often find the voices of the less powerful.

2. Louis Gottschalk, *Understanding History: A Primer of Historical Method* (New York: Alfred A. Knopf, 1950), 46.

3. J. H. Powell, "Preface to the 1949 Edition," in *Bring Out Your Dead: The Great Plague of Yellow Fever in Philadelphia in 1793* (1949; repr., Philadelphia: University of Pennsylvania Press, 1993), xvii.

Primary versus Secondary Sources

The distinction between "primary" and "secondary" sources for historical research dates back to the early twentieth century.[4] As Louis Gottschalk helpfully explains, "A *primary* source is the testimony of an eyewitness . . . of one who or that which was present at the events of which he or it tells. . . . A secondary source is the testimony of anyone who is not an eyewitness—that is, of one who was not present at the events of which he tells. A primary source must thus have been produced by a contemporary of the events it narrates." Significantly, a source can be fantastically old and still be a secondary source. As Gottschalk notes, Livy's history of Rome, now more than two thousand years old, covers events that took place centuries before Livy's birth. For those events, Livy is a secondary source. It may be an "original source": the earliest extant source for those events. But it will never be primary.[5]

Differentiating between primary and secondary sources helps distinguish types of historical scholarship. The chief purpose of a work based on primary sources, especially those never before consulted by a historian, may be to lay out the basic facts of a story. And part of the interpretive power of the argument is likely to be rooted in newly discovered facts. By contrast, the value of works based mostly on secondary sources lies in their presenting known facts in new configurations, to reveal new insights. W.E.B. Du Bois's 1935 book *Black Reconstruction in America*, for instance, remains one of the most influential texts in the historiography of the United States. "If I had had time and money and opportunity to go back to the original sources in all cases," Du Bois writes, "there can be no doubt that the weight of this work would have been vastly strengthened, and as I firmly believe, the case of the Negro more convincingly set forth." Yet even scholarship whose conclusions he rejected had facts he could rely on to support his claims.[6]

4. James Harvey Robinson, "The Newer Ways of Historians," *American Historical Review* 35 (1930): 245.

5. Gottschalk, *Understanding History*, 53–55.

6. W.E.B. Du Bois, *Black Reconstruction in America, 1860-1880* (1935; repr., New York: Touchstone, 1992), 724.

When historians understood history to be the record of state-craft and war, a primary source usually meant an official document preserved in a state archive. As history matured as a discipline, imaginative historians began to see the potential in other types of records. Edward Potts Cheyney, wrote an admirer, made use of literary and artistic sources "while most of us were limiting our attention to the State Papers, just as though there were not more of Tudor England in Shakespeare than in all the documents combined."[7] Newspapers—now routinely consulted by researchers from middle school students to the most senior scholars—were uncommon as historical sources until John Bach McMaster demonstrated their value.[8]

The line between primary and secondary sources can get blurry as we widen the definition of an event. Few of the characters in Martha Hodes's book *Mourning Lincoln* witnessed the April 14, 1865, shooting of Lincoln or his death the following morning, so their letters are not primary sources for the assassination. But a great many recorded their own reactions to news of that death, or the public displays of grief that followed. Their diaries and letters are primary sources for those reactions.[9]

Or consider one of the events that inspired Hodes: the 9/11 attacks on the World Trade Center and the Pentagon. The members and staff of the National Commission on Terrorist Attacks Upon the United States (better known as the 9/11 Commission) had not witnessed those events directly, so their 2004 report should be read as a secondary source for events of September 2001 and before. Indeed, the executive director of the commission staff, Philip Zelikow, had taught history at the University of Virginia, and the report is a work of history. Yet if we consider the event "9/11" to include not only the attacks and their antecedents but also the *effects* of those attacks, we must ask how the commission report came to be, and how it shaped both public policy and public perception. Indeed, the report was

7. Conyers Read, "Edward Potts Cheyney as a Writer," in *Edward Potts Cheyney: Portrait of an Historian*, ed. William E. Lingelbach (Philadelphia: University of Pennsylvania Press, 1935), 22.

8. Richard H. Shryock, "Medical Sources and the Social Historian," *American Historical Review* 41 (1936): 458.

9. Martha Hodes, *Mourning Lincoln* (New Haven, CT: Yale University Press, 2015).

so significant to that perception that a *New York Times* reporter, Philip Shenon, devoted a book to the commission's work: a history of a history. For Shenon, Zelikow and his team were most certainly eyewitnesses to the creation of the report, so their report (as well as their interviews with Shenon) served as a primary source.[10] We are all witnesses to history, and every record we make is potentially a primary source to someone.

Similarly, a great many primary sources are secondary sources as well. In 1965, Saul Benison argued that "the autobiography gathered by oral history methods is not merely an addition or a supplement to other extant documents; actually it stands as an attempt at a first interpretation of a series of given events. It is also the first reduction and ordering of a mass of primary and secondary material germane to a particular man's life."[11] The same is true of written autobiographies, which frequently mix the writer's recollection of past events and their current understanding of those events' meaning.[12] We cannot tell our own stories without some interpretation.

Legal historian Hendrik Hartog once claimed that "what makes a legal historian a legal historian might be nothing more than the difference between assuming that law is a window and assuming that you have to understand the window as an artifact and as having a shaping effect on what you see through it. Legal historians are curious about the windows."[13] I like the metaphor but reject the implication that legal historians are unique in this regard. Every historian, regardless of specialty, must regard sources as windows, remembering to look *at* the window as well as *through* the window. No window is wholly transparent, and without understanding the way a source frames the view and distorts the light, we cannot trust our eyes.

10. United States Government Printing Office, *9/11 Commission Report: The Official Report of the 9/11 Commission and Related Publications* (Washington, DC: USGPO, 2004); Philip Shenon, *The Commission: The Uncensored History of the 9/11 Investigation* (New York: Grand Central, 2008).

11. Saul Benison, "Reflections on Oral History," *American Archivist* 28 (1965): 74.

12. Jennifer Ritterhouse, *Growing Up Jim Crow: How Black and White Southern Children Learned Race* (Chapel Hill: University of North Carolina Press, 2006), 111.

13. Gautham Rao, "Friends in All the Right Places: The Newest Legal History," *Uncommon Sense—The Blog*, October 8, 2019, https://blog.oieahc.wm.edu/friends-in-all-the-right-places/.

Balancing Your Use of Secondary Sources

Some important histories rely entirely on secondary sources. Practitioners of what William McNeill called "macrohistory"—stories that span multiple continents and centuries—must get most of their information from other scholars. No single set of primary sources could capture movements and events too big to be perceived even by the people who took part in them, and no mortal historian could hope to learn all the languages and subjects needed to tell these stories from scratch.[14] Writers of reference formats are even more dependent. The writer of an encyclopedia entry or a textbook is generally expected to sum up current knowledge on a topic, not to break new ground, even if they occasionally interpret a primary source themselves along the way.

Historians working on smaller scales, however, must balance secondary and primary sources. You could start a project by hitting the library and securing every book and article related to your topic written since the event itself, then write a first draft based only on those sources before determining what there is left to say. I suspect, however, that this would be psychologically quite difficult, doing all that work without knowing what you would contribute that is new. On the other hand, writing a draft based only on primary sources could be equally terrifying. What if you have done all this work, only to find that someone else has marked that path before?

Fortunately, there are other possibilities in between. It is certainly a good idea to familiarize yourself with the existing literature, including its source bases. For instance, as I worked on the Philadelphia riots of 1844, I hoped to gain insights beyond those achieved by Michael Feldberg in his 1975 book on the topic.[15] Seeing how heavily he relied on one newspaper, the *Public Ledger*, I could feel more comfortable knowing that I was breaking new ground when I read other newspapers, without having to check back each paragraph to see what Feldberg said. You can also write a draft based

14. William H. McNeill, *Mythistory and Other Essays* (ACLS Humanities E-Book, 2008), 86–90.

15. Michael Feldberg, *The Philadelphia Riots of 1844: A Study of Ethnic Conflict* (Westport, CT: Greenwood Press, 1975).

on primary sources, then compare it to previous accounts to see if there is anything you missed or misunderstood. With luck, these will be few enough that you can happily cite the secondary source for the gaps and still feel you have done something original. Secondary sources can be particularly useful for information that is adjacent to your topic. If I am writing about Pennsylvania, I want most of my information about Pennsylvania to come from primary sources. But I may need a sense of what was going on in New York, Canada, and the United Kingdom, and I am happy to rely on secondary sources for that.

You will need to evaluate the merit of each secondary source on which you rely. Finding works published by a reputable press or journal is a good start, but some valuable works appear elsewhere, while some of the best publishers occasionally publish junk. Finding reviews and citations to works can give you a sense if other researchers trust them.

Sets of Sources

Any important event may leave traces in records scattered across the globe. Consider again Hodes's history of reactions to the assassination of Abraham Lincoln in 1865. Along with the accounts left by those who witnessed the shooting and Lincoln's death, we have accounts of the hunt for the assassin, his coconspirators, and their trials and execution. And even beyond that, we have the reactions of untold numbers of contemporaries in the United States and in other countries, just a sample of which Hodes tapped.[16] To try to gather every possible source would take more than a lifetime.

To make their job manageable, most historians focus their efforts by identifying *sets of sources* that can be found and read relatively quickly (and even this can mean years). A set might be an archival collection, a run of a periodical, published government documents, or any other group of sources that can all be found in the same place. For seminar papers or even journal articles, a single set of sources may be enough. Collections of letters sent to a mayor or a prominent prisoner, though addressed to the same recipient,

16. Hodes, *Mourning Lincoln*.

may express a range of views.[17] A set of children's books—written and illustrated by various authors and illustrated but published around the same time and sharing similar themes—can help us understand the "definition of masculine courage, chivalry, and self-sacrifice" that shaped the American boys who became soldiers in World War I.[18]

A truly rich set of sources may fuel a whole book. Theodore Rosengarten won the National Book Award for *All God's Dangers: The Life of Nate Shaw*, based on his remarkable interviews with a remarkable man.[19] He followed up with *Tombee: Portrait of a Cotton Planter*, the core of which was the plantation journal kept by Thomas B. Chaplin between 1845 and 1858. For the latter book, Rosengarten and his research assistant, Susan Walker, "stalked Chaplin in public and private archives, reconstructing the world he took for granted, filling in the gaps in his story."[20] Still, the journal is central to the story, and Rosengarten includes it as the second part of his book.

More commonly, historians seek multiple source sets to view events from more than one perspective. "I have assumed that each document might reflect a particular agenda and have taken certain precautions as a result," writes Kathleen Belew. "When possible. I use multiple sources to corroborate information. If, say, a fact appears in a redacted FBI file, an undercover reporter's interview with a white power activist, and a mainstream press report, it probably can be relied upon."[21]

It can be helpful to juxtapose sources reflecting the views of one set of actors against those reflecting the views of their antagonists.

17. Michael Willrich, "'Close That Place of Hell': Poor Women and the Cultural Politics of Prohibition," *Journal of Urban History* 29 (2003): 555–74; Jon Shelton, "Letters to the Essex County Penitentiary: David Selden and the Fracturing of America," *Journal of Social History* 48 (2014): 135–55.

18. Vanessa Meikle Schulman, "'The Books We All Read': The Golden Age of Children's Book Illustration and American Soldiers in the Great War," *Lion and the Unicorn* 41 (2017): 206.

19. Nate Shaw and Theodore Rosengarten, *All God's Dangers: The Life of Nate Shaw* (New York: Knopf, 1974).

20. Theodore Rosengarten, Thomas Benjamin Chaplin, and Susan W. Walker, *Tombee: Portrait of a Cotton Planter* (New York: Morrow, 1986), 11.

21. Kathleen Belew, *Bring the War Home: The White Power Movement and Paramilitary America* (Cambridge, MA: Harvard University Press, 2018), 14.

For instance, in *The Dead Will Arise*, Jeffrey Peires uses correspondence between two British officers to understand the point of view of the colonizers, while he uses articles by a Xhosa historian of the nineteenth century and journals of a British clergyman to understand events from the perspective of the colonized.[22] Alternatively, a historian might use one set of sources to document an actor's public statements while others reveal more private thoughts. Rachel Shelden, for example, contrasts the theatrical speeches that congressmen bellowed in order to please constituents back home with personal correspondence suggesting that fellow representatives discounted the bombast.[23]

Where records are scarce, a historian may need to move from one type of source to another, like a traveler who rides an electric scooter to the nearest bus stop, takes a bus to the subway to the airport, gets on a plane, and takes a cab to their final destination. Scott Heerman's *Alchemy of Slavery* covers nearly two centuries, and no one set of observers recorded that entire sweep. For the earliest period, Heerman relied on European diplomatic records, then moved on to local legal records, and, toward the end of his story, to local newspapers as they were founded. "Each set of sources offers its own window on the contours of slavery and freedom in Illinois," Heerman explains, "and each has its own set of limitations." But taken together, the sets get him from start to finish.[24] For her history of disability, spanning a century, Sarah Rose needed to tap a new set of sources for almost every chapter.[25] Despite discouraging advice from other labor historians, Seth Rockman was able to use multiple sets of sources to tell the story of unskilled workers of the early nineteenth century. "The archive *is* there," he concludes,

22. Jeffrey B. Peires, *The Dead Will Arise: Nongqawuse and the Great Xhosa Cattle-Killing Movement of 1856-7* (Bloomington: Indiana University Press, 1989), x–xi.

23. Rachel A. Shelden, *Washington Brotherhood: Politics, Social Life, and the Coming of the Civil War* (Chapel Hill: University of North Carolina Press, 2013), 39–40.

24. M. Scott Heerman, *The Alchemy of Slavery: Human Bondage and Emancipation in the Illinois Country, 1730-1865* (Philadelphia: University of Pennsylvania Press, 2018), 15.

25. Sarah F. Rose, *No Right to Be Idle: The Invention of Disability, 1840s-1930s* (Chapel Hill: University of North Carolina Press, 2017), Appendix A: Note on Sources.

"but it requires a willingness to see bigger stories in smaller evidentiary fragments."[26]

The more you learn, the clearer an idea you will get of what you are looking for. Jean O'Brien, for example, wanted to find nineteenth-century New Englanders writing about Indians. She "started by creating a comprehensive bibliography of local histories of all the towns and cities of Connecticut, Massachusetts, and Rhode Island published between 1820 and 1880," and added additional items that she thought might mention Indians. But she did not let those early selection principles confine her research, nor did she force herself to read everything on her initial list. "Once I settled down to read the texts," she explains, "I noticed some patterns and further modified my list. Fairly early on I concluded, for example, that church histories, manuals, and anniversaries rarely included Indians; sermons or historical discourses delivered at churches also likely did not. . . . And by no means did I look at every Forefathers' oration delivered at Plymouth (although I did consult many of them)." Eventually she had a source base that gave her confidence that a few additional sources here or there "would not alter the story I saw emerging from the texts I already had consulted."[27]

It is rare to find a finished work of history that relies solely on its main sets of sources, for historians must build some passages from varied scraps of information. To write a one-paragraph description of the appearance and contents of a typical dwelling around 1900 in the "Mexican Town" of Clifton, Arizona, Linda Gordon used photographs, interviews she conducted, interviews conducted by previous scholars, published scholarship, unpublished dissertations, an unpublished letter, and a historical society pamphlet.[28] Still, a glance through the notes for her book as a whole shows the importance of a few sets of sources that Gordon uses again and again, such as the New York Foundling Hospital Archives and such periodicals as the *Arizona Bulletin* and *Copper Era.*

---

26. Seth Rockman, *Scraping By: Wage Labor, Slavery, and Survival in Early Baltimore* (Baltimore: Johns Hopkins University Press, 2009), 352.

27. Jean M. O'Brien, *Firsting and Lasting: Writing Indians Out of Existence in New England* (Minneapolis: University of Minnesota Press, 2010), ix.

28. Linda Gordon, *The Great Arizona Orphan Abduction* (Cambridge, MA: Harvard University Press, 1999), 361n11.

Sources as Records of the Powerful

When Martha Jones entered the Baltimore Bar Library to trace the efforts of antebellum African Americans to assert their legal rights, she found that she would need to do her research in a room dominated by a portrait of Chief Justice Roger Taney, author of the infamous Supreme Court opinion holding that African Americans "had no rights which the white man was bound to respect." "The portrait of Taney haunted me," Jones reflected. "I could not reconcile how, despite the gracious accommodation that was extended to me, I wasn't sure I belonged. Or did I mean my research topic did not belong?"[29]

Jones's discomfort at Taney's portrait reminds us that no source, library, or archive is a neutral record of history. Literacy itself is a form of unequally distributed power, and it takes even more power to create, organize, and preserve records. In the United States we have vast buildings designed to store the papers of a few twentieth-century presidents, while ordinary folk may be lucky to find a stray reference to their great-grandmothers in a genealogical database. Long before it became a T-shirt slogan, Laurel Thatcher Ulrich's observation that "well-behaved women seldom make history" expressed an insight about uneven historical sources: the keepers of records in seventeenth-century New England were more likely to write about a woman if she were charged with heresy or witchcraft than if she lived her life as the ministers wished.[30] And since most women, like most men, are well behaved, that makes it hard to study the lives of ordinary folk in any age.

Rather than give up, historians have developed tools to find the voices of less powerful people in the archives of the powerful. Often, this takes the form of unusual intrusions by the state—that great creator of records—into the lives of people whose words have otherwise vanished. As noted in chapter 6, whole subgenres of history are based on trial records or census data, which themselves record moments when the state cared enough about taxation, conscription,

29. Martha S. Jones, *Birthright Citizens: A History of Race and Rights in Antebellum America* (New York: Cambridge University Press, 2018), 159.

30. Laurel Thatcher Ulrich, "Vertuous Women Found: New England Ministerial Literature, 1668–1735," *American Quarterly* 28 (1976): 20.

or social order to take notice of the poor. In writing her history of the cotton gin, Angela Lakwete found ample papers recording the career of wealthy manufacturers, such as Eli Whitney. To include the stories of less prominent craftsmen, she relied on patent extension files, which, she explains, "include biographies of the applicants, business histories, broadsides and trade catalogs, along with the petition, substantiating evidence and counterevidence."[31]

Nongovernmental actors also record the lives of the less powerful, and the less literate. Middle-class reformers left us their observations of gamblers and prostitutes.[32] To hear voices of Indians of the seventeenth and eighteenth centuries, Nancy Shoemaker relied on the records of "travelers, traders, missionaries, or soldiers," who wrote in European, not Native, languages. Yet she offers reasons to believe that those Europeans captured more than their own preconceptions. For one thing, different nations and even individuals appear distinct in the records. "If European record keepers had imagined their conversations with Indians," Shoemaker argues, "then we should expect Indians to act and speak alike, and in these records they do not." Moreover, she continues, "Indian complaints of greed, lies, and treachery appear openly in accounts written by the alleged perpetrators of the greed, lies, and treachery. If European functionaries wantonly doctored the records, surely they would have edited out these unflattering depictions of themselves."[33]

Some records of the powerless survive through the oddest of chances, and emerge from the greatest of ingenuity. Thomas Cope was a wealthy Philadelphia merchant whose five ships connected Liverpool and Philadelphia at the height of the Irish Famine. A century and a half later, Matthew Gallman picked through Cope's papers and found notes that Irish immigrants in Philadelphia had written on the backs of the tickets they were sending to friends and relatives who were preparing to cross the Atlantic. Since the

---

31. Angela Lakwete, *Inventing the Cotton Gin: Machine and Myth in Antebellum America* (Baltimore: Johns Hopkins University Press, 2005), 220.

32. Mara Laura Keire, *For Business and Pleasure: Red-Light Districts and the Regulation of Vice in the United States, 1890–1933* (Baltimore: Johns Hopkins University Press, 2010).

33. Nancy Shoemaker, *A Strange Likeness: Becoming Red and White in Eighteenth-Century North America* (New York: Oxford University Press, 2006), 10.

tickets were torn in half when used, Gallman often found only half a message. Still, he was able to glean details of the lives of desperately poor people, who needed to avoid con men and thieves, but were advised not to purchase clothing, which would be cheaper in America.[34]

It can be frustrating to see the lives of the powerless only through the eyes of the powerful. "Police, bureaucrats, folklorists, priests, teachers, agronomists, and men of letters looked on, even probed," Eugen Weber explains, "but whether critical or sympathetic they cannot tell us what went on as true participants" in the lives of the more humble villagers Weber wishes to study.[35] Paul Thompson notes the irony that classic works on bottom-up history depend on "reports by paid government informers," so that "socialist historians are reduced to writing history from the records of government spies."[36]

Worse still is the utter lack of records about many people whose stories we would like to tell. "I went to Barbados searching for something I would never find," writes Marisa Fuentes of her search for the voice of enslaved women of the eighteenth century.

> There were none of the voices I sought to document, no whole figures emerged that I could trace beyond a momentary mention. The women I did find were battered, beaten, executed, and overtly sexualized. They were listed on estate inventories only as Phoebe, Mimba, or "Broken Back Betty," and sometimes only as "negroe"—stripped bare of all that was meaningful in their lives. Bequeathed in wills and deeds, or counted and dying on slave ships, they could not tell me about these conditions or what they thought, how they loved, or from where they came. The permanent loss of this knowledge was harrowing.[37]

34. James Matthew Gallman, *Receiving Erin's Children: Philadelphia, Liverpool, and the Irish Famine Migration, 1845–1855* (Chapel Hill: University of North Carolina Press, 2000), 2–3; 229n1.

35. Eugen Weber, *Peasants into Frenchmen: The Modernization of Rural France, 1870–1914* (Stanford, CA: Stanford University Press, 1976), xi.

36. Paul Thompson and Joanna Bornat, *The Voice of the Past: Oral History*, 4th ed. (New York: Oxford University Press, 2017), 5.

37. Marisa J. Fuentes, *Dispossessed Lives: Enslaved Women, Violence, and the Archive* (Philadelphia: University of Pennsylvania Press, 2016), 145.

Fuentes does what she can with the sources she has. For instance, when she finds white men's descriptions of other white men's beating enslaved women, Fuentes keeps the details but retells the episodes from the women's point of view. Yet while she does all she can to tell these women's stories, Fuentes remains frustrated by "the historical impossibilities of representing and historicizing their pain."[38]

No Source Speaks for Itself

No source speaks for itself; the historian must ask questions, which will in turn determine the answers. Consider, for instance, the interviews of formerly enslaved Americans, conducted in the 1930s by Works Progress Administration (WPA) workers. Some scholars have been wary of the interviews. How well could elderly African Americans describe a world they had known only as children, seventy or more years before? Moreover, as John Blassingame points out, in most states, the WPA hired only white interviewers, whom the narrators likely did not trust enough to offer candid accounts of their lives under slavery, and who appear to have left doctored transcripts of what they did hear.[39] Other scholars acknowledge these shortcomings but note that every historical source is problematic. "If they were in some respects tainted," note the editors of one volume of excerpts, "so too were other sources of slavery—including the records produced by slaveholders and their white supporters. The historian's task was, as always, to employ them in ways that maximized their utility. The best scholars of slavery have used them critically and cautiously, carefully evaluating the quality of each narrative, verifying the ex-slave's memory against other sources, and sometimes even sifting through multiple versions of the same interview."[40]

---

38. Fuentes, *Dispossessed Lives*, 128. See also Saidiya Hartman, "Venus in Two Acts," *Small Axe* 12 (July 17, 2008): 1–14.

39. John W. Blassingame, "Using the Testimony of Ex-Slaves: Approaches and Problems," *Journal of Southern History* 41 (1975): 473–92.

40. Ira Berlin, Marc Favreau, and Steven F. Miller, eds., *Remembering Slavery: African Americans Talk about Their Personal Experiences of Slavery and Emancipation* (New York: New Press, 2011), xxii.

While many historians have read the narratives for clues about how African Americans experienced slavery, others have mined them for information about the behavior of white people who claimed African Americans as property. "Serving as metaphorical flies on the walls of southern households, formerly enslaved people talked about some of the most violent, traumatic, and intimate dimensions of life for those who were bound and those who were free," notes Stephanie Jones-Rogers. "They heard and saw things that typically remained obscured from view, details that white slave-owning couples often left out of personal correspondence or public communications—that is, when they were able to write at all."[41] While many historians' instinct has been to read the narratives for information about the 1850s, Stephanie Shaw notes that interviews conducted in the 1930s can also yield information about the 1930s. It seems obvious once it is put that way, but it requires a shift in perspective.[42]

Languages and Specialized Reading

As part of the imagining process, you may need to ask what languages you are willing to learn in order to complete the research. "If you don't know Russian, you don't really know what you're missing," notes Timothy Snyder, whose reading knowledge of ten European languages enables his scholarship. "Imagine that you're in a huge country house and you have keys, but your keys only open some of the rooms. You only know the part of the house that you can wander in. And you can persuade yourself that that's the whole house, but it's not. We can only see as much, and we can only go as far as our languages take us."[43] For the most part, historians need only reading, not conversational, knowledge in order to conduct research. On the other hand, they may need specialized training (called paleography) to read centuries-old handwriting. And while linguistic ability is obviously important for multinational studies,

41. Stephanie E. Jones-Rogers, *They Were Her Property: White Women as Slave Owners in the American South* (New Haven, CT: Yale University Press, 2019), xviii.

42. Stephanie J. Shaw, "Using the WPA Ex-Slave Narratives to Study the Impact of the Great Depression," *Journal of Southern History* 69 (2003): 623–58.

43. "The Q&A: Timothy Snyder, Historian," *Economist*, June 3, 2011.

all countries have linguistic minorities, not to mention visitors who recorded their observations in other languages.

Technical knowledge is also a kind of language. While some historians may need to read German or Korean, others may need to know how to read a legal brief, a garden journal, a medical chart, a military service record, a diplomatic cable, or a patent application—and perhaps how to read some of these documents in German or Korean. Business historian Caitlin Rosenthal's years of reading spreadsheets as a management consultant, for example, prepared her to ask questions of and extract answers from ledgers kept by men seeking to extract the most labor from the workers they enslaved.[44] Would you recognize a telex if you saw one, and, if so, could you understand why someone in your story chose that mode over a letter or telegram?

Each language you learn, or other specialized knowledge you acquire, is an investment in future research. If you are planning a career in legal history or Korean history, then spending years on a law degree or Korean-language study is a reasonable investment. If all you need is a few pages of a language you do not read, it may make more sense to consult an online computer translation (I suggest using multiple services and comparing the results), then—once you have identified the passages you care about—running them past a friend or colleague who reads the relevant language. If you quote a passage that someone else translated, be sure to credit the translator in your notes.

Choose Sources That You Love

Sources are a matter of taste. Some scholars find joy in close reading of a small number of sources, while others prefer to find patterns in vast collections. Some take pride in deciphering handwriting while others avoid the study of eras before the invention of the typewriter.

Just as it is a good idea to model the structure of your project on works of history that you enjoy reading, so should you consider the

---

44. Caitlin Rosenthal, *Accounting for Slavery: Masters and Management* (Cambridge, MA: Harvard University Press, 2019), xi.

source bases of your favorite works by other historians. If you love reading books based on personal letters, look for a cache of personal letters to write about. If you are more persuaded by quantitative analyses, look instead for a dataset. And if you admire cutting-edge historians who construct narratives out of sources that previous scholars had considered worthless, seek a comparable challenge.

CHAPTER SIX

Texts as Sources

STEREOTYPICAL IMAGES of historians feature them surrounded by old books, old papers, and, perhaps, old microfilm. That is not wrong; historians, by and large, consume enormous amounts of text. While chapter 7 is about the use of nontextual sources, in this chapter we will consider those more traditional forms. While these chapters reflect some of the types of sources most frequently used by historians, they do not present a complete list. It is up to each researcher to determine what sources will best inform a particular project.

Tips

- Read every source critically. Even a participant or eyewitness may not be the most trustworthy source.
- Look to newspapers, magazines, and journals as some of the richest sources for the past few centuries, and some of the easiest to access.
- Understand the power and promise of digitized texts, but also their limits.

First-Person Accounts

One might imagine that the most reliable accounts of an event are the participants' own words. In practice, historians have long known that first-person testimony is not always reliable. Ever since

bias

Thucydides, historians have sought to read first-person accounts as critically as any other source.[1] "I have often had to choose between very conflicting statements," wrote John Kaye in 1870, "and I have sometimes found my informants to be wrong, though apparently with the best opportunities of being right, and have been compelled to reject, as convincing proof, even the overwhelming assertion, 'But, I was there.' Men who are personally engaged in stirring events are often too much occupied to know what is going on beyond the little spot of ground which holds them at the time, and often from this restricted stand-point they see through a glass darkly."[2] The eyewitness, writes Oscar Handlin, "may have been a bystander with only limited opportunity to see; or a participant with a stake in acceptance of his own version of the event; or a traveling passerby regarding an imperfectly perceived landscape; or a dupe; or a swindler."[3] Exaggerations can be harder to spot than outright lies.[4]

Sheldon Stern gives a particularly disheartening set of examples in his masterful book *The Cuban Missile Crisis in American Memory: Myths versus Reality*. Stern gathers accounts of the crisis from the memoirs of several key participants—special assistant for national security affairs McGeorge Bundy, defense secretary Robert McNamara, and attorney general Robert Kennedy among them—and mercilessly compares them to the recordings made of the Executive Committee of the National Security Council (ExComm) as the crisis unfolded. These advisers, Stern finds, had tried to dissuade President John F. Kennedy from the agreement that ultimately defused the crisis and averted nuclear war. After the president's death, they had engaged in "manipulation and half-truths" to present themselves in more heroic roles, and

1. Thucydides, *The History of the Peloponnesian War*, trans. Richard Crawley, Internet Classics Archive, http://classics.mit.edu/Thucydides/pelopwar.html; Alice M. Hoffman, *Archives of Memory: A Soldier Recalls World War II* (Lexington: University Press of Kentucky, 1990), 1.

2. John William Kaye, *Kaye's and Malleson's History of the Indian Mutiny of 1857-8*, ed. G. B. Malleson, vol. 2 (London: W. H. Allen, 1892), xii.

3. Oscar Handlin, *Truth in History* (Cambridge, MA: Harvard University Press, 1979), 124.

4. Roger Connor and Alex Calta, "The Lies of Elmo Pickerill," *Air & Space Magazine*, April 2018.

only by listening to the original recordings could the historian tell the true story.[5]

While historians must therefore read first-person accounts critically, they have tools for the job. Eugen Weber advises that the historian "rely most freely on evidence that appears to be purely incidental to the main purpose of the witness or better still, contrary to his or her apparent interest."[6] Holocaust historian Christopher Browning adopts this "self-interest" test and adds three more: "the vividness test" (the better the witness can describe an event, the more likely it is to have happened), "the possibility test" (other sources do not disprove the claim), and "the probability test" (the accounts "coincide with or fit a pattern of events suggested or established by other documentation"). With such tests, Browning argues, the historian can extract truths even from accounts left by the lying, murderous Nazi Adolf Eichmann.[7] The historian need not read every source with the same skepticism they would bring to the claims of a genocidal killer, but they must understand the sources they deploy.

DIARIES

If you want to be remembered by posterity, keep a diary. (In good handwriting, please, or typed, on acid-free paper.) "Without her diary," writes Laurel Thatcher Ulrich, our knowledge of Martha Ballard's life "would be little more than a succession of dates": the date of her marriage, the dates on which her children were born and died, and her own death in 1812.[8] But thanks to the diary that she kept for more than twenty-seven years, and Ulrich's brilliant contextualization of its contents, Ballard is now one of the best-known New England women of her generation. Samuel Pepys of seventeenth-century London, Sidney George Fisher of

5. Sheldon M. Stern, *The Cuban Missile Crisis in American Memory: Myths versus Reality* (Stanford, CA: Stanford University Press, 2012), 7.

6. Eugen Weber, *Peasants into Frenchmen: The Modernization of Rural France, 1870–1914* (Stanford, CA: Stanford University Press, 1976), xii.

7. Christopher R. Browning, *Collected Memories: Holocaust History and Postwar Testimony* (Madison: University of Wisconsin Press, 2003), 12.

8. Laurel Thatcher Ulrich, *A Midwife's Tale: The Life of Martha Ballard, Based on Her Diary, 1785–1812* (New York: Knopf, 2010), 5.

nineteenth-century Philadelphia, and Victor Klemperer of Nazi-era Dresden all have similar claims to fame.[9] Fisher filled his diaries with expressions of regret that he was not doing more with his life. Ironically, by devoting his time to his diaries, rather than to more public activities, Fisher won immortality, since historians cannot resist quoting him.

LETTERS

Faithful diarists are relatively rare; most people do not take the time to write to themselves. A great many more, however, write to family, friends, and colleagues. To be sure, neither literacy nor paper are universal, and for most epochs, letter writing has been an elite occupation. But with the spread of literacy, even common folk—soldiers and housewives, cowboys and college students—have joined statesmen and intellectuals in writing and sending letters. Even today, one often hears complaints from people who are buried in email, or whose children stay up all night sending texts. I would not know how to quantify it, but I would guess that the vast majority of existing first-person accounts of historical events take the form of letters, dispatches, or some other kind of person-to-person communication.

Letters tell stories. Today's literature evolved in part from *epistolary novels*: collections of letters written by one or more fictional characters that the reader can connect into a plot. A woman who has followed her husband to a new town, or a diplomat reporting back to his minister, will describe many of the same people and concerns from week to week or month to month. They tend to date their letters, if not always with the complete date and year, allowing the historian to track quarrels and illnesses and ideas across time.

Letters are also often quite candid. People crafting a public pronouncement, court testimony, or memoir expect their statements to be carefully examined by strangers, so they choose words to bolster their own reputations. Sometimes this is true with letters as well.

9. John Lewis Gaddis, *The Landscape of History: How Historians Map the Past* (New York: Oxford University Press, 2002), 119; Sidney George Fisher, *Philadelphia Perspective: The Diary of Sidney George Fisher* (Philadelphia: Historical Society of Pennsylvania, 1967).

Dwight Eisenhower's letters to his boyhood friend Swede Hazlett reveal a great deal about what Eisenhower was thinking as general and president, but they were likely dictated to a secretary and contain, writes their editor, "an element of circumspection. . . . In his correspondence, as in his public utterances, Eisenhower was careful not to criticize others or to put to paper words that might, if revealed, prove embarrassing."[10] Even letter writers who do not expect their correspondence to become public may be just as circumspect. A soldier writing to his mother may downplay the horrors he has seen; a lover may deceive a lover.

But it is quite common for writers to use letters to say just what they think. Diplomats write home with brutally frank assessments of the governments to which they are accredited.[11] Friends share with friends assumptions and beliefs that they might hide from the wider world. In 1912, for instance, activist Joe Lee avoided mention of race and ethnicity in his public statements in favor of barring illiterate people from immigrating to the United States. Daniel Okrent compares those statements to Lee's private correspondence, in which Lee disparages Jews and Italians, and judges that the private letters better reflect Lee's true motives.[12] If letter writers describe an event, they often do so while memory is still fresh and uncontaminated by a knowledge of what is going to happen next.

In addition to letters written by characters in a plot, letters can set a scene. Many people travel specifically for the thrill of seeing a new place and have both the time and inclination to write up their impressions for the folks at home. Moreover, a newcomer to a place may notice things too mundane to capture the attention of people who have lived there all their lives, and record these observations in a journal, in letters home, or in published accounts of the journey. A lifelong resident of a place may have no idea if its

10. Dwight David Eisenhower, *Ike's Letters to a Friend, 1941–1958*, ed. Robert Griffith (Lawrence: University Press of Kansas, 1984), 6.

11. Abraham Ascher, *Was Hitler a Riddle? Western Democracies and National Socialism* (Stanford, CA: Stanford University Press, 2012).

12. Daniel Okrent, *The Guarded Gate: Bigotry, Eugenics and the Law That Kept Two Generations of Jews, Italians, and Other European Immigrants Out of America* (New York: Simon & Schuster, 2019), 180.

streets are clean or dirty relative to other places; a visitor may remark on that in print. Of course, travelers may also form mistaken impressions or seek information that conforms to their preconceptions. Philip Stevick gives the example of Ralph Waldo Emerson, who saw one chess game being played and generalized that observation to the bizarre claim that "in Philadelphia, they play chess in all houses."[13]

Some prominent people (Dolley Madison, Albert Einstein) leave letters so valuable that many researchers will want to see them, leading scholars to prepare annotated editions of their correspondence, either as bound volumes or digital resources.[14] In many other cases, working with letters means long hours in the archives, as described in chapter 9.

MEMOIRS

A third kind of first-person account is the memoir, written or dictated years or decades after an event. These may appear as published works, unpublished manuscripts, or other formats, such as privately printed texts circulated only to friends and family.

Memoirs make troublesome primary sources. Some memoirists hand some of the work over to ghostwriters, making it hard to determine which words truly reflect the views of the putative author.[15] Memories fade or get interwoven with impressions from other people, books, even movies. More conscientious memoirists will compare their memories to documents from the period, even citing them, but this happens too rarely. As Stern's Cuban Missile Crisis example shows, memoirists may unintentionally or deliberately shade their reminiscences to present themselves as having been right all along.[16] In his history of World War II, Winston Churchill sought not only to celebrate his actions and those of Great

13. Philip Stevick, *Imagining Philadelphia: Travelers' Views of the City from 1800 to the Present* (Philadelphia: University of Pennsylvania Press, 1996), 3.

14. Holly C. Shulman, ed., "The Dolley Madison Digital Edition," https://rotunda.upress.virginia.edu/dmde/; The Collected Papers of Albert Einstein, https://einsteinpapers.press.princeton.edu/.

15. Paul Farhi, "Who Actually Wrote That Political Memoir?," *Washington Post*, June 9, 2014.

16. Stern, *The Cuban Missile Crisis*. See also Hodes, *Mourning Lincoln*.

Britain, but also to charm Britain's postwar allies and obey the British government's insistence that he keep secret the code-breaking that had so shaped British strategy.[17] Some memoirs do not even pretend to tell the straight truth. Robert Capa's biographer, Alex Kershaw, warns readers that Capa's 1947 memoir, *Slightly Out of Focus*, was originally intended as a movie treatment. While it offers some insights, Kershaw finds that "some sections . . . are unreliable and a few are completely fabricated."[18]

On the other hand, it is hard to completely disregard the voice of a participant in events you are narrating. In the 1990s, historians fiercely debated the wisdom and morality of the American decision to use atomic weapons against Japanese cities, as well as the truthfulness of former secretary of war Henry L. Stimson's 1947 explanation of that decision. But historians on both sides of the debate could agree that the Stimson article was a valuable source, worthy of careful reading.[19]

Some memoirs may be valuable not for their accounts of specific events but for their evocation of a particular place and time. "Those memoirs that are deeply redolent of place and genuinely pungent, like Carlos Eire's," notes Paula Fass, "soak the reader in the smell, taste and sweat of Cuba before, during, and after the Revolution. Eire describes houses, vegetation, cars, streets, and school and household routines with verve. Even if many of these details are imaginative recreations, rather than pure memory, they are a rich source for historians." Still, she cautions, "no historian would settle exclusively for such partial views to understand and evaluate the larger subject."[20]

17. David Reynolds, *In Command of History: Churchill Fighting and Writing the Second World War* (New York: Random House, 2012), 502–7.

18. Alex Kershaw, *Blood and Champagne: The Life and Times of Robert Capa* (New York: Macmillan, 2003), 91.

19. J. Samuel Walker, "History, Collective Memory, and the Decision to Use the Bomb," *Diplomatic History* 19 (1995): 319–28; Robert P. Newman, "Hiroshima and the Trashing of Henry Stimson," *New England Quarterly* 71 (1998): 5–32; Henry L. Stimson, "The Decision to Use the Atomic Bomb," *Bulletin of the Atomic Scientists* 3 (February 1947): 37.

20. Paula S. Fass, "The Memoir Problem," *Reviews in American History* 34 (2006): 110, 111.

INTERVIEWS

As described in a later section, some historians have the good fortune to meet and interview the people about whom they write, while others rely on existing interviews conducted by journalists, government agencies, or other historians. Regardless of their origin, interviews—like memoirs—may offer more or less reliable accounts than contemporary records, depending on the circumstances.

Some narrators may become more candid as the years pass. In my book *Ethical Imperialism*, for instance, I quote retired federal official Charles McCarthy, who in 1981 faced the challenge of persuading the incoming Reagan administration to promulgate regulations crafted under the defeated Carter administration. In 2004, McCarthy told an interviewer how he had exploited the Reagan team's pledge to deregulate, and the inattention to a relatively minor issue shared by both Reagan and Carter staff:

> We went to the transition team, and we said would the transition team endorse regulations that are less stringent than the previous regulations? And, of course, they weren't, but they looked like they were because we wrote some exceptions. And so when we sent the package down to Harris, we said "Diminished Regulations for the Protection of Human Subjects." And that was the title. And, of course, we knew nobody down there in the last weeks of the Harris administration getting ready to leave office would actually read it. So they didn't know what all that was about, but they could read the title.[21]

Had McCarthy told that story to the *Washington Post* in January 1981, presumably the Reagan team would have immediately canceled the new regulations. Twenty-five years later, that was water under the bridge, so McCarthy could speak more freely without adverse consequences. I am therefore inclined to trust McCarthy's 2004 version of events.

21. Charles R. McCarthy, interview by Patricia C. El-Hinnawy, Oral History of the Belmont Report and the National Commission for the Protection of Human Subjects of Biomedical and Behavioral Research, July 22, 2004, https://www.hhs.gov/ohrp/education -and-outreach/luminaries-lecture-series/belmont-report-25th-anniversary-interview -cmccarthy/index.html.

On the other hand, even the most candid narrators may have trouble recovering the sentiments they once held, or at least sharing them with historians. The Mexicans who claimed, in the 1560s, that the arrival of the Spanish in 1519 had been foretold were likely fitting their memories to the reality of military defeat.[22] When, in the late 1950s, William Sheridan Allen sought interviews with former Nazis in a German town, he persuaded only two former adult members of the Nazi Party to speak with him, and one of those claimed to have resisted the party's program even as he remained a member. For a true understanding of their actions in the 1930s, Allen needed documents from that period and interviews with their opponents, not ex-Nazis' self-serving justifications crafted after Hitler's death.[23]

WORKADAY DOCUMENTS

Some first-person accounts emerge almost accidentally. We document our lives in appointment calendars, bank statements, and business records, probably never pausing to consider how they will reflect on us in the future, and thus leaving a more accurate, if skeletal, record of our actions than we do in anything we write with an eye for posterity. Annette Gordon-Reed begins *The Hemingses of Monticello* with a description of Thomas Jefferson's Farm Book, where she found his handwritten notes on "the names, births, family configurations, rations, and work assignments of all the people enslaved on his plantations." As Gordon-Reed observes, it is "highly unlikely that it ever occurred to Jefferson that his record of the lives of his slaves would become the subject of scholarly interest, even a passion among some—that his slaves' lives would be chronicled and followed in minute detail, the interest in them often unmoored from any interest in him. No, this was a workaday document to tell him what he had to buy from year to year, to keep some

22. Camilla Townsend, *Malintzin's Choices: An Indian Woman in the Conquest of Mexico* (Albuquerque: University of New Mexico Press, 2006), 46.

23. William Sheridan Allen, "Thalburg: The Nazi Seizure of Power in a Single German Town, 1930 to 1935," PhD diss., University of Minnesota, 1962, 15.

sense of what would be needed to continue operations."[24] That very workaday essence of the document meant that Jefferson was more likely to record the plain truth about the people he enslaved than he would in any letter or publication.

Such workaday documents gain the most value when compared to other sources. A single account book from a Spanish convent or monastery might tell us a little, but by comparing the prices that dozens of institutions paid for dried and salted codfish, economic historian Regina Grafe can construct a larger picture of market integration.[25] Similarly, Mary Dublin Keyserling's appointment books from the 1930s would not appear significant to the untrained eye. By comparing them to Keyserling's 1948 testimony that she had not socialized with communists, Landon Storrs can show that Keyserling did not tell the full truth.[26]

Periodicals

If a historian were to imagine the perfect primary source, it would have the following characteristics. First, it would be printed, not handwritten, since printed text is more easily read by human eyes or by a computer. Second, it would bear the complete date—day, month, and year—of its creation, sparing the historian the need to guess. Third, it would be produced shortly after the events it recorded, so that the historian could know what people were thinking in the moment. Fourth, it would record a variety of voices and perspectives. Finally, it would be fairly plentiful, providing abundant coverage of events as they unfolded, and existing in multiple libraries for historians to find. Newspapers, magazines, and journals—collectively known as periodical literature, or simply as periodicals—often meet some or all of the criteria, earning historians' enduring love.

24. Annette Gordon-Reed, *The Hemingses of Monticello: An American Family* (New York: W. W. Norton, 2008), 15–16.

25. Regina Grafe, *Distant Tyranny: Markets, Power, and Backwardness in Spain, 1650–1800* (Princeton, NJ: Princeton University Press, 2012).

26. Landon R. Y. Storrs, *The Second Red Scare and the Unmaking of the New Deal Left* (Princeton, NJ: Princeton University Press, 2013), chapter 5.

Periodicals themselves can contain important clues—letters to the editor, circulation figures, and advertisements—about the people who read them. Historians also seek references to periodicals in letters, diaries, memoirs, and other sources to understand periodicals as part of a conversation among editors, writers, advertisers, and readers.[27]

NEWSPAPERS

Newspapers can be fantastic starting places, the lowest-hanging fruit of historical research. A few hours of newspaper research can establish a basic timeline of events and the names of the key characters in those events. The most accessible biography of a prominent historical figure may be a newspaper obituary, while the only easily found mention of a more obscure person may be a newspaper advertisement or wedding announcement. While historians need to understand the limit of newspapers, they should also appreciate their value.

As Oscar Handlin tartly observed, "it is ludicrous to consider the newspaper as a type of evidence. It is a medium or vehicle that assembles various types of evidence—advertisements and market reports which record transactions effected or putative; the testimony of reporters; the rhetoric of editorials, commentators, and letter-writers, and such artifacts as appear in comics, cartoons, and photographs."[28] Historians can use each of those for different ends, or juxtapose items from different sections. Thus, Marcia Chatelain notes that different sections of the newspapers reported two events of April 21, 1965: the initial public offering of the McDonald's corporation and a speech by Martin Luther King Jr. calling for "the economic power structure of our nation" to be used against racist violence. It is up to Chatelain to show how those two stories later converged.[29]

27. Tony Michels, *A Fire in Their Hearts: Yiddish Socialists in New York* (Cambridge, MA: Harvard University Press, 2005), 91–114; Kelly Schrum, *Some Wore Bobby Sox: The Emergence of Teenage Girls' Culture, 1920–1945* (New York: Palgrave Macmillan, 2004), 154–55.

28. Handlin, *Truth in History*, 134.

29. Marcia Chatelain, *Franchise: The Golden Arches in Black America* (New York: Liveright, 2020), 57.

News articles establish the sequence of events, identify major characters, and often contain within themselves some of the multiple points of view needed to write analysis as well as narrative. And there is much more to a newspaper than the articles by its paid staff. Depending on the time and place, a newspaper may include government documents, shipping news, weather reports, stock prices, fiction, poetry, and cartoons. Letters to the editor and paid advertisements preserve the voices of nonprofessional writers and may give us glimpses of the lives of enslaved people, children, or others who can otherwise be hard to find. Even prominent voices are sometimes preserved only in print. A condolence letter sent (though probably not written) by Abraham Lincoln to Lydia Bixby, the mother of sons slain in battle, is a widely admired work of prose. Yet we have the text only due to its publication in the *Boston Evening Transcript*, the original having vanished soon after its creation.[30]

All kinds of newspapers can add value. Every newspaper offers the perspective of a particular ethnic, religious, occupational, or political group. The most prominent, prosperous papers are often owned by families with ties to the business community, and that depend on advertising revenue from local merchants. Read them in that light, and compare them to papers published by less powerful groups. Noenoe Silva, for example, notes seven newspapers published in Hawai'i in the 1850s and 1860s, and categorizes their politics as Calvinist, establishment, government, and resistance.[31] Such broad categorizations are useful, but no newspaper is a monolith. In the 1960s, for instance, the *Pittsburgh Courier*—like most of the African American community it served—supported the civil rights movement, but associate editor George Schuyler dissented and was pushed out of the newspaper as a result.[32]

Local newspapers may provide vivid descriptions of the main industry in an area; a coal town newspaper will describe life in the mines, while a farm town paper will describe work in the fields.

30. Jack Grieve et al., "Attributing the Bixby Letter Using N-Gram Tracing," *Digital Scholarship in the Humanities* 34 (2019): 493–512.

31. Noenoe K. Silva, *Aloha Betrayed: Native Hawaiian Resistance to American Colonialism* (Durham, NC: Duke University Press, 2004), 56.

32. Oscar R. Williams, *George S. Schuyler: Portrait of a Black Conservative* (Knoxville: University of Tennessee Press, 2007), 144–45.

Even the filler text that editors used to make columns reach the bottom of the page can be valuable. In her book on the Midwest, for instance, Kristin Hoganson kept an eye out for occasions when the *Urbana Courier* mentioned distant lands, then she fashioned these snippets of text into a series of "archival traces" that appear in between each chapter.[33] Thus, if the time and place you are studying was covered in any newspaper, it is almost certainly worth your time to identify and track down which newspapers had reporters on the spot, or editors writing commentary, and how you might get ahold of those newspapers.

Newspapers can exist in many forms. Some research libraries maintain bound volumes of the original newspapers themselves; depending on the composition of the paper used, these may be in excellent shape after centuries, or crumbling into dust. Others exist on microfilm. This is generally easier to access, since microfilm editions often (though not always) exist in multiple copies, and librarians are often less protective of microfilm reproductions than they are of one-of-a-kind originals. However, microfilm can be harder to skim than a paper original, and any images—cartoons, photographs, illustrations, maps—will lose some of the detail and all of the color of the print version.

In the twenty-first century, various libraries and private companies began scanning newspaper microfilm and running it through optical character recognition (OCR) software, allowing users to search specific terms. Because OCR struggles with the tiny, often broken type of newspapers, you cannot count on it to find every search term, and you can expect a fair number of false hits.[34] Search for "riot," for instance, and you will get many articles with the word "not," with the "n" slightly cracked. Other searches will produce false negatives. Still, this is a nearly magical technology, allowing historians to find relevant articles and advertisements that would have been impossible before its introduction.[35]

---

33. Kristin L. Hoganson, *The Heartland: An American History* (New York: Penguin, 2019).

34. Ian Milligan, "Illusionary Order: Online Databases, Optical Character Recognition, and Canadian History, 1997–2010," *Canadian Historical Review* 94 (2013): 540–69.

35. Liz Covart, "Sharon Block, How to Research History Online," Ben Franklin's World, https://benfranklinsworld.com/episode-092-sharon-block-research-history-online/.

Some newspaper digitization projects, such as Chronicling America at the Library of Congress or Trove at the National Library of Australia, are free for all to use. Others, especially those that include material still under copyright, require an institutional or individual subscription. Among the latter are sites that are aimed at genealogists and ask for names in their search engines, but historians can also make good use of these. The subscriptions are not cheap, but a year's access may still be less expensive than a short research trip. Since the companies have overlapping but distinct holdings, it is worth spending some time figuring out which has the most number of relevant newspapers before you invest.

Finally, if you are lucky, an archival collection may include a clipping file of relevant stories, which is vastly more convenient than trying to track down all the mentions of your subject in an array of periodicals. If there is a title you cannot find in databases of newspapers, it may be worth trying archival listings as well.

Beware of relying on newspaper reportage too much. Since the 1940s, journalists have been boasting of their output as the "first rough draft of history," and while we honor journalists for writing that first draft, historians must also take note of the roughness of their work.[36] First rough drafts are often factually incorrect, or biased in some manner, or mistaken about the significance of some key point. Publishers, editors, and reporters all have their own agendas and are prone to human error, especially when rushed to make a deadline. One would not want to take at face value Walter Duranty's fawning *New York Times* coverage of the Soviet Union in the 1930s, nor the *Chicago Tribune*'s famous headline that Dewey had defeated Truman.[37]

Beyond questions of factual accuracy, learn about the conventions of newspaper reporting and publication in the time and place you are studying. Was a particular newspaper editorially independent, or did it support a political party? Was the item you are reading written by the newspaper staff, or republished from a distant

36. Jack Shafer, "On the Trail of the Question, Who First Said (or Wrote) That Journalism Is the 'First Rough Draft of History'?," *Slate*, August 31, 2010.

37. S. J. Taylor, *Stalin's Apologist: Walter Duranty; The New York Times's Man in Moscow* (New York: Oxford University Press, 1990), 220.

city? This latter question has grown in importance with the mass digitization of newspapers. The first hits you get in a database search may be from a newspaper far from the main events that reprinted a story from an eyewitness reporter. Whenever possible, try to identify the original source. Read newspaper editorials especially critically. Compared to factual reporting, a blistering editorial can be refreshing to read and tempting to quote, but it may also represent just one editor's opinion, or a cynical effort to attract subscribers by being outrageous. While newspapers can be a wonderful starting place, it is best not to stop there.

MAGAZINES

Along with daily and weekly newspapers, for centuries people have published an array of magazines, journals, yearbooks, and other serialized literature. These are wonderful sources: far easier to find and use than unique letters and diaries, yet often as revealing. For example, Ruth Rosen devotes more than ten pages of *The World Split Open*, a history of the women's movement, to the early history of *Ms.* magazine, recounting its origin, its editorial content, and—most importantly—the letters it received, which provide fascinating, first-person accounts of women's daily experiences at home, at work, and on the street in the 1970s.[38] Like newspapers, magazines are packages of sources that you can read together. "In the early cold war decades," writes Michael Adas, "the very layout of popular magazines such as *Look* and *Life* suggested the stark contrasts in the levels of consumer comforts provided by capitalist and communist systems. Articles on shortages behind the iron curtain were routinely flanked by ads for the latest models of American cars, TV sets, dishwashers and other household appliances, and variety packs of breakfast cereals."[39]

Many popular magazines are essentially advice manuals, telling people what to eat, what to wear, how to raise children, and how

---

38. Ruth Rosen, *The World Split Open: How the Modern Women's Movement Changed America*, rev. ed. (New York: Penguin Books, 2006), 208–17.

39. Michael Adas, *Dominance by Design: Technological Imperatives and America's Civilizing Mission* (Cambridge, MA: Harvard University Press, 2006), 233.

to succeed in romance and at work. These are particularly valuable sources to understand elements of daily life, such as the range of acceptable emotions.[40] As magazines shrink or disappear in the age of digital media, it is not clear that historians of the twenty-first century will find an easy substitute.

SPECIALIZED PERIODICALS

Some of the most valuable periodicals are the most specialized. In 1972, *Monty Python's Flying Circus* imagined a television show called *Storage Jars*, which would relay the day's events to an audience fanatically interested in those containers. "On tonight's programme," the anchor promises, "Mikos Antoniarkis, the Greek rebel leader who seized power in Athens this morning, tells us what he keeps in storage jars. From strife-torn Bolivia, Ronald Rodgers reports on storage jars there. And closer to home, the first dramatic pictures of the mass jail-break near the storage jar factory in Maidenhead. All this and more in storage jars!"[41]

The Python sketch is an absurd extension of the truth that every news outlet shapes its coverage to appeal to a specific audience. The "mainstream press" may appeal to a country's majority, defined in racial, ethnic, class, or religious terms. Other periodicals serve specific political factions, professions, social groups, cities, regions, hobbies, institutions, and industries. For historians seeking the perspective of people in those categories, this record is invaluable.

While probably no one has ever really broadcast a television news program devoted to storage jars, enough people care about the latest developments in beverage containers to have inspired the publication of *American Brewer*, *National Bottlers' Gazette*, and *American Bottler*, later renamed *American Soft Drink Journal*. Robert Friedel mined these and other specialized journals to understand why Americans abandoned a working system of bottle deposits—which encouraged people to return empty bottles to be

---

40. Peter N. Stearns, *American Cool: Constructing a Twentieth-Century Emotional Style* (New York: New York University Press, 1994), 12.

41. Graham Chapman et al., *The Complete Monty Python's Flying Circus: All the Words* (New York: Pantheon Books, 1989), 2:140.

cleaned and reused—in favor of throwaway containers that consume resources and litter the landscape. While Friedel found useful context in less specialized periodicals like *Business Week* and the *New York Times*, those did not cover changes in bottling with anything like the depth and frequency of the more targeted journals that make up the bulk of his sources.[42]

Beyond their detail, specialized journals and books may offer a level of candor not found elsewhere; these are members of a group writing to each other, not presenting themselves to a possibly hostile outside world. Starting in the late 1960s, Stuart Ewen read advertising executives' journals (primarily *Printers' Ink*) and books, and he was surprised and delighted by their frankness. Decades later, he reflected that while doing research "I felt like a spy, following a mass consumer culture and the commercial propaganda machinery that propelled it. What blew me away, what still blows me away, was the extent to which the people I was uncovering, who never expected their words to be scrutinized except by their peers, were remarkably candid about their thoughts and intentions."[43]

Just one or two specialized periodicals can tell a rich story. Arwen Mohun read British and American laundry trade journals, finding in them not only technical discussions of how best to clean fabrics but also "jokes, anecdotes, remembrances, descriptions of social events such as conventions, and news of members." In these she found laundrymen's understanding of their gender.[44] To trace debates over eugenics, Sharon Leon read the periodicals *Eugenics* and *Eugenical News*.[45] Joy Lisi Rankin based her account of networked computing in Minnesota schools largely

42. Robert Friedel, "American Bottles: The Road to No Return," *Environmental History* 19 (July 2014): 505–27.

43. Stuart Ewen, *Captains of Consciousness: Advertising and the Social Roots of the Consumer Culture*, 25th Anniversary Edition (New York: Basic Books, 2008), 7.

44. Arwen Palmer Mohun, "Laundrymen Construct Their World: Gender and the Transformation of a Domestic Task to an Industrial Process," *Technology and Culture* 38 (1997): 101.

45. Sharon Leon, "'Hopelessly Entangled in Nordic Pre-Suppositions': Catholic Participation in the American Eugenics Society in the 1920s," *Journal of the History of Medicine and Allied Sciences* 59 (2004): 6.

on runs of two particularly obscure periodicals: the newsletter of the Total Information for Educational Systems network, and the *Systems Update* of the Minnesota Educational Computing Consortium.[46]

Specialized periodicals can be especially useful if you can play them against each other. Consider, for example, Pan American Airways' entry into Africa in the years during and after World War II. Along with Pan Am itself, the expansion involved the US government, the British government, Africans living under British colonial rule, American employees stationed in Africa, and African workers at Pan Am bases, as well as outside observers, such as newspapermen passing through or American schoolchildren reading of the new routes. Jenifer Van Vleck gets Pan Am management's version of this story from *New Horizons*, a magazine published by the airline. But rather than rest there, she supplements that account with selections from mainstream US newspapers, African American and labor newspapers, and African newspapers. Thanks to this triangulation, she can tell us not only what Pan Am thought of Africans, but also what Africans thought of Pan Am, and what other observers thought of them both.[47]

Identifying and finding specialized periodicals is harder than locating major newspapers, so seek a librarian's help if you can. Back issues of periodicals may be held in specialized engineering libraries, business libraries, or agricultural libraries. The best runs may exist only in an archive. For instance, Rankin read *Systems Update* on microfilm at the Minnesota Historical Society. Depending on the place and period you are researching, you may find indexes to multiple periodicals, such as *Poole's Index to Periodical Literature* (1802–1906) or *Applied Science & Technology Index* (which has covered engineering since 1914).[48]

46. Joy Lisi Rankin, *A People's History of Computing in the United States* (Cambridge, MA: Harvard University Press, 2018), chapter 5.

47. Jenifer Van Vleck, *Empire of the Air: Aviation and the American Ascendancy* (Cambridge, MA: Harvard University Press, 2013), chapter 4.

48. "Abstracts, Indexes, and Bibliographies for Finding Citations to Periodical Articles," Library of Congress, https://www.loc.gov/rr/main/ab_index.html.

Government Documents

Since King Hammurabi ordered a clerk to preserve his code by carving it into a basalt stele, governments have been particularly good at creating and maintaining records. While peasants and laborers, mothers and servants tell stories that vanish when the last listener dies, the police officer, court clerk, and tax assessor may be compiling ledgers that will endure for centuries. Whether you are interested in state actors themselves or in the people they observed, such records offer crucial evidence of past lives.

CRIMINAL INVESTIGATIONS AND TRIALS

Some of the most spectacular official records are trials for murder or other serious offenses, since they could lead government officials to the unusual step of recording in great detail how people spent their time and what they had to say. Classic microhistories, such as Carlo Ginzburg's *The Cheese and the Worms* and Natalie Zemon Davis's *Return of Martin Guerre* depend on the records of the trials of their protagonists, who otherwise would have left scarcely a record.[49] In other cases, historians mine trial records for information to feed a larger story. Lisa Tolbert, for example, wanted to know how residents of small towns in antebellum Tennessee moved through the streets and buildings and understood the physical world they inhabited. For white women and men, she was able to rely on their own words, recorded in letters and diaries that were carefully preserved for decades, but she had no such documents created by enslaved Tennesseans. Instead, she relied on the murder trial of an enslaved butcher and tanner named Henry, during which officers and lawyers carefully investigated his movements on February 24, 1850. Only due to this unusual intrusion of the state into

49. Carlo Ginzburg, *The Cheese and the Worms: The Cosmos of a Sixteenth-Century Miller,* trans. John Tedeschi and Anne C. Tedeschi, reprint ed. (Baltimore: Johns Hopkins University Press, 1992); Natalie Zemon Davis, *The Return of Martin Guerre* (Cambridge, MA: Harvard University Press, 1983). See also Paul E. Johnson and Sean Wilentz, *The Kingdom of Matthias: A Story of Sex and Salvation in 19th-Century America* (New York: Oxford University Press, 2012).

Henry's life do we get a glimpse of his typical routine: the place he slept, the clothes he wore, the chores he performed, and the people he encountered.[50] Economic historian Hans-Joachim Voth wanted to know what hours people worked, so he searched London trial records for witnesses who indicated whether they were at work at a given hour of a given day. He used these to estimate a rise in working hours between 1750 and 1800, followed by a long decline over the next two centuries.[51]

Riots are not bad either; a government that has long neglected its slums may become quite interested in conditions there after the slum-dwellers arise. In 1929, for example, residents of Makokoba— the African district of Bulawayo in colonial Zimbabwe—attacked people and property. In part as a response to this event, the government chartered a commission to examine life in Makokoba. Decades later, Moses Chikowero used the testimony of commission witnesses, both European and African, to reconstruct the Africans' frustrations at inadequate street lighting, frustrations that likely would never have been recorded in the absence of the violence and the subsequent investigation.[52]

Keep in mind that such sources may be tainted by the investigators' wish for a particular outcome. In 2001, Michael Johnson questioned established accounts of the slave uprising allegedly planned by Denmark Vesey in Charleston, South Carolina, in 1822. He noted that the evidence against Vesey came from the testimony of black men who had been confined, likely beaten, and informed that authorities were in the process of hanging accused conspirators. Any testimony they gave, Johnson argues, was coerced and therefore unreliable. He concludes that Vesey "was

50. Lisa C. Tolbert, *Constructing Townscapes: Space and Society in Antebellum Tennessee* (Chapel Hill: University of North Carolina Press, 1999), chapter 6. See also Elaine Frantz Parsons, *Manhood Lost: Fallen Drunkards and Redeeming Women in the Nineteenth-Century United States* (Baltimore: Johns Hopkins University Press, 2003).

51. Hans-Joachim Voth, "Time and Work in Eighteenth-Century London," *Journal of Economic History* 58 (1998): 29–58.

52. Moses Chikowero, "Subalternating Currents: Electrification and Power Politics in Bulawayo, Colonial Zimbabwe, 1894–1939," *Journal of Southern African Studies* 33 (June 2007): 295n42.

the victim of a conspiracy of collusion between the white court and its cooperative black witnesses, both eager for their own reasons to pay homage to the enduring power of white supremacy."[53]

CENSUSES

Censuses are among the most complete government records, sweeping in rich and poor, criminal and law-abiding, educated and illiterate. Like any other source, they have their limits, and it is good to consider the circumstances under which they were compiled. "Not only was it virtually impossible to canvass every family in the United States," writes Loren Schweninger, "but census takers also misspelled names, wrote in the wrong age, color, or gender, included families outside their district, and worse, sometimes failed to complete the canvasses of their assigned districts. In the midst of the racial and political violence during the summer of 1870 they probably missed 6 to 7 percent of the black population in the South." Nonetheless, Schweninger concludes, "census marshals produced a remarkable set of documents" that help us understand the American economy of the mid-nineteenth century.[54]

Genealogists depend on censuses to track people across space and time, while social historians can use them to build portraits of a neighborhood—What kind of people lived there, in terms of age, sex, race, nativity, wealth, occupation, or other indicators? Census data may not tell the whole story, but they can point you to a story that can be researched using other sources. Dylan Gottlieb used data from the 1970s and 1980s to map the changes in residences of professional workers in the New York City region. "Right away," he explains, "I noticed a growing concentration of finance folks in one small area: Hoboken, New Jersey. What were all these bond traders doing in this small city of brownstones right across from Lower Manhattan? I knew there had to be a story there." There was.[55]

53. Michael P. Johnson, "Denmark Vesey and His Co-Conspirators," *William and Mary Quarterly* 58 (2001): 915–76.

54. Loren Schweninger, *Black Property Owners in the South, 1790–1915* (Champaign: University of Illinois Press, 1990), 372.

55. Dylan Gottlieb, "Hoboken Is Burning: A Conversation on Gentrification, Arson, and Displacement," *Process: A Blog for American History*, December 12, 2019, http://www

While national censuses (such as those conducted every ten years in the United States) get most of the attention, specialized censuses are valuable as well. For his study of changing rural life in the early twentieth century, Jack Temple Kirby relied on the county-level data collected every five years by the farm census, introduced in 1920.[56] Subnational censuses, such as those conducted by many states in the nineteenth century, may also pick up data or years not caught by national counts.

OFFICIAL REPORTS

Occasionally—and with increasing frequency since the beginning of the twentieth century—governments have commissioned official reports on matters of interest. These can be wonderful resources: thousands of pages compiling quantitative information, sociological observation, and other data. Yet they are often complicated creations, representing not objective truth but a collaborative effort among various actors with their own agendas, expertise, and resources. Indeed, historians have devoted whole books to untangling the origins of reports that had particular impact in shaping policy or public understanding.[57] That is not always needed, but do read carefully and critically, understanding the report not as a neutral observation but as an intervention in a debate.

LETTERS AND PETITIONS

Fortunately for historians, governments not only archive texts that they produce but also preserve texts they *receive*, including some from people whose voices would otherwise be lost. In 1978, Eric Foner asked South Carolina state archivist Wilma Waites if she had

.processhistory.org/hoboken-is-burning-a-conversation-on-gentrification-arson-and -displacement/.

56. Jack Temple Kirby, *Rural Worlds Lost: The American South, 1920–1960* (Baton Rouge: Louisiana State University Press, 1986), 361.

57. Katherine Benton-Cohen, *Inventing the Immigration Problem: The Dillingham Commission and Its Legacy* (Cambridge, MA: Harvard University Press, 2018); Steven M. Gillon, *Separate and Unequal: The Kerner Commission and the Unraveling of American Liberalism* (New York: Basic Books, 2018).

any materials on Reconstruction. "Well," she replied, "you know we've got these Governor's Papers no one has ever looked at." As Foner later related the story:

> She brought a few out, and I knew no one had ever looked at it because you could barely open it up. This stuff had been stuffed into these boxes in the 1870s and when you took it out, you couldn't get it back in. And in those papers—a lot of it is total junk (someone wanting to get a job, and "My cow got lost, can you do something about that?")—are the voices of ordinary people—Black, white, rich, poor, planters, poor whites, free Blacks from before the Civil War, ordinary slaves, things about the Klan, things about land, about local level politics; it was fascinating.

Inspired by these documents, and comparable letters sent to other Southern governors, Foner wrote *Reconstruction: America's Unfinished Revolution*, which has shaped all subsequent interpretations of the era.[58]

In her history of the Erie Canal, Carol Sheriff boasts of working through dozens of cubic feet of materials so nondescript that even an archivist considered them "dull beyond belief." "While it is true that the official documents pertaining to the New York canals are in many ways tedious," Sheriff concedes, "they nonetheless have buried within them—sometimes in quite unexpected places—invaluable information about daily life in the Canal corridor." She prizes one letter favoring the adoption of steamboats as a way to displace "the 'profain' boys who drive the horses who pull the boats." And, Sheriff notes, "when other citizens filed claims enumerating, for page after dense page, the contents of their flooded cellars, they unwittingly left detailed records of their consumption patterns."[59]

Many of the letters read by Foner and Sheriff were likely written at the initiative of the writer, who sought redress for some grievance. In other cases, historians take advantage of state efforts to solicit information. To understand the lives of propertyless Southern

---

58. Eric Foner, "Black History and the Reconstruction Era," *Souls* 8 (2006): 198.

59. Carol Sheriff, *The Artificial River: The Erie Canal and the Paradox of Progress, 1817–1862* (New York: Hill and Wang, 1997), 226.

whites in the years before and during the Civil War, Keri Leigh Merritt read the veterans' questionnaires that the state of Tennessee started collecting in 1915. "Although the questionnaires rely heavily on memory," Merritt notes, "they are one of the only sources that allow the voices of poor whites to be heard."[60] For his study of the World War II home front, James Sparrow mined the materials collected by the Office of War Information, a government agency. By sending representatives to collect rumors in cities around the country, and archiving the results in the Library of Congress, the agency enabled Sparrow, decades later, to give us the voices of relatively ordinary Americans, who feared that the war was empowering African Americans and Jews.[61]

INSTITUTIONAL RECORDS

Public institutions often preserve records as well. To understand the lives of some of early Baltimore's poorest residents, Seth Rockman tracked them to the penitentiary and almshouse, whose records survive in the Maryland State Archives. "These records allow a social historian to create collective portraits of groups of people otherwise under the radar," he explains.[62] For good reason, however, institutions are wary of sharing case files with anyone other than authorized officials or, perhaps, members of the inmates' families. Some destroy records or seal them forever. Even when historians gain access, they often use partial names or pseudonyms to identify individual cases, either on their own initiative or to respect agreements with the institutions.[63]

60. Keri Leigh Merritt, *Masterless Men: Poor Whites and Slavery in the Antebellum South* (New York: Cambridge University Press, 2017), 27.

61. James T. Sparrow, *Warfare State: World War II Americans and the Age of Big Government* (New York: Oxford University Press, 2011), chapter 3.

62. Seth Rockman, *Scraping By: Wage Labor, Slavery, and Survival in Early Baltimore* (Baltimore: Johns Hopkins University Press, 2009), 351.

63. Miroslava Chávez-García, "Youth of Color and California's Carceral State: The Fred C. Nelles Youth Correctional Facility," *Journal of American History* 102 (2015): 47–60; Susan C. Lawrence, *Privacy and the Past: Research, Law, Archives, Ethics* (New Brunswick, NJ: Rutgers University Press, 2016).

Scholarship

Yesterday's scholarship can become today's primary source. "Places of rest, relaxation, recreation, and restoration rarely maintained archives or recorded the everyday conversations and noises that filled bars, dance halls, blues clubs, barber shops, beauty salons, and street corners of the black community," notes Robin Kelly. But "folklorists, anthropologists, oral historians, musicians, and writers fascinated by 'Negro life' preserved a relatively large body of cultural texts which have allowed scholars access to the hidden transcript." He goes on to cite research in sociology and economics from the 1930s.[64]

Like any primary source, such scholarship rewards critical reading. An undergraduate essay by Daniel Williford, for instance, analyzes articles published between 1870 and 1895 in *La Revue Africaine*, finding that "scholars in the *Revue* projected their particular interpretations of Algerian historical and physical space onto the reality of the colonial situation in Algeria, thus becoming participants in the creation of this reality."[65] Similarly, Sara Gregg reads the sociology of the 1930s in part for what it tells us about the people studied by the sociologists, but even more for what it tells us about the sociologists and the officials who used their work. She notes, for instance, that the Vermont Commission on Country Life originated as the Eugenics Survey of Vermont, suggesting a somewhat racist agenda. And she explains how one official used a sociological study to show that the people living on land slated to become Shenandoah National Park were "literally the scum of the mountain people" whose homes were not worthy of preserving.[66]

Technical reports, too, have their own histories. David Stradling notes that a main goal of WPA pollution surveys was "to provide employment to technical and clerical persons" during the

---

64. Robin D. G. Kelley, *Race Rebels: Culture, Politics, and the Black Working Class* (1994; repr., New York: Free Press, 1996), 44–45.

65. Daniel Williford, "Visions of Pre-Islamic Algeria in the Revue Africaine, 1870–1896," *Rhodes Historical Review* 13 (2011): 68.

66. Sara M. Gregg, *Managing the Mountains: Land Use Planning, the New Deal, and the Creation of a Federal Landscape in Appalachia* (New Haven, CT: Yale University Press, 2010), 58–59, 126.

Depression, so when World War II created better jobs for such experts, many pollution surveys were abandoned, unfinished.[67] And textbooks, which seek to present the consensus view of a body of scholarship, suggest the values and viewpoints of the leaders of a scholarly field.[68]

Today's scholarship can also be useful to understanding the past. Just as paleontologists study the behavior of extant reptiles and birds for clues about the behavior of long-extinct dinosaurs, so can historians gain insight about past human behavior by considering the findings of today's social scientists. For instance, Jennifer Ritterhouse was studying the ways that Southern children learned "racial etiquette" in the late nineteenth and early twentieth centuries. She could not observe the process directly, but she could read a 2001 study by two sociologists who had observed children in a day care center. Though the setting was more racially integrated than the Southern locales of previous decades, the stories told by the sociologists resembled those told by earlier generations and helped Ritterhouse make sense of her older sources.[69]

Fiction

Even explicitly fictional works can inform history. Some works of art are inextricably part of history because they themselves shaped historical events. Harriet Beecher Stowe's 1852 novel, *Uncle Tom's Cabin*, affected not only American readers in the 1850s but also those who viewed illustrations, attended staged versions, wrote competing narratives, or encountered the story far from the United States or decades after the Civil War.[70] That work's impact is perhaps

67. David Stradling, *Smokestacks and Progressives: Environmentalists, Engineers, and Air Quality in America, 1881–1951*, rev. ed. (Baltimore: Johns Hopkins University Press, 2003), 161.

68. Susan C. Lawrence and Kae Bendixen, "His and Hers: Male and Female Anatomy in Anatomy Texts for U.S. Medical Students, 1890–1989," *Social Science & Medicine* 35 (1992): 925–34.

69. Jennifer Ritterhouse, *Growing Up Jim Crow: How Black and White Southern Children Learned Race* (Chapel Hill: University of North Carolina Press, 2006), 12–13; Debra Van Ausdale, *The First R: How Children Learn Race and Racism* (Lanham, MD: Rowman and Littlefield, 2001).

70. Susan Belasco, "*Uncle Tom's Cabin* in Our Time," *Legacy* 29 (2012): 318–28.

incomparable, but later social novels, as well as paintings, plays, films, and other artworks, have all shaped history as much as any speech or manifesto. In Ellen Baker's *On Strike and on Film*, a miners' strike and the film made about it get equal weight, for each tell us important stories about labor in the 1950s.[71]

Fiction can also give us insights about how people in the past understood their world. While most Americans read F. Scott Fitzgerald's *Great Gatsby* for what it tells us about America, John Stilgoe reads it for what it says about train travel. "That's my Middle West—not the wheat or the prairies or the lost Swede towns, but the thrilling returning trains of my youth," exclaims the novel's fictional narrator, Nick Carraway. As Stilgoe shows, that passage reveals the *meaning* of the train for Americans like Nick, reared in the Midwest but transplanted to the East, and dependent on fast trains to connect the two landscapes of their lives.[72] In *A Covenant with Color*, Craig Steven Wilder quotes the novel *Brown Girl, Brownstones* to note Paule Marshall's distinction between those "lucky" domestic workers who had a steady employer and those who "wandered those neat blocks or waited on corners—each with her apron and working shoes in a bag under her arm until someone offered her a day's work."[73]

Some art expresses the values of particular occupations. In *Making Technology Masculine*, Ruth Oldenziel devotes several pages to Rudyard Kipling's 1907 poem "The Sons of Martha," not because she particularly likes or dislikes the poem but because the engineers who are the protagonists of her work "responded to the poem with pangs of recognition."[74] By reading the poem, we see the world through their eyes. Similarly, Joshua Specht uses cowboy songs to get glimpses of life on the trail. "Prairie Fires, won't you please

71. Ellen R. Baker, *On Strike and on Film: Mexican American Families and Blacklisted Filmmakers in Cold War America* (Chapel Hill: University of North Carolina Press, 2007).

72. John R. Stilgoe, *Metropolitan Corridor: Railroads and the American Scene* (New Haven, CT: Yale University Press, 1985), 51.

73. Craig Steven Wilder, *A Covenant with Color: Race and Social Power in Brooklyn, 1636–1990* (New York: Columbia University Press, 2000), 140.

74. Ruth Oldenziel, *Making Technology Masculine: Men, Women and Modern Machines in America, 1870–1945* (Amsterdam: Amsterdam University Press, 1999), 128.

stop? / Let thunder roll and water drop," runs one. "It frightens me to see the smoke / unless it's stopped / I'll go dead broke."[75]

The historian may want to compare people's actions to the standards of their culture. Advice manuals are great sources for this, but so are works of literature. As Cynthia Kierner notes of the literature of late eighteenth-century America, "in novel after novel, the young heroine becomes pregnant and, abandoned by her lover, dies alone and in shame. Sentimental heroines became prey to unscrupulous men because they lacked paternal protection or maternal guidance, and usually both." Reading those novels helps Kierner understand how the real people in her narrative would have reacted to the pregnancy of a young, unmarried woman.[76] Similarly, Thomas Piketty quotes the novels of Jane Austen and Honoré de Balzac to illustrate what it was like to live in a world where the wealth one could acquire by marriage or inheritance vastly exceeded what one could earn in a lifetime of hard work.[77]

Fictional works also shape historical perceptions in the present, so your readers may be eager to learn what is and is not true about the stories they have absorbed. Fredrik Logevall figures that many of his readers will have gotten most of what they know about early American involvement in Vietnam either from Graham Greene's 1955 novel *The Quiet American*, or one of its film adaptations. Logevall therefore devotes considerable space describing Greene's time in Vietnam, his writing of the novel, and its reception by various readers, as well as the story of how Hollywood altered the story in the 1958 movie, much to Greene's disgust.[78] In some cases, addressing popular representations can take the form of outright debunking. "Most of us are familiar with a well-entrenched stereotype of American women in the post–World War II years," writes Joanne Meyerowitz. "Domestic and quiescent, they moved to the suburbs, created the baby boom, and forged family togetherness. . . . The

75. Joshua Specht, *Red Meat Republic: A Hoof-to-Table History of How Beef Changed America* (Princeton, NJ: Princeton University Press, 2019), 84.

76. Cynthia A. Kierner, *Scandal at Bizarre: Rumor and Reputation in Jefferson's America* (Charlottesville: University of Virginia Press, 2006), 81.

77. Thomas Piketty, *Capital in the Twenty-First Century*, trans. Arthur Goldhammer (Cambridge, MA: Harvard University Press, 2014), 105–6, 238–40.

78. Fredrik Logevall, *Embers of War: The Fall of an Empire and the Making of America's Vietnam* (New York: Random House, 2012), 681.

stereotype persists today in television reruns of situation comedies, in popular movies, and sometimes in scholarly historical accounts of the postwar years. My students come to class with this image of womanhood set squarely in their vision." Meyerowitz titled her book *Not June Cleaver*, at once leveraging the reader's presumed familiarity with that sitcom housewife and alerting them that stereotypes can mislead.[79]

Of course, one must keep in mind that fiction is fiction, and cannot be used in the same way as source material whose creators sought to be wholly truthful. Indeed, historians must sometimes devote space to correcting the impressions of an event that a reader may have formed from a novel or movie. Yes, Kathryn Olmsted notes, John Steinbeck based his novel *In Dubious Battle* on stories he heard from real union organizers. But she also notes the distortions. "Women and people of color play no significant roles in Steinbeck's version of history," Olmsted writes. "Steinbeck's workers are Okie or native-born American migrants, while the Mexicans and Filipinos of the cotton strike have vanished. Moreover, the federal government does not make an appearance in Steinbeck's version of the cotton strike. . . . The New Deal does not exist as part of *In Dubious Battle*'s fictional California."[80]

Words

"Words are witnesses which often speak louder than documents," wrote Eric Hobsbawm, noting that in the period between 1789 and 1848, English speakers first used "such words as 'industry', 'industrialist', 'factory', 'middle class', 'working class', 'capitalism' and 'socialism' as well as 'railway', 'liberal' and 'conservative' as political terms, 'nationality', 'scientist' and 'engineer', 'proletariat' and (economic) 'crisis'. 'Utilitarian' and 'statistics', 'sociology' and several other names of modern sciences, 'journalism' and 'ideology', are all coinages or adaptations of this period. So is 'strike' and

---

79. June Meyerowitz, *Not June Cleaver: Women and Gender in Postwar America, 1945–1960* (Philadelphia: Temple University Press, 1994), 1.

80. Kathryn S. Olmsted, *Right Out of California: The 1930s and the Big Business Roots of Modern Conservatism* (New York: New Press, 2015), 103.

'pauperism.'"[81] By tracing words, historians can get glimpses of daily life and subtle changes of thought that otherwise went unrecorded. "Seventeenth-century sex words look earthy, vigorous, often big on metaphor or on body parts, and sometimes baffling," writes Sarah Knott. "Yielding. Sporting. Tumbling. Clipping. Clapping. There's a way to reread such words now that can slip between shame and prurience, and reveal something of past sexual moments, even at great distance. . . . Some of these terms sound passionate or wild, others exploratory or possessive, others loving."[82]

In a moving passage from *Killing for Coal*, Thomas Andrews describes the dangers of stinkdamp, blackdamp, afterdamp, and firedamp, each of which plagued Colorado coal miners. Andrews uses modern scientific terms as well—hydrogen sulfide, carbon dioxide, carbon monoxide, and methane—to explain the properties of the various damps. But by highlighting the historic names, he evokes the knowledge that miners passed on to one another, rather than the book-learning of a mining engineer.[83] Words reveal power relationships as well. When automobile owners wanted to clear pedestrians out of the street—or at least escape liability if they crashed into those pedestrians—they invented the slur "jaywalker" to suggest that streets belonged to motor vehicles.[84]

Place-names can record histories otherwise forgotten. Describing the founding of Natick, Massachusetts, Lisa Brooks considers its name. "'N'ahteuk,'" she explains, "means 'my land,' a deceptively simple phrase, which is more complex when viewed through the lens of Algonquian languages. . . . It is significant that the inhabitants of 'N'ahteuk' used the exclusive term, and not the inclusive term, *kdakinna*, which would suggest that this place was 'our [inclusive] land,' shared with many others, perhaps even including

81. Eric Hobsbawm, *The Age of Revolution: 1789–1848* (1962; repr., New York: Vintage, 1996), 1. For a brief history of such analysis, see Thomas Dixon, "Words in History: Mirrors or Motors?," *Cultural History of Philosophy Blog*, December 28, 2014, https://blogs.history .qmul.ac.uk/philosophy/2014/12/28/words-in-history-mirrors-or-motors/.

82. Sarah Knott, *Mother Is a Verb: An Unconventional History* (New York: Sarah Crichton Books, 2019), 23.

83. Thomas G. Andrews, *Killing for Coal: America's Deadliest Labor War* (Cambridge, MA: Harvard University Press, 2010), 144–45.

84. Peter D. Norton, "Street Rivals: Jaywalking and the Invention of the Motor Age Street," *Technology and Culture* 48 (2007): 331–59.

the English settlers. When the people of the falls renamed their town, they emphasized delineated bounds that would be registered in an English legal system."[85]

Metaphors, too, reveal patterns of thought. Greg Grandin devotes an entire chapter to the way that nineteenth-century Americans used the term "safety valve," first discussing the development of actual valves as a response to steamboat boiler explosions, and then exploring how Americans imagined their society as a vessel that might explode if the forces that powered it had no release.[86] The development of full-text databases of books, newspapers, and other materials has opened new opportunities for this kind of analysis. Economist Robert Shiller, for instance, has used the ProQuest newspaper databases to trace the history of such terms as "maximize shareholder value" and "highest tax bracket" as evidence for Americans' shifting understandings of the economy.[87]

Researchers must understand the terminology of previous places and times. A search for "abortion" in nineteenth-century newspapers may not produce information on how to terminate a pregnancy, but readers could find advertisements for products promising to "unblock menses."[88] Similarly, Americans of that era dared not write openly of same-sex desire. By tracking down the quotations and references (e.g., "a sight of comfort") in letters written between women, and showing that they were taken from stories of romantic love, Rachel Hope Cleves persuasively argues that the women were expressing erotic longing for each other, and not simply platonic friendship.[89]

85. Lisa Brooks, *Our Beloved Kin: A New History of King Philip's War* (New Haven, CT: Yale University Press, 2018), 174.

86. Greg Grandin, *The End of the Myth: From the Frontier to the Border Wall in the Mind of America* (New York: Henry Holt, 2019), chapter 4.

87. Robert J. Shiller, *Narrative Economics: How Stories Go Viral and Drive Major Economic Events* (Princeton, NJ: Princeton University Press, 2019), 47, 49.

88. Karin Wulf, "What Naomi Wolf and Cokie Roberts Teach Us about the Need for Historians," *Washington Post*, June 11, 2019; Lauren MacIvor Thompson, "Women Have Always Had Abortions," *New York Times*, December 13, 2019.

89. Rachel Hope Cleves, *Charity and Sylvia: A Same-Sex Marriage in Early America* (New York: Oxford University Press, 2014), 83–84.

Big Data

In 1950, Louis Gottschalk marveled that American records of the European theater of World War II were arriving in Washington "by the freight carload." "The future writer of monographs from this material," he speculated, "will have to devise categories and sampling techniques that may now seem fantastic to the conventional historians."[90] Since then, the challenge of abundance has only grown. "Digital information is mounting at a particularly daunting rate in science and government," observed Roy Rosenzweig in 2003. "Digital sky surveys, for example, access over 2 billion images. Even a dozen years ago, NASA already had 1.2 million magnetic tapes (many of them poorly maintained and documented) with space data. Similarly, the Clinton White House, by one estimate, churned out 6 million e-mail messages per year."[91] No historian could read them all; they can at best sample.

Historians do some sampling simply by choosing what to read and what to ignore. Michael Pfeifer, for instance, did not think he had the time to track every postbellum lynching in every state, but studying just one state would not let him explore the full phenomenon, which varied by region. So he examined seven states, spread across the United States, blending the thoroughness of a case study with the broader claims of a national study.[92] Walter Licht wanted to get a sense of how many "Help Wanted" advertisements appeared in Philadelphia's newspapers between 1850 and 1920. Had he wanted to read every ad appearing Monday through Saturday for that span of seventy years, he would have needed to scan roughly 22,000 issues of the *Public Ledger*, plus more from the *Bulletin* and the *Inquirer*, as those newspapers became important. Instead, he did some initial browsing, determined that the most advertisements appeared in May, and then read the May 1 issues for 1850, 1860, 1870, 1880, 1890, 1900, 1910, and 1920: only eight issues

90. Louis Gottschalk, *Understanding History: A Primer of Historical Method* (New York: Alfred A. Knopf, 1950), 77.

91. Roy Rosenzweig, "Scarcity or Abundance? Preserving the Past in a Digital Era," *American Historical Review* 108 (2003): 738.

92. Michael James Pfeifer, *Rough Justice: Lynching and American Society, 1874–1947* (Champaign: University of Illinois Press, 2004), 9–10.

per newspaper. That was enough to give him a sense of the broad trends.[93] Confronted with thousands of detailed prisoner case files—none of which he was allowed to photocopy—Joseph Spillane decided to open every tenth box and read every other file, thus sampling 5 percent of the total.[94]

Since the 1960s, some historians have programmed computers to do some of their reading and computation for them, allowing them to analyze sets of data and text otherwise too vast to handle. In the age of punch cards and magnetic tape, these were often data that could be reduced to numbers: birth and death registers, tax records, rents.[95] Data from some projects from this era, such as the Philadelphia Social History Project, are now available in formats used by today's computers.[96]

In the age of mass digitization, historians and other scholars in the humanities have supplemented earlier quantitative samples with computerized analysis of texts. Sometimes this simply means searching texts in ways one could not with paper or microfilm. For example, Sharon Block searched colonial American newspapers for ads that referred to runaway servants and slaves by their skin color, a task that would have taken far more labor and produced less quantifiable results had she only been able to skim the texts one page at a time.[97] Other historians engage in "text-mining": using computer algorithms to identify patterns in corpuses of texts too vast to be read by individuals in a human lifetime. Lincoln Mullen, for example, used a computer to identify "over 866,000 quotations of the Bible or verbal allusions to specific biblical verses" among the millions of newspaper pages digitized by the Library of Congress.[98]

93. Walter Licht, *Getting Work: Philadelphia, 1840–1950* (Cambridge, MA: Harvard University Press, 1992), 133–38, 291n101.

94. Joseph F. Spillane, *Coxsackie: The Life and Death of Prison Reform* (Baltimore: Johns Hopkins University Press, 2014), 286.

95. Emmanuel Le Roy Ladurie, *The Territory of the Historian*, trans. Ben Reynolds and Siân Reynolds (Chicago: University of Chicago Press, 1979), 3–6.

96. "Philadelphia Social History Project Series," Institute for Social Research, University of Michigan, https://www.icpsr.umich.edu/icpsrweb/ICPSR/series/229.

97. Covart, "Sharon Block, How to Research History Online"; Sharon Block, *Colonial Complexions: Race and Bodies in Eighteenth-Century America* (Philadelphia: University of Pennsylvania Press, 2018), appendix 1.

98. "America's Public Bible: Biblical Quotations in U.S. Newspapers," http://americaspublicbible.org/.

Similarly, Jo Guldi mined decades of parliamentary debates to identify moments when British politicians paid attention to infrastructure.[99] These methods are still new, and historians debate the value of such "distant readings." At Columbia University, a team of historians and statisticians analyzed the metadata of diplomatic cables to identify spikes in traffic, presumably indicators of significant events. The computer was able to spot some periods that, decades later, indicate important events. But, the team concluded, "successful predictions will be increasingly outnumbered by events that seem insignificant at the time, but which come to be viewed as important by future historians in part because of events that have not yet taken place."[100]

For historians of the age of print, digital methodology is a choice. For historians of events from the 1990s and later, digital methodology may be a necessity, since they will have no other way to explore the terabytes of email, word-processing documents, text, and other electronic formats left behind by the people they wish to study.[101] Moreover, they will need to understand that born-digital sources function differently from physical objects. Whereas a historian of the twentieth century might compare multiple paper drafts of a document to understand its evolution, historians of the twenty-first may need to reveal the changes in a single word-processing file.[102] And, thanks to the flexibility of digital formats, they may need to become ever more comfortable writing about sources other than texts.

99. Jo Guldi, "Parliament's Debates about Infrastructure: An Exercise in Using Dynamic Topic Models to Synthesize Historical Change," *Technology and Culture* 60 (2019): 1–33.

100. Joseph Bernstein, "Can an Algorithm Do the Job of a Historian?," *BuzzFeed News*, June 15, 2015; Joseph Risi et al., "Predicting History," *Nature Human Behaviour*, June 3, 2019.

101. Helen McCarthy, "Political History in the Digital Age: The Challenges of Archiving and Analysing Born Digital Sources," *Impact of Social Sciences* (blog), March 31, 2016, https://blogs.lse.ac.uk/impactofsocialsciences/2016/03/31/political-history-in-the-digital -age-born-digital-sources/.

102. Trevor Owens and Thomas Padilla, "Digital Sources and Digital Archives: Historical Evidence in the Digital Age," *International Journal of Digital Humanities*, May 4, 2020, 1–17.

CHAPTER SEVEN

Sources beyond Traditional Texts

HISTORIANS ARE INTELLECTUAL OMNIVORES, with the teeth and bellies to turn just about anything into usable food. You will find historians reading in libraries, but you will also find them peering at coins under magnifying glasses, brushing dirt away from cemetery headstones, firing replica muzzle-loaders, arranging tours of abandoned factories, bidding on eBay for vintage funeral home fans, and recreating old recipes in their kitchens. This guide cannot begin to catalog all the possibilities, but it can suggest a few of the most common types of sources other than straight text.

Tips

- Use quantitative sources to complement qualitative sources. Quantification can require masses of data, but sometimes others have done the bulk of the work for you.
- Read images with the same critical eye with which you approach texts. Ask about the choices made by the creator.
- With artifacts and places, use as many of the five senses as you can.

Numbers

While historians mostly deal in words, they can enrich their stories by incorporating quantitative evidence as well. For one thing, numbers can impose a rigor absent from purely qualitative analyses. In a large body of evidence, you can find isolated examples of all kinds of things, so how do you know what is a trend? Quantitative research can also give the voice of the silent. Election analysts cannot see individual votes, but they can make statistical inferences based on the demographics of the voters in each precinct. Similarly, while historians do not know much about the lives of individual peasants, perhaps we can use data to make generalizations about peasants as a group.

Quantitative history became particularly popular in the decades after World War II, as historians began using newly available computers to make calculations based on census data, military musters, election returns, weather reports, and prices. But converting printed or handwritten texts into machine-readable data series proved to be tedious and expensive, and it sometimes produced findings already known from more traditional sources. By the 1970s, fewer historians were training in quantitative methods, leaving scholars trained in economics as the primary analysts of historic datasets.[1] That was an overreaction, since historians should not shy away from numbers. As Claire Lemercier and Claire Zalc have argued, "quantification is a valuable addition to our investigative toolset—with standing equal to that of other methods, neither more nor less."[2]

Historians mostly rely on two ways of counting things in the past: first, by relying on tabulations and calculations made at the time, and second, by conducting their own counts. The first is

1. Margo Anderson, "Quantitative History," in *The SAGE Handbook of Social Science Methodology*, ed. William Outhwaite and Stephen Turner (London: SAGE, 2007), 248–64; Jacques Barzun, *Clio and the Doctors: Psycho-History, Quanto-History & History* (Chicago: University of Chicago Press, 1974), 24–27; Claire Lemercier and Claire Zalc, *Quantitative Methods in the Humanities: An Introduction* (Charlottesville: University of Virginia Press, 2019), chapter 1; John F. Reynolds, "Do Historians Count Anymore? The Status of Quantitative Methods in History, 1975–1995," *Historical Methods: A Journal of Quantitative and Interdisciplinary History* 31, no. 4 (1998): 141–48.

2. Lemercier and Zalc, *Quantitative Methods in the Humanities*, 26.

obviously less laborious and is the best path if you trust the data, or at least think it cannot be improved on. For instance, in *The Pox of Liberty*, Werner Troesken trusts smallpox data from publications of the 1890s and 1900s, providing them mostly without comment.[3] In my own work, I could have devoted months—possibly years— to acquiring the skills and data needed to explain the ballooning construction costs of the Washington Metro system in the 1970s. Instead, I reproduced a table prepared by the US General Accounting Office in 1979. My tax dollars at work![4]

But historians cannot always trust data from the past, which may be incomplete or misleading. For example, in the decades after the Civil War, journalist Ida B. Wells-Barnett and sociologist Monroe Work began tabulating lynchings based on reports in prominent newspapers. Their research was vitally important to debates of the day, and it continues to inspire those who pursue justice with data. But Wells-Barnett and Work were limited by the resources available to them. In the twenty-first century, scholars are using computers to search many additional newspapers, finding previously unreported lynchings and weeding out duplicates to produce more accurate data.[5] In between the extremes of trusting existing numbers and redoing the counts from scratch, scholars can read quantitative sources critically, determining when to trust them and when to doubt. Get to know your datasets, learn who collected them and for what purposes, and cross-check them against other evidence whenever possible. The result may be a blend between the past's accounting and your own.[6]

Historians might benefit from more frequently deploying a third method of quantification: engaging with the scholarship in related

3. Werner Troesken, *The Pox of Liberty: How the Constitution Left Americans Rich, Free, and Prone to Infection* (Chicago: University of Chicago Press, 2015), notes to chapter 4.

4. Zachary M. Schrag, *The Great Society Subway: A History of the Washington Metro* (Baltimore: Johns Hopkins University Press, 2006), 173.

5. Gianluca De Fazio, "Improving Lynching Inventories with Local Newspapers: Racial Terror in Virginia, 1877–1927," *Current Research in Digital History* 2 (2019); Charles Seguin and David Rigby, "National Crimes: A New National Data Set of Lynchings in the United States, 1883 to 1941," *Socius* 5 (January 2019).

6. "Essay on Sources and Methodology" in Loren Schweninger, *Black Property Owners in the South, 1790–1915* (Champaign: University of Illinois Press, 1990), 371–91.

fields. As economic historian Eric Hilt has noted, for example, economic history and recent studies in the "history of capitalism" take distinct approaches that could complement each other. Among several differences he identifies are economic historians' greater use of quantitative data, which others could do well to incorporate into their work.[7]

Maps

As a rule, historians adore maps. If you are writing about a specific place, whether a neighborhood, state, or continent, it can be crucial to understand where people were in relation to one another. Some historians seek maps for the hard facts they reveal. Starting in 1867, for instance, the Sanborn Company mapped American cities in precise detail, mapping the footprints of individual buildings and noting their height, construction, and usage. The original customers were fire insurance companies, who needed to know not only details about a building they were considering insuring, but also the likelihood that any building nearby would catch fire. Today, these maps—whether as paper originals, microfilm editions, or increasingly as digital editions—are beloved by historians and historical geographers trying to construct past landscapes.[8]

Other historians read maps for what they tell us, not about the physical world but about the mental space of their characters. Scholars have noted how decisions about scale, symbols, and even colors create a "visual rhetoric" by which mapmakers have defined such problems as urban poverty.[9] Daniel Immerwahr notes how, following the US annexation of Puerto Rico, Hawai'i, and the

7. Eric Hilt, "Economic History, Historical Analysis, and the 'New History of Capitalism,'" *Journal of Economic History* 77 (2017): 511–36.

8. Cheryl Lederle, "Learning Beyond the Original Purpose with Sanborn Fire Insurance Maps," *Social Education* 81 (2017): 351–55; Anne E. Mosher, *Capital's Utopia: Vandergrift, Pennsylvania, 1855–1916* (Baltimore: Johns Hopkins University Press, 2004).

9. Miles A. Kimball, "London through Rose-Colored Graphics: Visual Rhetoric and Information Graphic Design in Charles Booth's Maps of London Poverty," *Journal of Technical Writing and Communication* 36 (2006): 353–81; Laura Vaughan, *Mapping Society: The Spatial Dimensions of Social Cartography* (London: UCL Press, 2018).

Philippines, both government and commercial mapmakers added the new territories to maps of the United States, leading mainland Americans to rethink the nature of their country.[10]

Like other sources, maps are the products of power, becoming distorted by power relationships, but also revealing them. For instance, four years after the 1864 massacre at Sand Creek, Colorado, Lieutenant Samuel Bonsall prepared a detailed map of the ground. Bonsall's technical training, and the fact that he prepared his map relatively soon after the event, made some historians consider him a reliable source. But Bonsall had been an officer in the same US Army that had perpetrated the massacre, and he himself had callously collected body parts. More than a century later, Laird Cometsevah—a descendant of a Cheyenne survivor of the massacre—argued against trusting evidence created by a "grave robber."[11] A 1908 survey of Egypt, argues Timothy Mitchell, "did not produce, necessarily, a more accurate knowledge of the world, despite its claims, nor even any overall increase in the quantity of knowledge." But it did help the central government tax landholdings.[12]

Even cartographers who purport to display only objective reality have to make decisions about what to include and what to exclude, which requires some assumptions about what is important to show on a map. As Denis Wood has noted, the US Geological Survey claims to consider "the permanence of the features" when deciding what to include on its maps, yet it would not map the "trash and broken bottles" that linger more-or-less permanently on the sidewalks and in the yards of burned-out neighborhoods in Detroit.[13] The historian, like the geographer, can thus use maps as records of what mapmakers valued and did not value.

10. Daniel Immerwahr, *How to Hide an Empire: A History of the Greater United States* (New York: Farrar, Straus and Giroux, 2019), 74–75.

11. Ari Kelman, *A Misplaced Massacre: Struggling over the Memory of Sand Creek* (Cambridge, MA: Harvard University Press, 2013), 145.

12. Timothy Mitchell, *Rule of Experts: Egypt, Techno-Politics, Modernity* (Berkeley: University of California Press, 2002), 92.

13. Denis Wood, *The Power of Maps* (New York: Guilford Press, 1992), 81–84.

Images

Histories sometimes use images merely as illustrations: pictures that enliven rather than drive a story or argument. Even if you do not think a major character's appearance changed the course of history, it still could be nice to include a portrait in order to help your reader visualize the events you narrate. But images can do far more than illustrate. They also record history: the story of people and the choices they made. The scholars best trained to understand these choices are art historians, but the line between history and art history is indistinct. Art historians do not confine themselves to image analysis, and even historians without specialized training in art history can use images as evidence, much as they use texts.[14] (As a longtime member of a university department of history and art history, I have found the commonalities between the two disciplines more striking than the differences.)

Image analysis can go in the main text or in a caption, or sometimes both. Either way, it is nice to place the image alongside the most relevant text in a book or article. Even more important is placing images on the same or facing pages when you want your reader to compare and contrast them. In *The Secret History of Wonder Woman*, Jill Lepore frequently juxtaposes a political cartoon or news photograph with a panel or two from the early years of *Wonder Woman*, suggesting how the former may have inspired the latter. She and her publisher took care to place these images within a single page spread, in order to drive the point home.[15]

Some visual evidence can be taken at more or less face value. For instance, Sarah Jo Peterson sought to explain the design changes that Ford Motor Company engineers imposed on the B-24 bomber as they adapted another company's design for mass production. The text of her four-paragraph explanation is eloquent, but it gets even clearer when accompanied by her reproduction of a Ford photograph comparing early and later versions of the same airplane

14. Peter Burke, *Eyewitnessing: The Uses of Images as Historical Evidence*, 2nd ed. (London: Reaktion Books, 2014).

15. Jill Lepore, *The Secret History of Wonder Woman* (New York: Alfred A. Knopf, 2014). See, e.g., 100–101.

component. On the left is a part composed of several smaller pieces, the kind of thing a machinist might be able to bolt together using general-purpose tools. On the right, the same part is composed of fewer, more elaborate pieces, suggesting that someone had devoted the time and expense needed to craft a specialized jig. We immediately see the difference between a labor-intensive and a capital-intensive path to the same outcome, just as the Ford photographer wanted us to.[16]

In other cases, historians must read more critically, seeking information not as intentionally or explicitly communicated by the image creator. Davin Henkin, for example, acknowledges that designers of antebellum banknotes were primarily interested in devising forms of currency that facilitated economic exchange while deterring counterfeits. Yet by comparing their designs to other graphics, he finds additional meanings. "The volume and variety of bills circulating in the streets of Manhattan did not simply condition New Yorkers to the vicissitudes of the currency market or the instability of an inchoate banking system," he argues, "it also conditioned them to the kind of impersonal relations between strangers that we now take for granted. Banknotes evoked both the frenetic anonymity of urban life and the highly fraught social and economic interdependence that such anonymity obscured."[17]

A first step in analyzing images is to inventory who and what is included in the image. For example, Rosemarie Zagarri compares two painted depictions of elections: John Lewis Krimmel's *Election at the State House* (ca. 1815) and George Caleb Bingham's *The County Election* (1852). Among several contrasts, she notes that Krimmel included "lower-class men, African Americans, white women, and children, none of whom could vote," whereas "Bingham did not include either black people or women in the scene. All those present are white males." She concludes that in the intervening generation, American artists had "highlighted voting as the defining act of citizenship. Both in the image and

16. Sarah Jo Peterson, *Planning the Home Front: Building Bombers and Communities at Willow Run* (Chicago: University of Chicago Press, 2013), figure 1.3, 185.

17. David M. Henkin, *City Reading: Written Words and Public Spaces in Antebellum New York* (New York: Columbia University Press, 1998), 164.

FIGURE 7.1. A Jacob Riis photograph is at once documentary evidence of life in
New York in the 1890s, a Progressive Era argument for housing reform, a portrait, a
technical achievement (Riis was a pioneer of flash photography), and a work of art.
Jacob A. (Jacob August) Riis (1849–1914), "Ready for Sabbath Eve in a Coal Cellar,"
Museum of the City of New York. 2008.1.46.

in reality, the result was the virtual erasure of women from the
electoral scene."[18]

Photographers make similar choices about what to include in an
image. Analyzing a Jacob Riis photograph of a Jewish man preparing for the Sabbath in the coal cellar where he dwelt, Peter Bacon
Hales notes that Riis has pointed his camera to include the fingers of an otherwise unseen figure holding a shovel. "That shovel
must be in the picture," Hales writes, "for it signals the inappropri-
ateness of the coal cellar as a dwelling. We are, apparently, watching a devout Jew interrupted from his devotions by the rude work

18. Rosemarie Zagarri, *Revolutionary Backlash: Women and Politics in the Early
American Republic* (Philadelphia: University of Pennsylvania Press, 2011), 161–64.

around him. To include more than the hands of the shoveler, however, might detract from the presence of that lone human figure; it would also decrease the symbolic force of that shovel."[19]

In other cases, an image includes something more of interest to the historian than the image's creator. Eric Yellin notes both the presence of African American men in a 1901 photograph and their absence in the accompanying caption. The image, he concludes, "was meant to capture the rise of female employment in lower-level clerical work in federal departments. It also, unwittingly, illustrates the mixing of black men among white women common at the time."[20]

Having listed everything in an image, you can now consider other questions. For instance, which elements of an image does the artist feature most prominently? Which do they display with admiration, which with disdain? Did they shoot from below, making the subject look taller, more powerful? Or from above, to make them look helpless? Consider also the context in which an image appears. The same image can appear in multiple newspapers with different placement, cropping, and captioning.[21] Or an image might be hidden. As Sally Stein has noted, most photographs of Franklin Roosevelt in his wheelchair were snapshots seen only by family and friends until decades after Roosevelt's death. While they accurately depict the physical reality of Roosevelt's disability, they are not representative of a public image dominated by images of an active, smiling, and often standing Roosevelt.[22]

Like creators of texts, creators of images choose to respect or reject convention. In the 1830s, volunteer firemen commissioned artists to decorate engines and buckets with figures recalling the ideal nudes of classical and Christian art.[23] Even photojournalists

19. Peter Bacon Hales, *Silver Cities: Photographing American Urbanization, 1839–1939*, rev. ed. (Albuquerque: University of New Mexico Press, 2005), 315.

20. Eric S. Yellin, *Racism in the Nation's Service: Government Workers and the Color Line in Woodrow Wilson's America* (Chapel Hill: University of North Carolina Press, 2013), 101.

21. Ellen Wiley Todd, "Photojournalism, Visual Culture, and the Triangle Shirtwaist Fire," *Labor* 2 (2005): 18–19.

22. Sally Stein, "The President's Two Bodies: Stagings and Restagings of FDR and the New Deal Body Politic," *American Art* 18 (March 2004): 32–57.

23. Ross Barrett, *Rendering Violence: Riots, Strikes, and Upheaval in Nineteenth-Century American Art* (Oakland: University of California Press, 2014), 96–99.

frame their images according to traditions inherited from fine art.[24] As he created his immortal portrait of Ella Watson, a charwoman for the federal government, Gordon Parks deliberately posed her to make his image resemble Grant Wood's 1930 painting *American Gothic*.[25] "A woman is sometimes not just a woman but rather a Roman deity transformed into revolutionary symbol," write Jack Censer and Lynn Hunt. They caution historians to "learn the collective codes that shape artistic representation, whether in a crude woodcut made for plastering on a wall or a fine line engraving sold by subscription to the well off."[26]

Also like texts, images further agendas. Joshua Brown argues that *Frank Leslie's Illustrated Newspaper* did not merely reflect reality but sought to shape it. For example, in the 1870s it published urban scenes in part to prepare its readers to understand what they would see on city streets. "The pictorial press played a crucial role in making the city seem decipherable," Brown writes. "The customs and manners of the city were portrayed through a range of social types (and their subcategories) stretching across the classes: Wall Street types tussled in the financial district; middle-class types thronged the ferries on weekend excursions; polite society types attended banquets and fancy balls; and a panoply of ethnic types engaged in their customary pastimes."[27]

Reproducing an image—especially in a published work—may require gaining permission or paying fees, either for copyright license, access to the image, or photography and scanning. As you collect images in your work, keep track of who controls the reproduction rights or how you might find out. The College Art Association produces helpful guidance on this topic.[28]

24. Peggy J. Bowers, "Through the Objective Lens: The Ethics of Expression and Repression of High Art in Photojournalism," *American Communication Journal* 10 (2008).

25. Gordon Parks, *A Hungry Heart: A Memoir* (New York: Washington Square Press, 2005), 65–66.

26. Jack Censer and Lynn Hunt, "Imaging the French Revolution: Depictions of the French Revolutionary Crowd," *American Historical Review* 110 (2005): 44.

27. Joshua Brown, *Beyond the Lines: Pictorial Reporting, Everyday Life, and the Crisis of Gilded-Age America* (Berkeley: University of California Press, 2013), 81.

28. College Art Association, *Code of Best Practices in Fair Use for the Visual Arts*, February 2015; College Art Association, "Intellectual Property | Standards & Guidelines," http://dev.collegeart.org/standards-and-guidelines/intellectual-property.

Portraits

As is likely obvious in the age of the selfie, a portrait depicts more than a person's physical appearance. It is a record of how they chose to present themselves, or were seen by others. Perhaps the first question to consider is the circumstances under which the portrait was created. If the sitter paid good money to commission an oil painting, we can expect them to have had a good deal of say about how the final product appeared. If the portrait is a police mug shot, perhaps it will say more about the police officer's view than that of the suspect, though even accused criminals can decide whether to glare, smirk, or gaze humbly at the camera. In between these extremes is an infinite variation. Even government identification photographs, for instance, can end up as records of the dignity of the person being photographed.[29] Conversely, a powerful public figure may detest his official portrait.[30]

Skilled historians can turn a portrait into a story by reconstructing the choices made by both sitter and portraitist. In describing an 1877 portrait centered on Ollokot, a Nez Perce leader, Daniel Sharfstein notes the choices made by photographer Charles Phillips, who likely chose the backdrop and instructed Ollokot to pose stiffly in order not to blur the image during a long exposure. But Sharfstein emphasizes Ollokot's own choices in dress and ornament:

> In the Dreamer fashion, Ollokot's thick hair was combed high from his smooth forehead. Long white feathers cascaded from a wavy sidelock down to his left shoulder. His plaid shirt was open to the middle of his chest, displaying the gentle arc of eight beaded necklaces. He wore a trade blanket wrapped around his leggings and draped a white fur down his left leg, perhaps a wolf, its tail lying across his moccasins. A wide-brim felt hat, lushly adorned with feathers, lay on his lap. . . . Even as the photograph recorded his strength, his pose, his clothing,

29. Eric S. Yellin, "'It Was Still No South to Us': African American Civil Servants at the Fin de Siècle," *Washington History* 21 (2009): 42; "The Real Face of White Australia: Experimental Browser," http://invisibleaustralians.org/faces/.

30. Simon Schama, *The Face of Britain: A History of the Nation through Its Portraits* (New York: Oxford University Press, 2016), chapter 1.

and the very fact that he was posing for a photographer all suggested that Ollokot had reconciled himself to a place in the settlers' world. He was the picture of a traditional warrior, but his shirt, hat, and blanket had been made in distant mills, workshops, and factories. His very image, in turn, would be pasted onto card stock and sold to white people near and far.[31]

Motion Pictures and Recordings

The development, in the late nineteenth century, of technologies to record sound and moving images has given historians unprecedented abilities to achieve sensory connections to the past. Hearing people talk, or seeing them in motion, can be particularly effective for classroom and public history presentations, and recordings can be quite useful for researchers as well. While acknowledging that listening to tapes of the deliberations during the Cuban Missile Crisis takes a lot more time than does reading the transcripts, Sheldon Stern argues that no serious historian of the event should pass up the opportunity. Not only are transcripts sometimes inaccurate about which words were used; they also fail to capture tone and nuance. Defense secretary Robert McNamara's "dismal tone, lost in even the best transcript," argues Stern, "momentarily exposed the raw depths of exhaustion, fear, and anxiety which he and his colleagues had endured around the clock since October 16."[32] On a less elite level, Christine Ehrick finds that a 1928 recording of Argentine comedian Tomás Simari—complete with Simari's comic portrayals of people of various backgrounds, as well as sound effects—captures far more than any radio script alone could convey.[33] Unfortunately, recordings are harder to preserve, find, and use than are texts and images. Recordings are fragile, and even a tape or disc kept in good condition

31. Daniel J. Sharfstein, *Thunder in the Mountains: Chief Joseph, Oliver Otis Howard, and the Nez Perce War* (New York: W. W. Norton, 2017), 206–7.

32. Sheldon M. Stern, *The Cuban Missile Crisis in American Memory: Myths versus Reality* (Stanford, CA: Stanford University Press, 2012), 4.

33. Christine Ehrick, "Comedy and Aural Modernity in Argentina: Tomás Simari's 'Un Viaje En Ómnibus,'" *Hispanic American Historical Review* 96 (2016): 217–23.

is useless without a working device to play it on.[34] And it takes far longer for a researcher to listen to a whole recording than to skim a transcript.

The same is true for film. Historians of the twentieth and twenty-first centuries know the enormous impact that film—from Hollywood blockbusters to home movies—has had on culture around the world, but using films as sources remains a challenge. Like sound recording, film is difficult to preserve. And scholars who want to analyze films may need to learn its conventions and technicalities. "The halo of light behind a character's head may not symbolise their holy status," cautions Mia Treacey. "It may just have been a badly placed Redhead (film light)."[35]

Television lurks as both a profoundly influential medium and an ephemeral one, so that today's historians may not be able to view programs once watched by millions. Early television shows were shown live and not recorded at all. Others were recorded on media that has deteriorated or for which playback equipment is hard to find. Around 1990, Paul Longmore asked friends and colleagues in different parts of the United States to record the local broadcast of Labor Day fund-raising telethons, and those cassettes are now preserved at San Francisco State University. But to trace the content of earlier telethons, Longmore had to rely on newspaper accounts.[36] Even when recordings exist, they may not be open to researchers. "Approaching *All in the Family*, I presumed that my access-related challenge would be paying the cost of the DVDs and waiting for the package to arrive in my mailbox," writes Kathleen Collins of her efforts to study the popular 1970s sitcom. Instead, she found that while the first six seasons were easy to view, "there are only three viewable episodes from the final season remaining and 20 episodes from the final season that are not accessible anywhere, or at least not anywhere that a hearty, resource-aware researcher would easily

34. Anthony Cocciolo, *Moving Image and Sound Collections for Archivists* (Chicago: Society of American Archivists, 2017).

35. Mia E. M. Treacey, *Reframing the Past: History, Film and Television* (London: Routledge, 2016), xvi.

36. Paul K. Longmore, *Telethons: Spectacle, Disability, and the Business of Charity* (New York: Oxford University Press, 2015); David A. Gerber, "Pity Party," *Reviews in American History* 44 (2016): 511–16.

find them."[37] Despite impressive efforts by archivists, television remains a challenge.

Artifacts

"Objects are more than mute physical things," writes Zara Anishanslin. "Objects connect people across space and time; mark commercial transactions; play symbolic political roles; relay stories of labor, gift giving, and purchase; and provide insight into shared cultural imagination and aesthetic taste."[38] Moreover, artifacts can be the best-preserved records of individuals or whole cultures. "Humans made tools before they wrote words," note Leonie Hannan and Sarah Longair. "Therefore, the study of material culture opens up centuries of history that leave no textual record."[39]

Archaeologists, anthropologists, art historians, and museum curators make such objects central to their work. Historians, even those who write a great deal *about* objects, are more likely to rely on written sources than on extant artifacts themselves. A detailed patent application, advertisement, or memoir may tell you more about how people invented, produced, marketed, and used an item than will the sight of that item in a museum case, especially if you are not allowed to pick it up and see how well it functions. That said, the appearance of an item, or an analysis of how it functions, can give clues to the stories of its creation and use.[40] And some scholars are fortunate to be able to handle the artifacts they write about. As Marcy Dinius notes, nineteenth-century viewers of daguerreotypes held them in their hands, and saw their own faces reflected in the shiny surfaces that held portraits of others. "I encourage you to seek

37. Kathleen Collins, "The Trouble with Archie: Locating and Accessing Primary Sources for the Study of the 1970s US Sitcom, *All in the Family*," *Critical Studies in Television* 5 (2010): 120–21.

38. Zara Anishanslin, *Portrait of a Woman in Silk: Hidden Histories of the British Atlantic World* (New Haven, CT: Yale University Press, 2016), 19; see also 313–17.

39. Leonie Hannan and Sarah Longair, *History through Material Culture* (New York: Oxford University Press, 2017), 30.

40. Joseph J. Corn, "Object Lessons/Object Myths: What Historians of Technology Learn from Things," in *Learning from Things*, ed. David Kingery (Washington, DC: Smithsonian Institution Press, 1996), 35–54; Hannan and Longair, *History through Material Culture*, 33.

out an actual daguerreotype as you read or after you have finished," she tells her readers. "Encountering one is an untranslatable multisensory experience."[41]

Historians who wish to use material evidence often benefit from collaboration with scholars in other disciplines, especially archaeology. Tyler Anbinder, for instance, uses archaeologists' excavations of New York's Five Points neighborhood as evidence that "the majority of the neighborhood's residents could afford more than the barest necessities," though he cautions against disregarding textual evidence of the misery of many of them.[42] Some historians operate historical objects or replicas—such as medieval weapons or machinery of the early Industrial Revolution—in order to see how they functioned. Such demonstrations can never recreate the full experience of the past, in part because no historian or archaeologist can afford the years of training that the original user might have invested in their craft. Still, the chance to handle the tools one otherwise only reads about can offer insights beyond what one would find in texts and images alone.[43] Even the creation of such objects can yield new knowledge. Pamela Smith, for instance, has led teams who follow craft recipes in a sixteenth-century manuscript to understand metalworking, color making, and other crafts.[44]

The emergence of eBay and other online marketplaces has made it possible for historians to acquire artifacts related to their work. Acquiring an object like this has the added bonus that you may not need anyone's permission to include an image in your published

41. Marcy J. Dinius, *The Camera and the Press: American Visual and Print Culture in the Age of the Daguerreotype* (Philadelphia: University of Pennsylvania Press, 2012), 6.

42. Tyler Anbinder, *Five Points: The 19th-Century New York City Neighborhood that Invented Tap Dance, Stole Elections, and Became the World's Most Notorious Slum* (New York: Simon & Schuster, 2001), 77; Tyler Anbinder, review of *Five Points Archaeological Project Web Site*, by Rebecca Yamin, *H-Urban, H-Net Reviews*, September 1997, https://networks.h-net.org/node/22277/reviews/22931/anbinder-five-points-archaeological-project-web-site.

43. Patrick Malone, "Experimental Industrial Archeology: Imitation in Pursuit of Authenticity," *IA: The Journal of the Society for Industrial Archeology* 26 (2000): 85–94; Paul Bourke and David Whetham, "A Report of the Findings of the Defence Academy Warbow Trials Part 1 Summer 2005," *Arms & Armour* 4 (April 2007): 53–81.

44. "The Making and Knowing Project: Intersections of Craft Making and Scientific Knowing," https://www.makingandknowing.org/.

work.[45] (Copyright can still apply.) Daniel Gifford has shown that you need not spend anything to use eBay as an "online archive." After looking at tens of thousands of eBay listings for old postcards, Gifford was able to find around two thousand that included detailed information about the recipient. He did not need to purchase the card to add it to his database, and his analysis.[46]

Buildings and Plans

Buildings and cities reflect the priorities of individuals, institutions, and societies, so historians can read them in much the same way that they read textual sources. Thomas Hanchett studies the houses built at the beginning of the twentieth century in a new subdivision in Charlotte, North Carolina, in order to understand the values of the people who purchased them. "Elizabeth's architecture embodied shared aesthetic assumptions that assured the neighborhood a distinctly suburban appearance," he writes. "Unlike mill villages and black districts, where houses often sat close to the road, white-collar dwellings were twenty to thirty feet from the street. Front lawns with purely ornamental plantings proclaimed the owner's prosperity and signaled his appreciation of Nature." Later, he deploys similar analysis to a neighborhood as a whole, as proposed by planner John Nolen. Nolen included playgrounds and parks, but he located them amid the houses, so that they would only serve neighborhood residents. Reading Nolen's maps, Hanchett finds in them "the Progressive Planners' desire to both shelter and connect."[47]

Individual buildings likewise can reveal the values of their creators. In *The Grand Domestic Revolution*, for example, Dolores Hayden traces the efforts by feminist designers to build housing that would reduce women's domestic workloads. While Hayden

45. See, e.g., Suzanne E. Smith, *To Serve the Living* (Cambridge, MA: Harvard University Press, 2010), 79.

46. Daniel Gifford, *American Holiday Postcards, 1905–1915: Imagery and Context* (Jefferson, NC: McFarland, 2013), 14–19.

47. Thomas W. Hanchett, *Sorting Out the New South City: Race, Class, and Urban Development in Charlotte, 1875–1975* (Chapel Hill: University of North Carolina Press, 1998), 158, 174.

makes great use of textual sources, she also reads plans, elevations, and perspectives of buildings both built and imagined, showing how the arrangement of rooms and even the absence of kitchens embodied designers' hopes for communal rather than individual labor.[48]

Places

Historians have long visited the sites of the events they write about. George Macaulay Trevelyan walked and bicycled through long stretches of Italy, following the path of Garibaldi's armies.[49] To write his biography of Christopher Columbus, Samuel Eliot Morison followed some of the explorer's routes in a three-masted sailing ship.[50] Recent scholars have followed their example. Adam Hochschild hired a helicopter to take him to the ruins of a gulag camp in a remote part of Siberia.[51] Zara Anishanslin ventured into a building that—nearly three centuries earlier—had been the home and workshop of silk designer Anna Maria Garthwaite. "As she sketched the designs that would become flowered silks," Anishanslin writes, "she could pause and look out the windows to see the church spire piercing the London sky." As evidence, Anishanslin offers a photograph of that spire that she herself took from Garthwaite's studio window.[52]

More ordinary places have value as well. In the 1950s, W. G. Hoskins and J. B. Jackson, among others, encouraged fellow scholars to "read the landscape," appreciating the landscape itself—hedges, walls, houses, farms, churches, paths, and trailer camps—as both a subject worthy of historical analysis and a primary source for

48. Dolores Hayden, *The Grand Domestic Revolution: A History of Feminist Designs for American Homes, Neighborhoods, and Cities* (Cambridge, MA: MIT Press, 1982).

49. Jonathan Marwil, *Visiting Modern War in Risorgimento Italy* (New York: Palgrave Macmillan, 2010), 211.

50. James D. Hornfischer, "Revisiting Samuel Eliot Morison's Landmark History," *Smithsonian*, February 2011.

51. Adam Hochschild, "Meanwhile, Back at the Ranch, Part 2: Setting," *Nieman Storyboard* (blog), March 28, 2011, https://niemanstoryboard.org/stories/meanwhile-back-at-the-ranch-adam-hochschild-vanderbiltpart-2-setting/.

52. Anishanslin, *Portrait of a Woman in Silk*, 66–67.

such analysis.[53] Since then historians and geographers have "read" mining districts and suburbs, roads and rivers, main streets and shopping malls.[54] David Gange has explored British and Irish coastlines by kayak.[55] These explorations typically include a good deal of library research, but the places themselves become important sources.

Unfortunately, not every historian has this opportunity. Travel is expensive, in both time and money. And some landscapes have been so altered that a visit tells today's historian little about how a place appeared in times past. As Peter Charles Hoffer has noted, the Old York, Maine, of today has colonial buildings, but many were rearranged in the 1890s, and today's Everglades have been so reshaped as to bear little resemblance to the swamp of the nineteenth century.[56] In some cases, it might be better to visit a place quite far from the object of your study. If you want to know what it was like to cough through a coal-choked London of the late nineteenth century, perhaps you should visit twenty-first-century Beijing.

53. D. W. Meinig, "Reading the Landscape: An Appreciation of W. G. Hoskins and J. B. Jackson," in *The Interpretation of Ordinary Landscapes: Geographical Essays*, ed. D. W. Meinig (New York: Oxford University Press, 1979), 195–244.

54. See, e.g., Paul Groth and Todd W. Bressi, eds., *Understanding Ordinary Landscapes* (New Haven, CT: Yale University Press, 1997).

55. David Gange, "Retracing Trevelyan? Historical Practice and the Archive of the Feet," *Green Letters* 21 (2017): 256–57.

56. Peter Charles Hoffer, *Sensory Worlds in Early America* (Baltimore: Johns Hopkins University Press, 2003), 9–10, 17.

CHAPTER EIGHT

Finding Sources

BECAUSE THEY are so heterogeneous and so scattered around the world, it is not easy to locate every source—or any source—relevant to a topic. Indeed, locating this material is one of the more challenging tasks of historical research, and historians applaud each other for especially clever finds. While there is no single method that can get you to the source you need, some tools have proven effective. Some tools and methods, such as lists of eighteenth-century imprints, are suitable mostly for finding primary sources. Others, such as current catalogs from university presses, are better for secondary sources. A great many tools, however, will identify both primary and secondary sources, so it is good to be ready to record your findings in each category. Some bibliographic aids are digital, some are analog, and the best are human. When possible, seek a librarian's assistance when crafting your bibliography, though you may want to do some preliminary work first.

Tips

- Keep track of the sources you consult, and the sources to which they refer, in a working bibliography.
- There is nothing wrong with using an internet search as your starting place, provided it is not the only place you look.
- Once you have done some initial work, ask a librarian for help.

The Working Bibliography

A published bibliography, whether appended to a book or article or as a stand-alone piece, is a polished jewel. Depending on the project, it may list all the works cited, all the works on a topic, or all of the most important works. The best ones include annotations explaining the origin and value of each item on the list.

A working bibliography is far rougher. As part of your project management, it is a list of sources that you have considered consulting, whether or not you have actually located them, read them, or found them useful. It is not enough to record the publication information. You need to note whether you have located the source and, if so, where. That way you can make efficient use of your trip, whether to the library or another city. Once you have gotten your hands on the source, make a note of whether you have read it, whether you have notes, whether you have the full text, or whether you took a look and decided the source is not helpful.

It is a good idea to keep track of not only what sources you want but what you hope to find in each source. You are writing notes to your future self, and your future self may not remember why or how a particular item ended up on the list. For instance, imagine that I make a note that I should consult Naomi J. Stubbs's *Cultivating National Identity through Performance: American Pleasure Gardens and Entertainment*. Imagine further that it is some weeks or months before I finally get hold of the book. Will I remember that I am looking for information on the Philadelphia balloon riot of 1819? Possible, but unlikely. Better that the note includes the instruction: "Balloon riot!" If you are tracing a footnote from a secondary source, put that in your working bibliography. For instance, a note to myself to consult *The War Within: America's Battle over Vietnam*, a seven-hundred-page text, would be less useful than a note that Sandra Scanlon's *Pro-War Movement* cites *The War Within*, 287–88, and I might want to look at those pages.[1]

---

1. Naomi J. Stubbs, *Cultivating National Identity through Performance: American Pleasure Gardens and Entertainment* (New York: Palgrave Macmillan, 2013); Sandra Scanlon, *The Pro-War Movement: Domestic Support for the Vietnam War and the Making of Modern American Conservatism* (Amherst: University of Massachusetts Press, 2013),

Every scholarly source you find can lead to several more, as you scour the footnotes and bibliography for leads. (Some call this "footnote-chaining.")[2] This is a mixed blessing, especially at the start of a project, when every article or book you actually find seems to point to another half dozen sources to find and read, soon producing a mountain of work. With luck, after a while you will start to find that new sources are referring back to things you have already read.

Pay attention to whose voices are represented in your working bibliography. If all your secondary sources were written by white men with ties to prestigious institutions, you may be relying too much on research tools that amplify such voices.[3] If writing about a particular place or community, look for works by historians and others who live in that community. If writing about another nation, include historians from that nation.

See chapter 11, "Project Management," for information about reference manager software, which can help you manage your working bibliography.

The Open Web

So where do you find sources? For most twenty-first-century college students, the search begins with an internet search engine, usually Google. That is not wrong. My first book began with a search for Darwin Stolzenbach, one of the early planners of the Washington Metro. Google told me that George Washington University had received federal funds to process Stolzenbach's papers. That led me to visit special collections at GW, where I learned that they held not only Stolzenbach's papers but several other significant collections of material relating to the Metro. By the end of that visit, I had a dissertation topic.

Not every search is so fruitful, but in many cases, a basic internet search will lead you to a more specialized resource that will

---

357n108, citing Tom Wells, *The War Within: America's Battle over Vietnam* (Berkeley: University of California Press, 1994).

2. Alexandra Chassanoff, "Historians and the Use of Primary Source Materials in the Digital Age," *American Archivist* 76 (September 2013): 460

3. Emily Prifogle and Karin Wulf, "Why Women Also Know History," *Journal of Women's History* 32 (2020): 113–17.

then lead you to ever more useful sources. Search on a Chicago history topic, and with luck your first page of results will include a relevant entry from the *Encyclopedia of Chicago*. That entry may give you the information you need, assembled by a credible writer, or it may point you to even more useful sources, both on and off the web.

Besides a general search of the web, Google offers two search engines of particular interest to historical researchers. The first is Google Books. In 2002, Larry Page, one of Google's founders, calculated that it would only take a few years to scan tens of millions of books into a searchable database. Google cut deals with major research libraries in the United States, borrowing books by the truckload and scanning them in specialized cradles that could photograph the books even if the pages were not fully flat. By 2015, the project had scanned thirty million volumes. Unfortunately, you cannot read most of those volumes in their entirety. Most of those books could still be under copyright, and no one has figured out how to identify the copyright owners or negotiate a license to display the text.[4] Thus, most searches on Google Books for works published since 1923 initially displayed only snippets of text. Yet even in its truncated form, Google Books is a powerful tool, allowing historians to find references that they never could have before. This is especially true for very specific searches, such as quotations, or the names of individuals. Some historians even use it to search for text in books that they own, since the database is more thorough than any index.[5]

Just as you should not stop with Google for general research, you should not stop with Google Books when seeking fully digitized texts. The HathiTrust, a partnership of dozens of institutions and libraries, offers copies of works digitized by Google but supplements them with sources digitized elsewhere. Other large-scale digitization efforts include the Internet Archive and Europeana (www .europeana.eu), a project of the European Union. The biggest winners from these digitization projects are historians of periods more

4. James Somers, "Torching the Modern-Day Library of Alexandria," *Atlantic*, April 20, 2017; Scott Rosenberg, "How Google Book Search Got Lost," *Wired*, April 11, 2017; Tim Wu, "What Ever Happened to Google Books?," *New Yorker*, September 12, 2015.

5. Jennifer Rutner and Roger Schonfeld, "Supporting the Changing Research Practices of Historians," *Ithaka S+R*, December 2012, 17–19.

than ninety-five years in the past, since published works from those periods have entered the public domain.[6] Google Books and other projects have made countless numbers of these works free to read, search, and copy. Rare books, once hidden away to preserve them, are now seen by thousands.[7]

Just as Google Books was getting started, Google engineer Anurag Acharya launched Google Scholar, which allows searches specifically within published academic literature. This is helpful in part because one can generally trust peer-reviewed scholarship more than the ordinary web content. To my mind, though, the most impressive feature of Google Scholar is the "cited by" link that appears at the bottom of each listing. By looking for scholarship that cites a given source, Google has created a form of reverse footnoting that complements traditional citation practices. Let's say, for instance, that you are interested in the role of consumers in shaping technology, and you come across Ruth Schwartz Cowan's 1987 essay "The Consumption Junction: A Proposal for Research Strategies in the Sociology of Technology." In the age of print, you could read Cowan's endnotes to find comparable scholarship published *before* 1987, but you would have struggled to find related scholarship published since. The best you could do would be to see what subject terms an indexer had used to describe the article and then seek other works with those subject terms. I confess that I rarely found such searches very useful. Now, however, you can look up Cowan's essay in Google Scholar and click the link to find hundreds of scholars who have cited her work, right up to the present. In other words, while Cowan's footnotes trace her topic from 1987 into the past, Google Scholar's "cited by" traces the topic from 1987 forward. By using footnotes and "cited by" together, you can locate a project in an active scholarly conversation.[8]

6. "Copyright Review Program," HathiTrust Digital Library, https://www.hathitrust.org /collaborative-programs.

7. "Latin American Collections Now Available in Digital Repository," *UT News* (blog), October 3, 2016, https://news.utexas.edu/2016/10/03/latin-american-collections-enter -digital-repository/.

8. Steven Levy, "The Gentleman Who Made Scholar," *Wired*, October 17, 2014; Ruth Schwartz Cowan, "The Consumption Junction: A Proposal for Research Strategies in the Sociology of Technology," in *The Social Construction of Technological Systems*, ed.

Limits of the Open Web

Google, and general-purpose search engines like it, pose two common dangers. The first is the false positive: a result that promises more information than it delivers. Fabricated or mislabeled sources are hardly new to the internet age. Previous generations were occasionally fooled by fabricated papers.[9] But such cases were rare, since it takes hard work and skill to craft a credibly forged manuscript.

In the twenty-first century, computers have made forgery easy, and fake historical documents flood the internet. Some of these are created as humorous pranks, but a great many are the products of people so invested in a particular historical narrative that they are willing to fabricate evidence in support of their claims. So many statements are falsely attributed to America's founders that the Fred W. Smith National Library for the Study of George Washington and the Thomas Jefferson Foundation maintain lists of spurious quotations, allowing for near instant rebuttal.[10] Other forgers go beyond fabricating quotations into inventing wholly fictitious narratives. Some, for instance, apparently hope to challenge the concept of white privilege by crafting a myth that Irish people were enslaved under terms as bad or worse than those endured by people of African descent. They go so far as to misleadingly caption paintings or photographs of non-Irish people under different conditions.[11] Historians have spent considerable effort debunking such claims, but they remain out there, traps for the unwary. Education experts Sam Wineburg and Sarah McGrew suggest that researchers should "*read laterally,* leaving a site after a quick scan

Wiebe E. Bijker, Thomas P. Hughes, and Trevor Pinch (1987; repr., Cambridge, MA: MIT Press, 2012), 253–72.

9. Robert Lindsey, "Dealer in Mormon Fraud Called a Master Forger," *New York Times*, February 11, 1987; Wayne Biddle and Margot Slade, "Ideas and Trends: 'Hitler Diaries' Flunk Tests," *New York Times*, May 8, 1983.

10. "Spurious Quotations," George Washington Digital Encyclopedia, https://www .mountvernon.org/library/digitalhistory/digital-encyclopedia/article/spurious-quotations/; Thomas Jefferson Foundation, "Spurious Quotations," Thomas Jefferson Encyclopedia, https://www.monticello.org/site/research-and-collections/spurious-quotations.

11. Liam Stack, "Debunking a Myth: The Irish Were Not Slaves, Too," *New York Times*, March 17, 2017.

and opening up new browser tabs in order to judge the credibility of the original site."[12]

Along with the danger of the false positive, researchers must beware of the false negative: the belief that if it is not on Google or Wikipedia, it does not exist. Wikipedia's design, such as its standard of "notability," has tended to encourage articles about famous men of the past at the expense of coverage about women and less prominent figures.[13] A vast amount of digital material is stored in databases inaccessible to Google's algorithms. And, of course, there are yet vaster troves of materials that have never been digitized. Before you give up, ask a librarian.

The open web remains a useful discovery tool. My sense is that *most* historical information on Wikipedia is accurate, and a great many entries have links to sources I would consider trustworthy. Blogs and Tumblr sites may not cite their sources, but at least they can give you a sense of what to look for; if you see a 1960s ad for Wonder Bread that could help your research, you may be able to find it on a more trustworthy site.

Bibliographic Databases

For a more select experience, historians turn to specialized bibliographic databases.[14] Two related products—America: History and Life (for the history of North America) and Historical Abstracts (for the rest of the world)—are particularly valuable, since they index several types of publications, including journal articles, dissertations, and book reviews, which in turn can lead you to books. Better still, they offer some tools specifically for historians, such as a filter that allows you to search only articles about a specific period. They are also very good at picking up scholarly journals

12. Sam Wineburg and Sarah McGrew, "Lateral Reading: Reading Less and Learning More When Evaluating Digital Information," SSRN Scholarly Paper (Rochester, NY: Social Science Research Network, October 6, 2017), 1, https://papers.ssrn.com/abstract=3048994.

13. Sadie Bergen, "Linking In: How Historians Are Fighting Wikipedia's Biases," *Perspectives on History*, September 2016.

14. Margaret Stieg Dalton and Laurie Charnigo, "Historians and Their Information Sources," *College & Research Libraries* 65 (2004): 400–425.

with narrower distributions, such as state-level history journals in the United States.

Depending on one's library, these indexes may offer full text of some of their listings, but they will also display many items not available online, or even through your library. While that provides less click-through convenience than full-text databases of scholarly literature—such as JSTOR and Project Muse—it also means that these indexes can pick up a greater range of publications, producing a more thorough shopping list. For books, the best starting place is WorldCat, which indexes the holdings of thousands of libraries worldwide. Because it searches so many libraries, it picks up even fairly rare, privately printed volumes. Better still, it tells you which libraries hold these items, making it possible to plan a trip or at least a loan. Journal databases—such as JSTOR and America: History and Life—index book reviews, which can lead you to the books themselves.

Full-Text Databases

Starting in the 1990s, government agencies, nonprofit institutions, and private corporations began digitizing historical documents, publications, and photographs, including many that previously would have required laborious travel and library research in order to be used. The formats and distribution systems have varied widely, from poor-quality image scans to error-ridden texts generated by optical character recognition (OCR) software to painstakingly edited transcriptions of hard-to-read handwritten originals. Some of these materials, especially those whose copyright has expired, are free to be used by anyone with a good internet connection. Others require expensive subscriptions, either individual or institutional. As you scout out sources, keep in mind that even a well-funded research university may not subscribe to a genealogical site with newspapers or other records that could be crucial to your topic. Depending on your situation, you may need to combine the resources your own institution possesses, visits to other libraries, and personal subscriptions.

At one level, the availability of these resources has not revolutionized historical research. Clicking the trackpad on my laptop to see the next page of a scanned newspaper is more comfortable than twisting the dial of a microfilm reader, and rather than trek to the library, I can do it at home. But it is pretty much the same task.

And yet, Lara Putnam observes, digitized sources make some questions so much easier to answer that they shift our stories. She offers her experience of reading the microfilm version of the *Limón Searchlight*, published in Costa Rica, and coming across a reference to "Benbow's Follies." "Three years later," she writes, "when I was turning my notes into a chapter about the racial politics of music and dance in the circum-Caribbean, it occurred to me to wonder who exactly these 'Benbow's Follies' were. Google Books allowed me—in the space of three minutes at my desk, rather than a day at the library—to find out enough about African American show-man William Benbow to know that I wanted to know more." Additional research, much of it digital, led her to conclude that Benbow and other performers like him "helped create the very idea of an 'African diaspora'" in the early twentieth-century Caribbean.[15] Similarly, genealogical websites, with their birth records, ship manifests, and newspaper advertisements, allow historians to trace lives beyond what might be a person's worst moment: an arrest or violent death.[16] Genealogy sites can also put you in touch with the descendants of your characters. As he wrote *Almost Citizens*, Sam Erman met Belinda Torres-Mary, the great-granddaughter of the plaintiff, in a lawsuit that reached the US Supreme Court and was key to Erman's narrative. "Perceiving Belinda's passion for Gonzalez's story inspired me to deepen my depictions of Gonzalez, her choices, and their consequences," Erman later reflected, "all to the book's benefit."[17]

Magical as such tools may appear, historians must remember that digitized, searchable texts represent only a fraction of the available evidence, even if that fraction is increasing. "It is now easy to search through hundreds of thousands of pages of 19th-century

15. Lara Putnam, "The Transnational and the Text-Searchable: Digitized Sources and the Shadows They Cast," *American Historical Review* 121 (2016): 387.

16. Julia Laite, "The Emmet's Inch: Small History in a Digital Age," *Journal of Social History*, https://doi.org/10.1093/jsh/shy118.

17. Sam Erman, "A Better Book: Living Descendants," *Legal History Blog*, April 9, 2019, http://legalhistoryblog.blogspot.com/2019/04/a-better-book-living-descendants.html.

magazines and books," marveled Richard Jensen in 2002. Finding only a handful of want ads with the phrase "No Irish Need Apply," he concluded that "apart from want ads for personal household workers, the [No Irish Need Apply] slogan has not turned up in the newspapers," and that probably no business or hiring hall ever posted such a sign on a wall or in a window.[18] Fourteen years later, Rebecca Fried repeated the search, using a significantly larger number of newspaper databases than had Jensen, many of which had not existed when Jensen did his search. Fried found dozens of want ads, directed to men, specifying "No Irish Need Apply," as well as a few news stories describing "No-Irish signs" being posted in public. At the time she published her findings, Fried was a high school student, and Jensen a senior professor. But Fried had the better grasp of the need to account for the incompleteness of every source pool.[19] (To be fair to Jensen, the story also suggests that a good question retains value, even if the first answer is incorrect.)

Wise historians use searchable texts as a place to start but not to finish. A full-text search might yield a brief news item in a digitized newspaper, which could then lead you to skim every page of every issue of that newspaper in the surrounding weeks or months, likely finding items that the computer missed. Or it could lead you to a library where you could read a local weekly that might have covered the event in greater depth.[20] As Trevor Owens and Thomas Padilla argue, showing that "something was said at a particular point in time . . . is a rather low bar for historical argumentation." The real work of history includes "the legwork required to understand the original context from which that source emerged and think through the limitations that come from why that source was digitized and not something else."[21]

18. Richard Jensen, "'No Irish Need Apply': A Myth of Victimization," *Journal of Social History* 36 (2002): 421n17.

19. Rebecca A. Fried, "No Irish Need Deny: Evidence for the Historicity of NINA Restrictions in Advertisements and Signs," *Journal of Social History* 49 (2016): 829–54.

20. Ian Milligan, "Illusionary Order: Online Databases, Optical Character Recognition, and Canadian History, 1997–2010," *Canadian Historical Review* 94 (2013): 540–69.

21. Trevor Owens and Thomas Padilla, "Digital Sources and Digital Archives: Historical Evidence in the Digital Age," *International Journal of Digital Humanities*, May 4, 2020, 1–17.

Historians need not merely be consumers of databases; some create their own websites in order to collect material about a given event. In some cases this means asking people to contribute memories and digitized sources about an event decades in the past, such as American air raids during World War II.[22] In other cases, institutions have sought to collect information more or less in real time about breaking news, such as Hurricanes Katrina and Rita of 2005, the #metoo movement of the 2010s, and the COVID-19 pandemic.[23] As historians begin to study decades in which much public discourse took place on the web itself, they will need new tools to filter out the noise and try to get some signal.[24]

Libraries

Before the internet, the most familiar research tool was the library. Even my children, born in the twenty-first century, were taught that to research a topic, you start at the local library and ask for books. In addition, libraries collected runs of periodicals, government documents, and other published matter.

Today's research libraries are not merely storehouses for the books they themselves possess but portals to even vaster collections. Major institutions, such as the New York Public Library and the Library of Congress, have run out of room for all the books they own and have established storage facilities on less expensive land. Researchers can still request books to be delivered to the traditional reading rooms, but that can take days and require advance planning. In addition, university libraries participate in interlibrary loan (ILL), allowing researchers to request books from other institutions. This is not cheap, and your library may ask you to exhaust other alternatives, or even to limit your requests.

Libraries offer two major gateways: the catalog and the librarian. From the mid-nineteenth century into the late twentieth century,

22. "Japan Air Raids.Org," http://www.japanairraids.org/.

23. "#metoo Project Schlesinger Library," #metoo project Schlesinger Library, https://www.schlesinger-metooproject-radcliffe.org; "Hurricane Digital Memory Bank," http://hurricanearchive.org/; Audra D. S. Burch, "What Historians Will See When They Look Back on the Covid-19 Pandemic of 2020," *New York Times*, April 15, 2020.

24. Seth Denbo, "Data Overload," *Perspectives on History*, May 2019.

visitors to libraries often first encountered the card catalog: rows of cabinets with drawers of cards, each one listing a book's author, title, subject, and location within the library.[25] These days, catalogs are a series of online databases, which may or may not connect to one another. The better you know your topic, the better you will be able to navigate these yourself. And with many or most catalogs now online, you can complete your preliminary research at home, arriving at the library with a list of materials to consult.

Even if you are able to prepare such a list, you can benefit from a librarian's advice. Librarians spend years learning how to find information and gain even more expertise through work experience. A librarian who is not a specialist in your field may still know what resources the library just acquired, or point you to tools in fields related to your work, or to material that exists only on paper, or to "vertical files" that collect sources by subject area.[26] They often know the intricacies of databases: which search terms to use and which filters to impose. As information becomes more abundant, librarians' expertise is all the more valuable at multiple stages of a project. "The real challenge now is how to chart the tectonic plates of information that are crashing into one another and then to learn to navigate the new landscapes they are creating," writes Anthony Grafton.[27] Librarians are the pathfinders.

Oral History

Oral historians have the superpower of creating primary sources. The work demands special preparation, and anyone interested should read a manual on interviewing, and ideally take a workshop or course in the practice.[28] But it can be intensely rewarding for scholarship.

25. Peter Devereaux, Carla Diane Hayden, and Library of Congress, *The Card Catalog: Books, Cards, and Literary Treasures* (San Francisco: Chronicle Books, 2017).

26. Lindsey Bestebreurtje, "Beyond the Plantation: Freedmen, Social Experimentation, and African American Community Development in Freedman's Village, 1863–1900," *Virginia Magazine of History and Biography* 126 (2018): 334–65.

27. Anthony Grafton, "Future Reading," *New Yorker*, November 5, 2007, 50–54.

28. Donald A. Ritchie, *Doing Oral History*, 3rd ed. (New York: Oxford University Press, 2014).

Oral history consists of two main approaches. The first, pioneered by Allan Nevins at Columbia University, consists of interviews with elite figures, the same kinds of people whose lives we might expect to be documented in archives and publications. The fortunate historian conducts research about events sufficiently far in the past that archives have opened and tempers cooled, but recent enough that participants are still alive and in command of their memories. This was my lot for my first two books, where I had the pleasure of reading original documents to find out what had happened, then tracking down the creators of those documents to ask follow-up questions. But in some cases, there is no overlap between the archive and the living memory, since records have been lost, or they remain sealed until everyone worth interviewing is dead. In 2007, noting the absence of open corporate archives in Latin America, the Harvard Business School launched an oral history program that has since expanded to Africa, Asia, and the Middle East.[29]

A second tradition of oral history focuses on people whose lives are generally not documented, or whose documents are not preserved.[30] Historians have interviewed factory workers, migrant laborers, homeless people, and other marginalized groups, securing them a place in history that more document-based methods could not.[31] For both approaches, interviews and documentary sources can complement each other. Veterans of the Greensboro, North Carolina, Black Power movement told William Chafe that a man had attended their meetings to promote violent actions. "It would have been impossible to suggest the likelihood of infiltration and provocation on the basis of oral testimony alone," Chafe later wrote, but that testimony was consistent with FBI records, leading him to conclude that "Mr. X . . . was acting as an agent provocateur."[32]

---

29. Geoffrey Jones and Rachael Comunale, "Oral History and the Business History of Emerging Markets," *Enterprise & Society* 20 (2019): 19–32.

30. Paul Thompson and Joanna Bornat, *The Voice of the Past: Oral History*, 4th ed. (New York: Oxford University Press, 2017), 6.

31. Peter Friedlander, *The Emergence of a UAW Local, 1936–1939: A Study in Class and Culture* (Pittsburgh: University of Pittsburgh Press, 1975), xi.

32. William Henry Chafe, *Civilities and Civil Rights: Greensboro, North Carolina, and the Black Struggle for Freedom* (New York: Oxford University Press, 1981), 266, 271.

Since the formalization of the field, oral historians have prided themselves on preserving their interviews as recordings and transcripts, so they may be used by future researchers. Oral history archives at universities, presidential libraries, and other institutions make such records available, and they are increasingly being posted online. Thus, even historians who do not conduct interviews themselves can still benefit from oral history.

CHAPTER NINE

Archival Research

IN OCTOBER 1827, Leopold von Ranke submitted a slip of paper to a government office in Vienna, describing state documents that he wanted to read. As Kasper Risbjerg Eskildsen has noted, this was a preposterous request: "Civil servants did not save secret notes, encrypted documents, and diplomatic correspondences to aid visiting historians." But Ranke had the backing of powerful government officials, including Chancellor Klemens von Metternich. At their urging, archivists—first in Vienna, and then others in Venice—haltingly gave Ranke access to documents that had previously been seen only by state officials. What Ranke found astonished him. By reading original papers from the early seventeenth century, he was able to reconstruct a story at odds with two centuries' worth of previous accounts, some of them, he concluded, based on forged documents.[1] Ranke built his career on study in the archives, gradually persuading more and more archivists to open their doors. By the 1840s, he could look forward to the day when "we shall base modern history no longer on the reports even of contemporary historians, except insofar as they were in possession of personal and immediate knowledge of facts; and still less, on works yet more remote from the source; but rather on the narratives of eyewitnesses, and on genuine and original documents."[2]

1. Kasper Risbjerg Eskildsen, "Leopold Ranke's Archival Turn: Location and Evidence in Modern Historiography," *Modern Intellectual History* 5 (2008): 436, 442.
2. "Introduction to the *History of the Reformation in Germany*," trans. Sarah Austin and Roger Wines, in Leopold von Ranke, *The Secret of World History: Selected Writings*

Nearly two centuries after Ranke's first efforts, historians are still submitting requests for documents, often on slips of paper. And they are still relying on those documents for the same reasons Ranke did, expecting them to record the past in greater detail and candor than other sources. Consider your own life. Which would provide a more thorough account of the past year: the performance report you write for your boss and the Christmas letter you circulate to your cousins, both of them written in hindsight and crafted to present yourself in your best light? Or a full compilation of every email, text message, and social media post you wrote, all of them written in the moment, and many of them written in the expectation that only an intimate would see them? In judicial archives of eighteenth-century France, Arlette Farge found police records that, she argues, captured daily life more directly than any printed document. "People spoke of things that would have remained unsaid if a destabilizing social event had not occurred," she explains. "In this sense, their words reveal things that ordinarily went unspoken. The archival document is a tear in the fabric of time, an unplanned glimpse offered into an unexpected event."[3]

Tips

- Learn the rules of archival research.
- Contact an archivist before you plan your trip.
- If your time is limited, you can use a digital camera to capture images to be read when you return home.

What Is an Archive?

The Society of American Archivists defines archives as "the permanently valuable records—such as letters, reports, accounts, minute books, draft and final manuscripts, and photographs—of people, businesses, and government. These records are kept because they have continuing value to the creating agency and to other potential

---

on the Art and Science of History, ed. Roger Wines (New York: Fordham University Press, 1981).

3. Arlette Farge, *The Allure of the Archives*, trans. Thomas Scott-Railton (New Haven, CT: Yale University Press, 2013), 6.

users. They are the documentary evidence of past events. They are the facts we use to interpret and understand history."[4] For historians, the key distinction is that while a book or journal in one library can often be found at another, an archive preserves unique documents. Most obviously this includes manuscripts: a handwritten letter or typewritten memo preserved by its recipient and never reproduced. But it can also include printed materials, such as handbills and posters, which were once common but are now rare.[5] Some archives even preserve three-dimensional objects, such as the LGBT-themed T-shirts so lovingly photographed by Eric Gonzaba for his website, Wearing Gay History.[6]

Whether the archive preserves secret diplomatic notes, love letters, complaints to elected representatives, angry exchanges between scientists, or long-forgotten college yearbooks, it is likely to preserve stories in ways that widely available published sources cannot. There is some overlap, as when archival materials are distributed as documentary editions, microfilm, or, most recently, in digital form. But even when published equivalents exist, historians often prefer the originals. Jennifer Burns, for example, found that "the published versions of [Ayn] Rand's letters and diaries have been significantly edited in ways that drastically reduce their utility as historical sources," so she turned to the manuscript originals.[7]

Not all history relies on archives; one can find important works based solely on published materials, interviews, and other sources. But pick up a scholarly journal article, and chances are that at least some of the footnotes will refer to sources the historian accessed slip by slip. Museum exhibits and public-history websites feature documents retrieved from the archives, and other forms of history, such as textbooks, rely on scholarship ultimately grounded in archival research. Whether or not you yourself follow in Ranke's footsteps, it is at least worth understanding the process of archival research, as well as its limits.

4. "What Are Archives?," Society of American Archivists, https://www2.archivists.org/about-archives.

5. Pamela Walker Laird, *Advertising Progress: American Business and the Rise of Consumer Marketing* (Baltimore: Johns Hopkins University Press, 2001), 453.

6. Eric Gonzaba, "About" section, Wearing Gay History, https://wearinggayhistory.com/about.

7. Jennifer Burns, *Goddess of the Market: Ayn Rand and the American Right* (New York: Oxford University Press, 2009), 291.

Archival holdings are often needles in haystacks. It is one thing to locate the papers of major participants in an event. But the letters of witnesses to that event, with vivid descriptions, may be scattered over many states. Databases of archives, such as WorldCat and ArchiveGrid, are helpful, but they cannot pick up every collection in every archive. Finding all the unpublished material relevant to a topic is therefore a research challenge in itself. Search every catalog you can find, and get help from a librarian or archivist. Read other scholars' bibliographies. Identify prominent figures in your stories—politicians, activists, intellectuals—and see if they deposited papers somewhere. Eventually, as you become expert in a topic, you may get a sense of which individuals or institutions might have collected relevant material.[8]

Archives and Access

Whatever archives you locate, it is worth learning something about the origins of the archives and the collections they hold. Manuscript collections do not preserve themselves; they exist only because someone thought that they were worth collecting and preserving, and that someone's choices to collect, preserve, discard, or burn will shape the stories you can tell.[9]

As a general rule, archives are the creations of the powerful, whether they are individuals, businesses, or governments.[10] Occasionally these powerful actors are forced to create archives, for example, when a legislature requires agencies to retain certain records. In many cases, however, they have some discretion about what goes into the archive and who gets access to it, allowing them to shape the writing of history. At times, the powerful prefer that

8. For a lucid account of what this looks like in practice, see Amanda I. Seligman, *Chicago's Block Clubs: How Neighbors Shape the City* (Chicago: University of Chicago Press, 2016), appendix 1, "Researching Block Clubs."

9. M. L. Caswell, "'The Archive' Is Not an Archives: On Acknowledging the Intellectual Contributions of Archival Studies," *Reconstruction* 16 (2016), https://escholarship.org/uc/item/7bn4v1fk;

Robert C. Ritchie, "Historians and Archivists: Can We Still Be Friends?," *Reviews in American History* 40 (2012): 349–54.

10. Antoinette Burton, ed., *Archive Stories: Facts, Fictions, and the Writing of History* (Durham, NC: Duke University Press, 2005).

records disappear. In the early twentieth century, New York City's corrupt Tammany machine resisted the creation of a municipal archives that could document its graft. When the city established a reference library anyway, Tammany managed to sell key records—like those documenting police appointments—to a paper mill.[11] Few records of the Nigerian Civil War survive. Defeated Biafran separatists destroyed records in order to avoid prosecution, while victorious federal forces destroyed records to erase Biafra from historical memory.[12]

Even when records survive, access to them fluctuates. Some archives are palaces, employing large staffs to gather records and make them available to researchers. In the United States, presidential libraries have historically been particularly nice places to conduct research, though the Obama Foundation's decision not to create a research library may mark the end of that era.[13] Other archives deter researchers. A century and a half after the Mexican-American War, historians wishing to present the war from the Mexican Army's point of view were stymied by the refusal of Mexico's National Defense Archive to allow them to review records from the 1840s.[14] In Calcutta, Durba Ghosh found records "largely uncatalogued and out of chronological order, tied up in bundles with bits of twine, putting documents from 1765 with documents from 1896 next to each other, lumping civil suits with criminal cases, cases of petty theft, vagrancy, and domestic violence." Yet these documents preserved the stories she was seeking better than the materials that had been judged higher priority and shipped to London.[15] In 2012, the state of Georgia almost closed its archives to researchers due to

11. Barry W. Seaver, "Rebecca Rankin's Campaign for a Municipal Archives in New York, 1920–1952," *Libraries & the Cultural Record* 45 (2010): 269, 274.

12. Samuel Fury Childs Daly, "Archival Research in Africa," *African Affairs* 116 (2017): 311–20.

13. Jennifer Schuessler, "The Obama Presidential Library That Isn't," *New York Times*, February 20, 2019.

14. Michael Hogan, *The Irish Soldiers of Mexico* (Guadalajara, Mexico: Fondo Editorial Universitario, 1997), 15–16.

15. Durba Ghosh, "National Narratives and the Politics of Miscegenation: Britain and India," in *Archive Stories*, ed. Antoinette Burton (Durham, NC: Duke University Press, 2005), 38.

budget cuts. Instead, it transferred the archives to the state university system, which was able to increase access and research.[16]

Public records laws—which vary by jurisdiction—can force the release of some public documents, but this can take years and produce sparse results. In the 1990s, Jessica Wang was able to get records of the FBI's surveillance of American scientists, but a large percentage of the records she requested were withheld or partially censored. Yet Wang found ways to make the fragments useful. "The historian is forced to think creatively about how to use the records as they are, not as one would like them to be," she explains. "Although censored documents often omit desirable details that historians usually take for granted when sorting through government records to reconstruct a series of events, FBI files still contain a great deal of usable information. In the FBI's files on the Federation of American Scientists, it is often not possible to tell *who* is doing what. It is possible, however, to say quite a bit about *what* it is that they are doing."[17] Asking her reader to share her pain, she reproduces a heavily censored memo from 1946.

At other times, governments declassify portions of their archives, creating new research opportunities. In 2002, Mexico released a wealth of documents about government counterinsurgency efforts, which Alexander Aviña incorporated into his history of that struggle.[18] Other archives open only to close again. In the early 1990s, Western researchers enjoyed unprecedented access to archives in the former Soviet Union, in part because Russia's new leaders hoped they would discredit the communist past. By the first decade of the twenty-first century, Russia had restricted access to many previously open sources.[19] Around the same time, the

16. Kristina Torres, "Georgia Archives Thriving under New Management," *Atlanta Journal-Constitution*, December 24, 2015.

17. Jessica Wang, *American Science in an Age of Anxiety: Scientists, Anticommunism, and the Cold War* (Chapel Hill: University of North Carolina Press, 1999), 59.

18. Alexander Aviña, *Specters of Revolution: Peasant Guerrillas in the Cold War Mexican Countryside* (New York: Oxford University Press, 2014), 15.

19. J. Arch Getty, "Russian Archives: Is the Door Half Open or Half Closed?," *Perspectives on History*, May 1996; Rachel Donadio, "The Iron Archives," *New York Times*, April 22, 2007.

implementation of the Privacy Rule of the Health Insurance Porta-
bility and Accountability Act closed off access to many medical records in archives in the United States.[20] In 2006, a courthouse clerk
pointed Heather Ann Thompson to the recent arrival of a collection
of thousands of pages about the 1971 uprising at Attica Prison and
the subsequent state investigation. "I took as many notes as I could
take," she writes, "and Xeroxed as many pages as they would let me."
Good thing, too. When a reporter asked to see the same documents
in 2015, they had vanished, and the courthouse clerks denied they
had ever been there.[21]

Private archives, which are not subject to public records laws,
can be even more secretive than state archives. Sharing information with historians, or preserving it for future generators, offers
little demonstrable reward to a firm, and increases the chances that
a researcher will find something that will embarrass the firm, or
even expose it to legal liability.[22] For rational reasons, relatively few
corporations are eager to invite scholars to explore their history,
though there are some notable exceptions. The Ford Motor Company, for instance, has donated extensive materials to the Benson
Ford Research Center, even at the cost of letting labor historians
air some of its dirty laundry.[23] Institutions other than corporations may value history more. In 2016, the Church of Jesus Christ
of Latter-day Saints released documents it had held privately for
172 years, fueling new histories of the early church.[24]

When a corporation or organization maintains possession of
its records, the historian may have to negotiate for access.[25] Some

20. Susan C. Lawrence, *Privacy and the Past: Research, Law, Archives, Ethics* (New
Brunswick: Rutgers University Press, 2016), 85.

21. Heather Ann Thompson, *Blood in the Water: The Attica Prison Uprising of 1971 and
Its Legacy* (New York: Vintage, 2017), xiv–xv, 580n4.

22. David A. Kirsch, "The Record of Business and the Future of Business History:
Establishing a Public Interest in Private Business Records," *Library Trends* 57 (2009):
352–70.

23. Stephen Harlan Norwood, *Strikebreaking & Intimidation: Mercenaries and Mascu-
linity in Twentieth-Century America* (Chapel Hill: University of North Carolina Press, 2002).

24. Benjamin E. Park, *Kingdom of Nauvoo: The Rise and Fall of a Religious Empire on
the American Frontier* (New York: Liveright, 2020).

25. Erik Conway, *High-Speed Dreams: NASA and the Technopolitics of Supersonic
Transportation, 1945–1999* (Baltimore: Johns Hopkins University Press, 2008), 353.

institutional archives ask that researchers get approval prior to publishing works quoting from their holdings.[26] Others deny access to researchers whose research may challenge the institution's preferred narrative.[27] "Historians favor free, open, equal, and non-discriminatory access to archival, library, and museum collections wherever possible," notes the American Historical Association, but the decision may not be up to the researcher.[28] When they can, historians try to enable later researchers to access some of the records, either by facilitating the deposit in a public archive or by quoting extensively.[29]

Some valuable manuscripts reside not in formal archives, or even institutional records storage, but in the attics and basements of the people you are writing about, or their descendants. Act with sufficient charm, and you may gain not only the chance to review those materials, but also the opportunity to suggest that the possessor might think about contacting a relevant repository, where the papers would be processed and stored safely.[30] Families may possess better records of ancestors than appear in any publication or library. Jill Lepore's *Secret History of Wonder Woman*, for example, relies heavily on documents held by the descendants of her main characters. After it was published, additional family members shared even more material, which Lepore incorporated into the paperback edition.[31] In other cases, descendants can impede

26. Vanessa Ogle (@vanessahistory), "#Twitterstorians: Has anyone ever dealt with an archive that required to see and 'approve' a text using materials from said archive prior to publication? Has anyone ever published without acquiring such approval? With or without problems?," Twitter, December 18, 2019, https://twitter.com/vanessahistory/status /1207322571613655040.

27. Burns, *Goddess of the Market*, 293.

28. American Historical Association, "Statement on Standards of Professional Conduct (updated 2019)," https://www.historians.org/jobs-and-professional-development /statements-standards-and-guidelines-of-the-discipline/statement-on-standards-of -professional-conduct.

29. Gerald Markowitz and David Rosner, *Children, Race, and Power: Kenneth and Mamie Clark's Northside Center* (New York: Routledge, 2013), 253; Steven M. Teles, *The Rise of the Conservative Legal Movement: The Battle for Control of the Law* (Princeton, NJ: Princeton University Press, 2012), 5.

30. See, e.g., Sarah A. Vogel, *Is It Safe? BPA and the Struggle to Define the Safety of Chemicals* (Berkeley: University of California Press, 2012), xx.

31. Jill Lepore, *The Secret History of Wonder Woman*, reprint ed. (New York: Vintage, 2015).

scholarly research. For decades, Stephen James Joyce, the grandson of writer James Joyce, limited scholars' access to his grandfather's papers, threatening them with lawsuits were they to quote them in ways of which he disapproved.[32]

Occasionally, archives open despite the wishes of their creators. At the close of World War II, for instance, Allied forces captured millions of German records, many of which were microfilmed by the United States before being returned to Germany.[33] (The Soviets captured Bulgarian records, which Russia has yet to return.)[34] As a result of lawsuits, countless records from the tobacco, lead, and vinyl industries have come to light, allowing historians—as well as courts—to tell the story of what leaders of those industries knew about the dangers of their products.[35]

In other cases, a determined historian can find a detour around seemingly blocked roads. Gabrielle Hecht's history of the French nuclear power industry centers on two agencies, the Commissariat à l'Energie Atomique and Electricité de France, neither of which permitted her access to their official archives. While that might have discouraged another historian, Hecht began interviewing veterans of the two agencies, some of whom shared not only their memories but also gave her access to their personal files. Moreover, municipal archives, union archives, and other repositories included extensive material about the two agencies, allowing her to craft a deeply detailed account.[36] Samuel Fury Childs Daly reports a similar experience. Failing to find a centralized archive of the Nigerian Civil War, he made do with "records of individuals—diaries,

32. D. T. Max, "The Injustice Collector," *New Yorker*, June 12, 2006.

33. "Captured German and Related Records on Microfilm," National Archives, September 12, 2016, https://www.archives.gov/research/captured-german-records; Astrid M. Eckert, "The Fight for the Files: Captured German Records after World War II," *GHI Bulletin*, no. 32 (2003): 144–48.

34. Margarita Assenova, "Moscow Refuses to Return Bulgarian Archives," *POLYGRAPH.Info*, March 7, 2019, https://www.polygraph.info/a/fact-check-bulgaria-archives-russia/29807418.html.

35. Allan Brandt, *The Cigarette Century: The Rise, Fall, and Deadly Persistence of the Product That Defined America*, reprint ed. (New York: Basic Books, 2009); Gerald E. Markowitz and David Rosner, *Deceit and Denial: The Deadly Politics of Industrial Pollution* (Berkeley: University of California Press, 2002).

36. Gabrielle Hecht, *The Radiance of France: Nuclear Power and National Identity after World War II* (Cambridge, MA: MIT Press, 2009), 17–19.

unpublished memoirs, and 'tin-trunk' collections of personal papers," along with interviews, memoirs, and local histories.[37] Kelly Lytle Hernandez found that the Los Angeles Police Department had destroyed almost its entire archive, while the Sheriff's Department "either does not have or will not share its records." Undeterred, she worked through newspapers, personal papers, and court records, finding the stories not only of the people who created Los Angeles's jail system but also of those who challenged it. "It was a grueling archival slog," she writes, "but the chase was rewarding."[38]

Not all archival restrictions are inappropriate. Medical and penal institutions may want to preserve the privacy of their patients and inmates in obedience to both ethical and legal codes.[39] Oral historians sometimes pledge to seal all or portions of interviews until after a narrator's death, or a specified period of time, and archives that acquire such interviews are bound to honor these pledges.

Even when documents do exist, and archivists are eager to help, it may be a challenge to find the right materials. Ann Laura Stoler notes that while the Dutch Algemeen Rijksarchief "is among the most accessible, ultramodern depositories," the record-keeping conventions of a previous century keep documents hidden. "Because the archives of the Ministry of Colonies (MK) are organized *chronologically* and not by topic, there is no easy entry by theme," she explains. "An interest in European paupers or abandoned mixed blood children gets you nowhere, unless you know how they mattered to whom, when, and why they did so." Historians have thus searched the records of 1848 looking for information about a demonstration that year, only to have missed the interviews generated by a later investigation of the demonstration.[40] Thus, while any archival discovery depends on the help of current and previous generations of archivists and collectors who have preserved a precious document

37. Samuel Fury Childs Daly, "Archival Research in Africa," *African Affairs* 116 (2017): 320.

38. Kelly Lytle Hernandez, *City of Inmates: Conquest, Rebellion, and the Rise of Human Caging in Los Angeles, 1771–1965* (Chapel Hill: University of North Carolina Press, 2017), 3.

39. Susan C. Lawrence, *Privacy and the Past: Research, Law, Archives, Ethics* (New Brunswick, NJ: Rutgers University Press, 2016).

40. Ann Laura Stoler, *Along the Archival Grain: Epistemic Anxieties and Colonial Common Sense* (Princeton, NJ: Princeton University Press, 2010), 10, 13.

through the years, the historian can take some pride in bringing to light a document that has not been seen for some time.[41]

Working in Archives

Working in an archive requires some planning. An archive may store millions of documents, typically organized into folders, which in turn are stored in boxes. Bound materials, such as ledgers, may get their own boxes as well. Boxes, in turn, are organized into collections, each of which is most often the records of an individual or institution. A collection may consist of a single sheet of paper or tens of thousands. All of these take effort to identify and retrieve, so you will not be able to just walk into the building and grab the materials you want off the shelf. The more you plan ahead, the more efficient your time will be. A researcher who has worked in a particular archive may give you key information you cannot easily get elsewhere. Do the archivists expect researchers to bring letters of introduction? Where is a good place to stay and a good place to eat? Is the archive scheduled to shut down for a summer while its holdings are moved to a new building? (Thank you, Tim Lombardo, for that particular tip.) The more you prepare for archival work, the more efficiently you can carry it out, and the more likely others will be to help you.

READ THE FINDING AID

The first step is to locate the *finding aid* to the collection that interests you. The finding aid is a description of the contents of each collection. The level of detail varies considerably. Some collections are unprocessed, meaning that no archivist has had the time to open up the boxes as they came from the donor to see what was inside. Other collections, especially small ones, or those of great interest to many

---

41. Suzanne Fischer, "Nota Bene: If You 'Discover' Something in an Archive, It's Not a Discovery," *Atlantic*, June 19, 2012; Helena Iles Papaioannou, "Actually, Yes, It *Is* a Discovery If You Find Something in an Archive That No One Knew Was There," *Atlantic*, June 21, 2012; "Rediscovering a Lost Treatise on Martial Law," *Yale Law School* (blog), August 12, 2019; Abby Mullen, "In Defense of Finding Things in Archives," *Abby Mullen* (blog), January 9, 2019, https://abbymullen.org/in-defense-of-finding-things-in-archives/.

researchers, may list each item, for example, noting the date, sender, and recipient on every letter in a box of correspondence. In between, a finding aid may describe the contents of each folder, without listing each item. For example, a congressman's papers includes a folder entitled, "Letters in Opposition to Prayer in Public Schools, 1971," which gives you a good sense of what to expect in the folder, though it does not list the name of each constituent who wrote.[42]

Archives are increasingly placing their finding aids online, allowing interested researchers to identify in advance what they would like to see. If that is the case, invest the time to draw up a detailed shopping list. This list will allow you to budget the time (and therefore money) you need for your visit. If a distant archive contains just a few documents that are important to your story, it is probably cheaper to pay the archive staff or a local researcher to make scans or photographs for you. Conversely, if the archive includes multiple, voluminous collections directly relevant to your topic, you may be in a good position to apply for a multimonth fellowship to use them. In between, you might find an archive with a few dozen relevant boxes: one or two weeks' work with a digital camera. While you cannot predict exactly how long it will take to get through a given number of boxes, or bound volumes, you can at least have some idea. This is particularly useful if you are applying for research funding: show the prospective funder that you have a reasonable chance of using the money efficiently.

You cannot always count on an online finding aid, or any finding aid at all. I have been to an underfunded archive where the initial step involved the records custodian walking me through a storage area, allowing me to look for potentially interesting records by reading the labels on the sides of the boxes.

FOLLOW THE RULES

Archives can be the most hospitable places on earth. Official archives are often open to the public by law, and even private archives, such as the special collections departments at university libraries, know

---

42. *Guide to the Gilbert Gude Papers, 1967–1976*, Special Collections Research Center, George Washington University, 2012.

that it would be silly to restrict their use to only people affiliated with that university, since it is unlikely that the specialists on a topic will happen to be affiliated with the institution with the best holdings on that topic, and researchers need to visit multiple archives to create a complete story. In 1999, I showed up at the special collections department at Gelman Library, George Washington University, and more or less announced that I wanted to spend the next year working there. The archivists—who had met me only once before, during an initial scouting trip—welcomed me and showed me to a table. For the next year, they coached me through my research, delivering hundreds of boxes and suggesting ever more strategies.

On the other hand, even the most welcoming archivist has a duty to the future as well as to the present. Bad as it would be to destroy a library book, in most cases the loss of one copy does not mean that its contents are lost forever. By contrast, archives store unique or rare manuscripts and other materials. If a handwritten ledger or the sole extant copy of a pamphlet is damaged, destroyed, or stolen, there will never be another like it.

To protect against such loss while also allowing research, archives have developed special rules. Food and drink, though sometimes tolerated in libraries, are firmly forbidden in archives reading rooms. So are pens, lest they leak on the documents. Instead, archives supply pencils and, generally, welcome laptop computers. To prevent theft, they forbid bags and overcoats, asking researchers to store those in lockers before they enter the reading room. (While you cannot wear an overcoat in the archives, you should pack a warm sweater, even in summer. Many archives set temperatures low to prolong the life of the materials they hold.)[43] Once you are in the reading room, archivists will ask that you read just one document at a time and keep them in the order in which you found them. While clean, bare hands are best for handling documents, photographs may require that you wear gloves.[44]

---

43. Colleen Flaherty, "How Cold Is That Library? There's a Google Doc for That," *Inside Higher Ed*, May 10, 2019, https://www.insidehighered.com/quicktakes/2019/05/10/how-cold-library-theres-google-doc.

44. Alexandra K. Alvis, "No Love for White Gloves, or: The Cotton Menace," *Smithsonian Libraries / Unbound* (blog), November 21, 2019, https://blog.library.si.edu/blog/2019/11/21/no-love-for-white-gloves-or-the-cotton-menace/.

Because it is expensive to hire staff to enforce these rules, special collections departments are commonly open fewer hours than the libraries that house them. To maximize their use of the scarce opening hours, historians have been known to skip lunch, or reduce it to a ten-minute break for a protein bar. Of course, you must wash your hands before returning to research.

Beyond these commonalities, each archive has its own rules. In some institutions, manuscripts and rare books are in the same department; in others they are separate. One archive lets you request three boxes at a time (one on your table, the rest on a cart) while another allows twelve. Archives may have specific citation rules as well. For instance, while most archives encourage readers to cite the number of the box in which they found an item, the US National Archives does not, since some of its record groups have duplicate box numbers.[45]

The first trip to the archives can be intimidating. Many graduate and even undergraduate programs in history bring students into archives where the archivists know that they will be dealing with novices and are prepared to answer basic questions. That makes the process much easier, like learning to ride a bike on a basketball court before your first trip into the street. If you do not have such a class, it may be a good idea to explain to the archivists that you are new at the task, and ask for their help. Sadly, even the best-prepared researcher may face harassment or other unfair treatment based on their age, sex, disability, or status.[46]

WORK WITH ARCHIVISTS

Historians and archivists depend on each other. Archivists search for important material, rescuing it from the landfill. They preserve it for posterity, process it so that it can be found and used, and guide researchers to the most useful material. They choose what to collect

45. National Archives and Records Administration, "Citing Records in the National Archives of the United States," 2010, 4.

46. Ashley D. Farmer et al., "How Gender Affects the Experience of Archival Research and Field Work," *Modern American History*, published online by Cambridge University Press, July 15, 2019, 1–8, https://doi.org/10.1017/mah.2019.15; American Historical Association, Task Force on Disability Final Report, 2011.

and preserve based in part on current trends in historical scholarship, and those choices in turn shape future research.[47] Without archivists, historians would not have access to the richest sources of historical knowledge, which they need to craft their scholarship. Without historians, archivists would still serve some institutional and personal researchers, but they would lose some of their most devoted visitors, including the ones most likely to share archival findings with a wider world.

Unfortunately, mutual dependence does not always produce mutual respect and harmony. Historians can get frustrated with archivists who are the human representatives of institutions that may deny access to materials, either from scarcity of resources or a desire to restrict knowledge. Archivists can get frustrated with historians who fail to recognize their hard work and professional training. "Archival studies scholars and practicing archivists are more than willing to meet humanities scholars halfway," writes M. L. Caswell, "but there has to be a willingness to engage and a baseline of respect in interdisciplinary exchange that is currently lacking."[48]

One part of that baseline is, whenever possible, contacting archivists in advance of a research trip. For really big institutions, like the National Archives, this may not matter much, since the archivists may be too busy to prepare anything special for your visit. For a small archive, it can be quite important. At the very least, the staff can alert you to the rules and hours of the reading room and put in orders for materials held offsite. Or they may do more; I have contacted an archive or rare books room in advance, then arrived to find the materials I requested already laid out for my use. (These are among the happiest moments of my professional life.) Moreover, advance communication can alert the archivist to the scope of your project, letting them know that you are not a title researcher or genealogist looking for a single bit of information but rather a historian who might want to range rather freely. Advance

47. Liz Covart, "Peter Drummey, How Archives Work," Ben Franklin's World, https://benfranklinsworld.com/episode-075-peter-drummey-archives-work/.

48. M. L. Caswell, "'The Archive' Is Not an Archives: On Acknowledging the Intellectual Contributions of Archival Studies," *Reconstruction* 16 (2016), https://escholarship.org/uc/item/7bn4v1fk.

communication is not always possible; you might, for example, finish work in one institution sooner than you expected and decide to spend your newly found free time in another archive in the same city. But getting in touch is never a bad idea.

The other part of the baseline is acknowledging aid. Whenever you have an interaction with an archivist beyond the most routine document retrieval (suggesting a new source, finding a box that had been misfiled), get their name and contact information, so you can thank them twice. First, in a thank-you note following your visit, and again in the acknowledgments of your published work.

Beyond these basic courtesies, historians should recognize archivists as fellow professionals and scholars who shape the historical record by appraising, collecting, preserving, and cataloging material, as well as making it available to researchers.[49] They can lead you to new sources, help you understand what you are seeing, and shape your interpretations. With your permission, they can put you in touch with researchers working on related topics. Even without such a formal introduction, researchers are often helpful resources. If you hear someone requesting a collection related to your work, it is not too bold to introduce yourself.

Research with Digital Photography

"The introduction of digital cameras to archival research is altering interactions with materials and dislocating the process of analysis," wrote Jennifer Rutner and Roger Schonfeld in 2012, "with potential impacts not only for support service providers but for the nature of history scholarship itself."[50] Where archival research once required long trips, or even residential fellowships, the ability to photograph hundreds of pages in a single day now allows historians to conduct quick raids and review their booty at leisure. Long sojourns in the archive—with time to read, reflect, and even write—still offer advantages. But for historians with work or family responsibilities that limit their time away from home, or who simply lack funds

49. Caswell, "'The Archive' Is Not an Archives."

50. Jennifer Rutner and Roger Schonfeld, "Supporting the Changing Research Practices of Historians," *Ithaka S+R*, December 2012, https://doi.org/10.18665/sr.22532.

for extended stays, the digital camera can allow archival work that would otherwise be impossible.

Beyond this most basic advantage, the introduction of the digital camera could have further implications down the road. When historians took notes by hand or by typing on computers, their citations to archival documents were essentially claims to be taken on faith; no fact-checker was likely to request the same box and folder to verify the information. Now, it may be reasonable to ask the historian for a copy of the document in question. If archives were to loosen their policies, it would become easier for historians to share their images, so that future researchers might make even shorter trips, or not visit the archives at all. If we could get to a stage where historians routinely avoided requesting documents that have already been photographed, we could prolong the life of fragile paper. And if, God forbid, an archive were to be destroyed in flood or fire—as does happen now and then—we could still have a digital record. In 2020, as archives closed their reading rooms in response to the coronavirus pandemic, archives and researchers collaborated to help researchers share their digital files.[51]

In reality, few historians have the time to photograph every page in a collection, and many archives explicitly forbid the practice. Thus, the historian with the digital camera shoots the pages that are most likely to answer their own questions, and the next historian, who has their own questions, will prefer to go through the collection themselves. Oral historians have long confronted this challenge: Do they ask only the questions they care about for their own projects, or do they try to serve future historians by trying to get a full life history from everyone they interview?[52] Since archives generally last longer than memories, the historian with the camera has less of a duty to the future. Let the future take its own pictures.

Some archives restrict the use of digital cameras, charge high fees for their use, or ban them entirely; this may especially be the case in countries with traditions of secrecy, or in institutions that rely on the fees they collect for making reproductions. Even

51. Ashley Bowen, "Peer-to-Peer Research Exchange," *Perspectives Daily* (blog), June 10, 2020, https://www.historians.org/publications-and-directories/perspectives-on-history/summer-2020/peer-to-peer-research-exchange-shafrs-archival-records-discussion-group.

52. Saul Benison, "Reflections on Oral History," *American Archivist* 28 (1965): 75.

archives that allow unrestricted use of digital cameras for research purposes may ask that a researcher seek special permission if they want to reproduce the image in print or on a website. They will generally have the policy written out and will perhaps ask you to sign a copy to acknowledge it. Go ahead and photograph that as well; now you have a copy. (Some archives request that you place a card with an abbreviated copy of the policy along with every document you photograph, so that every photograph will bear a reminder of the restrictions.) Policies vary. For instance, some archives might require permission for the use of an image on a permanent website but not for use in social media. Still, because archival photography has become a major technique of historical research, it is worth spending some time discussing the practice.

TYPES OF CAMERAS

Enter a busy archive today, and you will likely see historians using a variety of optical equipment. With new products hitting the market every month, I cannot pretend to offer up-to-date information, but I can suggest some considerations.[53]

On one end of the spectrum are digital single-lens reflex (DSLR) cameras, the digital descendants of the 35mm film cameras so popular among photojournalists and hobbyists in the decades after World War II. DSLRs support lenses that are much larger and more sensitive than the tiny lenses available on smartphones, bringing in more light and producing sharper images. You can add filters, such as close-up filters that allow you to photograph tiny details. DSLRs often have large batteries—enough to last all day—and it is easy to swap in a spare when needed. With the right settings, DSLRs can produce images of great quality, which matters when you have just one chance to capture documents you will need for your research. (In one survey of historians, 8 percent of respondents reported that more than 25 percent of the images they shot were unusable—a

53. For additional introductions, now somewhat dated, see Kirklin Bateman et al., "Taking a Byte Out of the Archives: Making Technology Work for You," *Perspectives on History*, January 2005; Emily VanBuren, "6 Tools to Make Archival Research More Efficient," *Inside Higher Ed*, November 9, 2014, https://www.insidehighered.com/blogs/gradhacker /6-tools-make-archival-research-more-efficient.

troubling loss of information.)[54] Image quality can be especially important, for example, if you want to capture a lot of small print at once, or if the archive has poor lighting. But DSLRs are also expensive, heavy, and bulky. And they are a bit noisy, so some institutions forbid their use.

At the other end of the spectrum are smartphones, whose cameras improve with every new model. You may already own such a phone and carry it around, making it no additional investment in cost or weight. They weigh little and make no noise, providing you have silenced them in the settings. However, smartphone cameras do not produce the same quality images as DSLRs, especially in poor light, and it can be heartbreaking to return from an archive or library to find that your images are too blurry to read. Many models, such as iPhones, cannot take fresh batteries easily. Some researchers have reported poor results with folder control, making it a challenge to figure out which archival folders an image came from. And just as some archives allow cell phones but not DSLRs, some apparently allow DSLRs but not cell phones.[55]

Some archives allow flatbed scanners, though these are slow and cannot be used for bound materials. Finally, many research libraries now offer machines that allow users to create digital scans of microforms, and some also have machines for scanning books. Depending on how many pages you want, it may make sense to use one of these machines, or just use your own camera to photograph a few pages or a few screens of the microfilm reader.

I know of no archive that allows flash photography, which could damage their materials and distract fellow patrons. Archives vary widely in their policies on tripods, so ask in advance. If you are considering a tripod for use in archives, look for one with a horizontal arm that will allow you to mount your camera pointing straight down. Some specialized table mounts also allow this. This setup allows you to shoot at slow shutter speeds but with small apertures and low ISO settings, producing especially crisp, focused images.

54. Ian Milligan, "Becoming a Desk(top) Profession," January 2020, https://www .ianmilligan.ca/talk/aha-2020/.

55. Milligan, "Becoming a Desk(top) Profession."

HOW MUCH TO SHOOT?

Making a digital photograph is essentially free. Yes, it requires some tiny fraction of a cent's worth of electricity, as well as adding to the wear and tear on the camera. But that is nothing compared to the twenty-five or fifty cents archives once charged for each photocopy. The result is a fundamentally different logic. In the age of the photocopier, the historian had to choose only the most important documents. In the age of the digital camera, the rule is when in doubt, shoot. You would not pay fifty cents to photocopy the one line of text on the tab of a file, but you would be foolish *not* to photograph it, given the chance. And if you think you might have jerked your hand, blurring the image, then go ahead, shoot again. Keep in mind, however, that your future self (or possibly your future research assistant) will have to review every photograph you take. Be kind to that future self by exercising some control over what you shoot. While it is tempting to try to scan or photograph everything, in reality, it is usually more practical to be at least a bit selective as you go.

At the very least, before photographing a document, check to see if it has already been digitized. Mass digitization projects, such as Google Books and the Internet Archive, increase the probability that the fragile, yellowed pamphlet you just found already exists in digital form, so there is no need for you to photograph it again.

Also beware of becoming overreliant on the camera. Even if you are mostly taking pictures to be reviewed later, you should also take notes on what you see. If you come across something really good, make a note of that separately. Do not count on your future self, who may be tired and impatient, to notice it again, or to find it among the thousands of photographs you have taken. Also take notes on what is missing in the archive. When your future self notices a gap in the photographs, they will be grateful for a note like, "April issue not in holdings," or "did not photograph folder 10: nothing of value."

While most of your photographs will be close-ups of individual pages, it is worth taking a few shots of archival boxes, massive bound volumes, and even some selfies of you during the research process. These can be great illustrations for presentations of your research, as well as entries in your family album.

It is important to maintain some organization as you go. Many historians like to replicate an archive's organizational structure on their own computer. For instance, they might end up with a computer folder called "box 15," and within that folders with labels "folder 1, folder 2," and so on. Or, with periodicals, you could have a folder marked "Daily Chronicle," and within that one marked "1844," and within that folders for each month. If you are making multipage PDFs (the preferred output of many microfilm scanners), the same principle applies. Start a new file every few dozen images, whether that represents a week, a month, or some other useful division. That will make it easier to find things later on.

Uploading images to a cloud system, such as Google Drive or Dropbox, can free up space on your phone or computer or provide a backup. These systems may also provide optical character recognition (OCR) of printed or typewritten text, allowing searching later on.

Once you have images on your computer, you have additional choices to make about how to view them and incorporate them into your workflow. Computers and cameras often come with software for manipulating and organizing images, and my colleagues have created a specialized application called Tropy, designed specifically for historians using images photographed in archives. As with note-taking in general, there is no one best way to deal with the hundreds, thousands, or tens of thousands of images you may accumulate. It does help to have a large monitor, so you can view an image on one part of the screen and take notes on it in another, whether within the same application or in a second application on the side.

Managing Expectations

"I found the archival research to be unexpectedly similar to doing an archaeological excavation, except that it involved digging through paper rather than dirt," writes archaeologist and historian Eric Cline. "Just as with a dig at an ancient site, where the presence (or absence) of a single item can sometimes make a tremendous difference, trying to resolve a specific issue at an archive often raised a whole host of other questions even while answering the original query. There was also the same thrill of finding something, especially the unexpected; the same dejection at coming up dry despite a promising beginning; and the same satisfaction that comes from putting together enough puzzle pieces to yield a plausible hypothesis for a past event." Perhaps because of his long experience in archaeology, Cline appears—in print anyway—to accept disappointment with astonishing aplomb. Searching for one particular letter, described by its recipient as "the most sordid document ever to reach this office," Cline finds instead a sheet of pink paper recording the sordid document's removal. "When the letter comes to light in the future, as it undoubtedly will," writes Cline, "it will be interesting to see what it specifically says."[56] May we all respond to archival gaps with such confident grace.

Archival research is some of the most unpredictable work a historian can do. Some boxes open to reveal marvelous treasures. Others contain useless materials or copies of documents you have already seen. Still others offer tiny portions of the story that the historian can, with patient determination, build into something larger. One trip to the New-York Historical Society produced nothing of value for my research except for a 1921 pamphlet with an arresting six-word phrase: "The bus is young and honest," which I used for an article title. That was an afternoon well spent.[57]

Some days you find nothing. Some days you find sources that change your understanding of your project. You cannot control or predict what kind of day you will have. You can only open the next box.

56. Eric H. Cline, *Digging Up Armageddon: The Search for the Lost City of Solomon* (Princeton, NJ: Princeton University Press, 2020), xii, 176.

57. Zachary M. Schrag, "'The Bus Is Young and Honest': Transportation Politics, Technical Choice, and the Motorization of Manhattan Surface Transit, 1919–1936," *Technology and Culture* 41 (2000): 52n2.

CHAPTER TEN

Interpreting Sources

SOURCES DO NOT ANSWER questions by themselves; it is the task of the historian to analyze sources in ways that answer the questions that they posed at the start of a project, or developed along the way. Again, this is rarely a matter of logical proof so much as the presentation of enough evidence to persuade the reader that your explanation of events is the best available. Sometimes this simply requires documenting a pattern in the sources you have found. Frequently, however, you must analyze the sources for messages their creators might not have wished to convey, a practice known as *critical reading*.

Tips

- Look for patterns, and for deviations from those patterns.
- Read sources critically—finding messages that may not have been intended by the creator.
- Aim for plausible causal claims, knowing that you likely cannot *prove* your assertions.

Pattern Recognition

Much of historians' analytical work consists of reading enough material to recognize the patterns in what people did and said. "The historian is essentially a bringer of order to the past, a perceiver of patterns," writes John Cannon. "The events of the past are myriad in number, most of them neither recoverable nor of interest. Even the tiny fragment which survives in the shape of historical evidence presents the most bewildering variety of sequences, connections, relationships, parallels, contrasts and irrelevancies. In order to function at all, the historian must simplify."[1] Pattern recognition is subjective. Not every fact will fit any pattern, and you may need to flag some as mere outliers.[2] If you keep an open mind—as you should—your own views on the shape of the pattern will change as you proceed. If you read the same evidence in a different order, the story might come out differently.[3]

WORLDVIEW

One particularly important effort at pattern recognition is the reconstruction of a system of beliefs held by an individual or group. Variously called mind-sets, worldviews, ideologies, or perhaps *mentalités*, these belief systems form a more-or-less coherent way of understanding the world and one's place in it.[4] For instance, in her influential 1966 article, "The Cult of True Womanhood: 1820–1860," Barbara Welter sampled a wide range of antebellum women's magazines, lectures, gift books, and other texts that sought to explain to white, middle-class American women who they were and how they ought to behave. "The attributes of True Womanhood, by which a woman judged herself and was judged by her husband, her neighbors and society," writes Welter, "could be divided into four cardinal virtues—piety, purity, submissiveness and domesticity. Put them all together and they spelled mother, daughter, sister, wife—woman."[5]

Whereas Welter uses a religious metaphor—*cult*—to describe the web of beliefs about the role of women, Joanne Freeman prefers

1. John Cannon, *The Historian at Work* (London: Allen and Unwin, 1980), 2.

2. Peter Thorsheim, *Inventing Pollution: Coal, Smoke, and Culture in Britain since 1800* (2006; repr., Athens: Ohio University Press, 2018), 5.

3. Aili Mari Tripp, "Transparency and Integrity in Conducting Field Research on Politics in Challenging Contexts," *Perspectives on Politics* 16 (2018): 728–38.

4. Clifford Geertz, "Ethos, World-View, and the Analysis of Sacred Symbols," 1957, reprinted in *Antioch Review* 74 (2016): 623.

5. Barbara Welter, "The Cult of True Womanhood: 1820–1860," *American Quarterly* 18 (1966): 152.

a linguistic metaphor to describe the thoughts of an earlier generation of American men. "In early national America," she writes, "honor, democracy, and republicanism joined to form a distinctive political culture, governed by a *grammar of political combat*: a shared understanding of the weapons at one's disposal—their power, use, and impact. This grammar was no defined rule book, no concrete tactical guide. It was a body of assumptions too familiar to record and thus almost invisible to modern eyes."[6] In both cases, it is not a single belief but a collection of reinforcing ideas that defines the pattern.

Worldviews shade into patterns of action. Thus, when Wayne Lee describes three eighteenth-century "ways of war" (European, Native, and Militia), he must describe not only conceptions of war but also the specific forms of violence that both shaped those conceptions and were shaped by them.[7] And Sarah Seo explains the emergence of a motorized police force in the 1910s as a reflection of a progressive worldview that promoted the nonpartisan, professional regulation of "everything from the fat content of milk and the construction of factories to the sale of securities and the payment of child support."[8]

DUCK, DUCK, GOOSE

In the children's game of "Duck, Duck, Goose," one child walks calmly around a circle of playmates, tapping each on the head and saying, "duck." At some point, the child will instead say "goose," then try to run around the circle before being caught by the child they have tagged. The premise of the game is that having been lulled by a series of calls of "duck," it will be hard for the "goose" to notice the change until it is too late to catch the child who tagged them.

Historical research is a lot like that. You need to learn the patterns well enough both to sit still when nothing is happening and

6. Joanne B. Freeman, *Affairs of Honor: National Politics in the New Republic* (New Haven, CT: Yale University Press, 2002), xxii; emphasis in original.

7. Wayne E. Lee, *Crowds and Soldiers in Revolutionary North Carolina: The Culture of Violence in Riot and War* (Gainesville: University Press of Florida, 2001), chapter 4.

8. Sarah A. Seo, *Policing the Open Road: How Cars Transformed American Freedom* (Cambridge, MA: Harvard University Press, 2019), 66–68.

leap up when you hear something unusual. "Individual entries may seem flat and unrevealing," writes Laurel Thatcher Ulrich of Martha Ballard's diary.

> Taken together, they provide an unparalleled record of an eighteenth-century practice. Even the most routine and formulaic pieces of information are useful. Rare comments on obstetrical complications mean more when seen in relation to hundreds of bland notations that say simply "delivered" or "safe delivered"; a twenty-four-shilling fee acquires new significance when framed with all those other entries recording six shillings or a plain XX, while the appearance of a doctor at a delivery becomes more noteworthy when the hundreds of other deliveries in which no one thought to call a physician are considered. In midwifery as in so many other aspects of Martha Ballard's diary, it is the combination of boredom and heroism, of the usual and the unusual, that tells the story.[9]

Neither half of this is easy, since every type of source has its own conventions. For instance, a historian familiar with newspapers of the twentieth and twenty-first centuries—with their front-page headlines for the most urgent news—might be surprised to find an important story on the second page of a newspaper printed in the eighteenth or nineteenth century. But a historian accustomed to those earlier newspapers would know that front pages were printed in advance, and breaking news almost always appeared on page 2. Thus, an important story on page 2 would not be a goose, just another duck.

Should we take Andrew Jackson's "adoption" of an orphaned Creek boy as evidence of a peculiar tenderness on Jackson's part or an expression of sympathy for Indians in general? No, notes Laurel Clark Shire, drawing on the work of Dawn Peterson. Indian adoption was "a common practice among elite white families" and could express a wish to dominate rather than unusual sentiment.[10] Similarly, Katherine Benton-Cohen notes that anthropologist Franz Boas, who detested racism, worked alongside prominent

9. Laurel Thatcher Ulrich, *A Midwife's Tale: The Life of Martha Ballard, Based on Her Diary, 1785-1812* (New York: Knopf, 2010), 169.

10. Laurel Clark Shire, "Sentimental Racism and Sympathetic Paternalism: Feeling Like a Jacksonian," *Journal of the Early Republic* 39 (2019): 111–22.

eugenicists of the early twentieth century. Should we be surprised? No, Benton-Cohen tells us, just another duck. "Boas's participation in early eugenics is less an indictment of him than evidence of the movement's centrality in scientific developments of the era. . . . So Boas's joining the eugenicists did not mean he was joining some racial cult (which is how it seems in retrospect). Rather, it indicates that he was engaged in the professional life of a physical scientist."[11]

Conversely, historians need to spot the anomalies, the geese. You can get help by finding reactions to an event by observers at the time. For example, in January 1864, Confederate general Patrick Cleburne proposed "the emancipation and enrollment of negroes" into the Confederate army. Was this an expression of conventional wisdom at the time or a new and shocking idea? Kevin Levin shows it to be a goose. He notes that Cleburne's superiors in the army and Confederate president Jefferson Davis himself found the idea so outrageous that they ordered it suppressed. By showing that Cleburne's contemporaries regarded his proposal as scandalous, Levin demonstrates that the idea of arming African Americans remained unusual in the Confederacy until late 1864.[12]

Prescriptive literature is another aid, for it serves as a record of how at least some people in a culture expected their fellows to behave. "As the demand for [the Department of Housing and Urban Development] homeownership programs swelled," writes Keeanga-Yamahtta Taylor, "some fee appraisers were doing as many as five appraisals a day, churning them out in fifteen-minute intervals—despite the fact that industry standards suggested that appraisals should take at least two hours. In the inner city, however, 'windshield inspections' were 'more often the rule than the exception.'"[13] Perhaps this shoddy work is not surprising per se, but by pointing out the deviation from the stated norm, Taylor alerts us of the significance of the appraisal's brevity.

11. Katherine Benton-Cohen, *Inventing the Immigration Problem: The Dillingham Commission and Its Legacy* (Cambridge, MA: Harvard University Press, 2018), 177.

12. Kevin M. Levin, *Searching for Black Confederates: The Civil War's Most Persistent Myth* (Chapel Hill: University of North Carolina Press, 2019), 57–60.

13. Keeanga-Yamahtta Taylor, *Race for Profit: How Banks and the Real Estate Industry Undermined Black Homeownership* (Chapel Hill: University of North Carolina Press, 2019), 152.

Critical Reading

In his book *Historical Thinking and Other Unnatural Acts*, Sam Wineburg describes the beginning of a history of religion course with Professor Jacob Neusner. "'What is the text doing,' [Neusner] asked about Genesis 1, as a hundred students or so collectively quaked in their seats. One after another, baffled freshmen summarized the text, only to have Neusner strike his fist on the podium: 'Doing, not saying. What is the text doing?'"[14] That distinction, between saying and doing, lies at the heart of critical reading. To read critically means to extract information actively from a text, rather than taking the author's own statements as the truth, the whole truth, and nothing but the truth. In some cases, it can mean doubting the factual accuracy of the author's statements. More commonly, it means asking what we can learn from the way the author selected and arranged facts the way they did.

To read critically is to seek information beyond what the creator of a source intended to convey. This is often easiest to explain with advertisements as an example. If one were to grow up in an industrialized country believing every claim made in advertisements for consumer goods, one would quickly go broke purchasing every bit of junk that promised clear skin, warm friendships, and the thrill of a lifetime. Instead, we learn at an early age that advertisers' claims must be read or viewed with skepticism, that the jacket will not look as good on us as it does on the model, and that the fancy sports car will go no faster than the rest of the traffic on the congested freeway. Historians learn to read every document with equal skepticism, teasing out meanings despite the best wishes of the source itself.

The amount of critical reading in a work of history varies greatly depending on the project. In practice, historians mostly read primary sources for the facts they contain, and they assemble stories from the patterns they find. But historians must always be alert to the possibility of extracting more information from a source than its creator wished to convey. For instance, Fredrik Logevall's *Embers of War: The Fall of an Empire and the Making of America's Vietnam*

14. Sam Wineburg, *Historical Thinking and Other Unnatural Acts: Charting the Future of Teaching the Past* (Philadelphia: Temple University Press, 2001), x.

is based largely on documents prepared by French and American military and civilian officials who were trying desperately to craft a more optimistic assessment of the situation in Southeast Asia than reality permitted. Logevall must therefore read almost everything critically. "Nixon's confident pronouncements masked deep private chagrin," he writes of one typical example. "There was candor here, but also a seeming unwillingness to face the obvious paradoxes."[15]

AGENDA

Neusner asked, "What is the text doing?" A more precise question is "What was the source's creator *trying* to do, that is, what is the source's agenda?" To answer that, we need to consider several smaller questions.

1. What is the question?

Let us postulate that every primary source is created to fill a specific need. What question was the author trying to answer; what problem were they trying to solve? Sometimes the author will tell you explicitly. A party platform is designed to win votes. An advertisement is designed to persuade someone to buy a product or service. In other cases, the historian may need to make educated guesses. When an immigrant wrote home to his family, was he trying to persuade them to come join him, or was he emphasizing the hardship of his new life?

A source need not be made of words to suggest a question. A landscape painter may ask, How does a railroad shape the American countryside? A census taker begins with a list of questions: How many people live in the household? What are their occupations? and so on. The historian can then ask, Why did the Census Bureau decide that those were the important questions rather than others?

2. Who is the audience?

Aside from the most intimate of diaries, most sources are created to inform or persuade someone other than the creator. Figuring out the intended audience can reveal much about both speaker

---

15. Fredrik Logevall, *Embers of War: The Fall of an Empire and the Making of America's Vietnam* (New York: Random House, 2012), 375–76.

and listener. For example, Larrie Ferreiro coyly, but persuasively, describes "a document addressed to King Louis XVI of France and King Carlos III of Spain," the two individuals whose support the Continental Congress most needed. "Neither Louis XVI nor Carlos III would openly take sides in a British civil war," Ferreiro elaborates, so the remaking of the United States as an independent nation "was in fact an engraved invitation to France and Spain asking them to go to war alongside the Americans." By presenting the Declaration of Independence in this unfamiliar way, he helps us understand how dependence on France and Spain helped lead Americans to declare independence from Great Britain.[16]

3. What is the answer?

Just as sources generally present some kind of question, they also present some kind of answer. Again, sometimes the source is explicit. A court decision or law is itself an answer to a question. Did John Scopes violate a Tennessee law against teaching "that man has descended from a lower order of animals"? Yes, he did (though the Supreme Court of Tennessee voided his fine). Likewise, whatever problem is posed by an advertisement—sick children, unrequited love, ring around the collar—the suggested answer is always the same: buy our product.

In other cases, the author may not have so precise an answer, but may only suggest a way of thought. A portrait, whether a painting or photograph, often suggests how the subject wishes to be perceived. He may not want the viewer to do anything specific but to think about him in a certain way. In the years after World War I, US Army Air Corps officers developed the doctrine of precision bombing with both the *explicit* agenda of national defense and the *implicit* agenda of justifying the establishment of an independent air force.[17]

---

16. Larrie D. Ferreiro, *Brothers at Arms: American Independence and the Men of France and Spain Who Saved It* (New York: Vintage, 2017), xvi.

17. Michael S. Sherry, *The Rise of American Air Power: The Creation of Armageddon* (New Haven, CT: Yale University Press, 1989), 50.

CREDIBILITY

The most critical of critical readings will show that a source says something that is factually inaccurate. Sometimes a historian simply wants to set the record straight. "Although colonial and antebellum southern newspapers are replete with advertisements for timepieces by 'Clock and Watch Makers,'" writes Mark Smith, "such pronouncements are grossly misleading." He compares the advertisements placed by such self-styled "watchmakers" with the surviving business records and finds them to have been occasionally involved in cleaning and repairing timepieces, but more likely to alter jewelry or repair an umbrella than actually make a watch.[18]

Historians sometimes point out inaccuracies to hold historical figures to account for their misdeeds. In other cases, the goal is not to condemn the creator of the source but to use the inaccuracies or fallacies to understand better that person's view of the world.

The source is lying

Some sources are outright mendacious. Richard White, for example, caught railroad magnates and their bankers telling investors that "the financial and business prospects of your Company were never brighter" even as they wrote to each other that they would soon be unable to make interest payments.[19]

The source makes unfounded claims

Arguing that a source lacks evidence for its claims is less contentious than charging it with outright falsehood or contradiction, but it can still be a useful track. Whitney Strub compares a claim in a congressional report that "the impulses which spur people to sex crimes unquestionably are intensified by reading and seeing pornographic materials" to a small-print footnote in the same report that concedes, "There are no studies of the relationship of pornographic

---

18. Mark M. Smith, *Mastered by the Clock: Time, Slavery, and Freedom in the American South* (Chapel Hill: University of North Carolina Press, 1997), 24–25.

19. Richard White, *Railroaded: The Transcontinentals and the Making of Modern America* (New York: W. W. Norton, 2011), 86.

literature to sexual offense."[20] Be careful not to read too much into a lack of evidence, and be sure to consider the genre of the source. A scientific paper published without citations is an oddity; a magazine article without footnotes is not. Similarly, if a writer is making arguments based on what they believe to be commonly accepted facts, it is not a surprise if they do not devote space to demonstrating the validity of those facts.

The source's evidence undercuts the source's claims

Some sources undercut their own claims. Cathleen Cahill quotes the memoirs of Corabelle Fellows, a federal agent on the Cut Meat Creek reservation. In her account, Fellows boasts that she civilized the Indians in her charge by planting a garden and teaching effectively. But Cahill points out that Fellows also threatened Indians with confinement in the guardhouse, suggesting that Fellows relied on "the threat of coercive power" more than persuasion. Thus, Cahill extracts from Fellows's memoir a message quite different from the one Fellows wished to convey.[21]

The source's logic contradicts itself, or at least reveals a tension

In other cases, the historian questions the source's logic, rather than its facts. "In keeping with the complicated relationship Silicon Valley had with the government that had helped create it," writes Margaret O'Mara of a 1982 report, "their language mixed celebrations of free enterprise with pleas for more aggressive state planning and subsidy. 'California shows that the spirit of risk-taking is alive and well in America,' the report proclaimed, and government 'must do whatever is necessary to guarantee that our cutting-edge industries—like semiconductors, computers, telecommunications, robotics, and biotechnology—retain their competitive lead.'"[22]

20. Whitney Strub, *Perversion for Profit: The Politics of Pornography and the Rise of the New Right* (New York: Columbia University Press, 2013), 27.

21. Cathleen D. Cahill, *Federal Fathers and Mothers: A Social History of the United States Indian Service, 1869–1933* (Chapel Hill: University of North Carolina Press, 2011), 76–78.

22. Margaret O'Mara, *The Code: Silicon Valley and the Remaking of America* (New York: Penguin, 2019), 214.

The source makes unwarranted assumptions

Be careful when charging a source with "bias," a slippery term, often hard to define. As Seán Lang has noted, "All sources have an in-built bias, some more marked than others, and some more obvious than others, but none are exempt from it."[23] Thus, arguing that a source is "biased" risks either saying nothing (since all sources have bias) or claiming too much (falsely implying that one particular source is biased while others are not). Also avoid using "biased" to describe any source with a strong opinion or argument. If the creator of the source based their arguments on a reasoned examination of the available evidence, that is a case of *findings*, not bias.

It may be more precise to delineate the *assumptions* underlying a particular claim. "Like many economic concepts," writes Katherine Benton-Cohen of a Progressive Era report, "the 'American standard of living' paradigm sounded scientific—it sounded like a real thing—but it was constructed out of opinion and assumption. It hid assumptions about women's and men's roles, housing choice, consumer culture, and morality and ethics. . . . Americanization reformers often targeted immigrant women, assuming that converting them to American ways would bring the rest of the family along with them."[24]

NUANCE

Even sources that are factually accurate and logically sound are worthy of exploration, for every person must make choices when presenting information or argument. Look for the following, and use them to understand the source's creator's views.

Some sources make surprising choices about what facts to present, and how to present them. As Alan Brinkley explains, the films produced by Henry Luce reveal as much about Luce and his values as they do about their nominal subjects.

> The films, like the magazines, had one cultural standard that they used
> consistently to interpret and explain events: the progressive outlook

23. Seán Lang, "What Is Bias?," *Teaching History*, no. 73 (1993): 13.
24. Benton-Cohen, *Inventing the Immigration Problem*, 127.

of the Anglo-American world, reflecting Luce's own consistent views. Almost everything carried in *The March of Time* either displayed that world or made invidious comparisons with it. One example was an otherwise pointless piece about Lake Tana in Ethiopia, the source of the Blue Nile. "High in the mountains of northeast Africa," the narration boomed over shots of the landscape, "fed in the rainy season by the drainage of a vast plateau, likes a lake seldom visited by white men but of vital importance to one great white nation." The importance of the lake, in short, was that it irrigated cotton fields that were important to the British textile industry.[25]

Pay special attention to the metaphors used, since they can reveal assumptions and beliefs. As Marilynn Johnson observes, when people describe other people as animals, it reveals the depths of their contempt. "In highlighting the animal-like traits of policemen—most of whom came from working-class backgrounds—elite critics drew on popular ethnic and class stereotypes of lower-class people as bestial and subhuman," she writes. "These derogatory characterizations would persist into the late twentieth century, with middle-class radicals of the 1960s casting police as 'pigs' and 'brutes.'"[26]

Also pay attention when a source makes concessions to an opponent's view or acknowledges failure. Alan Taylor notes that in 1814, Major General Jacob Brown "vowed that his troops would fight to 'gain a name in arms worthy of our selves or the gallant nation in whose name we fight.'" Taylor reads this critically to suggest that Brown had, by this point, abandoned hope of conquering Canada, and instead simply hoped to restore the military honor of the United States.[27] On the surface, Brown is calling on his troops to fight hard. But Taylor reads between the lines to see that by this point, Brown has already abandoned hope of his army's initial objective.

25. Alan Brinkley, *The Publisher: Henry Luce and His American Century* (New York: Vintage, 2011), 186.

26. Marilynn S. Johnson, *Street Justice: A History of Police Violence in New York City* (Boston: Beacon Press, 2004), 37.

27. Alan Taylor, *The Civil War of 1812: American Citizens, British Subjects, Irish Rebels, & Indian Allies* (New York: Knopf, 2010), 382.

CONTEXT

People create sources in conversation with other people. Sometimes this is literally true; a letter or email is as much an element in conversation as a sentence uttered in a face-to-face discussion. At other times, "in conversation" is more of a metaphor, as when a diarist reacts privately to a book whose author they will never meet. In between are cases where a variety of actors state their views, perhaps, but do not necessarily listen to one another. How does a given source fit in that conversation?

By reading multiple sources, a historian can understand an event better than did the participants at the time. In 1911, for instance, the Smoke Abatement League of Cincinnati sent questionnaires to countries around the world, hoping that each might have some wisdom to share. The German consulate in Cincinnati, however, did not realize that so many countries had received the questionnaire, and took it as evidence that "the Americans regard Germany as a model country in matters of urban order and administration." Only by juxtaposing the Smoke Abatement League's report and the German consulate's correspondence could Frank Uekötter expose the somewhat comical miscommunication.[28]

In other cases, historians must use their knowledge of a longer history to explain the significance of a source. For instance, Thomas Sugrue and John Skrentny explain the words of Barbara Mikulski and other angry "white ethnics" of the early 1970s by comparing them to those of black power advocates of the same era. "A history of group oppression, of shared suffering," they write of the newly self-identified white ethnics, "would allow them to gain political recognition on the same terms then enjoyed by blacks—as well as a widening circle of other aggrieved minorities, including Latinos, American Indians, and Asian Americans."[29] The ability to craft such analyses depends on a reasonably wide knowledge of the

28. Frank Uekötter, *The Age of Smoke: Environmental Policy in Germany and the United States, 1880–1970*, trans. Thomas Dunlap (Pittsburgh: University of Pittsburgh Press, 2009), 65.

29. Thomas J. Sugrue and John D. Skrentny, "The White Ethnic Strategy," in *Rightward Bound: Making America Conservative in the 1970s*, ed. Bruce J. Schulman and Julian E. Zelizer (Cambridge, MA: Harvard University Press), 178.

period one is studying. This is why it can be silly to debate whether history education should focus on facts or skills; real historical understanding requires both.

CHANGE

As noted earlier, history has been defined as "the analysis of change over time."[30] Accordingly, historians seek sources that document this change. Some sources boldly announce changes. Revolutionaries proclaim new orders, legislatures pass laws, baseball teams trade players. Since reporters and editors are always eager for news, periodical literature is particularly good at noticing—and often exaggerating—such changes. But historians are equally eager to find hints of subtler changes, to watch as concessions, doubts, and new perspectives creep into the record before the change blossoms for all to see.

One of the joys of archival research is that it is sometimes possible to track such subtle change over time by comparing multiple versions of the same document. For instance, Steven Gillon read the official records of the Kerner Commission, as well as the papers of several members of the commission and its staff, to reconstruct the process and debates that led up to its famous 1968 report. Those drafts reveal the paths not taken—which findings and proposals were rejected as too radical, too conservative, or too distracting from the commission's central concern—in a way that the final report alone does not.[31] In *Downtown America*, Alison Isenberg compares the photographs that towns and cities sent to the Curt Teich postcard company with the finished postcards the company printed. "With tiny paint brushes," she finds, "artists touched up photographs to repair broken-down sidewalks, to remove offending utility poles or signs, and to pave streets—improving the streets' physical realities." These comparisons allow her to deduce what urban boosters considered ugly and what they considered beautiful,

30. Social Science Research Council, Committee on Historiography, *The Social Sciences in Historical Study: A Report* (New York: Social Science Research Council, 1954), 24.

31. Steven M. Gillon, *Separate and Unequal: The Kerner Commission and the Unraveling of American Liberalism* (New York: Basic Books, 2018).

in a way that neither the source photograph nor the finished post-card alone could indicate.[32]

Some sources hide change, trying to slip in something new so quietly that no one notices. Thus, Peter Bacon Hales notes that "ideology of technological progress upon which the [Manhattan Engineering] District based its programs posed a rosy future in which engineers and scientists would render neutral, or reclaim to benevolent use, the toxins of atomic bomb production. This had been an assumption from the beginning." By 1946, however, "District officials confessed that the materials 'cannot be disposed of by ordinary means.'" Rather than address the implications of this change, district officials kept assuming that a method to dispose of radioactive waste safely was bound to emerge.[33] At other times, the real story is an *absence* of change. As Manning Marable explains, the title of Malcolm X's famous speech, "The Ballot or the Bullet," may have "seemed incendiary," but "at its core the speech actually contained a far more conventional message, one that had defined the civil rights movement as far back as 1962: the importance of voting rights."[34]

Causation

As historians map patterns and read critically to extract information from sources, they work to answer the *why* questions that are driving their projects. Ultimately, that requires them to make claims about motive, causation, and influence that leave behind the realm of demonstrable fact and enter the realm of inference and interpretation. It is a big leap, but one that many historians make quietly, unencumbered by the theoretical apparatus borne by scholars in other disciplines. Observing historians at work, anthropologist Bernard Cohn surmised that "a historian starts with a model of

32. Alison Isenberg, *Downtown America: A History of the Place and the People Who Made It* (Chicago: University of Chicago Press, 2005), 43. The electronic edition of Joshua Brown, *Beyond the Lines: Pictorial Reporting, Everyday Life, and the Crisis of Gilded-Age America* (Berkeley: University of California Press, 2013) similarly compares preliminary sketches and final published versions of news engravings.

33. Peter Bacon Hales, *Atomic Spaces: Living on the Manhattan Project* (Champaign: University of Illinois Press, 1999), 140.

34. Manning Marable, *Malcolm X: A Life of Reinvention* (New York: Viking, 2011), 302.

what cultures and societies are and how they work. He continually fits his facts into this model, even though at a common-sense level," in contrast to the anthropologist who "tries to be as explicit as possible about what the model is."[35] David Hackett Fischer laments "the unfortunate tendency of historians to hide their causal models from everybody—including themselves."[36]

As Fischer notes in his chapter on "fallacies of causation," we can at least try to avoid some of the worst mistakes in attributing causation.[37] Two strike me as particularly noteworthy. The first is the assumption of causation based on simple chronology. Often known by its Latin form, *post hoc ergo propter hoc* (after this, therefore because of this), this fallacy suggests that if one event followed another, the earlier event caused the latter. For instance, many prominent figures have asserted that Nick Ut's June 1972 photograph of a nine-year-old girl wounded by napalm hastened the end of the war in Vietnam. As Joseph Campbell has shown, however, the United States had begun drawing down its troops in Vietnam years before the photograph was taken, and the fighting in the country continued for years afterward. He finds no evidence that the photograph was particularly influential in changing opinion or policy about the war.[38]

The other common error is to identify a single factor and seize on it as the *only* factor causing an event. If you look for communist influence on the New Deal, you will indeed find it. But if you keep looking for policies in other countries adapted by the New Dealers, you will end up with a list ranging from old-age pensions in New Zealand to cooperative creameries in Ireland.[39] Serious historians trace back all the branches of the family tree. Only after having considered all factors do they make claims about which factors mattered the most.

35. Bernard S. Cohn, *An Anthropologist among the Historians and Other Essays* (New York: Oxford University Press, 1987), 7.

36. David Hackett Fischer, *Historians' Fallacies* (New York: Harper Torchbooks, 1970), 186.

37. Fischer, *Historians' Fallacies*, chapter 6.

38. W. Joseph Campbell, *Getting It Wrong: Debunking the Greatest Myths in American Journalism*, 2nd ed. (Oakland: University of California Press, 2016), chapter 8.

39. Daniel T. Rodgers, *Atlantic Crossings: Social Politics in a Progressive Age* (Cambridge, MA: Harvard University Press, 1998), 55, 333.

Rather than relying on explicit models, historians generally offer a *plausible* account of why people acted as they did. "Narrative can satisfy most of the time," writes philosopher David Carr, "as long as we do not expect too much of it. The satisfaction we normally feel with a narrative explanation should not be taken at face value, nor should it close off further inquiry. But there is no reason why we should not take it for what it is, a valuable and useful implement for understanding human action."[40]

40. David Carr, "Narrative Explanation and Its Malcontents," *History and Theory* 47 (2008), 30.

PART IV

Projects

{⚜}

YOU HAVE FORMED a question and identified the sources you will use to answer that question. You have a plan. Now you must execute.

There is no one right way to do this. In *Star Wars* canon, every Jedi youngling must gather their own kyber crystal and build their own lightsaber.[1] Similarly, every historian must design their own research tools, since what works for one may fail another. Indeed, a system that works for one project may not work for the next, so historians often tinker with their methods and swap ideas. That said, historians have some common goals, and some tools and techniques have proven their worth for a great many researchers.

1. "Jedi Youngling," Wookieepedia, https://starwars.fandom.com/wiki/Jedi_youngling.

CHAPTER ELEVEN

Project Management

A RESEARCH PROJECT, whatever its scale, is an enterprise. A project undertaken by a paying client, or funded by a specific grant, may require some of the attributes of a business, or a vast public works project, with lines of authority and designated work roles for multiple people, plus specific schedules, budgets, and financial reports. A student term paper may lack those obvious project management features, but it too requires a deliverable by a specific deadline. Either way, research requires some project management, and it can help to make that explicit.

Tips

- Paying attention to your own work rhythms can help you stay productive.
- No one computer system is best for everyone, but every computer user needs to back up their data.
- Word count is your friend.

Goals of Project Management

While all historians must find their own ways of managing a project, keep in mind some functions that any system should perform.

AVOID CATASTROPHE

As discussed in greater detail below, the most likely catastrophe to befall a research project is the loss of electronic data, through the failure of hardware or software; the disappearance of a computer or drive due to theft, fire, or flood; or your own human error. Plan from the start to avoid this, preferably with online backup, though an external hard drive backup can also be helpful. A second type of disaster is faulty note-taking, which can result in inaccuracy or plagiarism. Consider both your note-taking system and any work with research assistants, to be sure that you and they fully attribute all the material you gather. Finally, guard against embarrassing misunderstanding by planning to have peers check your work at some point. If you can conceive of other disasters, guard against those as well. In other words, imagine the worst thing that could happen to your project, and take measures to prevent that outcome.

COMPLETE TASKS—IDEALLY JUST ONCE, AND IN THE RIGHT ORDER

In an ideal world, you would enter the supermarket with a list of everything you need, organized by aisle. You could start at the entrance and work your way up one aisle and down the next, never navigating the same aisle twice. An ideal research plan would work the same way. You would visit each source, each library, and each city only once and get what you needed, no less and no more.

In practice, supermarkets are deliberately designed to tempt us to linger and purchase items we had not considered in advance.[1] And the act of shopping itself may change our desires; the sight of tortilla chips in the snacks aisle may send us back to the produce aisle in search of avocados. Similarly, it would take heroic research skills never to return to the same source, either because you missed something on the first pass, or because you got everything you could get but did not realize it. However, a good project

---

1. Rebecca Rupp, "Surviving the Sneaky Psychology of Supermarkets," *National Geographic*, June 14, 2015, https://www.nationalgeographic.com/people-and-culture/food/the-plate/2015/06/15/surviving-the-sneaky-psychology-of-supermarkets/.

management plan will reduce the frequency of such wasted efforts, while also ensuring that you pick up the milk and other staples you wanted at the start. If your project will rely on some sources in a particularly distant place, a solid plan is all the more important.

It is also worth pondering the order in which you need to complete the various tasks. To extend the supermarket analogy a bit, you likely want to buy ice cream last, minimizing the time it spends between the grocer's freezer and your own. The same logic applies to historical research. For instance, you might delay doing oral histories until you have done enough background research to ask informed questions. But you should probably not leave them until the end, since a narrator might give you insight into the sources you have located, or point you to sources you had not known to look for. Written sources can behave the same way. If you are writing about a topic that was covered, however ineptly, by the newspapers, it may make sense to read through them for major dates and controversies before hitting the archives to discover the stories behind those controversies.

Historians writing narratives often like to write from start to finish, which helps put them in the mind-set of actors who do not know what is coming next. But this is not always possible. Perhaps the sources you need for chapter 3 are in a distant city that you cannot visit until you get more funding, but sources for chapter 4 are right at hand. Write chapter 4 while waiting for the grant. Or maybe your sources inform multiple chapters, so that rather than writing one chapter at a time, you are applying layers of sources, one coat after another, over the entire project.

MAINTAIN MOMENTUM

Researchers must take breaks, if only to sleep. In addition, other tasks impose longer interruptions, making it hard to resume where you left off. Find ways to remind yourself where you were before the interruption. This can be as simple as a comment in a working draft or a paper note left on a desk, or more elaborate, such as a research diary or time-stamped database that can show you what you were working on before you had to stop.

Writing history can be fun, but it can also be terrifying. You may invest months or years of your life in the uncertain hope that strangers will like what you write. Some days you may think your topic is so unimportant that no one will care, and on other days you will think it is so good that if someone else has not published the definitive study, it is because they are about to. Breaking down a big project into smaller tasks can make it easier to manage these moments of panic or despair. Your project management system may remind you that today's job is not to fret over the project as a whole but just to read the contents of three archival boxes and write five hundred words. If one kind of task gets too tedious, it can point you to something else to work on, then guide you back to the previous task when you have had that break.

Tools of the Trade

European artists traditionally depicted Clio, the muse of history, with a stylus, a tablet, and a trumpet, the last of which would proclaim the fame of the heroes in Clio's tales. Today's historians are less likely to carry trumpets, but they still rely on some version of the stylus and tablet.

HARDWARE

Into the twenty-first century, some historians prefer pen and paper, both for taking notes and writing drafts. While some are writers who came of age before the diffusion of personal computers, even those adept with digital methods find that writing on paper can help them get through writer's block. Then, when they type up notes or drafts, they have the chance to revise.[2] In addition to possibly aiding deliberate thought, practice in writing cursive has the added benefit of improving one's ability to read handwritten documents.[3]

Most current historians, I would wager, use a computer at least some of the time. Since they often work in libraries and archives, something portable is helpful: either a laptop or perhaps a tablet

---

2. Jessica Otis, email to author, January 15, 2020.

3. If your penmanship needs improvement, I recommend Barbara Getty and Inga Dubay, *Write Now: The Complete Program for Better Handwriting* (Salt Lake City, UT: Continuing Education Press, 2005).

with a keyboard. Along with that basic machine, a few other bits of hardware are particularly handy.

Backup

Computers are vulnerable to multiple types of failure: file corruption, mechanical failure, fires, floods, and theft. If you are working on a project for long enough, expect to suffer some kind of failure. Just days after I completed a first draft of my dissertation, I woke up to find that my laptop would not boot. I used another computer to check my backup drive and found that the latest backup had finished at 3:00 a.m. that morning; I had lost exactly zero bytes of work. I got a new hard drive for the laptop (still under warranty), restored from the backup, and was back in business. I would have lost more work had my apartment burned with both the laptop and backup drive in it; at the time, my only offsite backup was the series of CD-ROM discs I sent every month or so to a friend in Vermont. These days, you can back up overnight to an internet service, which can protect you even if you lose your entire home. Armed robbers attacked one of my graduate students, taking his laptop with his dissertation and all his notes. The student, however, was unharmed, as he had had the foresight to back up all his files to the cloud. He lost at most a few hours of work, and five months later, he defended his dissertation. For long-term backup, consider M-Discs, the data equivalent of a Blu-ray disc. They do not require annual subscriptions, they do not rely on magnetic particles or moving parts, and they may last up to one thousand years.[4]

Smartphone

By 2020, more than 80 percent of American adults owned smartphones, with even higher percentages in some other countries. The right apps can make a smartphone a powerful tool for historical research, beyond the photographing of archival documents mentioned earlier. First, get a scanner app to capture documents. This can be as useful in an ordinary library as in an archive. If you just need a few pages from a book or article, you do not need to check

---

4. John L. Jacobi, "M-Disc Optical Media Reviewed: Your Data, Good for a Thousand Years," *PC World*, August 2015.

out the book, or even walk it over to a photocopier; you can capture the pages right there. (If you do this, do not reshelve the book. By leaving it on a reshelving cart, you are helping the librarians show that the book has been used, thus justifying future purchases.) Some scanner apps create PDFs with the images of the documents, while others perform optical character recognition (OCR) to convert printed materials into editable text. This is great when you want to capture a paragraph or two, but it tends not to work as well with tightly bound paperbacks. Second, foreign-language dictionaries are obviously helpful, though you may need a historical dictionary more specialized than the versions available for smartphones. An expense tracker can be useful for reimbursements or tax deductions for research trips and other expenses. If you only occasionally record interviews, the voice recorder app on a phone may suffice, though dedicated oral historians will likely prefer something fancier.

USB flash drive

Get a big one. Libraries often have public terminals that allow you to download material, including material in databases to which you might not otherwise have access. In addition, microfilm readers and book scanners may allow you to store scans onto a flash drive. But do not count on a flash drive for long-term storage; it is too easily lost or damaged. Transfer files as often as you can, preferably at least once per day.

Monitor

One of the challenges of the shift from paper to digital research has been the revolution in format. For centuries, people have been writing and printing documents that are in "portrait" orientation, that is, taller than they are wide.[5] Yet most computer monitors are set up in "landscape" orientation, wider than they are tall. This can make it hard to see a whole page at once, whether that page is a photograph of a centuries-old letter or the PDF of a journal article that has yet to be published. To avoid scrolling down to see the bottom

5. "Magna Carta 1215," British Library, https://www.bl.uk/collection-items/magna
-carta-1215.

half of each of the thousands or tens of thousands of pages you will likely read in the course of a project, it helps to have a monitor that can display at least 1440 pixels from top to bottom. This could be a twenty-four-inch monitor that rotates; you will see these attached to microfilm readers. Or it could be a twenty-seven-inch monitor that has 1440 pixels on its shorter side; this has the advantage of letting you see two or three full pages side by side, depending on your preferences. The best of both worlds is a twenty-seven-inch monitor that rotates into portrait mode; these can be particularly helpful if you end up with a lot of PDFs or photographs of newspapers, printed in long, narrow columns in small type. While such monitors do represent a significant investment, they can run for years and do not become obsolete as quickly as other computer technology— though you may need to buy new cables or adaptors if you switch to a new computer. Also, a good monitor reduces the need to print and eases strain on the eyes, shoulders, and back.

KINDS OF SOFTWARE

Historians, like people in a wide array of pursuits, face a range of software choices. To start with, software emerges from multiple business models, each of which has its own pros and cons for users. Major brands, such as Microsoft and Adobe, have been around for years or decades. You can expect to find many other people running their software and able to open files generated on it. On the other hand, these firms tend to update their products frequently, often insisting on expensive upgrade fees or subscriptions for new releases whose added features slow the operations while serving few users. If you only need a particular product occasionally, it may make more sense to purchase a cheaper competitor. For instance, while Adobe so dominates photo editing that "Photoshop" risks becoming a generic verb, other companies offer photo-editing products that do most of the work of Photoshop for less money.

Some commercial products are free, at least for a while. Google offers Google Docs, Google Sheets, and Google Slides as part of its Google Drive service, which is free to use for storage up to 15 gigabytes. Note, however, that companies may grow tired of giving away free services. Google killed the popular Google

Reader in 2013. Evernote, which once allowed free, unlimited syncing across devices, started charging for that feature in 2016, leading millions of users to seek alternatives. Two years later, Flickr did something similar, cutting free storage from one terabyte to one thousand photos. Of course, even paid software can disappear. Many lawyers still mourn the demise of WordPerfect as a standard word processor.

Other software emerges from nonprofit ventures, who release products that are free to use, and often to modify. Such "open source" software has the advantage of community support. Lots of people may adopt it quickly, making it likely that someone will write updates, and others will volunteer to help out with tech support. However, open source software may be less polished, or less powerful, than commercial versions.

WORD PROCESSORS

In the 1990s, Microsoft Word beat out WordPerfect to become the dominant word processor. The word processors offered by Apple, Google, and OpenOffice are largely similar in function, and they can swap files with Word.[6] Many universities provide Word for their faculty and students, and journals and publishers expect submissions in Word-compatible formats. Moreover, Microsoft Word works well with Zotero and other reference managers (described below). It is therefore worth learning to use Word or something like it, including some mildly advanced features, like the navigation pane.

That said, Word has its limits. It bogs down with long files, and its many icons and buttons and ribbons can be a distracting clutter. Some historians prefer more minimalist editors, particularly for short projects. If you are writing a blog, it is probably worth learning an application that handles Markdown, a syntax that is easy to learn and to export to HTML, the syntax used by blogs and websites. Some historians have used it for lecture notes, CVs, and

---

6. Tony Lystra, "The New Word Processor Wars: A Fresh Crop of Productivity Apps Are Trying to Reinvent Our Workday," *GeekWire*, December 2, 2018, https://www.geekwire.com /2018/new-word-processor-wars-fresh-crop-productivity-apps-trying-reinvent-workday/.

other purposes as well.[7] The LaTeX system allows exact control over typesetting, image placement, and other visual features.[8]

This book was written in Scrivener, a word processor specifically designed for long texts. As developer Keith Blount has explained, the software allows users to "split up a long manuscript into smaller sections, and to view each chunk in isolation or together with the other sections as part of the whole."[9] Though Blount created Scrivener to help him write a novel, that ability to navigate immediately to whatever section of the text you are working on, without opening or closing any files, can be of enormous help to historians. Scrivener is particularly helpful for revision. By dragging icons up or down on the outline, I can reorder sections of the text. It is also easy to split a section that has grown too long, or to merge two sections that belong together. Or to drag a section to an "outtakes" folder, from which it can be quickly retrieved if I change my mind. As political scientist Alexandra Samuel explains, whereas "Word is fundamentally a tool designed to facilitate . . . modest changes," Scrivener "encourages writers to slice their work up into the smallest viable units: not just chapters or even sections, but individual scenes, quotes or arguments. . . . It's much easier to undertake ambitious restructuring—not just technically easier, but conceptually easier, because you can see the parts that make up the whole."[10] And Scrivener is wonderful for writers who rely on word counts to measure their productivity and to make sure they are allocating the right amount of attention to each topic. It is easy to see how long a section, a chapter, or a whole manuscript has grown, and Scrivener even tracks how many words you have written each day.

7. Ben Schmidt, "Markdown, Historical Writing, and Killer Apps," *Ben Schmidt* (blog), September 5, 2014, https://benschmidt.org/2014/09/05/markdown-historical-writing-and-killer-apps/.

8. rjgunning, "Three Ways Historians Can Use LaTeX—HTTP," *History to the Public* (blog), June 22, 2015, http://historytothepublic.org/three-ways-historians-can-use-latex/.

9. Francesco Cordella, "Scrivener and Me," *L'avventura è l'avventura* (blog), May 2013, https://web.archive.org/web/20140427081859/http://www.avventuretestuali.com/interviste/keith-blount-english/.

10. Alexandra Samuel, "Better Writing Begins with the Right Tools," *JSTOR Daily*, January 9, 2018, https://daily.jstor.org/better-writing-begins-with-the-right-tools/.

MEANS OF ENTRY

Most historians of the twenty-first century can expect to do a lot of typing, but it is worth knowing about some alternatives to typing every letter. Word processors and other software may have built-in auto-correct or auto-completion functions, allowing you to type an abbreviation and have it expand to a longer word. Better still are software utilities—known as text expanders—that allow you to use the same abbreviations across applications. For instance, "Cadwalader" is one of the major characters in my story, whose name (and the name of a street named for his family) appears hundreds of times in my manuscript and thousands of times in my notes. Not wanting to type that out every time, I set up my shorthand application so that every time I type the letters "cadw," followed by a space or punctuation mark, in any application, it is replaced by the name. This saved me many thousands of keystrokes, as well as preventing misspellings. Text expanders can also be useful for tasks like date-stamping records (three letters gets you today's date in the format of your choice), avoiding typos (if I type "aiport" I get "airport"), and even storing longer phrases, like the title of your work in progress.

A second alternative is to skip the keyboard by using OCR. Sources published in recent decades are increasingly likely to be available in full-text digital form, allowing for copying and pasting into your own notes. (The relationship between age and this kind of access is not guaranteed. One can copy and paste from digitized versions of George Washington's correspondence but not from some twenty-first-century e-books.) Be warned that in some cases, the pasted text will need cleaning up. Texts from Google Books, for instance, lack punctuation, while the same text on another platform, such as HathiTrust, may be cleaner. You can also make your own editable digital versions of printed or typewritten sources using optical character recognition (OCR) software.

OCR can take place at several stages. Some smartphone apps convert the pictures you take of books or documents into text, which you can then transfer to a computer. I find this particularly useful for library books. If I see a passage longer than a couple of sentences, I snap the picture with the OCR app, send the text to my laptop, and paste it into my note-taking database.[11] For larger-scale conversion, note that some cloud storage systems, such as Google Drive, will automatically recognize text in the documents you place there, even if you upload tens of thousands of documents, allowing you to search later. This can be helpful for photographs you take in the archives or screenshots you take of published sources. Both of these options may be free.

Desktop OCR applications can cost up to a hundred dollars, but these applications may have more powerful features, such as correcting for skewing if you took the picture at an angle, or recognizing only parts of an image, which is quite useful if you are photographing newspaper or other texts set in columns. Even if you have to pay, OCR software offers tremendous return on investment if it saves you the effort of typing long passages from PDFs, screenshots, or digital photographs. Still, because OCR remains imperfect, it is important to check over every quotation to avoid embarrassing errors. One scan I made of a newspaper article rendered "Christian love" as "Christian Jove," a nonsensical phrase that a colleague flagged before too many people had seen it. (Thanks, Lincoln.)

A final method of text entry is dictation software, which can be indispensable for historians who cannot type, and useful even for those who can. For instance, if I have written notes in the margins of a book I own, I find it is sometimes easier to hold the book in my hands while I read the notes into the computer, rather than try to hold the book open with a weight to free my hands for typing. That said, I have found dictation software to be the most error-ridden of any entry method I have used, so I must carefully proofread any dictated text before using it in a draft.

Productivity

Various scholars have recommended schemes for making progress even when challenged by other responsibilities and distractions. Some set aside an hour each morning to write; others one day of the

11. See Heather Ann Thompson, "The Writer's Studio with Heather Ann Thompson," *Modern American History* 2 (2019): 82.

week. Others care less about how many hours they put in than how many words they get out. If they hit their quota, they can knock off for the day. My colleague Peter Stearns, who kept cranking out books while serving as a provost of a large research university, took advantage of short gaps between meetings. If he had fifteen minutes, he tells me, he could write a page. (The same advice—to learn to write in fifteen-minute increments—is sometimes given to new parents.) Others go long stretches without writing, then write in bursts. "Productivity," writes Helen Sword, "is a broad church that tolerates many creeds."[12]

A GOOD DAY'S WORK

Rather than advocate for any particular scheme, I would merely encourage researchers to pay some attention to what counts as a good day's work, and what circumstances allow them to achieve that.

Gathering information

Historians are mostly filter feeders, taking in vast volumes of primary sources in order to extract a tiny bit of nourishment from each. Part of the work is swimming through the oceans, coating your baleen with plankton. In some cases, you can measure progress fairly easily. If you have five working days in an out-of-town archive, and you have identified forty boxes that you want to explore, then getting through ten of them on your first day is a good day's work. With luck, you will finish that last box early on the afternoon on your last day and have an hour or two to congratulate yourself on finishing the task. For other forms of gathering, progress can be illusory. It is easy to spend a lot of time checking books out of a library or downloading articles from a database, but if you do not get around to reading them, you are not advancing your project.[13]

12. Helen Sword, "'Write Every Day!' A Mantra Dismantled," *International Journal for Academic Development* 21 (October 2016): 312–22.

13. Umberto Eco, *How to Write a Thesis* (1977; repr., Cambridge, MA: MIT Press, 2015), 125.

Taking notes

Chapter 12 will offer more detailed guidance on note-taking, but expect to spend a fair amount of time at this task. Here, too, you can set goals for yourself. Today I will read such-and-such book that I checked out of the library, or read the five of the forty boxes I so smugly photographed on that research trip in the previous paragraph. If you are lucky, this process will add some words to your working draft, but you cannot always count on that. Background reading in secondary sources, in particular, may require many hours but produce relatively few words, if your goal is a paper based mostly on primary sources.

Writing words

In 2013, Princeton historian Anthony Grafton boasted of writing "about 3,500 words per morning, four mornings a week."[14] L. D. Burnett realized she could not possibly match that output, but she could set a daily goal for herself, a more manageable 555 words a day.[15] That seems to be about right for most historians not named Anthony Grafton, and historians' Twitter feeds often include expressions of satisfaction with a 500-word day. At that rate, it takes only twenty good days to draft a 10,000-word seminar paper or article, or two hundred good days to draft a 100,000-word book or dissertation. Few days are as satisfying as a good writing day, and I encourage you to try tracking how many words you write each day. If you are feeling especially good, try boasting about the results on social media.

Not every day of work can be such a good writing day, since historical research takes many steps. For instance, you might spend a day reading an important secondary source and write no words of your own. Conversely, you might have a truly exceptional day, on which, after long preparation, you write thousands of words. David Maraniss, for instance, endured a cold winter in Green Bay, Wisconsin, getting a sense of the place and its weather. After that, he

14. Noah Charney, "Anthony Grafton: How I Write," *Daily Beast*, July 17, 2013.

15. L. D. Burnett, "The Grafton Line," *Saved by History* (blog), July 21, 2013, http:// savedbyhistory.blogspot.com/2013/07/the-grafton-line.html.

was able to draft an entire chapter on the 1967 NFL Championship in a single day, writing from 6:00 a.m. until midnight.[16]

Solving problems

Sometimes you will be plugging along, on track to write five hundred, maybe a thousand words that day, when you come across something you do not understand: an unfamiliar name that sounds important, a lawsuit whose outcome you do not know, or a whole group of people whose social status you would like to analyze. If you want to keep up the momentum, just drop a note to your future self: Who is this guy? How did this turn out? and so on. Later, you may need to consider it a good day if you spend the whole day just writing that one sentence that answers the query.

This last point is a reminder that one of the pleasures of historical research is its variety. Some days you may feel like writing, but other days you may not. Some days you may get tired at looking at a computer screen and prefer to read a physical book, or print out a draft and revise it. While the best good days are the ones that substantially add words to your project, some days you may not have the time, energy, or mood for that, and instead work on another stage of research. Give yourself credit for those good-enough days.

Not writing

You may have some days when you are simply not in the mood to read or write. You can still be productive by cleaning up footnotes, or perhaps rethinking information by making a map or a table. But beware of allowing too many days like this. Strive for relentless forward motion.

WORD COUNT IS YOUR FRIEND

Every historian has their own preferred methods, and for the most part I have tried to write this guide to present ideas and options, not to prescribe specific choices. Here I will make an exception and urge you to pay attention to word count at every stage of the process.

---

16. David Maraniss, *Into the Story: A Writer's Journey through Life, Politics, Sports and Loss* (New York: Simon & Schuster, 2010), xvii.

Your editor cares

Even if you do not care about word count, someone else will. Whether it is a professor with a lot of papers to read, a newspaper opinion editor with only so much space on the op-ed page, a museum director who knows precisely how many words a visitor will read before moving on, or a book publisher with a budget for paper, printing, and shipping, you will encounter someone who will be grateful if you can stick to agreed-upon limits—and be miffed if you cannot. The one partial exception is scholarly journals, which have a bad habit of announcing a maximum length for manuscripts that is shorter than anything they actually publish.

A feeling of progress

Lynn Hunt tells the story of her grandmother, a gardener. "Every day in the summer she would call my mother and inform her of the number of radishes in her garden at that moment, a number that grew steadily over time until the end of the season," writes Hunt. "You want the number of your pages to increase steadily over time, culminating in the completion of a first draft."[17] Robert Caro keeps a chart of his progress, measured in words, on a closet door.[18] Ten thousand words or 100,000 words may be too many to contemplate. But if you can write 500 in a day, you will reach those milestones.

Relative weight

Perhaps most importantly, word count reflects your priorities. Reviewing a new biography of Napoleon, Ferdinand Mount writes that author Adam Zamoyski "gives more space to Napoleon's formative years than to his time in power, and much less to his military campaigns than other biographers have. Blink and you miss the battle of Jena, Wagram is over before you know it, and even Waterloo is done within a couple of pages."[19] By taking words away from battles and devoting them instead to his subject's youth, Zamoyski argues for the relative importance of the latter to understanding

---

17. Lynn Hunt, "How Writing Leads to Thinking," *Perspectives on History*, February 2010.

18. Robert A. Caro, *Working* (New York: Knopf, 2019), xi.

19. Ferdinand Mount, "An Ordinary Man," *New York Review of Books*, April 4, 2019.

Napoleon. Similarly, every time you use more words to tell one story and fewer words to tell another, you are implicitly arguing that the first story is more important. Devote words to topics that you think matter more; trim them from those that matter less.

MANAGING RESEARCH ASSISTANTS

Given the massive amount of effort taken to gather and synthesize material, historians can be tempted, if they have the opportunity, to hire research assistants. But it is not easy to delegate research tasks. "I don't care how good they are," Eugene Genovese once exclaimed. "I would never trust anybody to do my research. Even the very best assistant can't read the stuff through your eyes. You can't trust it." Instead, he used assistants to check his drafts against the original sources, making sure that he had not only correctly quoted them, but that he had also provided the needed context.[20] Some historians ask research assistants to assemble secondary readings on particular topics. They might deliver a few articles or book chapters, as well as brief summaries, but it would be up to the author to craft the paragraphs synthesizing the findings. If a research assistant is making decisions about the relevance of sources, finding new primary materials, or developing interpretations, it may be worth considering whether they should be listed as a coauthor.

When hiring a research assistant, be as clear as you can about deadlines and deliverables. If you can, start by giving the assistant a relatively small task. Depending on how well they manage that, they may be able to handle more or less responsibility.

RESEARCH DIARY

Many historians keep a "research diary," in which they record the progress of their work. Such a diary can be a stand-alone document, either electronic or paper, or you can integrate it into a note-taking

---

20. Judith Lee Hallock, John C. Waugh, and Drake Bush, *How Historians Work: Retelling the Past—From the Civil War to the Wider World* (Buffalo Gap, TX: State House Press, 2010), 238.

database, making it one of the sources on which you take notes. Whatever its form, such a diary can fulfill several functions.

Tasks

Most scholars probably have the experience of downloading the same article repeatedly, or despairing that another patron has the library book they want, only to find that it is charged to their own account. It may be too much to hope to avoid such duplication entirely, but one can at least try to track one's progress through the sources, to avoid both duplication of effort (reading the same source twice) and oversight (reading it not at all). Lists of tasks are especially helpful if you are working in fits and starts, returning to research after attending to other duties. If you have been working on one kind of task to the point of boredom, see what else you could be doing and still make progress. Whether you list your tasks on paper or electronically, leave room not only for a box to check when a task is completed but also for the date on which you completed it. It can be most satisfying to look back on such lists when all the boxes are checked.

Ideas

The purpose of historical research is to find answers to questions— the more surprising the better. If nothing you find in your research surprises you, you are probably doing it wrong. Conversely, if something does surprise you, it is worth recording that surprise. As you share your findings in conversations and in print, you will want to explain how your research brought you a better understanding of your topic, to tell a story of discovery. A research diary recording your intellectual journey is a great source for such a tale.

Progress

Historical research can be a long, slow trip toward a destination that never seems to get nearer. Rather than staring at the always-distant horizon, it can be comforting, from time to time, to turn around and see how far you have come. A research diary listing the books you have read, the sources you have found and uncovered, and the words you have written can reassure you that you are making progress.

Some historians share their progress. As doctoral students, Natalia Mehlman Petrzela and Sarah Manekin "sent each other daily emails that contained our goals for the day, a tentative schedule for how we would achieve those goals, and the occasional rambling reflection on the particular analytical question that had us in knots. Over the course of that two-year period, we kept each other on task, modeled for each other perseverance and life balance, and inspired each other to continue forward on the long marathon that constitutes completing a dissertation."[21] Others form dissertation groups that meet in person, or post their daily word count on Twitter for all the world to see.

Debts

Scholars know that even single-authored works are the products of many hands; that is why journal editors and book publishers leave space for acknowledgments. Start a list of names as soon as you begin a new project and update it every time an archivist suggests a new source, a friend reads a draft, or a stranger agrees to join your conference panel. Take pride in acknowledgments as thorough as your footnotes.

When to Stop

No work of history is ever complete. Every event, however small, has infinite contexts, infinite possible comparisons. Whatever it is you are writing, you will not write the definitive account. Nor will you answer all of your questions. You will never find the omniscient reader who can tell you that your work is finished, or correct. Even if you share a draft with the people about whom you wrote, none of them will know the whole story; no one can write *100 percent!* at the top of your paper the way your second-grade teacher did when you aced your geography quiz. So when do you stop?

21. Natalia Mehlman Petrzela and Sarah Manekin, "The Accountability Partnership: Writing and Surviving in the Digital Age (2012 Revision)," in *Writing History in the Digital Age*, ed. Jack Dougherty and Kristen Nawrotzki (Ann Arbor: University of Michigan Press, 2013).

If you are on assignment—for a class or a publisher—the answer is easier. When the deadline is near, or when the word count is reached, you need to stop researching and writing and use your remaining time to revise what you have. Walter Prescott Webb decided he needed to finish *The Texas Rangers* in time for the centennial of the institution. "No more research," he told himself. "I will not be lured away by new material. I will write this damned thing now."[22]

For more open-ended projects, stop when additional research only confirms what you have already learned. "This study is based upon thousands of letters and diaries, written by hundreds of men and women, a small fraction of the Virginia gentry but a large enough group to yield distinct patterns," writes Jan Lewis. "I knew my research was complete when I was no longer surprised by what I read, that is, when newly discovered letters or diary entries fell into the patterns already suggested by others."[23] Martha Hodes agrees: "I stopped not only in the interest of producing the book in a timely manner but also because I reached a point where new material no longer altered or challenged the patterns I had identified."[24] Or, as Kenneth Jackson told his students, "You don't have to drink the ocean to know it's salty."

22. Walter Prescott Webb, "History as High Adventure," *American Historical Review* 64 (1959): 275.

23. Jan Lewis, *The Pursuit of Happiness: Family and Values in Jefferson's Virginia* (New York: Cambridge University Press, 1985), 280.

24. Martha Hodes, *Mourning Lincoln* (New Haven, CT: Yale University Press, 2015), 275. See also Linda Gordon, "The WRITER'S STUDIO with Linda Gordon," *Modern American History* 1 (2018): 124.

CHAPTER TWELVE

Taking Notes

IN THE MID-TWENTIETH CENTURY, note-taking was simpler. The basic tools were the pen and pencil, the index card and the notebook—tools so elementary that research manuals of the day could explain their use in a few pages.[1] Since then, historians have gained access to a vast array of new tools, from photocopiers and digital cameras to laptops and online databases. While these new options bring many blessings, they have left each historian to find their own way of taking notes, making it a particularly difficult skill to teach or explain. The suggestions in this chapter present some factors for you to consider as you develop your own system.

Tips

- Take good-enough notes: notes that distinguish your words from others, and that can guide you back to sources if you need more information.
- There is no off-the-shelf computer software that is right for all projects. Do try to keep notes in one or two applications, to make searches easier.
- A working draft can be a great complement to your notes, showing you what you have learned so far and what gaps remain.

1. Jacques Barzun and Henry F. Graff, *The Modern Researcher* (New York: Harcourt, Brace, 1957), 25–31.

Goals

The purpose of note-taking is to answer your research questions by extracting relevant information from your sources. I offer two alternative metaphors for this process: mining and assembly.

NOTE-TAKING AS MINING

A finished work of history presents a fraction—usually a very small fraction—of the information potentially relevant on a topic. Thus, one purpose of note-taking is to separate that useful fraction from the much larger volume of material the historian has gathered, read, or simply glimpsed. Such separation is analogous to the production of valuable minerals through extraction and refining. As Timothy LeCain notes, it can take "almost three tons of ore to produce enough gold to make one small wedding band."[2] Historical research is not quite that bad; I need not read one million pages of source material in order to write seven of my own. (Though some days it does feel like it.) What I must do, however, is to compact the massive piles of manuscripts, newspapers, and books into a more usable form, like the gold ingot that is the step between the pile of ore and that wedding band. A note is that ingot: an intermediate step between a source—primary or secondary—and a passage in your finished text.

To find the gold, you must know it when you see it. In John Huston's 1948 film *The Treasure of the Sierra Madre*, novice gold-seekers Fred C. Dobbs (Humphrey Bogart) and Bob Curtin (Tim Holt) ride into the Mexican mountains with no particular idea of what they are looking for. First, they waste precious water rinsing boulders containing only pyrite: fool's gold. Sometime later, they are discouraged enough to propose going back. Their companion, seasoned prospector Howard (Walter Huston), knows better. "You're so dumb," he mocks them, "you don't even see the riches you're treading on with your own feet!" They are, he explains,

---

2. Timothy LeCain, *Mass Destruction: The Men and Giant Mines That Wired America and Scarred the Planet* (New Brunswick: Rutgers University Press, 2009), 209. For a mixed metaphor of mining and paleontology, see Samuel Eliot Morison, "Faith of a Historian," *American Historical Review* 56 (1951): 262–63.

already walking on gold dust, and if they climb a little higher, they will hit even richer deposits. Gold dust does not glitter like pyrite. "You've got to know how to recognize it."[3]

Daniel Vickers describes this wonderfully. He wanted to understand how colonial New Englanders, lacking the precious metals or crops to pay for slaves or indentured servants, "constructed labor systems adequate to their needs." He therefore sought to "catch working people in the act; this study is scrupulous in limiting itself to documented work experiences. It is a history of people who were working on an actual date in a known town at an identifiable task." He found thousands of such work experiences recorded in the ledgers of employers or in court records, though eventually only a few hundred were detailed enough to allow the kind of analysis he wanted. The point, though, is that as he sifted through those ledgers and depositions, he knew exactly what he was looking for.[4]

Of course, if you are looking for gold and keep finding silver, that is worth some attention. As you read for some kinds of information, you will no doubt encounter others, gaining in the process a more complete view of the world in which your people lived. The challenge is to balance too close a focus, at the risk of ignoring information that could later prove useful, and insufficient focus, that does not allow you to skim material quickly enough. When in doubt, you can split the difference by taking notes that summarize material that you do not think you will use, but that might just come in handy. For instance, had Vickers been reading for his "working people in the act" and taking detailed notes on each "identifiable task," yet noticing that the ledgers also had mysterious entries about, say, horse trades, he could note that the ledgers had a lot of horse trades without bogging down by trying to record each horse trade in detail. He would then have the information he or some other historian could use for a future project on horse trading.

Take notes that will support the style in which you intend to write up your findings. The more you consider yourself a storyteller, the more carefully you will look for descriptions of your characters,

3. John Huston, *The Treasure of the Sierra Madre* (Warner Brothers, 1948).

4. Daniel Vickers, *Farmers and Fishermen: Two Centuries of Work in Essex County, Massachusetts, 1630–1850* (Chapel Hill: University of North Carolina Press, 1994), 7, 10–11.

physical depictions of settings, and instances of verbatim dialogue. Conversely, the more quantitative analysis you do, the more you may care about any numbers. Any two historians examining the same source would emerge with distinct sets of notes based on what they were seeking.

The sad answer is that you will never get this just right. You will spend a good amount of time, especially at the beginning of a project, taking detailed notes that will prove unimportant to your final set of questions. And at the end of the project, you will find yourself remembering something you saw early on, but failed to note, and now you cannot find it again. (Historians swap stories of the one that got away.) Resign yourself to these inevitable frustrations, and aim not to take perfect notes but good-enough notes.

NOTE-TAKING AS ASSEMBLY

While the mining metaphor usefully suggests the importance of condensing a great deal of source material into something both smaller and purer, it fails to convey a second function of note-taking: the reordering of material from the way the historian finds it into a new structure that suits the needs of the researcher and reader.

Let me offer a different movie analogy. In the 1980 film *My Bodyguard*, the hulking Linderman (Adam Baldwin) spends his spare time rebuilding a motorcycle from discarded parts. As he assembles it piece by piece, Linderman can see its shape emerge. He knows with ever greater precision what parts he already has and what parts are left to find. By the time that we first see the project, Linderman is missing only one part: "Cylinder. I can't find the right one. They don't make them anymore." So he wanders junkyards, getting progressively filthier. Because he knows how far along he is in his project, Linderman does not stop to look for gas tanks, shock absorbers, or wheel hubs. Or, if he does see one, he can mentally compare it to the one he has already installed and decide if it is worth swapping in. He can instead devote almost his whole attention to cylinders, and even explain to a research assistant more or less what he is looking for, though Linderman will make the final decision about whether it fits. (Again, be ready for surprises.

Imagine an alternative version, where Linderman comes across a pair of skis and some tracks and decides to convert his emerging motorcycle into a snowmobile.)[5]

Like Linderman, you can start building your motorcycle even before you have all the parts, so that the unfinished structure helps you know what you are looking for in the junkyard and what you can ignore. That partial motorcycle can take many forms. Some historians start straight into a working draft. "The more I write, the more I know what I am looking for," explains E. H. Carr, "the better I understand the significance and relevance of what I find."[6] I myself also start writing as soon as I can, so that my working draft reflects my understanding of the topic at any given time.

Other historians assemble information in equally organized but less finished outlines, as if Linderman were laying out all the parts he had collected onto a diagram of the motorcycle without actually fitting them together until he was ready.

The Good-Enough Note

Notes do not need to be perfect; they need to be good enough for the job. We can identify some functions of a *good-enough* note-taking system.

IDENTIFY THE SOURCE, SO YOU CAN GO BACK AND CONSULT IF NEEDED

A note is likely worthless, or even harmful, if you cannot figure out where the information came from; the essence of scholarship is the ability to attribute each fact and quotation to a primary or secondary source. Each note therefore needs to include enough bibliographic information to write a full footnote later on. Typically, however, this does not mean that you need to write out that full footnote for each note you take. If you are taking notes on a book, the author's last name, title, and page number ("Hughes, *American Genesis*, 130") will usually suffice. For newspapers, include the newspaper, date,

---

5. Tony Bill, *My Bodyguard* (20th Century Fox, 1980).
6. Edward Hallett Carr, *What Is History?* (New York: Vintage, 1961), 33.

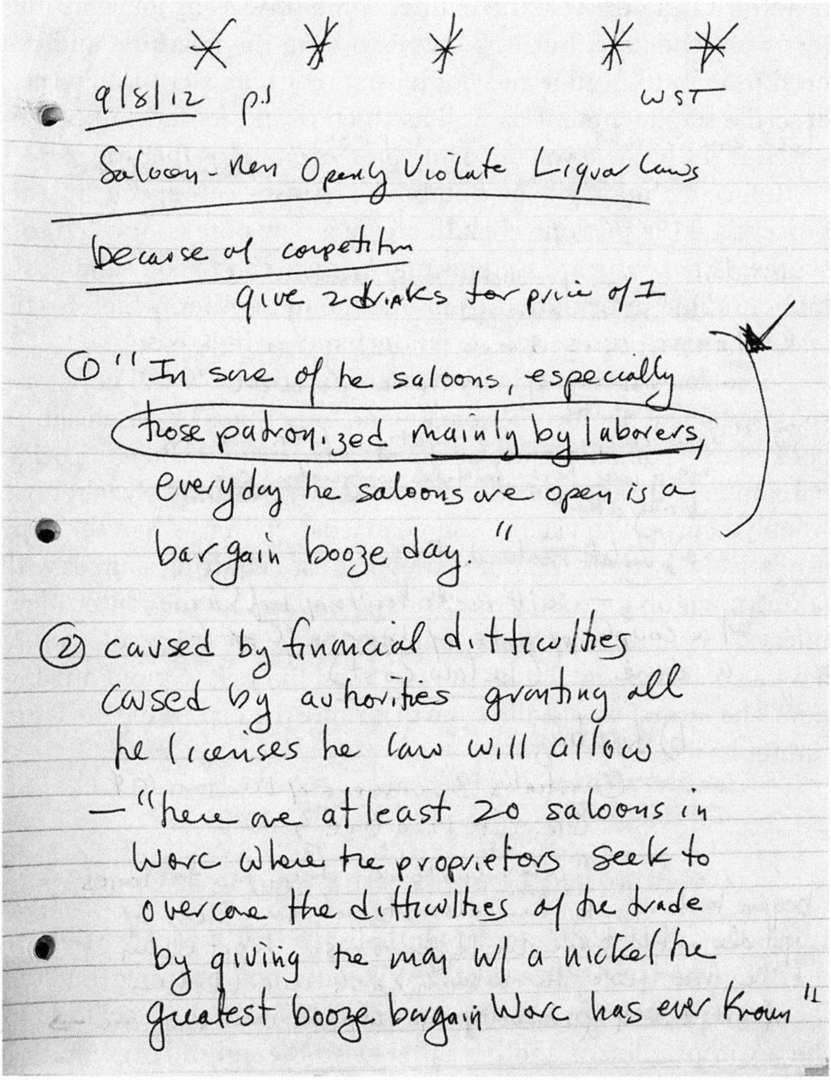

9/8/12 p.1 WST

Saloon-Men Openly Violate Liquor Laws

because of competition

give 2 drinks for price of 1

(1) "In some of the saloons, especially those patronized mainly by laborers, everyday the saloons are open is a bargain booze day."

(2) caused by financial difficulties caused by authorities granting all the licenses the law will allow

— "there are at least 20 saloons in Worc where the proprietors seek to overcome the difficulties of the trade by giving the man w/ a nickel the greatest booze bargain Worc has ever known"

FIGURE 12.1. A good note includes three levels of information. Here, Roy Rosenzweig starts with the metadata (the date, title of the newspaper in abbreviated form, headline, and subheadline). Then he summarizes the article, including some direct quotations carefully set off in quotation marks. The third layer is Rosenzweig's own reaction, which in this case consists of the circled phrase, arrow, and stars that mark his excitement at finding explicit evidence that temperance reformers focused on working-class saloons. The phrase "patronized mainly by laborers" made it into his book *Eight Hours for What We Will: Workers and Leisure in an Industrial City, 1870–1920*. Roy Rosenzweig Papers, Collection #C0038, Special Collections Research Center, George Mason University, box 14, folder: Drink Notes, 1890–1920, 3 of 3.

headline, and, if listed, the byline. Some presses or journals may just want the date, but it is better to have the headline and not need it, than to need it and not have it. For manuscript materials, describe the document as well as the box and folder number, or series, if the archive you are using prefers citations that way.

Reference manager or database software can speed up this process, taking just one click to create a new note connected to a source. Other software systems may require you to copy and paste bibliographic information from one file to another, which is still faster than writing everything out by hand each time.

Sometimes it may be appropriate to acquire a full copy of a source, using a photocopier or camera, or perhaps by purchasing a book. Such acquisitions are obviously most helpful when the original source is distant from your home—so you are unlikely to return, when you expect to use the source extensively, and when the copy is relatively inexpensive. But do not confuse acquiring sources with taking notes on those sources. And remember that the source identification is more important than the source copy. I would rather have a good citation and no full text than full text without attribution. The former would allow me to acquire the text, while the latter cannot be used.

DISTINGUISH OTHERS' WORDS AND
IDEAS FROM YOUR OWN

It is better to have no note at all than one that misleads you into thinking you wrote a passage that you did not, opening the door for plagiarism, defined by the American Historical Association as the "expropriation of another author's work, and the presentation of it as one's own."[7] Occasionally a historian deliberately passes off another's text as theirs, but I would wager that the vast majority of plagiarism results from sloppy note-taking that mixes up old and new material. There are two basic ways to avoid this mix-up: set off direct quotations with quotation marks or other indicators

7. American Historical Association, "Statement on Standards of Professional Conduct (updated 2019)," https://www.historians.org/jobs-and-professional-development /statements-standards-and-guidelines-of-the-discipline/statement-on-standards-of -professional-conduct.

and assume that everything else is your own words, or assume that everything in the note is text from someone else and set off your own words, for example, with brackets. If you are typing notes rather than cutting and pasting, you may need to distinguish among three types of texts: verbatim quotations, paraphrases, and your own thoughts. If you are using a database, you can set up separate fields.

In the age of handwritten note-taking, copying verbatim passages required extra effort, and thus was the exception rather than the rule. Research manuals advised researchers to set off such passages with "prominent quotation marks."[8] In the age of digital cut-and-paste, it may be easier to make verbatim copying the default and your original words the exception that needs to be set apart. As long as you are careful, copying verbatim passages may be better than writing paraphrases as you go. That way, you can later compare your drafts to the original passage and decide whether you need citation or quotation marks.[9]

Beyond this basic task of avoiding plagiarism, you should have some way to record your own thoughts about the material you gather. At the moment you create a note, you have some reason to believe that your future self, the writer of history, will find the information valuable. Rather than assume that your future self will remember what it is that you found so striking, record your reactions to what you learn. This could be on the note itself (a passage from a source, then your reaction, with some means of distinguishing the two), in a separate document (my bibliographic database includes a source called "Misc. notes," and I take notes on that like any other source), or in a working draft.

ALLOW SORTING AND RETRIEVAL OF
RELATED PIECES OF INFORMATION

A note gains value when placed alongside other notes. If many pieces of information align, you have identified a pattern. If two or more pieces of information present contrasting views, or change over

8. Thomas Edward Felt, *Researching, Writing, and Publishing Local History* (Nashville: American Association for State and Local History, 1976), 14.

9. Peter Charles Hoffer, "Reflections on Plagiarism, Part 1: A Guide for the Perplexed," *Perspectives on History*, February 2004.

time, you may have identified a turning point in a narrative, a debate among actors in your story, or a tension within the views of a single person or group. To achieve such juxtapositions, you need to be able to organize your notes by time, theme, or some other system.

On paper, this can mean bundling stacks of index cards or assembling files. Judith Walkowitz has described how she assembles a two-inch loose-leaf notebook, about three hundred pages, of notes for each chapter she writes.[10] The computer version of such a system is to organize electronic documents into folders, either within an application (such as a database or reference manager) or in the operating system itself.[11]

Keywords or tags—equivalent to subject headings in library catalogs—function the same way. If you tag all of your notes by topic, then searching for that topic will give you a virtual loose-leaf notebook like Walkowitz's. For instance, you might assign the tag "gender" to all notes on sources that display assumptions about the proper roles of men and women, regardless of whether the source itself uses the word. Using separate tags for notes about Bishop John England and the country of England, and using the same tag for references to England and Great Britain, will produce results that could baffle a simple full-text search. Developing a list of tags is work, and that list will evolve in the course of your project, which could require you to go back and add tags to previously tagged notes. Whether the return justifies the investment depends on the project, and the number of notes.

Consider two extreme cases. If you want to minimize the work of entering, you could keep all of your notes in a single document, like the scroll Jack Kerouac fashioned so he could type without pausing to add pages.[12] The typing would go quickly, and, assuming you used a word processor rather than a paper scroll, you could search for individual words and phrases. But as the document grew, it would be slower to load and navigate, especially if you started pasting in images and PDFs. It would be easy to lose track of which information

10. Judith Walkowitz, "On Taking Notes," *Perspectives on History*, January 2009.

11. Rachel Toor, "Scholars Talk Writing: T. J. Stiles," *Chronicle of Higher Education*, October 1, 2019.

12. Howard Cunnell, "Fast This Time: Jack Kerouac and the Writing of *On the Road*," in Jack Kerouac, *On the Road: The Original Scroll* (New York: Viking, 2007), 24.

came from which source—a catastrophe for a scholar—and it could not answer many types of queries you might wish to answer.

Conversely, you could fashion all of your notes in the format specified by the Text Encoding Initiative, which offers standards by which all manner of words and phrases can be tagged for future analysis. For instance, the guidelines suggest that the Montgomery Bus Boycott could be entered as

```
<event xml:id="eMBB" from="1955-12-01"
  to="1956-12-20">
  <label>Montgomery Bus Boycott</label>
  <desc>A political and social protest campaign
  against the policy of racial segregation on the
  public transit system of the city of <placeName
  ref="#MONT">Montgomery</placeName>.</desc>
</event>[13]
```

If you were to mark up every person and event in your notes to such exactness, you could later perform magnificent searches, perhaps listing all the events in your note by start date or city. But the time required to craft all those tags would be immense, which is why the format is better suited to metadata rather than full-text notes, or the intensive study of fairly short texts.

Even if you do not intensively structure most of the information you find, it may be useful to do so for some subsets. If you find yourself making lists of arrests for murder, or ships' voyages, or any other event that generates a predictable set of data points, it will likely help to be able to take notes in table form, such as a spreadsheet or, better still, a database.

PROVIDE THE RIGHT LEVEL OF DETAIL

Note-takers must find a balance between capturing too much information and too little. Of all the facts staring at you from the source, which will end up in your finished work? At the start of a project, everything is new, so everything seems equally important,

---

13. P5: Guidelines for Electronic Text Encoding and Interchange, version 3.6.0, last updated on July 16, 2019, revision daa3ccob9.

or unimportant. "It's kind of like walking into a room of strangers," Laurel Thatcher Ulrich says of confronting a list of names in a diary. "You don't know who they are, and not sure if you care."[14] The more research you do, the more you will recognize those names, know if you care, and be able to distinguish between what is new and what you already know. At that point, your notes will become more efficient.

If you are not sure if some information is important, you can hedge your bets by writing general descriptions rather than detailed notes, the way that archivists write container summaries on finding aids. For instance, if you come across a published report or archival box with detailed financial records, it might be better to write a note along the lines of, "1882 sales figures here; come back if needed," rather than take down the whole table. You can also take comfort in knowing that every historian gains from the countless words read but noted only by the mind, not the hand. By immersing yourself in sources, you will get a sense of time and place.

The availability of born-digital texts and the capacity to convert older texts into digital formats makes it tempting to capture the entirety of a text into one's notes. And there are advantages to this approach. Say, for instance, that early in your work you start coming across documents—membership lists or petitions—with long lists of people's names at the end. As Ulrich notes, you may have no idea which of these people will be important to your story, or whose presence on a committee with someone else will prove to be a significant connection. If it is just a matter of cutting and pasting, or dragging and dropping, you may as well grab what you can and decide later if it is important.

Write down anything that surprises you. For example, if you can find someone changing their mind on an issue, that is a rare event, regardless of the time and place you are studying. Also record any particularly shocking or amusing stories that might enliven your work or a party conversation. In the 1940 film *His Girl Friday*, a newspaper editor played by Cary Grant screams at his printers to make room for a big scoop by clearing the front pages of lesser

14. Richard P. Rogers, *A Midwife's Tale* (Watertown, MA: Blueberry Hill Productions, 1997).

stories—the European war, Hitler, and the rest. But after listening for a moment, he relents on one item. "Keep the rooster story," he concedes. "That's human interest." Take notes on all rooster stories.

Extensive note-taking has its rewards. For example, in February 2018, I received a message from a *Washington Post* reporter who wanted to know why the designers of the railcars for the Washington Metro had decided to place carpeting on the floors. While researching my book *The Great Society Subway*, I had built a File-Maker Pro database of about 8,500 notes about the Metro system, representing years of research into primary and secondary sources. I searched this database for the term "carpet" and within a second was given twenty-eight results. With these results, I was able to quickly read all of those notes and call the reporter back. When we realized we had some questions I could not answer with my notes, I went to the library and consulted one of the original sources. The reporter got what he wanted.[15] By grabbing a great deal of information and assembling it in one place, I had built a thin encyclopedia on my topic. When I ask a question, it should spit out an answer that is neither too big (sixteen million hits) nor too small (zero).

There are dangers, however, to grabbing too much information. First, the more information you incorporate into your note-taking system, the more extraneous results you will get when you search. Thus, if I had included in my Metro database the full text of every article and book I could find that mentioned any person in the story, I might well have cluttered it with references to carpets in buildings, carpet bombing, and all the rest, making it harder to find the information I needed. Second, as noted earlier, you must take care to distinguish your words from others, so that you quote and cite appropriately in your finished project.

Third, you must take care with copyright. You own the copyright to notes that you write yourself, and short quotations come under fair use provisions.[16] Moreover, the terms of service of many commercial databases allow authorized users to download whole articles for their own research. Thus, you can store copies of such

15. Faiz Siddiqui, "The Story behind the Carpeting in Metro's Rail Cars? It Stinks," *Washington Post*, February 8, 2018.

16. Michael Les Benedict, *A Historian's Guide to Copyright* (Washington, DC: American Historical Association, 2012).

articles or other texts with your notes. The problem comes if you ever want to share your notes with others, for example, by depositing them in a university repository for the use of future researchers. Since all historians should have an eye on posterity, it may make sense to keep copyrighted material separate in your note-taking system. The same would go for other kinds of privileged information, such as the transcript of an oral history interview, parts of which the narrator has asked to be sealed until a future date.

Finally, keep in mind that cutting and pasting does not require careful reading and thinking, and thus may give a false sense of progress. I recommend that as you take notes, you take the time to figure out if and how each new piece of information changes your story. This may not be possible in a rushed trip to a distant archive, but it is a good habit when time allows.

Sometimes, then, you may not want the full text at all. This may be especially true toward the end of a project, when each new document repeats things you already know. In that case, a brief summary can suffice. The thirtieth time I read someone complain that standing armies are bad, I might just type "standing armies are bad." If I need more detail, I will know where to find it. An in-between option would be to write a summary and include a key quotation.

Simple Tools for Notes

Historians take notes using a range of tools. There is no off-the-shelf solution with powerful features, so any choice has its pros and cons. Many historians rely not on a single tool but on a combination of tools to create a workflow. For instance, you might use one software application (or a paper notebook) to take short-term notes, like making a list of books to consult on your next trip to the library, while another application stores longer-term information. Or you might use a reference manager to store the full bibliographic information on the published sources you consult, even if you end up storing your notes on those sources in another application. The challenge is to use as few applications as possible, to minimize cutting, pasting, and searching operations. This last is particularly important. While computer operating systems allow full-text searches across applications, you may not get the most relevant results, or be able to refine your search. Limiting your notes to one or two applications will likely allow more powerful queries.

I hesitate to recommend any particular software, since in any given week, one application might massively raise its prices or end its support, while another application, though previously disappointing, suddenly adds the functions that make it useful. For up-to-date information on how historians are using a specific tool, try an internet search for "historians" with the name of that tool. Here I provide more general—and I hope more durable—thoughts on categories of tools.

No one system will suit every project, since some choices will depend on the sources you will use and the product you hope to produce. There is no single form that such notes have to take, nor any single way to create them.[17] Each form and method has its own advantages and disadvantages—some methods make it easier to take notes, others to retrieve them. Some tools take a long time to learn but can complete more tasks, others are simple to learn but relatively constrained in what they can do. Some are nice because you customize them to your own needs, while others are nice because they rely on widely shared standards. But whatever means you choose, keep in mind the ends: easy retrieval of relevant information, answers to the questions *you* pose, and not too much nor too little.

For example, reference-manager software is very good at handling published sources, especially those whose metadata have already been entered into online databases, such as library catalogs. If most of your citations for a given project will be to such sources, it could make sense to depend primarily on a reference manager. For instance, this book relies primarily on recent, published sources, and only uses short passages from each. I needed a workflow that emphasized the capture of metadata from existing sources and the conversion of printed material into editable text. By contrast, during my work on the Philadelphia riots of 1844, I accumulated tens of thousands of digital photographs of newspapers and manuscript documents from the 1840s. What I needed most was a way to quickly catalog sources—especially newspaper articles—not in

17. Jennifer Rutner and Roger Schonfeld, "Supporting the Changing Research Practices of Historians," *Ithaka S+R*, December 2012, https://doi.org/10.18665/sr.22532.

existing databases. That meant using tools for which I could write scripts, something not available in some software packages.

NOTEBOOKS AND INDEX CARDS

Even in the age of the internet, paper has its advantages. Paper will not suddenly crash—erasing all their stored information—the way a computer can. It remains readable for generations, unlike those floppy disks and Iomega Zip drives that seemed so grand not many years ago. Paper can also be good for thinking. Taking notes by hand may force you to think about what you are reading in ways that typing or, far worse, copying and pasting does not. And some archives may require you to take notes by hand. In the early twenty-first century, one historian entered all his notes into a database, but then printed that database out on index cards, which he sorted by hand to form the notes for a chapter.[18] Writing out a list of tasks and then checking them off with a thick black stroke—sometimes with the date on which the task was finally completed—offers a sense of satisfaction that I have yet to achieve by clicking a check box on a screen. Paper pages or cards can be spread out on the floor in a way that is hard to replicate on a computer without spending thousands of dollars on monitors.

Even software companies recognize the pleasures of paper, naming their products after paper goods (Notepad, FileMaker), imitating the appearance of paper on computer screens (the "Notebook Layout" in old versions of Microsoft Word, or the "corkboard" view in Scrivener), or offering "cut" and "paste" commands to youngsters who may never lay out a newsletter with a pair of scissors and a glue stick.

The two major forms of paper notes—notebooks and index cards—illustrate a basic trade-off that carries through to digital notes as well: Do you want easy data entry or easy data analysis? Notebooks are great for data entry. If you are working through a source, you need only enter the bibliographic information once, then you have dozens or hundreds of pages on which to write. (Taking notes in the margins of a book that you own can be considered

18. Rutner and Schonfeld, "Supporting the Changing Research Practices of Historians," 25.

a version of writing in a notebook. Please do not write in library books, or attach sticky notes to them, since those can damage the book.) The problem with notebooks is that when it comes to writing your own story, there will be no easy way to reorder those notes, to interweave the information you have gathered from multiple sources, or to keep track of what you have included.

Index cards, by contrast, require more work as you enter information, but they are better for extracting it. As you create them, each needs at least a shortened form of bibliography, so if you find a source that will fill many cards, you will need to write the same information at the top of each one in order to keep track of where you found it. But once you have your cards ready, you can sort them into stacks that reflect the order in which you will introduce the information in your own work.

The two forms can work together. Some research manuals from the age of paper recommend 5 × 8-inch note cards, 8½ × 11-inch pages folded in half, or some combination of the two, since the size is about the same.[19] (Europeans have an advantage; A5 cards are *exactly* the size of folded A4 sheets.) That way, you can take notes in notebooks, tear out the pages, and fold them in half to combine them with index cards. Other manuals recommend writing in notebooks in chunks that can later be cut up into card-like slips.[20]

Much as we can respect the power of paper systems, and the centuries of scholarship they produced, we can also note their disadvantages. Entering information can be much slower than on a computer, especially if one is working with digitized sources that can be copied and pasted, or if one never got proper penmanship instruction in grade school. Compared to digital media, paper is relatively hard to back up, and hard to share with others. Paper records *can* be searched; the reason index cards are called index cards is that they can be used to create an index: a guide to more extensive holdings. But obviously they cannot be searched as rapidly as can a computer file.

Most historians, then, will seek to take notes with a computerized system that maintains most of the benefits of a paper system

19. Felt, *Researching, Writing, and Publishing Local History*, 13; Louis Gottschalk, *Understanding History: A Primer of Historical Method* (New York: Alfred A. Knopf, 1950).
20. Barzun and Graff, *The Modern Researcher*, 25.

while adding new functions. In some cases that means a hybrid system: either scanning or transcribing paper documents to create computer files or printing computer files onto paper.

WORD PROCESSORS FOR NOTE-TAKING

Any text editor or word processor can serve as a note-taking system. The advantage is that you likely already have a word processor and are familiar with its major functions. Unlike a paper system, a word processor can store a more-or-less infinite amount of text in a small space. You can search your notes, copy and paste passages into your draft, and easily make copies for backup or sharing.

The big disadvantage of most word processors is their inability to sort. Eventually, you want to reorder the information, to get it out of the order in which you encountered it and into the order you want your reader to encounter it.[21] As Mary Beth Norton has argued, the Salem witch hunt of the 1690s looks different depending on whether you order the documents according to the suspects, by their date of creation, or by the date of the events they purport to describe.[22] A word processor wants to keep text in one order, making it the electronic equivalent of a bound notebook. What you want is the equivalent of a stack of cards or a file of loose sheets that can be pulled out and sorted as needed.

Some historians who enter information on a computer then fall back on paper when it comes time to sort their notes, in the manner of Judith Walkowitz and her binders. Brad Gregory describes digital note-taking followed by analog sorting. "I print hard copies of all my notes and work by reading, rereading, annotating in the margins, and cross-referencing what might be relevant to a particular chapter," he explains. "Then I think about patterns, or thematic clusters, or specific chronology, depending on what it seems the chapters require, and write out abbreviated references to sources for potential placement within a chapter."[23]

21. Thanks to Sam Lebovic for his insights here.
22. Mary Beth Norton, "Essex County Witchcraft," *William and Mary Quarterly* 65 (2008): 486.
23. Brad Gregory, "Managing the Terror," *Perspectives on History*, January 2009.

It is possible to do some of this work of sorting within a word processor. Scrivener, for instance, lets you import PDFs or texts and display them in one pane of the application while you write in another. You can slide your notes up or down, much as you might manually sort cards, or the way Walkowitz arranges pages within a binder. But storing notes together with one's draft, especially if you are including PDFs or image files, results in very large files, making performance slower and backup more cumbersome. Moreover, you will probably not have automatic sort functions, like sorting all documents by their date of publication with a single click. For historians, it may be best to take notes in one application and write in another, displaying them side by side on a monitor as needed.

PLAIN TEXT AND MARKDOWN

Plain, or unformatted, text files have the advantages of taking up little space and being readable by the widest range of software. If you want to take a note today and read it on a computer twenty years from now, your best hope is a plain text file. Plain text can store information about formatting—not only basics like italics and boldface but even citation information and links to images. The Markdown language, developed by John Gruber and Aaron Swartz, adds basic formatting and hyperlinks, allowing one to connect notes together by theme (the digital equivalent of a binder or stack of cards), but still produces files that are readable by any editor. Some historians use simple text editors to write Markdown, while others prefer more specialized apps.[24]

24. Ben Schmidt, "Markdown, Historical Writing, and Killer Apps," *Ben Schmidt* (blog), September 5, 2014, http://benschmidt.org/2014/09/05/markdown-historical -writing-and-killer-apps/; Sarah Simpkin, "Getting Started with Markdown," *Programming Historian*, November 13, 2015, https://programminghistorian.org/en/lessons/getting -started-with-markdown; Dennis Tenen and Grant Wythoff, "Sustainable Authorship in Plain Text Using Pandoc and Markdown," *Programming Historian*, March 19, 2014, https://programminghistorian.org/en/lessons/sustainable-authorship-in-plain-text-using -pandoc-and-markdown.

Database Software

A database application is designed to store, organize, and retrieve information. If we use a loose definition, this includes not only applications marketed as "databases" but also spreadsheets (probably the most familiar database application), reference managers, note-taking applications, and highly customizable relational database platforms. Each has its virtues, and you can find historians using each of these.

REFERENCE MANAGERS

Reference managers, or citation managers, are specialized databases that store metadata—the author, title, date, and the like—about a source. Because they are designed specifically for scholarly research, they offer some of the most immediate returns on investment; an hour spent learning a reference manager will likely save you an hour of work before too long. One of the most popular—Zotero—is free to download. However, in the long term they may be less flexible than other options.

Reference managers are fantastically helpful for published sources, especially when article databases include full-text PDFs of the article; a reference manager can often capture that, saving you the trouble of figuring out where to store the PDF on your hard drive so you can find it later. Even if you cannot get the full-text version, you can often import metadata into your reference manager, saving countless keystrokes and, perhaps, some typographical errors as well. When you are ready to write, reference managers can format notes and bibliographies according to the specific style in which you are citing your work. This is particularly helpful if you want to submit works to journals or publishers with varied demands. If one journal wants Chicago-style notes and another insists on APA, a reference manager can make the change in a few clicks, while it could take hours by hand.

Reference managers also have their limits. They can often pull in information that a style guide tells you to ignore, or miss information that you are supposed to have, such as the city in which a book was published. Or the database from which you are pulling metadata may simply have incorrect or incomplete information. In particular, the electronic versions of books are often produced from reprint editions, so citation managers often fail to capture the original date of publication. For historians, who care about dates, this is a serious problem. While great for published sources, whose metadata is relatively predictable and often already digitized, reference managers may struggle with archival collections.

In addition, the basic unit of information in a reference manager is the reference, not the note. It is easy enough to take one note per book or article, but what if a book contains dozens of facts that will be scattered through your own outline? Or, to put it the other way, what if you want to organize your notes on a subject that will draw on multiple references? A reference manager may not allow you to take the equivalent of index-card notes to be reshuffled and ordered independently of the original reference.

NOTE-TAKING APPS

Note-taking applications—such as Evernote, OneNote, Apple Notes, and Google Keep—are designed to allow easy note-taking. Liz Covart has described Evernote as a "digital filing cabinet," a place to put all one's materials on a project. Indeed, these applications excel at ease of entry.[25] You can type a note on a keyboard, save a link with a browser extension, take a picture with a smartphone, record a voice memo, or import a PDF; it all goes to the same cloud-based account, so you can pull it up on any device. Unlike spreadsheets, which are optimized for numbers, note-taking applications can store text and images equally well. Some will convert images of books and articles into machine-readable texts for easy searching.

These applications are great for relatively short-term task management. For instance, if I consult my university library catalog and find the call number of a book, I can paste that into the relevant note in my notes application, and it will be waiting on my phone the next time I enter the library. If I see a relevant news story or

25. "3 Ways Evernote Makes Research Easier: A Historian's Notes," *Liz Covart* (blog), February 13, 2012, https://www.lizcovart.com/blog/evernote-and-historical-research.

tweet on my phone, I send it to notes, and it is waiting on my laptop the next time I have the chance to write. When I have secured that news story or tweet into a more permanent place, such as my Zotero citation manager, I can delete it or put it in a "done" file.

With some investment of time, historians have also found ways to use these products for multiyear research projects. DevonThink, a particularly powerful note-taking application for Mac, seems to be particularly popular, but historians have also made Evernote and OneNote work for them.[26] Each of these applications can store a vast amount of information in digital notebooks, with individual entries tagged to indicate subject matter.

While more flexible than citation managers, these applications also have their limits. You often cannot set up custom fields, or write footnotes, or run advanced queries. For that, you need a full-fledged relational database.

RELATIONAL DATABASES

In the 1980s and 1990s, major software vendors defined the "office" suite—word processor, spreadsheet, and slideshow—which remains standard to this day. Not included was a database program. Microsoft Access has always been an add-on to the Office package, and Microsoft never developed a Mac version. Apple's HyperCard, released to great acclaim in 1987, slowly faded over the following decade.[27] There is no standard platform for nonexpert computer users to organize qualitative information. That is a great pity, since relational databases can be powerful tools for research.

A relational database is a tool that allows you to connect two or more tables of information. In the most basic use, the historian can

26. Gökser Gökçay, "How I Used OneNote for My PhD," *Apps for Research* (blog), August 2, 2015, https://appsforresearch.wordpress.com/2015/08/02/how-i-used-onenote -for-my-phd/; Rachel Leow, "DevonThink, Digital Research, and the Paperless Dream," *Perspectives on History*, October 2012; Emily VanBuren, "Building a Research Database with DEVONthink Pro Office," *Inside Higher Ed*, October 1, 2013, https://www.insidehighered .com/blogs/gradhacker/building-research-database-devonthink-pro-office; Avigail S. Oren, "DEVONthink for Historians," http://www.avigailoren.com/about-the-guide.

27. Leander Kahney, "HyperCard Forgotten, but Not Gone," *Wired*, August 14, 2002; Samuel Arbesman, "The Forgotten Software That Inspired Our Modern World," *BBC Future*, July 23, 2019.

set up one table of sources and a second table for notes, so that a quick search reveals all the notes taken from that source.[28] In other words, relational databases function a lot like the 5×8-inch index cards used by historians of the mid-twentieth century. Consider some of the things that index cards do well that word processors and spreadsheets do not.

Link a record to a source

In the old days, researchers kept one file of cards with complete bibliographic information on the sources they were using and a second file of cards with substantive notes. The substantive cards would need only an abbreviated reference to the bibliographic file, sparing the historian the need to write out full bibliographic information for every card. Word processors and spreadsheets are not set up to mimic this relationship, but databases are. Enter the bibliographic information once, then spawn as many notes from that source as you like.

Display one record at a time

A word processor wants to show you text as part of a steady stream, not a particular record. A spreadsheet wants to show you several records arranged in rows, with each cell offering just a few words before it becomes hard to read. Databases are happy to show you records in any form you like, but they are particularly good at showing records roughly the length of a 5×8 card.

Find relevant records

Imagine going through a stack of 5×8 cards and pulling out all the ones related to Albuquerque, or to dairy agriculture, or to eugenics, because that is the section you are working on, or because someone is asking you about that part of your research. Better still, imagine more specific searches, like all your notes about Albuquerque in the 1940s, or all mentions of eugenics in sources published before 1924 that *do not* also mention immigration. Those kinds of specific

28. Ansley T. Erickson, "Historical Research and the Problem of Categories: Reflections on 10,000 Digital Note Cards," in *Writing History in the Digital Age*, ed. Kristen Nawrotzki and Jack Dougherty (Ann Arbor: University of Michigan Press, 2013).

queries are beyond the reach of notes taken with a word processor, but database software can present you with those cards in a fraction of a second.

Sort records

Now imagine sorting that set of records by some criteria. Historians will often want to sort by date—perhaps the date of publication of a source, or the date of an event. But you can imagine other sorts: by chapter numbers you have assigned, or by the last name of historical characters. Again, software can do this instantly.

Database software also allows you to save scripts for searches, sorts, and other tasks that you do repeatedly. In the age of paper, a historian taking many cards of notes on a single source would have to write an abbreviated footnote at the top of each card. A database can do that with one click. If I am taking notes on a run of newspapers, one button will create a new record for an article taken from the same issue of the newspaper I am reading, while a different button will create a record for an article from the following day, and a third button (which I use for weekly newspapers) creates a record for an article published seven days later. If I am taking notes on an archival collection, a button will create a record for a document from the same box and folder that I have been reading.

Databases can generate specialized tables as well, which are particularly helpful for quantitative analysis. To understand how seventeenth-century New Englanders exchanged news, Katherine Grandjean built a database of 2,856 letters, coding each for "date; author; addressee; direction (how the letter was addressed); place of origin; destination; carrier's identity (if known); speed of delivery (if noted); and, of course, the subject of the letter (what news it contained)." This allowed her to see quantitative patterns, such as an apparent decrease in colonists' reliance on Indian couriers after 1655. To track the travels of a particular colonist, Thomas Minor, Grandjean built a second database "of every place that he mentioned visiting in the diary, including the date and Minor's reason for visiting (if given)."[29] Again, she looked for patterns.

---

29. Katherine Grandjean, *American Passage: The Communications Frontier in Early New England* (Cambridge, MA: Harvard University Press, 2015), 218, 266n40, 267n48.

And databases are great for project management. If you have a table of all your sources, linked to a table of your notes, it is easy to track what sources exist, what sources you have found, what sources you have mined or rejected, and/or what lies ahead. This helps avoid the embarrassment of recalling a book you have already checked out from the library, or finding that you have already taken notes on it. You can generate lists of all the books you have not yet consulted, organized by library and, within that, by call number, providing a handy shopping list the next time you are in the stacks. And you can set up a database to record the exact time when you create or modify every note, the way your email client automatically stamps the time on every message you send. While no substitute for a complete research diary, it can help fill in gaps.

Databases are also good at producing notes that record not only the actions of the people you are studying but also your own. As you come back to your notes on a source in the future, it can be helpful to know when you read it, and whether you got all the way through. I have my database set up to generate a date stamp and time stamp every time I create or modify a bibliographic note or record.[30] This is particularly useful when I need to figure out where I left off, either because I got distracted by some other task and want to know what I was doing an hour ago, or perhaps because I had to stop working through some source for several weeks, and I would like to know how far I had gotten. Other databases do this automatically. For instance, every time you create a reference in Zotero, it date-stamps it, allowing you to sort your references by the date they were added. This can help you resume where you left off after a break. It can also help to date-stamp any comments you make to yourself within a note.

SPREADSHEETS

Arguably, spreadsheets are a particular form of database software, and the most common. Along with word processors, spreadsheets have become a standard component of "office" software suites;

---

30. As I wrote this paragraph, out of curiosity I opened my Metro database and searched for the notes I had taken precisely twenty summers earlier. It turned out to have been a productive day.

Microsoft, Apple, and Google all offer versions. Many historians have experience using these for nonresearch purposes, such as preparing their tax returns or calculating student grades, so they can apply them to research without much additional learning.

Spreadsheets are great for managing quantitative information. You can make calculations, run statistical operations, and produce quick graphs, though the default settings on the graph functions can produce some ugly results. Historians should note that depending on the operating system, Microsoft Excel cannot recognize dates before 1900 or 1904.

More significantly, because they were designed to display and manipulate numbers, spreadsheets are pretty bad at displaying and manipulating text, a much more common task for historical research. While it is possible to alter their appearance with various plug-ins and templates, at a deep level, spreadsheets want to display multiple rows of data. That is like having to look at the top line of thirty index cards, when what you really want is to see an entire single index card at a time. It is possible to make a spreadsheet show you a long bibliographic citation, plus multiple paragraphs of text. But that is quite hard. It is also difficult to manipulate text in a spreadsheet. A reference manager has built-in functions to format a citation according to various style guides, and a database platform can be programmed to do the same.

To be sure, historians can and do use spreadsheets to track a range of textual information, and if that works for you, great. But if you are planning to spend years working with text, it may be worth exploring some alternatives.

Specialized Tools

Some types of information are most easily recorded apart from your main set of notes. Depending on your subject, you may find yourself juggling long lists of names, dates, places, or relationships that are most easily tracked in a separate document, perhaps in a separate format. For some projects, these documents will serve as temporary scaffolding: useful to you and your editor but not to be seen by outsiders. In other cases, you may want to present them as a permanent part of your finished project.

TIMELINES

While history is much more than a list of dates, a chronology of events can still be a great place to start. Writing down just a few dates is enough to break the blankness of a page, while a more elaborate timeline can serve as a reference, even if you end up not telling your story in strictly chronological order. Cite the sources for the dates you add to your timeline, since you are likely to find some dates in dispute, or multiple versions of the same event.

GLOSSARIES AND ALPHABETICAL LISTS

History is also much more than a list of names, but such lists can help you tell a story clearly and spell terms consistently. As you research, keep an alphabetical list of names, specialized terms, foreign or italicized words, and abbreviations, complete with capitalization, diacritics, and words to be set in italics. In many periods and places, people disagreed over how to spell place-names and personal names, so cite your sources as you build your working list, which will allow you to make an informed decision about which spelling to choose. If you add definitions to your terms, you are writing a glossary, which may be worth including in the final version of your work as an aid to the reader.[31]

IMAGE CATALOGS

As historians embraced the digital camera as a means to capture sources in archives and libraries, they faced the challenge of keeping track of thousands or tens of thousands of images and incorporating them into their work. Photo cataloging software can help with both tasks, organizing photos into folders; rotating, sharpening, and otherwise cleaning up images to make text more legible; and allowing the reader to zoom in or out as needed. General-purpose cataloging software, sometimes included with the purchase of a camera, may suffice. The Roy Rosenzweig Center for History and

---

31. For a good example of a helpful glossary, see Karl Jacoby, *Shadows at Dawn: An Apache Massacre and the Violence of History* (New York: Penguin, 2008), 285–90.

New Media has also released Tropy, a free application specifically designed for those who use digital cameras for historical research. As of 2020, it was still relatively new software with additional features being added, so its full potential was not clear.

For fewer images, slide presentation software may be adequate. If you create a slide deck of your favorite images—complete with citation information in the notes area—you can easily extract the slides you want when it comes time to give a presentation.

MAPPING

Maps can be a form of note-taking. Instead of organizing notes by the date of an event or the name of the person most involved, maps organize them by place. The results may cover a single neighborhood or a whole continent.

If all you need is to position a few places in relation to each other, simple tools may work. *A Midwife's Tale*, a film based on the book of the same name, shows Laurel Thatcher Ulrich using a pencil to sketch a map on tracing paper, overlaid on a map of the region of Maine, where her story is set. Presumably sketches like these formed the basis for the more elegant, but still quite simple, maps by Karen Hansen that appear in the book.[32] The digital equivalent of this practice would be to open a base map of the place you are studying in a general-purpose graphics application, then draw the lines, arrows, markers, and text boxes that highlight the information that matters for your story. Such maps can help you understand the information you gather, and serve as material for a professional cartographer or illustrator—such as Hansen—if you are able to publish.

More sophisticated mapping software, such as a geographic information system (GIS), can require greater investment of time and money, but it also provides more tools. If you have a list of coordinates or street addresses, the software may be able to locate them automatically. (Keep in mind that street names and house numbering systems have the bad habit of changing over time.) Software may be able to measure the distance between two points or

---

32. Rogers, *A Midwife's Tale*; Laurel Thatcher Ulrich, *A Midwife's Tale: The Life of Martha Ballard, Based on Her Diary, 1785–1812* (New York: Knopf, 2010), 415.

the area of a particular place. And it can allow you to overlay multiple layers of data in order to make comparisons. One challenge with such projects, however, is keeping them up to date. Some of the most ambitious historical mapping projects of the early 2000s were defunct within fifteen years.[33]

OTHER SPECIALIZED FORMATS

Of course, ingenious people have developed all manner of other specialized record-keeping systems, analog and digital, for specific types of information. If you need to trace the family relations among various people in your study, genealogical software can help you craft a family tree. You could reconstruct a business's finances using accounting software, or use architectural software to recreate a vanished building or landscape. All of these are forms of note-taking, with different forms but the same basic goals.

The Working Draft

A working draft does a job distinct from your notes. Your notes should answer every question you think a reader might ask about your topic; if you find information that you think a reader *might* want, take a note. The working draft is a bit more selective. It includes only the material you think a reader *might well* want to know. Of course, that is only your guess, and you will not know what your readers *do* want to know until you start circulating drafts. Moreover, while there is rarely any reason to delete material from your notes, you will cut passages from your working draft fairly frequently. Keeping drafts and notes separate will give you the confidence to make those cuts. (Even then, do not actually delete the material. Just move it someplace out of the way.)

A workflow with a working draft might look something like this:

1. Read a source and notice something interesting in it.
2. Take a note of the interesting thing.

33. For an introduction to spatial history, see Richard White, "What Is Spatial History?," Spatial History Lab: Working Paper, submitted February 1, 2010, and the Stanford Spatial History Project more generally, http://web.stanford.edu/group/spatialhistory.

3. Consult your working draft. Where would this interesting thing go? Does it conform to what you already know or does it challenge it?
4. Add a sentence to the working draft or change one in light of the new information.
5. Repeat.

Step 3 is particularly important. Comparing the information in your note to the record of what you already know tells you the value of that information. Think again of Linderman's motorcycle. Each time he sees a brake lever in the junkyard, he can quickly ask himself: Do I already have a brake lever and, if I do, is the one I see now sufficiently better than the one I already have to justify picking it up and swapping it out for the existing part?

The working draft need not be elegantly styled. My colleague Scott Berg compares a rough draft to a pile of clay on a worktable. Once you have gathered that clay, you can shape it into something pretty. Nor do you need to write the draft in the order of the final product; it is fine to leave placeholders for material you will seek later. "I need more here about the experiences of children" might be a good note to yourself. Or, "Schiller cites Rowe, *Prophets of Rage*. I should look that up." Or, "I requested *Prophets of Rage* from the library. Here's where I might use it." Then, when the book arrives, you will know what to do with it. Depending on your word processor preferences, you might put such notes in a comment, or format them in bold so that you can see what work remains.

The working draft may include material that you know will need to be trimmed in subsequent drafts. If you find a paragraph-long block of text in a primary source that looks good, go ahead and paste the whole thing into your working draft. You can excerpt and integrate it into the text later. Just make sure to put quotation marks around it so you do not get it confused with your own words. Similarly, the working draft may include multiple arrangements of material. A primary source analysis, a conference paper, a list of themes, or an email to a friend where you try to explain your project— all of these can go in, for now.

While the working draft need not be easy to read, it should be carefully footnoted, likely in much greater detail than your final version will be. Even if you will eventually consolidate footnotes to have just one per paragraph, footnote every sentence in your working draft, so that if you move or delete a sentence, the citation will stay or go with it. Even if your final product will not have any footnotes (as would be the case, say, in a newspaper op-ed), footnoting your working draft will keep you honest and accurate.[34] If you have conflicting or uncertain information, write a long footnote explaining what each source says about the topic at hand. Later, you can review all of those notes and decide what version you believe best matches the available evidence. Or your first draft might offer seven examples to prove a point, and your eventual editor will want just two. Drafting footnotes that clarify which source supports which example will make it easy for you to delete the extra citation along with the extraneous information.

I should note an alternative workflow, preferred by some writers who aim for more stylish writing. That is to take all the notes, put them away, and start with a blank page. David Herbert Donald— admired for his style—explained that "you get a certain fluency in language that you do not have if you have your notes in front of you." Only after crafting a story the way he remembered it going from all his research would he then check his first draft against his notes.[35]

---

34. Samuel Eliot Morison, *History as a Literary Art: An Appeal to Young Historians* (Boston: Old South Association, 1946), 9.

35. Judith Lee Hallock, John C. Waugh, and Drake Bush, *How Historians Work: Retelling the Past—From the Civil War to the Wider World* (Buffalo Gap, TX: State House Press, 2010), 271.

CHAPTER THIRTEEN

Organization

EVERY WORK OF HISTORY IS UNIQUE, but its format need not be. Readers and listeners expect works of any genre to obey long-established conventions of format and style. "The unity of a novel is not the same as the unity of a treatise on politics," write Mortimer Adler and Charles Van Doren, "nor are the parts of the same sort, or ordered in the same way. But every book without exception that is worth reading at all has a unity and an organization of parts. A book that did not would be a mess."[1] The same is largely true of term papers, journal articles, and—to a lesser extent—documentary films, museum exhibits, and websites. Readers, viewers, and visitors arrive with expectations about a format, and the more you can meet those expectations, the more clearly your message will come through.

The advice in this chapter is straightforwardly, unapologetically formulaic. Of course, you are free to depart from convention, which may be necessary to tackle a new topic, to shake a reader out of complacency, or to find your own voice as a writer.[2] But such deviations can mean more work for both the writer and the reader. Moreover, even if you do not choose to follow conventions, others will, so understanding those conventions will help you read their work. It is worth knowing the rules before breaking them.

1. Mortimer J. Adler and Charles Van Doren, *How to Read a Book: The Classic Guide to Intelligent Reading*, rev. ed. (New York: Touchstone, 1972), 75.

2. Aaron Sachs, "Letters to a Tenured Historian: Imagining History as Creative Nonfiction—or Maybe Even Poetry," *Rethinking History* 14 (2010): 5–38.

Tips

- Prepare to work at multiple scales. If you know your major points, you should be able to summarize.
- If you can write a five-paragraph essay, you can write a ten-page paper, a thirty-page article, or a two-hundred-page book.
- Outlines can help at the beginning of the project, in the middle, and during revision.

Scale

In his 2015 book, *One Nation Under God*, Kevin Kruse argued that "the postwar revolution in America's religious identity had its roots not in the foreign policy panic of the 1950s but rather in the domestic politics of the 1930s and early 1940s," as "new evangelists for free enterprise promoted a vision best characterized as 'Christian libertarianism.'"[3] Eager to bring this finding to as many readers as possible and, one assumes, to persuade some of them to buy and read his book, he told the same story in an essay published in the *New York Times*.[4] At 1,400 words, the op-ed is about 1 percent the length of the book, not including the book's footnotes. But it uses the same basic structure: an introduction, some evidence in the form of stories, and a conclusion.

Historians are hardly the only scholars to work at multiple scales. Departments throughout the university encourage graduate students to hone their "elevator talk"—an explanation of their research they could deliver to a stranger in the time it takes to ride between floors—and sponsor "three-minute thesis" competitions, formalizing the time limit to 180 seconds and insisting that the talk be comprehensible to a nonspecialist.[5] On social media, researchers try to summarize their arguments in 280 characters, or using only emoji. At one level, such condensations can be an end in themselves. If you are

3. Kevin M. Kruse, *One Nation Under God: How Corporate America Invented Christian America* (New York: Basic Books, 2015), xiv.

4. Kevin M. Kruse, "A Christian Nation? Since When?," *New York Times*, March 14, 2015.

5. University of Queensland, "Three Minute Thesis," Three Minute Thesis, https://threeminutethesis.uq.edu.au/.

seeking to disseminate your work, or gain research funding, or get a job, you may well be asked to explain the significance of the work to someone who starts with no interest in your topic and has little time to invest in it. If you cannot spark an interest in the first few sentences of a proposal, you may lose your chance.

Moreover, if you can present your findings as a simple story, you reach more people than the longer version ever will. Peter Norton's story of how Americans redefined city streets as spaces dominated by motor vehicles runs for more than 250 pages, plus notes. But by summarizing it in shorter forms, he reached not only journalists but even comedian Adam Conover, who translated Norton's findings into a three-minute television segment that reached close to half a million viewers.[6]

The most important consumer of the short version may be you, as you craft longer, more complete versions of your work. If you can state your most important findings in 180 seconds, you will also be able to state them in an 800-word op-ed, a 20-minute presentation, a 45-minute public lecture, a 10,000-word article, and a 100,000-word book, the only difference being the level of detail, nuance, and evidence you can present. Robert Caro's books run hundreds of pages, but he starts them by writing a summary of at most three paragraphs. "Getting that boiled-down paragraph or two is terribly hard," he explains, "but I have to tell you that my experience is that if you get it, the whole next seven years is easier. . . . You can look over there and say, You're doing this whole thing on civil rights—let's take *Master of the Senate*—the whole history of the civil rights movement. Is this fitting in with those three paragraphs? How is it fitting in? What you just wrote is good, but it's not fitting in. So you have to throw it away or find a way to make it fit in. So it's very comforting to have that."[7]

The opposite of the one-paragraph summary is the encyclopedia that you must not write. A history of the Washington Metro is

6. Peter D. Norton, *Fighting Traffic: The Dawn of the Motor Age in the American City* (Cambridge, MA: MIT Press, 2011); Adam Conover, "Adam Ruins Cars," *Adam Ruins Everything*, TruTV, October 11, 2015; "UPDATED: SHOWBUZZDAILY's Top 100 Tuesday Cable Originals & Network Update: 10.13.2015," http://www.showbuzzdaily.com/articles/showbuzzdailys-top-100-tuesday-cable-originals-network-update-10-13-2015.html.

7. Robert A. Caro, *Working* (New York: Knopf, 2019), 199.

not the encyclopedia of the Washington Metro, I reminded myself again and again. Take any work of history off the shelf, and you can imagine a version that would be ten times longer. Quite possibly, the author assembled enough notes for that but found a way to tell the story, and make the key points, in a manageable length.

The reader who wants the longest version is probably you. As I was trying to decide whether to keep in some detail in my dissertation, one committee member—Betsy Blackmar—assured me, "if *you* don't care about this, no one does." That is not always true; there are critics who will be disappointed, even angry, if you leave out information on some topic about which they are passionate. But as a general rule, imagine a reader who is less fascinated by your topic than you are, and who will not wish your work to be any longer than you do.

The Foundational Five-Paragraph Essay

At any scale, you are likely to need an introduction, a conclusion, and some evidence in between. American high school students are introduced to this concept by being taught to write five-paragraph essays: an introduction, three body paragraphs in support, and a conclusion. Some writing instructors argue that this format is too constraining, but as both a teacher and a writer, I find it essential for three reasons.

First, it is important to be able to express yourself in 1,000- to 1,500-word chunks. That is the length of a newspaper op-ed, a brief article for a magazine, and many a blog post or encyclopedia entry. (For museum work, learn to write in even tighter 50–100 word chunks, suitable for wall panels.)

Second, a great deal of scholarly writing is composed of short essays, each not much longer than five paragraphs. For instance, Karin Wulf dissects a thirty-five-hundred-word review essay by Annette Gordon-Reed, finding it to consist almost entirely of three-paragraph sections strung together.[8] If you can master the five- or six-paragraph essay, you can likely stretch to ten or fifteen

8. Karin Wulf, "The Art and Craft of Review," *Scholarly Kitchen* (blog), January 9, 2017, https://scholarlykitchen.sspnet.org/2017/01/09/the-art-and-craft-of-review/.

paragraphs. A bundle of sections becomes a chapter, and a bundle of chapters becomes a book. I own shelves of history books built one fifteen-paragraph essay at a time. Thus, the first step to writing a book may be a five-paragraph essay.

Finally, the five-paragraph form is a microcosm of larger works. An article or chapter has an introduction, a conclusion, and a series of sections in between. A book has an introduction, a conclusion, and a series of chapters in between. Really long books organize these chapters into parts, again sandwiched between introduction and conclusion. For a museum exhibit, the units may be walls, which in turn are organized into rooms, which in turn make up the exhibit. More popular, narrative histories may swap out the introduction and conclusion for a prologue and epilogue, or a foreword and afterword, but it is still a sandwich. At any scale, then, the historian needs some kind of opening, a series of spaces in which to present and analyze evidence, and some kind of closure.

With its three body paragraphs, the five-paragraph essay form builds on the rule of three, which has shaped Western drama from Greek tragedies through the *Star Wars* trilogy of trilogies, and which many historians adapt for their own works. For example, Sam Bass Warner organized *The Private City: Philadelphia in Three Periods of Its Growth* into three parts: "The Eighteenth-Century Town," "The Big City," and "The Industrial Metropolis."[9] Similarly, Dell Upton divided his history of Philadelphia and New Orleans by theme: "The Lived City," "Metropolitan Improvements," and "Public Spaces and Private Citizens."[10] While Warner used chronology and Upton used themes, the three-part structure served both of them well. At smaller scales, a division into threes allows a thesis, antithesis, and synthesis. Section 1 could state one side's position in a debate, section 2 could state the opposing case, and section 3 could explain how the conflict was resolved. But there is nothing mandatory about threes; Shakespeare wrote his plays in five acts. Historians' books may well have anywhere from four to twelve chapters sandwiched between beginning and end; beyond

9. Sam Bass Warner, *The Private City: Philadelphia in Three Periods of Its Growth*, 2nd ed. (Philadelphia: University of Pennsylvania Press, 1987).

10. Dell Upton, *Another City: Urban Life and Urban Spaces in the New American Republic* (New Haven, CT: Yale University Press, 2008).

that number, it is likely best to group chapters into parts. For really long stories, plan multiple volumes.

VARIANTS: THE TEN- AND THIRTY-PAGE PAPERS

A ten-page term paper is merely an expanded version of the five-paragraph essay. Instead of an introductory paragraph, stretch the introduction into two paragraphs: a lede (explained below) and a thesis. Instead of three body paragraphs, write three body sections, each of six paragraphs. Instead of a paragraph conclusion, write a two-paragraph conclusion. Add those together and you have written twenty-two paragraphs, about ten or eleven pages. The thirty-page paper—roughly the length of a seminar paper, a journal article, or a somewhat short dissertation or book chapter—is only slightly more complex. The introduction can grow to around eight paragraphs, including lede, thesis, and historiography. The body may be about forty-five to fifty paragraphs total. These can range in size and number (three sections of sixteen paragraphs each, four of twelve, perhaps five of ten), and need not be uniform in size. If a background section is needed, keep it to about three paragraphs. The conclusion need not be longer than the two paragraphs of a shorter paper.

All of these paragraph counts are, of course, rough estimates, not rigid formulae. What matters is that you understand longer papers as expanded versions of shorter essays, and that you budget your time and your words to help your reader keep track of the flow of your argument and narrative.

Introductions

An introduction to an analytic work must state a thesis. It may also include two additional parts. First, a lede—the journalist's term for a short but provocative flash of narrative that, one hopes, will make the reader care enough about the people in the story to work through the more difficult analytical claims.[11] A good lede

11. Marc Lacey, "Watch Your Lapels: These Great Ledes Are Coming for Them," *New York Times*, January 15, 2019.

Table 13.1. Paragraph Budgets for Short, Medium, and Long Papers

	Five-Paragraph Essay	Ten-Page Paper	Thirty-Page Paper
Introduction	1	2	8
Body 1	1	6	16
Body 2	1	6	16
Body 3	1	6	16
Conclusion	1	2	2
Total Paragraphs	5	22	58

is particularly important for newspaper op-eds and other brief pieces meant to capture the attention of nonspecialists. Indeed, I often ask my own students to write six-paragraph essays instead of the traditional five paragraphs, splitting the introduction into a lede paragraph and a more analytical one to follow. The second optional part is the historiography, which highlights the novelty of the work's findings.

LEDES

In September 1986, Nancy Schrom Dye and Daniel Blake Smith tried to get the attention of readers of the *Journal of American History* with the following opening paragraph:

> American motherhood has only recently begun to acquire a past. Mothering is far more than a biological constant; it is an activity whose meaning has altered considerably over time. Changes in cultural values, maternal self-perceptions, and attitudes toward children—all these factors underscore the historical dimensions of motherhood. Indeed, the shifting status of women and the changing nature of the family in history cannot be fully understood without close study of the experience of mothering.[12]

In the following paragraphs, they made claims for the significance of the topic, argued that existing scholarship has left questions

12. Nancy Schrom Dye and Daniel Blake Smith, "Mother Love and Infant Death, 1750–1920," *Journal of American History* 73 (1986): 329.

unanswered, posed research questions, listed the sources they would use to answer the question, and presented a thesis of change over continuity—all very methodical, scientific, precise, and dispassionate, in a tone that could be found in historical journals dating back to the late nineteenth century. Was there another way?

Jacquelyn Dowd Hall thought so. In the very next article in the same issue of the same journal, Hall opened her article as follows:

> The rising sun "made a sort of halo around the crown of Cross Mountain" as Flossie Cole climbed into a neighbor's Model T and headed west down the gravel road to Elizabethton, bound for work in a rayon plant. Emerging from Stony Creek hollow, the car joined a caravan of buses and self-styled "taxis" brimming with young people from dozens of tiny communities strung along the creek branches and nestled in the coves of the Blue Ridge Mountains of East Tennessee. The caravan picked up speed as it hit paved roads and crossed the Watauga River bridge, passing beneath a sign advertising Elizabethton's newfound identity as a "City of Power." By the time Cole reached the factory gate, it was 7:00 A.M., time to begin another ten-hour day as a reeler at the American Glanzstoff plant.
>
> The machines whirred, and work began as usual. But the reeling room stirred with anticipation. The day before, March 12, 1929, all but seventeen of the 360 women in the inspection room next door had walked out in protest against low wages, petty rules, and high-handed attitudes. Now they were gathered at the factory gate, refusing to work but ready to negotiate. When 9:00 A.M. approached and the plant manager failed to appear, they broke past the guards and rushed through the plant, urging their co-workers out on strike. By 1:40 P.M. the machines were idle and the plant was closed.[13]

Here we have no grand claims, no discussion of the state of scholarship, no explicit research questions. Instead, Hall gives us a setting, characters, conflict, and events. Only after she has us desperate to know the fate of Flossie Cole and the hundreds of other striking women does she start writing about "female friendships and sexuality, cross-generational and cross-class alliances, the incorporation

---

13. Jacquelyn Dowd Hall, "Disorderly Women: Gender and Labor Militancy in the Appalachian South," *Journal of American History* 73 (1986): 354.

of new consumer desires into a dynamic regional culture" and citing Michel Foucault. By contrast, readers of the Dye and Smith article must get through nearly three pages of analysis before reaching the agonized words of an eighteenth-century clergyman whose infant daughter had just died.

Episode ledes like Hall's are a matter of taste, but they have grown quite popular among historians. In her survey of academic writing, Helen Sword found that 58 percent of historians' articles feature an "engaging opening," the highest percentage of any of the ten fields she studied.[14] Note, however, that not just any story can serve as a lede; it should focus attention on the main themes that will follow.[15] Thus, Hall's lede not only tells an exciting story but also introduces her emphasis on women workers' readiness to challenge authority.

When writing for newspapers and magazines, historians often start with a contemporary event, known as a "news hook." For example, near the start of his op-ed, Kruse observes that "just a few weeks ago, Public Policy Polling reported that 57 percent of Republicans favored officially making the United States a Christian nation." Occasionally one sees this in scholarship as well. In 1893, for example, Frederick Jackson Turner opened his now-classic essay, "The Significance of the Frontier in American History," by quoting the findings of "a recent bulletin of the Superintendent of the Census."[16] But he was pushing his luck; most such ledes seem dated after a while. Better to tell a story from the past. That census report will eventually no longer be recent, but Flossie Cole will forever head west.

THESIS STATEMENT

A thesis statement is a brief presentation of the main argument, or thesis, of a work of any length. Typically, historians present their thesis statements toward the beginning of a work, often at the end

14. Helen Sword, *Stylish Academic Writing* (Cambridge, MA: Harvard University Press, 2012), 17, fig. 2.1.

15. Barbara Young Welke, "The Art of Manuscript Reviewing: Learning from the Example of Peggy Pascoe," *Perspectives on History*, September 2011.

16. Frederick J. Turner, "The Significance of the Frontier in American History," *Annual Report of the American Historical Association*, 1893, 199.

of the introduction to a section, article, chapter, or book. Since the historian has not yet presented the key evidence, a thesis statement is a claim about what the following evidence will show. It is analogous to the opening statement of a prosecutor in a criminal case, or to the bid of a player in a game of bridge. As in bridge, the bolder the bid, the more points one gets for "making contract," that is, winning as many tricks as one has predicted. The challenge is to make as bold a claim as you can support with evidence.

A thesis statement can take many forms, but here I would like to offer a formula that historians, other scholars, and analytic writers often deploy, and that is at least worth considering for many works of history:

> [Why] did [people] do/say/write [something surprising]? [Plausible alternative explanation], but in fact [better or more complete explanation].[17]

I offer this formula to suggest that a good thesis has all five elements, not that they need to appear in that specific format. That said, historians not infrequently craft claims that take the form almost precisely. Often, this requires a full paragraph, or something close to it:

> Julia Gaffield: Why did Dessalines and Nugent fail to reach a trade agreement? Pivotal decisions changed the trajectory of the negotiations from 1803 to 1806. Jamaican authorities and the British government in London were less concerned about the consequences of dealing with a country governed by former slaves than much of the literature about the Haitian Revolution has suggested.[18]

> Pekka Hämäläinen: Why was it that only the Comanches—among the hundreds of Native American nations—managed to build an empire that eclipsed and subsumed Euro-American colonial realms? . . . What was it that made Comanches exceptional? The historian's instinct

---

17. I have adapted the idea of a thesis-statement template from the "magic thesis" presented by the UCLA Undergraduate Writing Center, "What, How, and So What?," https://wp.ucla.edu/wp-content/uploads/2016/01/UWC_handouts_What-How-So-What -Thesis-revised-5-4-15-RZ.pdf.

18. Julia Gaffield, "Haiti and Jamaica in the Remaking of the Early Nineteenth-Century Atlantic World," *William and Mary Quarterly* 69 (2012): 585.

suggests that the Comanches' extraordinary ascendancy must have intersected with parallel Euro-American weakness and disinterest, but in reality Comanches operated in one of the most fiercely contested imperial arenas in North America. . . . Rather than a reflection of Euro-American indifference, Comanches' rise to dominance stemmed from their own adaptive culture, their ability to harness Euro-American resources—both material and nonmaterial—to their own advantage.[19]

Matthew Karp: In the 1850s the proslavery South's leading politicians and intellectuals confronted a new and urgent set of domestic challenges, beginning with the eclipse of southern parity in the Senate, and accelerating into a sectional crisis of unprecedented intensity. Why, then, did so many of them bother to develop an opinion about labor relations in faraway South America? Unlike slavery in Kansas, the Southwest, or even Cuba or Mexico, the fate of Brazilian bondage had little direct bearing on the domestic politics of the United States. Southern thinkers and actors concerned themselves with the condition of labor in Latin America for reasons that went beyond the raging sectional struggle, immediate commercial interest, or even the anxious geopolitics that guided Tyler and Calhoun's foreign policy in the 1840s. South American slavery mattered most of all to southern elites because it gave concrete expression to a larger economic truth that they believed the world had only just begun to understand.[20]

Bartow J. Elmore: Why did the [Environmental Protection Agency] allow these pollution problems to go on for so long? In answering this question, one might posit the possibility that Monsanto, through cunning deception, kept critical information about contamination from both the government and the public. Such an account would mesh well with works such as Erik M. Conway and Naomi Oreskes's *Merchants of Doubt* or Gerald Markowitz and David Rosner's *Deceit and Denial*, which document the ways in which industries paid scientists to make deceitful claims about toxic pollution associated with industrial processes. But calculated corporate duplicity was not the key behind community acceptance of corporate contamination in Soda Springs. . . . In

19. Pekka Hämäläinen, *The Comanche Empire* (New Haven, CT: Yale University Press, 2008), 345, 346.
20. Matthew Karp, *This Vast Southern Empire* (Cambridge, MA: Harvard University Press, 2016), 148.

the end, many residents, with open eyes, agreed to accept certain health risks in exchange for remediation measures that would not fundamentally disrupt the economic vitality of the community.[21]

Each of the preceding passages has the following key elements.

Why?

History theses answer the question why or, occasionally, how. Who, what, where, and when are important too, but why and how make an argument.

People

History is about people. Abstract nouns (capitalism, war, society, etc.) are important, but a thesis without people lacks life. Historians write about individuals (Dessalines and Nugent), groups (the Comanches, politicians, and intellectuals), or institutions made of people (the Environmental Protection Agency).

Something surprising

The function of any scholarship is to explore the unknown and the mysterious. The failure of the negotiations is surprising because the negotiators had worked together for three years. The success of the Comanches is surprising because they alone succeeded where hundreds of Native American nations failed. Southern attention to Latin America is surprising because domestic concerns were more pressing. The passivity of the EPA is surprising because its very mission is to protect the environment. Challenge yourself with difficult questions.

Plausible alternative explanation

Each historian presents but then rejects an answer to their stated question; we are *not* to attribute the surprising thing to a reluctance to deal with a country governed by former slaves, Euro-American weakness and disinterest, the raging sectional struggle, or cunning deception. In these examples, historians refer to the work of other

21. Bartow J. Elmore, "Roundup from the Ground Up: A Supply-Side Story of the World's Most Widely Used Herbicide," *Agricultural History* 93 (2019): 107.

scholars: "much of the literature about the Haitian Revolution," "the historian's instinct," and, most explicitly, the works of Erik M. Conway and Naomi Oreskes and Gerald Markowitz and David Rosner. By positioning their own arguments against such established wisdom, the historians are showing that they are offering something new. In other cases, the plausible explanation might come from the historical actors, not other scholars. For instance, if eighteenth-century Spaniards, rather than "the historian's instinct," had attributed Comanche success to Euro-American weakness and disinterest, Hämäläinen would still have a foil against which to argue.

A better or more complete explanation

Finally, we have the factor that historians themselves believe best answers the question: the belief that British interests could be best served without an official treaty, the Comanches' adaptive culture, a confidence about slavery's role in the world, and a community's agreement to accept certain health risks. Though this is the part that the historian may treasure the most, only by framing it can they establish its value.

While historians sometimes summarize their theses in a sentence or two, they often take a full paragraph to present all five of these elements. (Even the somewhat long quotations above have been excerpted from longer paragraphs.) Of course, one need not follow the precise template. Some historians avoid rhetorical questions as a matter of stylistic preference, while others may not explain what interpretation they are arguing against with the clarity of these examples. Moreover, while most historians state their theses in a work's introduction, the formula sometimes appears in a conclusion, as it does in Hämäläinen's book. And even if your final product never contains a thesis in this format, it may be helpful as part of a working draft.

The template is also a tool to identify the theses in works you are reading, whether or not they adhere to the specific form. Look for the elements in a work's introduction and conclusion, and you can more easily determine its main argument. And the template is a research tool. Understanding a thesis statement as the weighing of two plausible, alternative explanations is a reminder that it is best to start a project with a question, not a firm answer. If you find yourself at equilibrium between two plausible explanations but think that more evidence would help you choose between them, you have framed a research question.

HISTORIOGRAPHY

Not all introductions include historiography. Most readers of newspaper or magazine articles do not care about debates among historians, and classroom instructors, especially at the secondary or undergraduate level, may want their students to focus on primary sources, not scholars' debates. Even published journal articles often compress the historiography to two or three paragraphs of the main text or even confine it to footnotes—sometimes long ones citing dozens of previous works. By contrast, seminar instructors and dissertation committees are likely to be quite interested in how your account builds on previous scholarship. Thus, the historiography of a seminar paper may be considerably longer than that of a journal article of equal length. For such papers, the historiography sections of books and dissertations may offer better models than do journal articles.

Regardless of length, a historiography section must achieve three tasks:

1. Explain how other scholars have approached the research question in general.
2. Explain how other scholars have approached (or ignored) the specific research question.
3. Explain how your work uses new questions or sources to answer the question.

Because the historiography can interrupt the flow from the introduction to the main body of a story, it may be helpful to restate the thesis at the end of the historiography section, with reference to other scholarship. For instance, Joel Black offers two versions of his argument that lawyer Richard Westbrooks relied on a theory of presumed or implied equality.

- Without historiography: "In an era when courts refused to decree Black equality, Westbrooks articulated a spectrum of individual and collective, and of partial and comprehensive,

citizenship statuses that derived from the implied equality of
local law."
- With historiography: "By proposing an alternative to legal
  liberal analyses of civil rights, this paper uses 'Legal Helps' to
  examine law away from courts, and carries forward discussions
  of popular justice by Elizabeth Dale and Donald Nieman to
  illustrate popular constructions of citizenship, and to highlight
  the efforts of civil-rights activists to make the constitutional
  presumption of equality a mechanism of social change."[22]

Though the arguments are the same, each version does distinct
work. The first is easier to read and remember, answering the question of why Westbrooks wrote what he did. The second is nearly
twice as long (and it comes with a much longer footnote), but it
answers an additional important question: If the reader is already
familiar with the existing scholarship on pre-1954 civil rights law,
what will they learn from this study?

Body

The body of your work should constitute about 75 percent of your
paper. It is the essence of your contribution, the pastrami of your
sandwich, to which the rest of the paper contributes only the pum-
pernickel bread that holds it together and the Russian dressing that
sets off the flavor of the meat. Whereas the background section
may cite mostly secondary sources, the body of the work should cite
mostly primary sources. Other parts of the paper can show what
other scholars have done; this is the chance for you to add new
sources to the collective account.

SECTIONS

Breaking a larger story or argument into parts will help you budget
your time as you write and help your reader keep track of the flow
of your argument and narrative. Some books and articles consist

22. Joel E. Black, "A Theory of African-American Citizenship: Richard Westbrooks,
The Great Migration, and the *Chicago Defender*'s 'Legal Helps' Column," *Journal of Social
History* 46 (2013): 897–98.

of relatively few, long chapters or sections, while others are broken into more, shorter divisions. The decision involves trade-offs. Longer sections make the structure clearer, dividing a story into three to five acts. Shorter sections mean more ledes, introductions, and conclusions. Thus, breaking up a project into more sections is like staggering the floor plan of a hotel to maximize the number of rooms with waterfront views. If you have a lot of characters to introduce, or your narrative is composed of many small, discrete episodes, this can work well. It is also possible to blend the two forms. Kate Brown's *Plutopia* has forty-three short chapters, an unusually high number. But by grouping them into four parts, Brown gives readers a sense of the big picture they might otherwise miss.[23]

However long your chapters or sections, it helps the reader if they are all roughly the same length. Making the longest chapter or section no more than 2.5 times the length of the shortest one is good. A 3:2 ratio is even better. Thus, for an article or chapter, you could aim for sections of between 1,500 and 4,000 words, or 1,000 and 2,500 words.

Books always signal new chapters with page breaks and titles, or at least numbers. Chapters and articles can signal new sections with headings or subheads, which are essentially titles for the multiparagraph essays that follow. Some journals even offer two levels of hierarchy—bold headings denoting major sections and headings in italics to distinguish subsections within those sections.[24] Others denote section breaks with blank lines, numbers, a row of asterisks, or ornamental characters, such as fleurons. It is a matter of taste, to be settled between author, editor, and publisher. As a teacher, I can report that my students have an easier time understanding articles and chapters with explicit subheads. Yet they learn to detect a story's internal structure from more subtle typographical cues, becoming more expert readers.

---

23. Kate Brown, *Plutopia: Nuclear Families, Atomic Cities, and the Great Soviet and American Plutonium Disasters* (New York: Oxford University Press, 2013).

24. See, e.g., Antony Adler, "The Ship as Laboratory: Making Space for Field Science at Sea," *Journal of the History of Biology* 47 (August 1, 2014): 333–62.

BACKGROUND

The first section of a stand-alone work (as opposed to a chapter of a larger work) often provides background, explaining all that has happened before the start of your story. This background section should be relatively brief, since you do not want to devote too much of your time or your reader's to someone else's work. For a book, a single chapter is likely enough. For a seminar paper or article, three paragraphs should do it. A good example is found in Ann Ziker's "Segregationists Confront American Empire." In about four paragraphs, Ziker tells the story of Hawai'i's annexation and statehood, from the 1890s through the 1950s, based largely on the work of Roger Bell and other scholars.[25] That provides the necessary background for her own contribution, a study of how white segregationists viewed the congressional debate from afar. That is, she uses secondary sources to speed through decades of history, then slows down to read carefully the primary sources from a debate that lasted just months. Often, the reader can find the end of the background section by seeing secondary sources give way to primary sources in the accompanying citations.

SECTIONS AS INDEPENDENT ESSAYS

With the background out of the way, each body section needs its own claim, one that supports the overall argument. For example, Kathleen Franz devotes one chapter of *Tinkering: Consumers Reinvent the Early Automobile* to "Women's Ingenuity." In the first section, "Motor Girls: Technological Heroines and Popular Feminists" (twenty-two paragraphs), Franz describes books that presented young women as technologically adept, able to swerve around children in the street or repair a radiator hose with strips of a torn-up mackintosh. The second section, "No Vacation for the Motor Wife" (fourteen paragraphs), offers a contrasting look at novels, advice literature, and magazine articles that told women

---

25. Ann K. Ziker, "Segregationists Confront American Empire: The Conservative White South and the Question of Hawaiian Statehood, 1947–1959," *Pacific Historical Review* 76 (2007): 442–46.

on car trips that their main responsibilities were cooking and cleaning at the campsite. A third and final section, "Undermining Women's Skills" (thirteen paragraphs), concludes the story with a victory for the enforcers of traditional gender norms. Franz then ends the chapter with a one-paragraph conclusion, noting that despite women's early efforts to "define women as equal to men in their claim to the automobile," the "window of opportunity for women to claim equal authority in driving and repairing or modifying the automobile, however, closed as male advice experts asserted that woman's place was not behind the wheel but in the passenger seat next to her husband, the real mechanical expert."[26] Scaled up, each chapter in Franz's book functions somewhat independently, with its own thesis, though the whole is more than the sum of its parts.

Note the clarity of Franz's headings for these sections. "No Vacation for the Motor Wife" is a lovely title, half concealing, half disclosing its argument. We get a hint of the tension within many marriages, and we even know the outcome of the story: the wife gets no vacation. But Franz also seeds curiosity by using the 1910s term "motor wife," making me, at least, eager to learn more about that role. For an extreme version of this kind of signposting, read a legal brief, such as the ones that historians occasionally submit as amici in important Supreme Court cases. Commenting on a gerrymandering case, one team of historians argued that the framers of the Constitution were aware of the evils of disproportionate representation in the British Parliament. That section of the brief is given the long but unambiguous title, "The Framers Rejected 'Corruption' of Representation in the British System and Sought to Prevent Similar Undemocratic Entrenchment By Factions in the American System."[27] While most published formats frown on such wordy headings, you can build your working outlines from equally clear, single-sentence summaries of the main argument or event in each section.

26. Kathleen Franz, *Tinkering: Consumers Reinvent the Early Automobile* (Philadelphia: University of Pennsylvania Press, 2011), 72.

27. Brief of Amici Curiae Historians in Support of Appellees, Gill v. Whitford, No. 16–1161, 2017, https://www.brennancenter.org/our-work/court-cases/gill-v-whitford.

TOPIC SENTENCES

A topic sentence—usually the first sentence of a paragraph—should fit evidence or analysis into a broader argument. To do so, it does three things.

1. A topic sentence holds facts together. When you have a series of facts on the same general subject, group them together and summarize them with a topic sentence.

2. A topic sentence relates the paragraph to what came before. It often will contain transition words showing continuity (next, another, more) or a turning point in the argument (despite, nevertheless, but). If you are writing a narrative, a topic sentence can signal a shift in time (in 1968, four years later), simultaneity (meanwhile, while), or even a flashback (five months earlier).

3. A topic sentence can relate facts to argument. Not all topic sentences do this; historians sometimes write paragraphs that merely lay out factual information, introducing people, places, and events. But in many cases, in addition to summarizing the facts within a paragraph, a topic sentence can show their relevance to your overall thesis. To do so, a topic sentence not only states facts but also makes claims about those facts, serving as the thesis statement of a one-paragraph essay.

For an example of topic sentences at work, see Robert Self's article "'To Plan Our Liberation': Black Power and the Politics of Place in Oakland, California, 1965–1977."[28] Self's overall thesis is that "black power as a political phenomenon was not primarily a response to the civil rights movement but a parallel development that sought to redistribute economic and political power within the increasingly divided metropolis without emphasizing integration." In the following passage, Self offers evidence in the form of examples of actions by the Black Panther Party:

---

28. Robert Self, "'To Plan Our Liberation': Black Power and the Politics of Place in Oakland, California, 1965–1977," *Journal of Urban History* 26 (September 2000): 759–92.

The Panthers' critique began with the physical destruction of West Oakland and moved, in an ever widening arc, to encompass the principal contradictions of the East Bay economy as a whole. Using the publications of the Oakland Project, the University of California's multiyear study of Oakland, the results of the federal government's 701 housing survey, and various reports and research papers produced by the Survey Research Center (affiliated with the University of California, Berkeley), the *Black Panther* documented for its readers the systematic demolition and redevelopment of West Oakland. Here were the familiar culprits: BART, the new freeways and federal post office, the closing of public housing projects, massive delays on West Oakland's biggest new housing project, Acorn, and residential displacement. "BART has spent over 20 million dollars," the newspaper cited as an example, "has literally dislocated thousands of people in West Oakland, offered few of the promised jobs to Blacks, and has the nerve to make one stop in West Oakland." The *Black Panther* published special editions on the cost of living, public housing (exposing problems in the Oakland Housing Authority), imbalances in urban and suburban public school budgets, urban renewal, and unemployment. It was a remarkably coherent body of critical journalistic work, concluded after its first year, 1972, with a special issue titled "Our Challenge for 1973." The latter became the political platform on which Bobby Seale and Elaine Brown ran for local office.

More than anything else, the party seized upon the Port of Oakland as a symbol of the city's failed priorities and the deep contradictions within local economic development. "While the Port thrives, Oakland stagnates," read the headline in a special edition of the *Black Panther* in 1972. "Its spiraling growth, which began a few years ago, has not brought about the same kind of increase in employment for Black and poor people in Oakland." Indeed, the Port of Oakland had become the West Coast's busiest and largest, doubling its annual income between 1968 and 1972. According to the Panthers, though, "the city gets little in return: no jobs and no access to Port income at a time when Oakland city government flirts with bankruptcy." In fact, the party contended, "tenants get special tax privileges to lower their property tax bills, and in some instances the Port actually pays their property taxes." The Panthers highlighted the odd independence of the Port. Its Board of Commissioners was appointed by the mayor, but city hall had little other official control over Port activities and revenue. The Port remained a public entity, technically owned by the city, but its operations and revenue were virtually untouchable. As the *Black Panther* observed, this arrangement meant that when public tax dollars were invested in the port—as had happened during its phenomenal growth—the proceeds redounded primarily to the benefit of private shipping companies, not the residents of Oakland. In all, the party argued, the Port's operation was another example of the city's "behind the scenes deals for millions of dollars, money that is never used to benefit us [Oakland citizens]."

The party's two-year campaign mixed its older anticolonial discourse with this new attention to local political and economic arrangements in Oakland. The Panthers linked the Port's growth, for instance, to the "imperialist war" in Vietnam, even likening Oakland to "other colonial cities of Asia or Africa: Shanghai, Singapore, Alexandria, and Hong Kong" because of the nearby army base and U.S. Naval Supply Center from which soldiers and materiel were shipped to Southeast Asia. Although the party's characterization of Oakland as a colonial outpost bordered on the fanciful and defined the outer limits of Panther discursive excesses, other "Base of Operation" critiques had more substantial merit. The party consistently emphasized the enormous percentage of the city's white workforce that lived outside of Oakland (more than 50 percent by some estimations), particularly the municipal police force and members of the fire department. Party journalists wrote countless articles on the failure of federal redevelopment and urban renewal projects to provide opportunity for local residents while nearby industrial suburbs boomed with new factory and construction jobs. In 1973, the Panthers urged a full reassessment of the city's tax structure and advocated raising taxes on the long-sheltered downtown properties and reducing the property tax burden on small businesses and residents in the neighborhoods. And, in preparation for the 1973 municipal elections, the party prepared a detailed spatial analysis of past Oakland voting patterns, exploring divisions between white and black neighborhoods on such issues as public housing and district versus at-large elections for city council, as well as about congressional and California Assembly candidates.

The topic sentences are as follows:

> The Panthers' critique began with the physical destruction of West Oakland and moved, in an ever widening arc, to encompass the principal contradictions of the East Bay economy as a whole. More than anything else, the party seized upon the Port of Oakland as a symbol of the city's failed priorities and the deep contradictions within local economic development. The party's two-year campaign mixed its older anticolonial discourse with this new attention to local political and economic arrangements in Oakland.

The first thing to notice is that strung together, the topic sentences *summarize the passage* as a whole. If the whole article is written in this way, then a reader can zip through the piece by reading only the first sentence of each paragraph, choosing to read full paragraphs only when they want to know more about the claim made in the topic sentence. Few if any books and articles are written entirely in this manner, but in most cases, one can get the gist of a paragraph by reading the first two sentences, or the first and last sentence. Aim for the same kind of summary. (This, by the way, is what makes it possible to skim an academic history book in two or three hours. Read all of the topic sentences, but only read the rest of each paragraph when the topic sentence makes you want to know more.)

The second point is that the topic sentences *support the overall thesis* about the importance of metropolitan debates to black power ideology. The first two paragraphs connect the Panthers' overall program to specific concerns about Oakland, while the last connects these to the anticolonial strand of black power thinking. Thus, each topic sentence serves as a more specific version of the thesis.

The passage presents a great deal of detail in the form of names, dates, and statistics, all of them important to Self's argument, but the topic sentences themselves *make arguments rather than stating facts*. You can think of topic sentences as the labels on drawers of a filing cabinet, while the facts are the files kept neatly inside.

Note in particular that Self's topic sentences do not include direct quotations; he saves those for the bodies of the paragraphs.

Historians only rarely use quotations in their topic sentences, since the topic sentences should present the scholar's voice, not the sources'.

Self presents each topic sentence in the active voice, with active verbs: began, moved, encompass, seized, and mixed—not a "was" or "were" in the lot. And while two of the three sentences have abstract nouns (critique and campaign) as their subjects, they are connected closely enough to a group of people—the Black Panthers—that the reader has no doubt about whose story this is.

Self is also careful about his use of transitions. The first sentence uses the verb "began," signaling that he is moving to a new topic, or a new chapter in his story. The next one uses "more" to hint that it is an elaboration on what just came before. That is, while the first paragraph discusses several places in the East Bay, the second one focuses on just one: the Port of Oakland. The third topic sentence's transitional word is "mixed." Self tells us to keep in mind what we have just read, because he is about to mix in a new element. Without these topic sentences, Self's careful research would be but a jumble of names and dates. With them, it becomes a powerful argument.

Conclusions

Not all histories have conclusions. Popular narratives, for instance, may end with epilogues, explaining what happened between the end of the main action and the deaths of all the major characters. But for analytical histories, a brief conclusion is critical. Even if it is only a couple of paragraphs—5 percent of an article-length work—a conclusion can do important work.

While I generally advise students to model their work on that of accomplished historians, this may not work with conclusions, since otherwise expert historians often fail at this task. I have read many fine works and articles that end abruptly, leaving me wondering what I was supposed to have learned from the story. This is also the most common critique I have gotten on my own work. Writing conclusions is hard.

The biggest challenge is to avoid repetition, since like the introduction, the conclusion presents the research question and the thesis. But it does so to a different reader. The reader of your introduction did not know much about your topic, and certainly had not been exposed to the stories and evidence you have so carefully compiled. By the time they get to your conclusion, they are conversant with the events you have studied. Remind them of what they have learned and why it matters. This is important both at the very end of a work and at the end of each chapter of a book or dissertation. You want the reader to leave you carrying your most important ideas.

ANSWERING QUESTIONS

An *ending* terminates the narrative of a story. A *conclusion* terminates the argument. The conclusion is not the place to introduce new evidence; it is the place to point out the big themes to readers who have followed you through a mass of smaller details. In *The Dead Will Arise*, J. B. Peires begins his conclusion by addressing those readers directly. "You probably began this book with a number of questions in mind," he writes, "and, as it draws to a close, you might be wondering whether any of these questions has really been answered."[29] To show that they have, he proceeds to list a dozen questions about the events he has narrated, along with answers ranging from two to seven paragraphs. In case that is not enough, each answer refers readers back to the chapter where Peires has laid out and analyzed the evidence at greater length. The conclusion even gets a catchy title: "Everything You Always Wanted to Know About the Xhosa Cattle-Killing."

Few if any historians write their entire conclusions in quite that question-and-answer format, though perhaps more should. And some do pose and answer questions as part of their conclusions. "Why did most men in Reserve Police Battalion 101 become killers," asks Christopher Browning at the start of his book's conclusion, "while only a minority of perhaps 10 percent—and certainly no more than 20 percent—did not?"[30]

To answer the questions you post in your conclusions, you need not restate all the evidence, only summarize it. "Our story began

29. Jeffrey B. Peires, *The Dead Will Arise: Nongqawuse and the Great Xhosa Cattle-Killing Movement of 1856-7* (Bloomington: Indiana University Press, 1989), 309.

30. Christopher R. Browning, *Ordinary Men: Reserve Police Battalion 101 and the Final Solution in Poland* (New York: HarperPerennial, 1998), 159.

in the 1970s," write Naomi Oreskes and Erik Conway, "when Fred Seitz was already retired from the Rockefeller University and began defending tobacco, although he was a solid-state physicist, not a biologist, oncologist, or physician. The story continued in the 1980s, when Seitz joined forces with Robert Jastrow and William Nierenberg. How much original research on SDI or acid rain or the ozone hole or secondhand smoke or global warming did any of them do? The answer is nearly none."[31]

Taken out of context, this passage is hard to follow. Who are these people, what does SDI stand for, and what do that and tobacco, acid rain, the ozone hole, secondhand smoke, and global warming have in common? Were they addressing people fresh to their topic, the authors would have to explain all of these terms and their connections. But they are not; they are writing a conclusion, aimed at readers to whom they have carefully introduced each scientist, each policy debate, and the relationship between those debates and accompanying debates about science. Having done all that work, they only need to remind readers of the topics they have covered before stressing a question they want the reader to ask, and giving the answer. Had dissenters from the scientific consensus done research of their own? No, they had not.

INVISIBLE BULLET POINTS

Advice books—such as those written for business managers—end chapters with bullet points or general "laws," then begin the following chapters with summaries of the wisdom the reader is supposed to have absorbed up to that point. This is great for those kinds of books; if a reader starts a chapter and realizes they have not, in fact, mastered the intended lesson, they can reread the preceding chapters before moving on.[32] Expository works in other genres can

31. Naomi Oreskes and Erik M. Conway, *Merchants of Doubt: How a Handful of Scientists Obscured the Truth on Issues from Tobacco Smoke to Global Warming* (New York: Bloomsbury Press, 2010), 270.

32. Michael Feiner, *The Feiner Points of Leadership: The 50 Basic Laws That Will Make People Want to Perform Better for You* (New York: Warner Business Books, 2004); David H. Maister, Robert Galford, and Charles Green, *The Trusted Advisor* (New York: Simon & Schuster, 2012).

pull similar stunts. Sociologist-psychiatrist Jonathan Metzl opens a chapter of his book *Dying of Whiteness* with the phrase, "To summarize where we've come thus far . . ." If the summary that follows does not sound familiar, it is a chance for the reader to review the previous chapter.[33]

Such signposting is too clunky for most history writing, but it can serve as a reminder of the purpose of a conclusion: to remind the reader of the most important findings of a chapter. Presented with those findings, the reader has two choices: accept them and move on to the next chapter or review the chapter to make sure they understood the reasoning and evidence supporting those conclusions. For example, Steven Teles promises to track the progress of the conservative legal movement from relative impotence in the early 1970s to great power thirty years later. In between, he uses chapter conclusions to check in with his reader, to make sure they understand how far the movement had risen by that point in the story.[34] Historians often follow such summations with a short cliffhanger that keeps the reader eager to continue. "Over the last two years, the Pokanokets and the Pilgrims had made each other stronger," writes John Turner, explaining his characters' position at the end of one chapter. Then he pivots to a preview of the next chapter: "In the years ahead, it would prove more difficult for the fortunes of both peoples to rise in tandem."[35]

THE PERILS OF POLICY PRESCRIPTIONS

Some historians, having described the historical origins of a problem, conclude their projects with suggestions for fixing that problem. The temptation is clear; you have your reader's attention and have established yourself as something of an expert, so why not take the chance to recommend action? As Karl Marx lamented in 1845, "philosophers have only interpreted the world differently, but the

33. Jonathan M. Metzl, *Dying of Whiteness: How the Politics of Racial Resentment Is Killing America's Heartland* (New York: Basic Books, 2019), 83.

34. Steven M. Teles, *The Rise of the Conservative Legal Movement: The Battle for Control of the Law* (Princeton, NJ: Princeton University Press, 2012).

35. John G. Turner, *They Knew They Were Pilgrims: Plymouth Colony and the Contest for American Liberty* (New Haven, CT: Yale University Press, 2020), 104.

point is to change it."[36] The problem with such an approach is that knowing the history of a problem does not necessarily point to any solution. I may be able to tell you in great detail how I dropped an expensive camera down an elevator shaft, but that does not mean I know how to retrieve the camera or repair the damage. Prescriptive conclusions can also distract readers from more valuable findings. I have given up trying to teach one important book because I have repeatedly found the students more focused on the book's ten-page conclusion—with its utopian vision for a reinvented America— than engaged with the preceding hundreds of pages of historical analysis. The same warning applies to predictions. Thomas Hughes ended his 1989 masterpiece, *American Genesis*, by predicting that the United States would turn away from large technological systems. The 2004 edition begins with his chastened reflections on those "flawed anticipations."[37]

Historians can offer better service to the present not by predicting or prescribing the future but by posing questions about the past that inform a contemporary problem. What forces are at play in this conflict? Who stands to benefit and who to lose? Do present structures reflect careful compromises by previous generations, in which case we might want to dismantle them only with great care? Or were they slipshod emergency measures whose prolongation should be suspect? Concluding one of the chapters of his 1955 classic, *The Strange Career of Jim Crow*, C. Vann Woodward argued that "the policies of proscription, segregation, and disfranchisement that are often described as the immutable 'folkways' of the South, impervious alike to legislative reform and armed intervention," had in fact been choices, and relatively recent choices at that. "The belief that they are immutable and unchangeable is not supported by history," he continued, not presenting a specific plan of action but nonetheless insisting that Americans of his day had the power to end segregation.[38]

---

36. Friedrich Engels, *Feuerbach: The Roots of the Socialist Philosophy*, trans. Austin Lewis (Chicago: Charles H. Kerr, 1908), 133.

37. Thomas P. Hughes, *American Genesis: A Century of Invention and Technological Enthusiasm, 1870–1970* (1989; repr., Chicago: University of Chicago Press, 2004), x.

38. C. Vann Woodward, *The Strange Career of Jim Crow* (1955; repr., New York: Oxford University Press, 2002), 65.

It is also worth remembering that historians can write in more than one voice, and in more than one venue. In the conclusion of his book *Know Your Enemy: The Rise and Fall of America's Soviet Experts*, David Engerman only briefly considers the lessons that Cold War support for Soviet studies could hold for post-9/11 support for studies of Islamic fundamentalism, and he challenges the parallels drawn by Secretary of Defense Robert Gates. "New enemies, in new times, require new solutions," he concludes.[39] Yet in an essay for *Foreign Affairs* published soon after the book's release, Engerman gave himself a longer leash, explaining how "the lessons of early Sovietology" could be applied to twenty-first-century challenges.[40]

Outlines

An outline is a map of a longer work, which can be anything from a brief essay to a full-length book. Some historians prefer to outline early, even if only to list a few topics that they know will become important. "I can never begin any major writing project without having already done an outline of the overall arc of the piece," reports Heather Ann Thompson. "When you have a solid outline of the overall project and then each section or chapter of it, that is the hardest part done. With that you know what to write and won't get lost in the weeds and head off on tangents. Of course outlines themselves need to be updated as they evolve. But they are the blueprint, the map, regarding what words, what evidence, needs to make it on the page."[41] Conversely, Linda Gordon prefers not to outline her work until she has gotten a fair amount written.[42] My own advice is to outline early and often, updating your outline as your project evolves.[43]

---

39. David C. Engerman, *Know Your Enemy: The Rise and Fall of America's Soviet Experts* (New York: Oxford University Press, 2009), 338–39.

40. David C. Engerman, "Jihadology," *Foreign Affairs*, December 8, 2009, https://www.foreignaffairs.com/articles/2009-12-08/jihadology.

41. Heather Ann Thompson, "The WRITER'S STUDIO with Heather Ann Thompson," *Modern American History* 2 (March 2019): 77.

42. Linda Gordon, "The WRITER'S STUDIO with Linda Gordon," *Modern American History* 1 (March 2018): 125.

43. Scrivener encourages this practice. As one writes, one can keep an outline—called the Binder—constantly in view.

An outline has two goals. The first is to organize a long work into smaller sections. This will be helpful to you as you write, since it will break an intimidating project into shorter, more manageable tasks. The second goal, one sometimes overlooked, is to highlight the major findings of a body of research, both for you and for anyone helping you with your work. The best way to do this is with what is sometimes called a "full sentence outline," listing not merely topics to be covered but claims to be made and supported with evidence, like the legal brief cited earlier.[44] By highlighting the key points that each section needs to make, it will help you craft a story or argument that draws readers' attention to those key episodes or arguments.

Classic outlines denote the major sections of a work with uppercase Roman numerals. Within each section, a subsection can be denoted with a capital letter, and smaller levels still with Arabic numerals, lowercase letters, and, if really necessary, lowercase Roman numerals. I have found, however, that it is easy to lose track of a section's place in such a hierarchy, and have come to prefer decimal outlines. In a decimal outline, the largest divisions are denoted with a single digit, the next-largest divisions with two digits (e.g., 1.1), and so on.

A Model (T) Outline

To show how this looks in practice, I have outlined Christopher Wells's article "The Road to the Model T: Culture, Road Conditions, and Innovation at the Dawn of the American Motor Age," which is possibly the most elegantly structured journal article I have ever read.[45] Most of this outline consists of sentences taken directly from Wells's article; to avoid clutter I have copied them without quotation marks.

The titles of the sections (indicated by single digits) are those of the headings in the published article. The lower-level headings (two-digit numbers) are topic sentences from Wells's essay that

44. "Types of Outlines," Purdue Writing Lab, https://owl.purdue.edu/owl/general
_writing/the_writing_process/developing_an_outline/types_of_outlines.html.

45. Christopher W. Wells, "The Road to the Model T: Culture, Road Conditions, and Innovation at the Dawn of the American Motor Age," *Technology and Culture* 48 (2007): 497–523.

summarize claims fleshed out in multiple paragraphs. This format makes for a good discussion document for a student and an instructor. If you want to outline a multichapter work, such as a dissertation, then you will need to add another level to the hierarchy. In that case, single digits represent chapters, two-digit headings represent sections, and three-digit headings represent clusters of paragraphs.

I crafted the Wells outlines based on the finished work, a process called reverse outlining.[46] No doubt Wells's working outline looked different, and perhaps he would outline the final project somewhat differently as well. (Though he tells me my version is pretty close to the one he used as he polished the piece for publication.) An outline need not be an exact map, only a rough guide to tell you where you have been and where you are going.

Please note the following about this outline:

Each section presents a thesis

I have started each section with its own thesis taken from the essay, one that supports the thesis of the article as a whole. Except for section 2, these do not appear at the start of the section in the article. The thesis for section 3 appears at the tail end of the previous section, while the thesis for section 4 appears in the final paragraph of that section. For student papers, and particularly for outlines, I suggest that you place the thesis for each section at the start of that section.

Notice how the section headings themselves suggest claims, not merely topics. Wells could have titled section 3 "Cars in Europe and America." By instead titling it "Updating the Horseless Carriage, Americanizing the Automobile," he emphasizes the choices faced by American consumers and designers.

Each cluster of paragraphs makes a claim

While this is a narrative history, Wells takes care to make claims for each section of the narrative and in almost every topic sentence. Note his use of transitional words and phrases (more, thus) and contrast words (however, although). Note also how a full-sentence outline shows how the various claims fit together to create a larger argument.

46. See "Reverse Outlines: A Writer's Technique for Examining Organization," *UW-Madison Writer's Handbook*, https://writing.wisc.edu/handbook/process/reverseoutlines/.

An article is built out of sections,
which are built out of five-paragraph essays

The article is essentially composed of a series of five-paragraph essays (designated by two-digit headings): the building blocks of so much formal writing. Sections (designated by single digits) can vary in length and complexity. But they do not vary all that much, and the range here (roughly ten to twenty paragraphs, or two to four subsections) is a good target. I outlined the entire article using only digits one through five, and you should not need to go much beyond that in your outlines. Occasionally you might need six, but if you hit seven, it is probably time to split whatever you are working on into two or more units.

Key terms hold it all together

In his introduction, Wells establishes a dialectic between the worldview of the horse-minded and that of the machine-minded. (Section 2 broadens the latter to the "mobility-minded.") Note how he keeps coming back to this crucial comparison by repeating terms relating to horse-mindedness or mobility-mindedness. In the full article, the term "-minded" appears twenty-nine times.

Box 13.1. A Model Outline

Christopher W. Wells, "The Road to the Model T: Culture, Road Conditions, and Innovation at the Dawn of the American Motor Age." *Technology and Culture* 48 (2007): 497–523; outlined by Zachary Schrag.

1 Introduction
    1.1 Lede: In 1920, a single vehicle dominated the American market for automobiles: Ford's famous Model T.
    1.2 Research question: Why did so many Americans buy Model Ts, making them the center of the American automotive revolution?
    1.3 Historiography: Many scholars, such as Rudi Volti, argue that the Model T "embodied few technological innovations, but was sturdy, reliable, and easy to drive by the standards of the time."
    1.4 Thesis: In fact, the Model T's design created a new type of motor vehicle— the lightweight automobile—that transformed the US market from one of disagreement and division into a broad mass market, focused largely (if not exclusively) on a single technology. In doing so, it reconciled two seemingly irreconcilable worldviews, one forged in the world of the horse and the other guided by enthusiasm for machines.

2 Competing Visions, Specialized Designs

   2.1 Thesis: As horseless carriages appeared more frequently on US streets, turn-of-the-century observers debated the role that such expensive new machines should play in everyday life.

   2.2 Most early commentators on horseless carriages fell into one of two broad groups: the "horse-minded," who compared motor vehicles specifically to horses, and the "mobility-minded," who compared them to all other forms of transportation.

   2.3 The fact that designers chose from three major motor types—steam, electric, and gasoline—underscores both the diversity and the uncertainties of early horseless-carriage design.

   2.4 The declining importance of the market for commercial motor vehicles, such as urban trucks and taxis, and the rapid expansion of the market for private, recreational vehicles, helped cause manufacturers and consumers alike to develop an overwhelming preference for gasoline-powered vehicles.

3 Updating the Horseless Carriage, Americanizing the Automobile

   3.1 Thesis: Despite its strengths, the adventure-machine thesis does not fully explain the development of automotive technology in the United States, where the split between mobility-minded and horse-minded buyers put the evolution of automotive technologies on a very different trajectory from the adventure-oriented path followed in Europe.

   3.2 Europe, particularly France and Germany, embraced gasoline carriages earlier and more fully than did the United States.

   3.3 Like most cultural imports, however, the social meanings that the French attached to the automobile were subject to subtle change when translated into the American idiom.

   3.4 Perhaps, however, the most important factor explaining why so many horse-minded consumers chose gasoline-powered runabouts and high-wheelers lies in an important factor that all manufacturers had to address: the poor state of US roads.

   3.5 Engineers thus began adapting Mercedes-style automobiles to US conditions by raising the chassis to provide greater road clearance.

4 Merging Worldviews in Ford's "Universal Car"

   4.1 Thesis: To label the Model T "the Universal Car" was grandiose marketing hype and yet, as a description of the first automobile to appeal to horse- and mobility-minded consumers alike, it contained more than a little truth.

   4.2 Although the prospect of an inexpensive, powerful, lightweight, full-sized automobile had wide appeal, automakers struggled to design such vehicles in the half-decade before 1908.

   4.3 After much trial and error, Ford's team developed a design—dubbed the Model T when it went into production—that finally seemed to thwart the circular curse of weight and power.

5 Conclusion

   5.1 The Model T's design allowed it to bridge the technological and social chasm that divided mobility- and horse-minded motorists—a signal accomplishment. Because of this fusion, the distinctions between horse- and mobility-minded motorists slowly began to blur and disappear.

Flexibility

If all of this sounds too rigid, keep in mind that it is downright anarchic compared to the conventions of other scholarly disciplines, in which researchers must report their findings in the standardized structure known as IMRAD: Introduction, Methods, Results, and Discussion.[47] And while structuring findings as the presentation of evidence to support a thesis is an important skill, historians can and do break with this form in service to another goal: telling a story.

47. Luciana B. Sollaci and Mauricio G. Pereira, "The Introduction, Methods, Results, and Discussion (IMRAD) Structure: A Fifty-Year Survey," *Journal of the Medical Library Association* 92, no. 3 (July 2004): 364–71.

PART V

Stories

{≈≈≈⟨᠍≈᠍⟩≈≈≈}

WHILE YOU SHOULD TAKE satisfaction in answering your own questions, you likely will want to share your findings with others. You have your choice of a range of formats, from traditional texts to multimedia productions, and scales, from short essays to career-long explorations. Yet some rules apply across genres and scale. Your audience will appreciate stories about people, clear language, and a willingness to listen to others. And storytelling can be fun. Many people are drawn to the study of history by the exciting, graceful storytelling of others. It can be deeply satisfying to practice that craft yourself.

CHAPTER FOURTEEN

Storytelling

BEFORE THE NINETEENTH CENTURY, historians mostly had no choice but to be storytellers; what else was history but a story well told? With the spread of a more "scientific" approach, however, historians had choices to make. If history were to be a science, perhaps historians should focus on presenting their findings in a straightforward, factual manner, much like a scientific paper. If, on the other hand, historians wanted to reach readers, they would need to preserve at least some of the literary techniques that had made history a popular genre. They would need to remain adept at storytelling or, to use a somewhat fancier term, narrative.[1]

The debate over which of these goals is more important has plodded along for more than a century, with one generation after the next pining for the good old days when serious historians were also good writers, while others insist there is no shame in writing specialized texts for a specialized readership.[2] Both sides make good points. On the one hand, no level of literary grace is going to make a best seller of a story that does not already appeal to a

1. Sarah Maza, "Stories in History: Cultural Narratives in Recent Works in European History," *American Historical Review* 101, no. 5 (December 1996): 1493.

2. Robert B. Townsend, "From the Archives: Why Can't Historians Write?," *Perspectives on History*, March 2008; Robert B. Townsend, *History's Babel: Scholarship, Professionalization, and the Historical Enterprise in the United States, 1880–1940* (Chicago: University of Chicago Press, 2013); Samuel Eliot Morison, *History as a Literary Art: An Appeal to Young Historians* (Boston: Old South Association, 1946); Evan Goldstein, "'The Academy Is Largely Itself Responsible for Its Own Peril,'" *Chronicle of Higher Education*, November 13, 2018.

mass readership. Many journals and academic presses are content to publish submissions that pose important questions and answer them with careful analysis of the evidence. Elegant writing is optional. On the other hand, even specialist readers deserve good writing. While most scholarly history I read is *competent*, I must occasionally strike books from a draft syllabus simply because the plot is too hard to follow, and a great many I do assign would be greatly improved by a little more attention to storytelling craft. As Aaron Sachs and John Demos argue, "artfulness is a great enhancer of relevance."[3]

Tips

- Even the most scientific, scholarly history can benefit from attention to storytelling.
- People like stories about other people. Get to know your characters, and introduce them to your readers.
- Shape your story with conflicts, turning points, and resolutions.

Characters

"Let us be sure that there are people in history," insisted Dexter Perkins in 1957. "Let us make them live; let us share their triumphs and frustrations; let us *know* them. History is a kind of introduction to more interesting people than we can possibly meet in our restricted lives; let us not neglect the opportunity."[4] Deborah Harkness agrees: "The most vital elements of any story well told are the characters," she reminds us. "By getting to know your characters, and following the plot as it unfolds through relationships your characters have with each other, you will find the story that you are trying to tell."[5]

Just as historians make choices about what events will make up their stories, they also have choices about which characters, and

---

3. Aaron Sachs and John Demos, introduction to *Artful History: A Practical Anthology*, ed. Aaron Sachs and John Demos (New Haven, CT: Yale University Press, 2020), xiii.

4. Dexter Perkins, "We Shall Gladly Teach," *American Historical Review* 62 (1957): 302.

5. Deborah E. Harkness, "Finding the Story," *Perspectives on History*, January 2009.

how many, to emphasize. Choices on characters may change along the way. "There are times when, to your horror, the main characters turn out to occupy minor roles in your story," advises Harkness.[6] Rather than trying to force a character about whom you know much into the narrative, it may be better to leave them out. In revising his dissertation for publication as a book, Sam Erman took his adviser's suggestion to replace "an ensemble cast" with the story of "three remarkable Puerto Rican men."[7] Other historians move in the opposite direction, adding characters until a small set becomes an ensemble.

PROTAGONISTS

Strong protagonists make the best stories. Writers of popular narratives know this; to keep her readers engaged through a six-hundred-page account of the Great Migration of millions of African Americans to the north and west, Isabel Wilkerson introduces us to just three of those migrants—Ida Mae Brandon Gladney, George Swanson Starling, and Robert Joseph Pershing Foster—and brings us along as they journey to Chicago, New York, and Los Angeles.[8] While not every work of history can be so centered on major characters, the more you can structure your story around a small number of protagonists, the easier it will be to keep your reader's attention.

Once you have identified your protagonists, give them the longest introductions. If you are only going to mention a person once, it is probably best to spare your reader the work of learning a name they will not need to know again. If the character reappears two or three times, a name and perhaps title will suffice. But if a character is going to appear throughout a chapter or even a whole book, go ahead and add biographical detail, a physical or character description, and perhaps even a portrait. "Get to know this person," you are telling the reader. "It will help you understand what's coming. It will be on the exam."

6. Harkness, "Finding the Story."

7. Sam Erman, "A Better Book: Mentors," *Legal History Blog*, April 4, 2019, http://legalhistoryblog.blogspot.com/2019/04/a-better-book-mentors.html.

8. Isabel Wilkerson, *The Warmth of Other Suns: The Epic Story of America's Great Migration* (New York: Random House, 2010).

Jessica Wang, for instance, devotes a chapter of *American Science in an Age of Anxiety* to the stories of two defiant scientists: Harlow Shapley and Edward Condon. Though she cares about them primarily because of the way they responded to congressional investigations in the 1940s, she wants the reader to know who they were as people, to help us understand why they braved political confrontation. So she tells us the stories of their lives: their births, their early education, their emergence as both scientists and political figures. She also includes photographs of each man alongside prominent political figures.[9] You can offer similarly detailed biographies of institutional actors. The more often you are going to mention the National Consumers League or the US Geological Survey, the more time you should invest in explaining how these entities came to be and what they stood for.

Along with such descriptors as age, appearance, social class, and the like, your main characters should appear with a *desire*. In a Shakespeare play, a new character may offer a soliloquy to the audience; in a Broadway or Disney musical, they sing an "I want" song, wishing for love, money, adventure, fame, or revenge.[10] Historians can deploy the same techniques. Thus, when she introduces detective William Burns, Beverly Gage describes his jowls, his red hair, and the triumphs that had won him a reputation as the "Sherlock Holmes of America." Then she ends the description by noting that "encomiums to Burns' genius . . . were noticeably less frequent in 1920 than they had been in 1911." His song is a wish for a case that will return him to glory.[11]

Individuals can also sing "I want" as representatives of a broader social group or institution. Introducing the "practical segregationists" of 1950s Mississippi, Joseph Crespino quotes Robert Patterson, who organized the state's first "Citizens' Council" as a response to the Supreme Court's decision in *Brown v. Board of Education*. In Crespino's telling, Patterson strides to the spotlight to sing of his

9. Jessica Wang, *American Science in an Age of Anxiety: Scientists, Anticommunism, and the Cold War* (Chapel Hill: University of North Carolina Press, 1999), chapter 4.

10. Jeffrey Hatcher, *The Art and Craft of Playwriting* (Cincinnati, OH: Story Press, 2000), 23–24.

11. Beverly Gage, *The Day Wall Street Exploded: A Story of America in Its First Age of Terror* (New York: Oxford University Press, 2009), 141.

wish for a respectable racism. If, Patterson warns, "our highest type of citizenship fails to supply a plan to maintain segregation and the integrity of the white race, then the wrong crowd will supply the leadership and there will be violence and bloodshed."[12] With that, Crespino sets up an antipathy between Patterson's movement and against both civil rights activists and "the wrong crowd."

ANTAGONISTS

Movie actor Lee Marvin made a career by convincingly portraying villains. Asked his secret, he explained, "I don't play bad people. I play people struggling to get through their day, doing the best they can with what life's given them. Others may think they're bad, but no, I never play bad people."[13] The best historians follow Marvin, doing their best to explain human behavior not as the result of someone trying to do evil, but of people doing the best they can with what life has given them.

Even mass murderers may be the heroes of their own stories. "To dismiss the Nazis or the Soviets as beyond human concern or historical understanding is to fall into their moral trap," writes Timothy Snyder. "The safer route is to realize that their motives for mass killing, however revolting to us, made sense to them. Heinrich Himmler said that it was good to see a hundred, or five hundred, or a thousand corpses lying side by side. . . . It was an instance, albeit an extreme one, of a Nazi value that is not entirely alien to us: the sacrifice of the individual in the name of the community."[14] Lower-level bad guys may deserve empathy as well. Hollywood movies often dress their legions of goons in masks or opaque helmets, so that we do not worry about the suffering caused by the heroes' rampages through the enemy camp. Historians can do better than this.

All of this takes work. Editor John Staudenmaier once advised me to devote the most time to trying to understand my villains, who almost by definition were the people whom I least understood.

12. Joseph Crespino, *In Search of Another Country: Mississippi and the Conservative Counterrevolution* (Princeton, NJ: Princeton University Press, 2009), 23.

13. Robert McKee, *Story* (New York: HarperCollins), 385–86, Kindle.

14. Timothy Snyder, *Bloodlands: Europe between Hitler and Stalin* (New York: Basic Books, 2012), 400.

His advice resembled journalists' practice of trying to give everyone mentioned in a story the chance to comment, even if they cannot shape the story overall.

Sometimes additional research will not challenge the nastiness of a character, but at least you can then demonize with confidence. While writing my dissertation, I got the impression that the late congressman William H. Natcher had acted out of stubbornness, vanity, and racism, tinged with some self-interest. To give him a chance to weigh in posthumously, I traveled to Western Kentucky University and spent a week reading the diaries that Natcher had methodically dictated to a secretary throughout his career. In those diaries, I found, Natcher had ranted about the District of Columbia in ways that made it clear he did not believe African Americans to be capable of self-government. The diaries only confirmed my previous impression of him, but at least I had given him the chance to speak back. History without good guys and bad guys would be tedious to read and to write, so the best we may be able to do is to offer our characters the presumption of innocence and a chance to testify in their own defense.

WITNESSES

Some characters do less to shape events than to lead readers through them. Richard Holmes notes that his book *The Age of Wonder* is "held together by, as a kind of chorus figure or guide, a scientific Virgil" in the character of Sir Joseph Banks, who, as president of the Royal Society, had some connection to most or all of the other figures in the book.[15] Joanne Freeman structures *Field of Blood* around the diaries of Benjamin Brown French, a congressional clerk. "Not only does he act as a kind of guide, offering an insider's view of Congress," she explains in an interview, "but his striking transition over the course of the book tells a larger story." (It also helps that French had a clerk's excellent handwriting.)[16] Jefferson Cowie opens his book *Stayin' Alive* with a profile of Dewey Burton,

---

15. Richard Holmes, *The Age of Wonder: How the Romantic Generation Discovered the Beauty and Terror of Science* (New York: Pantheon, 2008), xxi.

16. "Q&A with Joanne Freeman," C-SPAN, September 20, 2018, https://www.c-span.org/video/?451795-1/qa-joanne-freeman.

a Detroit autoworker who was repeatedly interviewed by the *New York Times* as a spokesman for America's working class. Though Burton mostly appears in the book's introduction, he returns throughout the book to comment on politics, busing, tax policy, and movies, as well as appearing on the book's cover.[17]

Similarly, though less prominently, Iowa merchant John Burrows appears every hundred or so pages in *Nature's Metropolis*, as William Cronon uses Burrows's memoir to humanize the stories of economic and technological changes that affected countless merchants like him. In his analytic voice, Cronon tells us that the railroad "elaborated the urban hierarchy by proliferating towns and villages beneath the emerging metropolis of Chicago, but also brought the layers of that hierarchy closer together." As a storyteller, he can say that "the coming of the Chicago and Rock Island was not good news for John Burrows, for it meant the end of the way of doing business on which he had built his life and fortune."[18] Eric Yellin—writing about the community of African American civil servants at the start of the twentieth century—keeps us posted about the fortunes and reactions of one such worker, Swan Kendrick, based on Kendrick's frequent and detailed letters to his fiancée Ruby Moyse.[19]

You cannot just pick any historical figure to be a witness; you must find someone who left an unusually detailed source base, such as French's diary, Burton's many interviews, Burrows's memoir, or Kendrick's faithful correspondence. Keep an eye out for candidates.

BIT PLAYERS

In theater and film, a bit player is an actor who speaks just a few lines of dialogue, then disappears from the main action. Historians sometimes include such bit parts as a way to illustrate the lived reality of trends that might otherwise dissolve into statistics and generalizations. Joshua Specht, for instance, wanted readers to

17. Jefferson Cowie, *Stayin' Alive: The 1970s and the Last Days of the Working Class* (New York: New Press, 2010), 1–19, 38, 74, 103, 234–44, 308, 311, 341, 353–54, 362, 372.

18. William Cronon, *Nature's Metropolis: Chicago and the Great West*, reprint ed. (New York: W. W. Norton, 1992), 325.

19. Eric S. Yellin, *Racism in the Nation's Service: Government Workers and the Color Line in Woodrow Wilson's America* (Chapel Hill: University of North Carolina Press, 2013).

understand the rise of large-scale meatpacking at the end of the nineteenth century. "Packing plants needed cheap, reliable, and desperate labor," he writes. "Fortunately, they found it in the combination of mass immigration and a legal regime that empowered management, checked the nascent power of unions, and limited liability for worker injury." All of that is important, but it is not the kind of story that will connect with the reader's emotions or linger in the reader's memory. So before offering that generalization, he narrates the events of June 30, 1892, when fourteen-year-old immigrant Vincentz Rutkowski was assigned to a task formerly handled by three teenagers. "Rutkowski fell behind the disassembly line's frenetic pace," Specht writes. "After just three hours of working alone, the boy failed to dodge a carcass swinging toward him. It struck his knife hand, driving the tool into his left arm near the elbow. The knife cut muscle and tendon, leaving Rutkowski gravely injured." Aside from the records of the subsequent lawsuit, which reached the Supreme Court of Illinois, and a couple of possible hits on Ancestry.com, Specht could find nothing about Rutkowski. But his four vivid paragraphs narrating Rutkowski's injury and failed search for compensation humanize Specht's longer section about the packing companies' power over their workers.[20]

CHORUS

Finally, we have the chorus: a group of characters whom we do not really register as individuals but who set the tone and comment on the decisions made by more prominent characters. Consider this chapter introduction from Meg Jacobs's *Panic at the Pump*:

> The winter was shaping up to be the coldest in nearly a hundred years; forecasts were predicting subzero temperatures and massive snowstorms for the weeks ahead. In Philadelphia, a man attempting suicide failed when he bounced off the frozen ice of the Schuylkill River. Miami had its first snow ever. . . . The Ohio governor ordered one million schoolchildren to stay home for a month. Minnesota, Tennessee,

20. Joshua Specht, *Red Meat Republic: A Hoof-to-Table History of How Beef Changed America* (Princeton, NJ: Princeton University Press, 2019), 179–81.

Virginia, Florida, Indiana, Pennsylvania, and New York declared a fuel emergency, as did New Jersey, where Governor Brendan Byrne asked housewives to leave laundry unwashed and requested that residents take short showers instead of baths. Ordering thermostats turned down, he said the state police would conduct compliance checks. "Damn right we're going to arrest people," snapped his aide.[21]

Neither the man bouncing off the Schuylkill nor the aide to Governor Byrne will appear again in the narrative, nor does Jacobs expect us to think too hard about their individual choices. Rather, their words and deeds vividly set the mood to help us understand what follows: the passage—with presidential support—of the Emergency Natural Gas Act of 1977.

Plots

"No given set of casually recorded historical events can in itself constitute a story," argues Hayden White. "The most it might offer to the historian are story elements. The events are made into a story by the suppression or subordination of certain of them and the highlighting of others, by characterization, motific repetition, variation of tone and point of view, alternative descriptive strategics, and the like—in short, all of the techniques that we would normally expect to find in the emplotment of a novel or a play."[22] In other words, by choosing which events to emphasize and which to ignore, the historian, like the novelist or playwright, inevitably builds events into a plot.

THE SHAPE OF THE STORY

Perhaps the most basic plot choice confronting the historian is whether the end point of the story leaves your protagonists in a better place than where they began. Partly this is a matter of the historian's own sympathies. "Too often economic historians see only the steamship's forward progress, while environmental

21. Meg Jacobs, *Panic at the Pump: The Energy Crisis and the Transformation of American Politics in the 1970s* (New York: Farrar, Straus and Giroux, 2016), 162.

22. Hayden White, "The Historical Text as Literary Artifact," in *The History and Narrative Reader*, ed. Geoffrey Roberts (New York: Routledge, 2001), 223–24.

historians see but the smokestack's plume," writes Mark Cioc. "Depending on perspective, a fishing village can be depicted as pleasingly arcadian or hopelessly backward, a factory as benignly progressive or rapaciously exploitative."[23] This choice is also the result of periodization, which all historians must impose on their works, and which is never neutral. "A narrative history of the First World War," notes Peter Burke, "will give one impression if the story ends at Versailles in 1919, another if the narrative is extended to 1933 or 1939."[24]

Historians must guard against triumphalism: the suggestion that the course of events that actually occurred were the best that *could* have occurred. "A properly constituted history of technology should consider artifacts that were 'failures' on the same par with artifacts that were 'successes,'" writes Ruth Schwartz Cowan. "The task of such a historical investigation is not to glorify the successes but to understand why some artifacts succeed and others fail."[25] Similarly, historians should be skeptical of claims that a particular political or economic system outpaced others because of unalloyed superiority.[26]

On the other hand, we should be equally wary of telling sad stories for their own sake. In the 1940s, Perry Miller used the term *declension* to describe the New England Puritans' sense that their once-holy community was collapsing into corruption and sin.[27] Since then, historians have themselves crafted other "declension narratives": thriving ecosystems ravaged by capitalist exploitation, nonviolent civil rights movements collapsing into separatist militancy. While these narratives are easy to follow—and while they do

23. Mark Cioc, *The Rhine: An Eco-Biography, 1815–2000* (Seattle: University of Washington Press, 2009), 17.

24. Peter Burke, *New Perspectives on Historical Writing*, 2nd ed. (University Park: Penn State University Press, 2001), 290.

25. Ruth Schwartz Cowan, "The Consumption Junction: A Proposal for Research Strategies in the Sociology of Technology," in *The Social Construction of Technological Systems*, ed. Wiebe E. Bijker, Thomas P. Hughes, and Trevor Pinch (1987; repr., Cambridge, MA: MIT Press, 2012), 255.

26. Ellen Schrecker, ed., *Cold War Triumphalism: The Misuse of History after the Fall of Communism* (New York: New Press, 2006).

27. Perry Miller, "Declension in a Bible Commonwealth," *Proceedings of the American Antiquarian Society* 51 (1941): 37–94.

reflect the truth that a great many things go to pot—they run the risk of oversimplification.[28]

In theater, tragedy is taken more seriously than comedy. The same is true of history. "While we instinctively shrink from a writer's adulation," cautions Tacitus, "we lend a ready ear to detraction and spite, because flattery involves the shameful imputation of servility, whereas malignity wears the false appearance of honesty."[29] Tacitus referred to writings about individuals, but the same goes for events and institutions. It is certainly possible to succeed with a happy ending, but I see a lot of book prizes going to stories of injustice, oppression, and suffering. Those are important, but business leaders and policy makers also need histories of successful problem-solving to emulate. If all historians can offer are tales of protest and failure, we have not done our job.[30]

THE CONTROLLING IDEA

Some people mistakenly believe that stories do not make arguments. In fact, some of the most vivid storytelling comes with explicit thesis statements. For instance, Adam Goodheart's *1861: The Civil War Awakening*—as eloquent a historical tale as you will find—includes an interpretive claim. "The war described here," he argues, "was not just a Southern rebellion but a nationwide revolution—fought even from within the seceding states—for freedom. . . . Swept away forever would be the older America, a nation stranded halfway between its love of freedom and its accommodation of slavery, mired for decades in policies of appeasement and compromise."[31]

More commonly, narratives imply, rather than state, their theses. Screenwriting master Robert McKee describes the "controlling

28. Ted Steinberg, "Down, Down, Down, No More: Environmental History Moves beyond Declension," *Journal of the Early Republic* 24 (2004): 260–66; Mark Joseph Walmsley, "Tell It Like It Isn't: SNCC and the Media, 1960–1965," *Journal of American Studies* 48 (2014): 291–308.

29. Tacitus, "The Histories," trans. Alfred John Church and William Jackson Brodribb, Internet Classics Archive, http://classics.mit.edu/Tacitus/histories.1.i.html.

30. Rit Aggarwala, conversations with the author.

31. Adam Goodheart, *1861: The Civil War Awakening* (New York: Alfred A. Knopf, 2011), 18.

idea" of a screenplay as "a single sentence describing how and why life undergoes change from one condition of existence at the beginning to another at the end." He offers such examples as the movies *Dirty Harry* ("Justice triumphs because the protagonist is more violent than the criminals") and *Jaws* ("The courage and genius of humanity will prevail over the hostility of Nature"), encouraging screenwriters to "shape your work around one clear idea."[32] That is not always easy, since storytellers may not be fully aware of the idea controlling their work. John Demos had already published his narrative *The Unredeemed Captive* when he came across a magazine article arguing that kidnapping's "unique horror" is its forcing parents to realize "that our children have a fate that is different from our own." "I read that, and broke into tears," Demos reports. "There it was in a nutshell, the 'generic' meaning of my own book."[33]

The controlling idea may be equally applicable to public history presentations. As Smithsonian curator Roger Connor argues, a Huey helicopter offers one set of meanings if displayed surrounded by mannequins representing US troops in Vietnam and accompanied by videos of interviews with veterans, and something else when displayed with minimal interpretation amid other military aircraft of its period.[34] And while I do not think I have ever taken a walking tour that began with an explicit thesis statement, the ones I best remember are those led by guides who clearly knew the idea they most wanted to convey with the stories they told.

Events

Once you know the shape of your story and its controlling idea, you can give your characters directions. While historians have less freedom than do fiction writers in this regard, they still face a wide range of choices about how to narrate events. To tell an effective story, they must put events in a meaningful order, prioritizing

32. McKee, *Story*, 115–245.

33. John Demos, "History in the Head, History from the Heart: A Personal Manifesto," in Sachs and Demos, *Artful History*, 275.

34. Roger Connor, "Huey 65–10126 Helicopter," in *Engaging Smithsonian Objects through Science, History, and the Arts*, ed. Mary Jo Arnoldi (Washington, DC: Smithsonian Institution Scholarly Press, 2016), 134.

some, skipping quickly past others, and leaving out a great many altogether. As Michel-Rolph Trouillot observes, "if the account was indeed fully comprehensive of all facts it would be incomprehensible." To make comprehensible history, the historian—already constrained by the silences of the archives—must make additional choices about what to silence and what to mention.[35]

ALCHEMY: TURNING SOURCES TO STORIES

A historian is an alchemist who turns paper and ink into flesh and blood. If you describe only the documents you find, you will bore your reader and lose the story. Instead, you must use deduction and imagination to reconstruct the events that led to the creation of the documents.

Martha Sandweiss, for instance, could have described a census return from 1900, listing the names, ages, and occupations of the neighbors of one of her main characters, Ada Todd. That would have been serviceable but dull. Instead, Sandweiss transforms the information on the return into a story about Mrs. Todd and the census taker, Edward Brown:

> As Brown made his way down North Prince Street, he encountered immigrants from Germany, England, Ireland, and Poland, families supported by men who worked as policemen, machinists, and clerks. At number 50, he met Mary Chase, a sixty-year-old widow from Rhode Island who ran a small boardinghouse, and took note of her black housekeeper, the widowed Deborah Peterson. He had counted seventy-two white residents on the street thus far, and Peterson, who descended from an African American family long resident in New York, was the first black person he had encountered. But then he walked next door and knocked at the large and comfortable home at 48 North Prince Street. Two black servants lived here. Phoebe Martin was a thirty-three-year-old widow, and Clarine Eldridge, just fourteen, was scarcely older than the children she had been hired to watch. It was afternoon, and Grace, age nine; Ada, age eight; and Sidney, age six, were home from school, perhaps playing with their three-year-old

35. Michel-Rolph Trouillot, *Silencing the Past: Power and the Production of History* (Boston, MA: Beacon Press, 1995), 50.

brother, Wallace. Whoever answered the door probably invited the census taker into the parlor; neither the servants nor the children could have answered his long list of personal questions about the family. And so Edward Brown entered the home to talk to Ada Todd, the lady of the house. Her husband, James, was away, she said, so she would answer the census agent's long list of questions herself.[36]

Or consider the way James Goodman reads the headlines in old issues of an African American newspaper of the 1930s, then turns them into a story of a person, editor Oscar Adams, and the choices he made. "Adams used ostensibly unrelated news stories and other people's words, drawn from the wire services and set on his front page, rather than explicit articles or his own editorials, to let his readers know what was on his mind," Goodman writes. "Juxtaposition was another of Adams's tricks: at the beginning of August he printed two stories of the same length, with the same size headline, both high and perfectly centered on page one, separated by a single column. One read: 'NEGRO BOY SAVES WHITE FRIEND FROM DROWNING'; the other, 'NEGRO BOY LYNCHED IN ALABAMA.'"[37]

CHRONOLOGY

When in doubt, tell a story in chronological order. Chronology is not everything, and historians dread the misconception that their craft is nothing more than memorizing a series of dates. But knowing the sequence of key events is enormously helpful to understanding most histories, whether they cover a single day or multiple centuries. For good reason, many textbooks, as well as the occasional monograph, feature timelines before or after the main text.[38]

Historians craft exceptions to this rule. Most commonly, especially in journal articles, a historian leads with an exciting story plucked from the middle of the chronology. Instead of ordering

36. Martha A. Sandweiss, *Passing Strange: A Gilded Age Tale of Love and Deception Across the Color Line* (New York: Penguin, 2009), 2.

37. James E. Goodman, *Stories of Scottsboro* (New York: Pantheon, 1994), 64.

38. See, e.g., Yevette Richards, *Maida Springer: Pan-Africanist and International Labor Leader* (Pittsburgh: University of Pittsburgh Press, 2004), xiii–xv; Francis Jennings, *Empire of Fortune: Crowns, Colonies & Tribes in the Seven Years War in America* (1988; repr., W. W. Norton, 1990), starts each chapter with a chronology of key events.

events 1-2-3-4-5-6, they order them 3-1-2-4-5-6. In other cases, historians tell stories that happen simultaneously, often bracketing them between beginning and ending chapters: 1-2a-2b-2c-2d-3. If you want to begin with the present day (a recent news story, the setting of your narrative as it now appears), fade back into time, and then end again with the present, you could write 10-1-2-3-4-5-10.

Nonfiction writers will sometimes violate chronology to be fancy, but this is risky. Edmund Morris, for instance, organized his biography of Thomas Edison into chapters, each of which covered one decade of the inventor's life. Then he organized those chapters in reverse chronological order, so that the chapter on the 1880s follows the chapter on the 1890s. "Nothing is gained by this approach, and much comprehension is lost," complained one reviewer.[39] Readers like their stories in order.

At the very least, you should generally try to preserve chronology within a chapter (even Morris understood this) and especially within a section of a chapter. Consider movies. Many great films include flashbacks or other manipulations of chronology. *Citizen Kane*, for instance, starts with the death of its protagonist, moves forward to journalists' trying to tell the story of Kane's life, jumps back to Kane's childhood, and then at various points shifts from vignettes of Kane's biography to the posthumous exploration of that biography. Within each scene, however, time flows forward. Similarly, even in a work of history that is not primarily narrative, or that plays with the order of events, readers will appreciate a chronological telling of shorter sequences within your larger story.

If you do use flashbacks, signal their start and end. Historians commonly do so by switching the past perfect tense, formed by writing the word *had* followed by a past participle. If you do this, be sure to get the reader back to the simple past tense, usually with the word *now*. Here again is the lede to Jacquelyn Dowd Hall's "Disorderly Women," describing the events of the morning of March 13, 1929.

> The machines whirred, and work began as usual. But the reeling room stirred with anticipation. The day before, March 12, 1929, all

39. Derek Thompson, "Thomas Edison's Greatest Invention," *Atlantic*, October 13, 2019. See also Scott Detrow, "End-to-Beginning Telling of Inventor's Story in 'Edison' Makes for a Circular Read," *NPR.Org*, October 25, 2019.

but seventeen of the 360 women in the inspection room next door *had* walked out in protest against low wages, petty rules, and high-handed attitudes. *Now* they were gathered at the factory gate, refusing to work but ready to negotiate.[40] (Emphasis added)

This passage begins on March 13, but to explain what people were thinking that morning, Hall flashes back to the previous day. Everything between *had* and *now* takes place on March 12. Once Hall writes *now*, we are back to March 13, and events will proceed in chronological order from there.

Flash-forwards are less common, but they are sometimes necessary to explain evidence. If all you are doing is quoting from a memoir or oral history recorded long after the event, you can signal that with a simple phrase like "she would later recall." But in some cases, you may need to discuss the future at length. For instance, Kai Bird and Martin Sherwin pause their biography of Robert Oppenheimer to discuss a dinner party, held in 1942 or 1943, at which Oppenheimer may or may not have been asked to share nuclear secrets with the Soviets. Because the accounts of the evening are so varied, the biographers take us out of the war years to describe FBI interrogations, sworn testimony, and interviews and memoirs written decades after the event. Then they bring us back to 1942 and resume the story.[41]

Some stories have multiple threads taking place around the same time, giving the author the choice of freezing one story and switching to a different thread. "I'm always looking for places where I can pause the action," writes Adam Hochschild. "Often they are times when in actual life as it was happening, there was indeed a period of weeks or months when people didn't know how things were going to turn out." Having placed some of his characters in imminent peril, he changes scene, leaving his readers in suspense until a later chapter.[42]

40. Jacquelyn Dowd Hall, "Disorderly Women: Gender and Labor Militancy in the Appalachian South," *Journal of American History* 73 (1986): 354.

41. Kai Bird and Martin J. Sherwin, *American Prometheus: The Triumph and Tragedy of J. Robert Oppenheimer* (New York: Alfred A. Knopf, 2005), 195–201.

42. Adam Hochschild, "Meanwhile, Back at the Ranch, Part 4: Plot," *Nieman Storyboard* (blog), April 11, 2011, https://niemanstoryboard.org/stories/adam-hochschild-vanderbilt-narrative-storytelling-part-4-plot/.

TURNING POINTS

"In the fall of 1901," writes Michael Willrich, "regulation [of vaccine production] was a controversial idea. A few months later, it was federal law."[43] That is a turning point: a distinct change from before and after.

Robert Caro describes encountering such a turning point in his research on the early congressional career of Lyndon Johnson. "Before [October 1940]," he writes, "Lyndon Johnson had been invariably, in his correspondence, the junior to the senior. After that month, and, it became clearer and clearer as I put more and more documents into date order, after a single date—November 5, 1940; Election Day, 1940—the tone was frequently the opposite. And, in fact, after that date, Johnson's files also contained letters written to him by middle-level congressmen, and by other congressmen as junior as he, in a supplicating tone, whereas there had been no such letters—not a single one that I could find—before that date. Obviously the change had had something to do with the election. But what?" Eventually, he found that Johnson had steered Texas oil money to other congressmen's campaigns, earning the gratitude of fellow legislators who had previously snubbed him.[44]

Look for such shifts in the flow of a story, and do what you can both to explain them and to emphasize their significance. This can be as simple as devoting more words to the events you consider more important. "One can race through a historical event or prolong it," writes Christopher Bram. "George R. Stewart draws out a few hours at the Battle of Gettysburg in *Pickett's Charge* much as Proust drew out Albertine's first kiss of the Narrator. It's the Proust trick of riding your bicycle as slowly as possible without falling over."[45]

For balance's sake, I should note that sometimes historians must emphasize more gradual change. "Nearly all American social studies and history students today learn of the student-led lunch counter sit-ins," laments Nancy MacLean, without learning of the

43. Michael Willrich, *Pox: An American History* (New York: Penguin, 2011), 171.

44. Robert A. Caro, *Working* (New York: Knopf, 2019), 87.

45. Christopher Bram, *The Art of History: Unlocking the Past in Fiction and Nonfiction* (Minneapolis: Graywolf Press, 2016), 85.

"the day-to-day, face-to-face organizing that sustained the movement and made substantive change possible." Similarly, "flashy youthful protests such as the 1969 Atlantic City demonstration against the Miss America pageant overshadowed the patient organizing by older women that yielded many of the movement's most noteworthy innovations in culture and achievements in policy."[46] And sometimes change of any kind is less impressive than continuity. Thus, Peter Baldwin argues that while Robert Koch's discovery of the comma bacillus in 1883 marked a milestone in human understanding of disease, it did not radically change efforts to prevent the spread of cholera, since disinfection "had become routine prevention two decades before Koch."[47]

AGONES

The English words *agony*, *antagonist*, and *protagonist* are derived from the ancient Greek *agon*, meaning "struggle" or "trial." The great Athenian dramatists structured their plays as a series of *agones*, scenes in which a protagonist (say, Electra) debates with an antagonist (Clytemnestra). Thucydides, the great Athenian historian, adapted this form for his work. For example, he presents the speeches that the Corcyraeans and the Corinthians delivered before the Athenian assembly, as each sought Athenian military aid. Having presented this contest, he then narrates the Athenian decision: offering the Corcyraeans a defensive alliance, rather than the full alliance they had sought.[48]

Today's historians use similar techniques to convert long and complex series of events into agones that a reader can follow. In *Cold War at 30,000 Feet*, for example, Jeffrey Engel tells the story of US and British aviation policy in the decades after World War II. Mostly the two powers struggle with each other, but in one agon—which goes on for seventeen pages—Engel narrates an asymmetrical contest

46. Nancy MacLean, *Freedom Is Not Enough: The Opening of the American Work Place* (Cambridge, MA: Harvard University Press, 2008), 342.

47. Peter C. Baldwin, *Contagion and the State in Europe, 1830–1930* (New York: Cambridge University Press, 2005), 166.

48. Elton T. E. Barker, *Entering the Agon: Dissent and Authority in Homer, Historiography, and Tragedy* (New York: Oxford University Press, 2009), chapter 4.

between two nominal allies: the United States and Pakistan. The former seeks to contain communist China, in part by denying it access to the latest civilian jet aircraft. The latter seeks better relations with China in an effort to counter India. As part of this effort, Pakistan wants to buy US planes to service Pakistan-China routes, despite US misgivings about storing the needed parts and supplies in communist territory. Who will win—the hegemonic superpower or the fiercely independent young nation? Having set up this question, Engel must answer it; he must show how the agon ended. In this case, the US government eventually agreed to let Pakistan International Airways purchase US jets for use on routes to China, but the Pakistanis, miffed by American bullying, ended up purchasing a single Boeing. Yet that single sale, Engel argues, marked a turning point: the end of "a quarter century of American aviation rigidity." Thus, in closing this particular agon, Engel explains its significance to his larger story.[49]

RESOLUTION

Just as every agon requires resolution, so does each story as a whole. This is not easy. "In a fictional universe," writes David Kennedy, "we have a right to expect catharsis, which has been a staple of the western literary tradition since the time of the ancient Greeks. The world of the novel, by the time we have read the last page, closed the covers, and put the book down for good, is a world that has typically been rendered finished and tidy, perfectly coherent and comprehensible. But the messy universe of real life with which we historians are compelled to deal rarely offers us the kind of neat resolutions that are permitted to the novelist."[50]

Thus, rather than ending for a complete victory for one side or the other, debates often result in some kind of synthesis or compromise. Rejecting a simple story of the triumph of British abolitionists over proslavery forces, Srividhya Swaminathan argues that "by the end of the eighteenth century, abolitionists and proslavery

49. Jeffrey A. Engel, *Cold War at 30,000 Feet: The Anglo-American Fight for Aviation Supremacy* (Cambridge, MA: Harvard University Press, 2007), 261–77.

50. David M. Kennedy, "The Art of the Tale: Story-Telling and History Teaching," *Reviews in American History* 26 (1998): 471.

writers had shaped and informed each others' argument in significant ways. Thus, the image of the 'Briton' that emerged from the debates contained attributes lauded by both sides."[51]

The best resolutions are those that let the reader know that something important happened between the start of a story and its end—hence the popularity of all those "and how it changed America" subtitles on books. Jack Temple Kirby ends *Rural Worlds Lost* with a description of Southern farmers after 1960 as mostly "dependent to various degrees upon corporate giants, whether as commuters to industrial jobs, as woodcutters, or as chicken farmers, those new-style rural hostages whose very existence was manipulated by forces beyond their reach and region. Thus had the modern South completed a circle of sorts, or perhaps a spiral, from undercapitalized colonial dependency to complex, well-capitalized colonial dependency, complete with motors of every sort and faceless coercion."[52] That is not a happy ending, but it does bring closure.

COUNTERFACTUALS

Sometimes historians narrate events that never happened but that could have. As Richard White argues, "we need to think about what did not happen in order to think historically. Considering only what happened is ahistorical, because the past once contained larger possibilities, and part of the historian's job is to make those possibilities visible; otherwise all that is left for historians to do is to explain the inevitability of the present." He maintains that historians should consider "hypotheticals about what might have happened," especially the "alternative worlds that people in the past themselves imagined."[53] The goal is not only to empathize with historical actors who did not know what was going to happen next but also to understand the consequences of the choices they made. As economic historian Eric Hilt notes, "all statements about causal

51. Srividhya Swaminathan, *Debating the Slave Trade: Rhetoric of British National Identity, 1759–1815* (Farnham, UK: Taylor & Francis, 2009), 173.

52. Jack Temple Kirby, *Rural Worlds Lost: The American South, 1920–1960* (Baton Rouge: Louisiana State University Press, 1986), 360.

53. Richard White, *Railroaded: The Transcontinentals and the Making of Modern America* (New York: W. W. Norton, 2011), 517.

relationships contain counterfactuals. To say that the gold standard caused the Great Depression is to say that absent the gold standard, the Great Depression would not have happened; these two statements are equivalent."[54]

Some historians interrupt their narratives, asking readers to pause and contemplate the what-if. "August 1945 was the open moment," writes Fredrik Logevall, "when so much hung in the balance, when the future course of the French imperial enterprise in Indochina was anyone's guess." While he argues that nothing President Harry Truman could have done would have dissuaded Ho Chi Minh from establishing a communist government in Vietnam, he suggests that a warmer response by the Truman administration could have led to a situation comparable to that developing at the same time in Yugoslavia: a communist country not aligned with the Soviet Union.[55]

Other historians explore counterfactuals by telling the story of proposals that died on the vine. "Let us start with what he did not paint," writes Julian Barnes, in his masterful essay on Théodore Géricault's monumental painting *The Raft of the Medusa*. Along with imagining many ways an artist could have depicted the scene, he explores some preliminary sketches that document the options that Géricault considered but rejected. Only by understanding what the artist did not paint can we appreciate what he did.[56] Similarly, Rosemarie Zagarri traces arguments made for women's participation in politics in the 1820s, nearly a century before the Nineteenth Amendment instituted women's suffrage nationwide.[57] Sara Elkind devotes an entire chapter to a failed 1950 federal water resources planning proposal.[58] These explorations show us that people faced real choices other than the ones they eventually selected.

54. Eric Hilt, "Economic History, Historical Analysis, and the 'New History of Capitalism,'" *Journal of Economic History* 77 (2017): 529.

55. Fredrik Logevall, *Embers of War: The Fall of an Empire and the Making of America's Vietnam* (New York: Random House, 2012), 104–7.

56. Julian Barnes, *A History of the World in 10½ Chapters* (New York: Knopf, 1989), 126–30.

57. Rosemarie Zagarri, *Revolutionary Backlash: Women and Politics in the Early American Republic* (Philadelphia: University of Pennsylvania Press, 2011), 181–82.

58. Sarah S. Elkind, *How Local Politics Shape Federal Policy: Business, Power, and the Environment in Twentieth-Century Los Angeles* (Chapel Hill: University of North Carolina Press, 2011), chapter 5.

Like a (Realist) Novel

In 1972, journalist Tom Wolfe argued that the "New Journalism" of which he was a part depended on the rediscovery of four basic "techniques of realism" earlier developed by novelists of the eighteenth and nineteenth centuries.[59] History that "reads like a novel" (words of praise from some readers, scorn from others) generally deploys some or all of the same techniques.

SCENE

Wolfe's first category is "scene-by-scene construction, telling the story by moving from scene to scene and resorting as little as possible to sheer historical narrative." Most scholarly journal articles are relatively devoid of action and full of that historical narrative. They may begin with a dramatic lede, in which someone nails a large placard to a tree or asks a doorman about his family.[60] After that, however, historical characters mostly traffic in ideas and words. They write, say, think, believe, persuade, argue, debate, accept, demand, concede, assert, agree, disagree, criticize, claim, explain, understand, and depict. Rarely do they cook a meal, build a house, or fire a gun.

By contrast, popular narratives are full of people doing these things. "When you go to watch a feature film," notes popular historian Adam Hochschild, "you don't expect a narrator standing there for 9/10 of the time telling you what's going to happen, and then a brief scene and then more narration. No, you expect the whole thing to be in scenes. The same thing applies when you read a novel."[61] One of the reasons military history sells so well, I suspect, is that so much of it consists of stories of people doing with their

59. Tom Wolfe, "Why They Aren't Writing the Great American Novel Anymore," *Esquire*, December 1972, https://classic.esquire.com/article/1972/12/1/why-they-arent-writing-the-great-american-novel-anymore.

60. Emily A. Remus, "Tippling Ladies and the Making of Consumer Culture: Gender and Public Space in *Fin-de-Siècle* Chicago," *Journal of American History* 101 (2014): 751–77, https://doi.org/10.1093/jahist/jau650; Barbara Young Welke, "The Cowboy Suit Tragedy: Spreading Risk, Owning Hazard in the Modern American Consumer Economy," *Journal of American History* 101 (2014): 97–121.

61. Hochschild, "Meanwhile, Back at the Ranch, Part 2: Setting."

bodies, not just with their words, making it easier for historians to write it as a series of scenes. But there are opportunities in other genres as well. Historians of sports, labor, leisure, medicine, and the like can all try their hand at writing scenes.

Part of the work is setting the scene, appealing to as many of the five senses as possible. Hochschild has explained his crafting the setting for the first interdenominational antislavery committee meeting, held in a Quaker bookstore and printing shop in 1787. "We know what happened at the meeting," he explains, "because we have minutes that were taken, but we don't have a description of the scene. However, there are building blocks that you can use to put together a scene like that." Hochschild found newspaper advertisements for a business adjacent to the printing shop and read about printing in 1780s London. So although he had no information on that particular shop, he could describe it. "We know that the compositors would be working at slanted wooden tables with big trays on them with compartments, one little compartment for each letter of the alphabet, large and small," he explains. "We know that it would have been lit by tallow candles, and that the ceiling would have been blackened by this candle smoke over time." He knew that the shop used ink, and he knew that shops of the time collected human urine to wash ink residue off of woolen pads. "From all these things," he concludes, "we can really assemble a picture—sight, sound, smell— and I'd like to think that that is something that carries the reader into the scene, the setting where the story took place."[62]

Narratives often show us a scene from the perspective of a particular character. Rather than simply describe a Cleveland neighborhood in the wake of a riot, Marcia Chatelain uses the chance to show what the devastation meant to one person in particular:

> Carl Stokes must have remembered the scenes from an intact Hough Avenue, one of the neighborhood's main arteries, as he strolled down the numbered side streets with the volunteer cleanup crews that gathered to collect rubble and mourn what had just been there a few days earlier. Swift Dry Cleaners' brick frame sides remained strong, but without a roof. The wire grate that was supposed to shield Al's Cut Rate Store off of Lexington was no match for the mobs, and the store that offered BEER

62. Hochschild, "Meanwhile, Back at the Ranch, Part 2: Setting."

TO GO was left dry. All that remained of the University Party Roller Rink Hall was the sign that helped mark it, like a headstone.[63]

DIALOGUE

Tom Wolfe's second technique is dialogue, which he found moves readers through a story and establishes character. Journalists try to capture dialogue, ideally by witnessing it directly, or, perhaps more commonly, by asking people to recall conversations. Historians writing about the dead lack such opportunities, so a lack of dialogue becomes one of the major stylistic differences between conscientious history and fiction or journalism. Still, historians can stay alert for chances to extract dialogue from written sources. As noted earlier, criminal trial transcripts can be particularly helpful. For example, while we do not have a lot of verbatim dialogue from seventeenth-century New England, the multiple investigations and trials of witchcraft in Salem left us with plausible accounts of what the accused said to their accusers.[64]

POINT OF VIEW

Wolfe's third device is the "third-person point of view," which he defines as "the technique of presenting every scene to the reader through the eyes of a particular character, giving the reader the feeling of being inside the character's mind and experiencing the emotional reality of the scene as he experiences it." Historians are often able to deploy this to good effect, telling only the parts of a story known to specific participants.

In *Malintzin's Choices*, for example, Camilla Townsend conceals information, choosing words that suggest how Indians may have construed the arrival of the Spanish conquistadors. She writes not of bullets, horses, or a priest but instead of "metal balls," "huge beasts, like deer," and "a well-dressed Spaniard to whom the others showed deference [who] conducted an unintelligible ceremony,

---

63. Marcia Chatelain, *Franchise: The Golden Arches in Black America* (New York: Liveright, 2020), 89.

64. Marion Lena Starkey, *The Devil in Massachusetts: A Modern Inquiry into the Salem Witch Trials* (New York: Knopf Doubleday, 1949), xii.

speaking a few words over each woman and anointing each with some water that he obviously believed held special power."[65] Yet Townsend is careful not to present the Indians as naive or fearful. They may never have seen horses before, but that does not mean they thought the Spaniards were gods.[66]

Historians can use the same device to tell a story from multiple viewpoints. Consider this opening passage from an article by Martha Hodes:

> It was summer in New York City, Saturday night turning into Sunday morning, and when Kid came back outside with the cigarettes, a white man was bothering May. Whatever Kid said or did next, the white man clubbed him, which made Kid reach for his knife and stab at his assailant. It was 12 August 1900, on the corner of 41st Street and Eighth Avenue, and a heat wave had overtaken the city.
>
> The white man was Robert Thorpe, patrolling in plain clothes that night. To Officer Thorpe, a black woman on the street in the middle of the night meant trouble.[67]

Hodes writes the first paragraph from Kid's point of view. She refers to the other characters by how Kid saw them: May (his lover), and a stranger, just "a white man." In the second paragraph, Hodes identifies the white man as Robert Thorpe and writes from his point of view. Since Officer Thorpe does not know May, now she is just "a black woman on the street."

Whereas Hodes starts a new paragraph to change points of view, others change points of view at chapter breaks. In *Stories of Scottsboro*, a tour de force for multiple points of view, James Goodman starts a new chapter every few pages, each time shifting to the perspective of a new set of characters.[68] The important thing is to signal changes in points of view with some kind of break, so the reader can follow the story.

65. Camilla Townsend, *Malintzin's Choices: An Indian Woman in the Conquest of Mexico* (Albuquerque: University of New Mexico Press, 2006), 30, 35, 36.

66. Townsend, *Malintzin's Choices*, 46.

67. Martha Hodes, "Knowledge and Indifference in the New York City Race Riot of 1900: An Argument in Search of a Story," *Rethinking History* 15 (2011): 61.

68. Goodman, *Stories of Scottsboro*.

SYMBOLIC DETAILS

Wolfe's fourth device is "the recording of everyday gestures, habits, manners, customs, styles of furniture, clothing, decoration, styles of traveling, eating, keeping house, modes of behaving toward children, servants, superiors, inferiors, peers, plus the various looks, glances, poses, styles of walking and other symbolic details that might exist within a scene. Symbolic of what? Symbolic, generally, of people's *status life*, using that term in the broad sense of the entire pattern of behavior and possessions through which people express their position in the world or what they think it is or what they hope it to be."

Take, for example, Kevin Boyle's description of an African American hospital of the 1920s:

> It was about two miles from Palace Drugs to Dunbar Memorial, just far enough to be inconvenient. But Ossian made the trip as often as time would allow, climbing into the rattletrap of a Model T he bought in the spring of 1922 and bumping through the streets. . . . Undoubtedly, the contacts Ossian made were casual: standing on Dunbar's broad stone steps, perhaps, chatting with the chief of surgery, Alexander Turner, while the good doctor's chauffeur kept the sedan idling at curbside; trading stories of Howard University with Dr. Ames, the last colored man to serve in the state legislature; asking H. Peyton Johnson, Tufts Medical Class of '96, for his opinion on a puzzling case. It was through such moments—so ephemeral as to seem almost meaningless—that a young man of no pedigree brought himself to the attention of the elite and taught himself their ways.[69]

Boyle includes not only physical objects—the cars, the stone steps—but also location, human relationships, and professional and political credentials to show us not only who Ossian Sweet was but also what he aspired to become. It is as good as any novel, and better than most.

---

69. Kevin Boyle, *Arc of Justice: A Saga of Race, Civil Rights, and Murder in the Jazz Age* (New York: Henry Holt, 2007), 117.

COMBINATIONS

Skilled storytellers combine scene, dialogue, point of view, and details to build vivid episodes. Here's Scott Berg, describing a fateful wagon trip in 1862:

> As they rode for mile after mile along the bluff, the river wound in curlicues to their left while to the right a sea of high grass filled the horizon. For long stretches their view was uninterrupted by a single tree, hill, or built structure. The third week of August was the height of the prairie's summer display, an immense quilt pattern created by pasqueflowers, golden alexander, bearded tongue, and goldenrod budding in color-rich waves. The expanse was beautiful but also so spacious as to be frightening. Sarah begged Gleason to hurry and to keep an eye out for ambush, but, she wrote later, "he would laugh, sing, shout, and when I would chide him and tell him how I felt, he would say I was nervous, and told me he would never take me anywhere again." Reaching a rise in the road they saw a "great body of smoke" rising ahead of them in the direction of the river, where the Lower Agency was situated. When Sarah asked Gleason one more time to turn back, he laughed and said, "Oh, no, it is the saw mill or the prairie on fire."[70]

It is all there. Sarah and Gleason are in a wagon, riding mile after mile. They talk, with verbatim dialogue. Berg supplies details—the uninterrupted views, the spacious expanse—that symbolize their isolation on the Minnesota prairie. And he tells the story from Sarah's point of view; indeed, the scene is based largely on her memoir. Along with a bit of foreshadowing ("so spacious as to be frightening") these devices create not only a vivid image but also narrative suspense.

Speculation

The ultimate technique in writing like a novelist is to write beyond the evidence, patching over gaps with speculation. Biographers may hit this most frequently, since they want to account for every year,

---

70. Scott W. Berg, *38 Nooses: Lincoln, Little Crow, and the Beginning of the Frontier's End* (New York: Pantheon, 2012), 30.

however poorly documented, in their subject's life. But all historians make some guesses, if not about observable facts, then about the motivations behind characters' choices.

Typically, historians try to get as close to the person or event as they can with available documentation. Thus, if they do not have a description of a particular moment in one character's life, they can offer a description of such a moment of someone else who lived in similar circumstances, or the traditions of such events in that person's culture. For instance, Camilla Townsend knows that in the autumn of 1521, her protagonist, Malintzin, gave birth. She has no description of the event itself, but she does have some information about Mexican childbirth customs in general, which she uses to suggest the ways that Malintzin experienced the milestone. "There is no doubt that as the pains escalated, reducing all the horrors that she had experienced before to mere nothings," writes Townsend, "her incoherent thoughts came to her in her native language. It is always the tongue of childhood that surfaces at such moments."[71] Sometimes historians must simply appeal to universal experiences. "Warnings notwithstanding, there are, in fact, some elements of the human condition that have existed forever, transcending time and place," writes Annette Gordon-Reed. "If there were none, and if historians did not try to connect to those elements (consciously or unconsciously), historical writing would be simply incomprehensible."[72]

Historians have choices to make about how to present their speculation. Most maintain the same voice they use for the rest of their story, dropping signals that they are speculating based on the limited evidence before them. Whether they choose words of possibility (may have, perhaps), probability (likely, probably), or even confidence (must have, surely, certainly, no doubt), the effect is much the same: without slowing down the narrative too much, the historian acknowledges the limits of their research. Each such sentence speaks both to the reader who just wants to know what happened next, and to the reader who is testing the historian's claims. It

71. Townsend, *Malintzin's Choices*, 5, 139.
72. Annette Gordon-Reed, *The Hemingses of Monticello: An American Family* (New York: W. W. Norton, 2008), 32.

is up to the author and editor to determine how frequently to use such signals. Too many can burden a story, while too few qualifications— or too many assertions of confidence—suggest a certainty that may not be warranted.[73]

Another common device is to present a character's situation as a series of questions. We may not know what someone thought, but we might be able to determine the choices that lay in front of them. Here's how Adam Goodheart presents the situation of Frank Baker, Shepard Mallory, and James Townsend, three enslaved men who, in May 1861, approached Fortress Monroe in the hopes that the Union troops there would not return them to their Confederate masters. "It cannot have been an easy decision for the men," Goodheart writes. "What kind of treatment would they meet with at the fort? If the federal officers sent them back, would they be punished as runaways—perhaps even as traitors? Even if they were allowed to remain inside, might this leave their families exposed to Colonel Mallory's retribution? How, and when, would they ever reunite with their loved ones?"[74]

Occasionally, one lets loose and dips into historical fiction. In his 1995 book, *The Unredeemed Captive: A Family Story from Early America*, John Demos deals with sparse evidence in one chapter by carefully labeling a series of "very bare facts" and then offering his best guesses about the life of one of his major characters. In another chapter, however, he seeks to explain her views even in the absence of evidence. "We can only speculate—only imagine—but that much, at least, we must try," he writes, before writing what is essentially a six-paragraph work of fiction.[75]

Such experiments remain controversial. In *The Half Has Never Been Told*, for example, Edward Baptist creates "vignettes" that appear to be the stories of single individuals but are in fact composites of multiple experiences from multiple sources. Baptist signals

73. Jacques Barzun, *Clio and the Doctors: Psycho-History, Quanto-History & History* (Chicago: University of Chicago Press, 1974), 45; Natalie Zemon Davis, *A Passion for History: Conversations with Denis Crouzet* (Kirksville, MO: Truman State University Press, 2010), 5–6; David Hackett Fischer, *Historians' Fallacies* (New York: Harper Torchbooks, 1970), 90.

74. Goodheart, *1861: The Civil War Awakening*, 298.

75. John Demos, *The Unredeemed Captive: A Family Story from Early America* (New York: Vintage, 1995), chapter 7 and 108–9.

his method with the usual qualifiers—"would have," "perhaps," "surely"—and explains it further in his notes.[76] But some argue he goes too far. "What Baptist calls 'evocative history,' I call made-up history," complains one reviewer. "Baptist creates biographies about people, describing what enslaved people did, thought and felt, out of virtually no evidence. The problem with this approach is that it is ventriloquism: Baptist is speaking for people who cannot speak for themselves. It may be a worthy sentiment, but it is patronizing in practice."[77] Historians who seek to write vividly thus walk a narrow path between imagining too much and imagining too little.

76. Edward E. Baptist, *The Half Has Never Been Told: Slavery and the Making of American Capitalism* (New York: Basic Books, 2014), 1–2, 428n1.

77. Trevor Burnard, "'The Righteous Will Shine Like the Sun': Writing an Evocative History of Antebellum American Slavery," *Slavery & Abolition* 36 (2015): 184.

CHAPTER FIFTEEN

Style

HISTORY IS A BROAD collection of genres, encompassing everything from exciting adventure stories to sophisticated debates about theory. No one style could be right for them all, and it is less important that you write to sound like someone else than it is for you to write clearly and keep your voice consistent within a project. Still, some conventions are especially important to writing about history, and these are emphasized in this chapter.

Tips

- Your choice of words is part of your argument. Choose terms that reflect your understanding of history, and define them for your reader.
- Write in the active voice, with active verbs. Limit your use of "was" and "were."
- All good writing requires multiple drafts.

Words

Just as historians are careful consumers of words, so should they be careful producers. Your choice of words will determine who reads your work and how they receive it.

IS YOUR JARGON REALLY NECESSARY?

Many historians take pride in relying on a less specialized vocabulary than other academic fields. The fact that many important scholarly works of history also become commercial successes shows that historians can make significant arguments for fellow scholars without deploying words known only to those specialists. But it is easier to decry "jargon" than to define it.[1]

Determining if a term is "jargon" is itself a matter of historical analysis. Take the word "commodification." The *Oxford English Dictionary* dates its first appearance to a 1974 article in *Theory and Society*, in which Dick Howard wrote that Habermas "points to the role of science in destroying any image of the totality, replacing it with fads based on partial evidence (e.g., ethology, not to speak of astrology, etc.); to the dilemma of modern art which, having lost the promise of happiness it once held, has reacted to its increasing 'commodification' by turning inward to an obscurity that protects its independence, but also makes it less meaningful to most people; and to the relativization of ethics, or their identification with positive law."[2] Based on the length and density of that sentence, not to mention the title of the journal, I would say that in 1974, "commodification" would count as jargon. Only specialists would use it, and even then in quotation marks that emphasized its novelty. But the word, and the concept, spread. By 2015, *Spin* magazine founder Bob Guccione Jr. lamented to the *New York Post* that "the commodification of music is so complete that artists these days create songs thinking they would make a good car commercial."[3] Could we agree that if a word appears in a tabloid newspaper without being mocked, it is no longer jargon?

That said, the historian's duty is to reach as many readers as possible, rather than to inject new words into the language. If you need a specialized term in order to communicate with the specialists you

1. John R. McNeill, "Jargon in History Writing Shuts Out the Public," *Perspectives on History*, May 20, 2019.

2. Dick Howard, "A Politics in Search of the Political," *Theory and Society* 1 (1974): 277.

3. Richard Morgan, "Spin Magazine Founder: Today's Music Isn't Any Good," *New York Post* (blog), August 9, 2015, https://nypost.com/2015/08/08/spin-magazine-founder-todays-music-isnt-any-good/.

want to reach, go ahead and use it. Just realize this comes at the cost of losing other readers. Conversely, if you can restrict yourself to the vocabulary of the newspaper and magazine, you can likely reach some readers who otherwise would not benefit from your insights, without losing any fellow scholars.

If your purpose in using an uncommon term is to deploy a theoretical concept developed by others, define that term and refer your readers to the body of theory from which it comes. For example, rather than merely asserting that twentieth-century scientists engaged in "boundary work," sociologist Kelly Moore explains the term and refers readers to the work of Thomas Gieryn, who popularized it, as well as other scholars who followed his usage.[4] Similarly, in order to argue that white power was a "social movement," Kathleen Belew needs to explain how she uses that term, and she cites three books about social movements, so interested readers can learn more about her understanding of the concept.[5]

Including an explanation like this, or at least pointing the reader to someone else's explanation, is the equivalent of IKEA's packing a 3 mm hex wrench with every item of furniture that needs it for assembly. Repeat customers may already have a drawerful of such wrenches, or fancy electric screwdrivers that do the job faster. But they lose little by having a new one included, and the first-time shopper depends on the included wrench to make the entire purchase useful.

DEFINING TERMS

Eliminating jargon is only one step toward choosing terminology that your reader can understand. Defining terms is just as important. The following paragraphs include some cases where you need to define your terms.

4. Kelly Moore, *Disrupting Science: Social Movements, American Scientists, and the Politics of the Military, 1945–1975* (Princeton, NJ: Princeton University Press, 2008), 9–10.

5. Kathleen Belew, *Bring the War Home: The White Power Movement and Paramilitary America* (Cambridge, MA: Harvard University Press, 2018), 10, 246n39.

When you are employing technical vocabulary

In the course of their research, historians may learn the words used by other disciplines and occupations, either currently or in previous epochs, and they should take care to translate those specialized terms for readers who have not made the same journey. In *Alongshore*, John Stilgoe devotes a paragraph to defining "gunkholing"—the practice of navigating in shallow water by feeling the bottom with a hand lead—before telling stories of vessels that succeeded or failed at the practice.[6] In *The American Synthetic Organic Chemicals Industry*, Kathryn Steen must teach her readers enough organic chemistry for them to understand how Americans and Germans discovered, sold, shipped, and taxed various compounds. "In the case of indanthrene blue GCD," she explains, "treating a basic indanthrene blue with nitric and hydrochloric acid added chlorine atoms to the molecule and shaded the blue slightly to green. These reactions created new chemical compounds from the organic (or carbon) base, which is what made them synthetic organic chemicals. Because manufacturers obtained their crude organic raw materials from coal tar for decades, synthetic organic chemicals were just as often called coal tar chemicals." This may not give the reader enough information to repeat the process in a lab, but it does give a sense of what Steen and her characters mean by both "synthetic organic chemicals" and "coal tar chemicals." With that established, we can get on with the story.[7]

Take care not to overwhelm your reader with terms they do not need. When a James Bond film devotes time for Q to explain every new gadget, viewers pay attention because they trust that the information will be important to the plot later on.

When you are inventing a term not used by
your historical characters or other scholars

Sometimes historians need to create terms to describe the phenomena they observe. Landon Storrs, for instance, writes about "a group of young radicals, male and female, who ascended with surprising

6. John R. Stilgoe, *Alongshore* (New Haven, CT: Yale University Press, 1994), 48.
7. Kathryn Steen, *The American Synthetic Organic Chemicals Industry: War and Politics, 1910–1930* (Chapel Hill: University of North Carolina Press, 2014), 20.

rapidity in the [Franklin D.] Roosevelt administration." What to call them, especially the women? Storrs finds that simply calling them "feminists" fails to distinguish them from those feminists who emphasized the equal rights amendment over the bread-and-butter issues of Storrs's group, "labor feminists" overlooks their antiracism, and "Popular Front feminists" suggests a closer relationship to the Communist Party than Storrs wishes to convey. Instead, she settles on the term "left feminists"—a term not used by the women themselves—as the clearest way to communicate with the reader. She goes on to define the "left feminist" as a member of a group of government women who "often knew one another, through shared interests in labor, poverty, housing, public health and health insurance, consumer rights, and international peace—interdependent causes that in their vision had a feminist subtext."[8]

When one historian invents a term like this and other historians borrow it, it is especially important for the borrowers to explain whether they are keeping the original meaning or modifying it. Historians may offer competing definitions of the "market revolution" or the "consumer revolution," terms unknown to the people living through those revolutions.[9] Without a common definition, or an explicit acknowledgment of disagreement, the scholars risk talking past each other.

When the term you use has multiple meanings

Some terms, especially abstract nouns, mean so many things to so many people that every writer who uses them must explain which meaning they have chosen. "The men and women of the Populist movement were modern people," writes Charles Postel. Knowing that "modern" is particularly slippery, he offers four paragraphs defining modern as both participation in a world market and embracing the change that came with such participation.[10]

8. Landon R. Y. Storrs, *The Second Red Scare and the Unmaking of the New Deal Left* (Princeton, NJ: Princeton University Press, 2013), 9.

9. Paul G. E. Clemens, "The Consumer Revolution: Now, Only Yesterday, or a Long Time Ago?," *Reviews in American History* 23 (1995): 574–81; Jill Lepore, "Vast Designs," *New Yorker*, October 22, 2007.

10. Charles Postel, *The Populist Vision* (New York: Oxford University Press, 2007), 9–10.

To explain the French concept of *terroir*, which she describes as "a term with no precise equivalent in English," Kolleen Guy traces the usage of the word from the thirteenth century to the time of her writing.[11]

Any use of a term ending in "-ism" will probably benefit from some kind of definition. As early as 1944, George Orwell observed that, because so many people used it carelessly, "the word 'Fascism' is almost entirely meaningless," though some meanings "are obviously very much more justified than others."[12] The same could almost be said for feudalism, nationalism, liberalism, conservatism, and socialism, just to name a few.[13] "Capitalism" is particularly slippery, since it can refer to relations of production, labor, exchange, or government.[14]

There is no need to restrict yourself to a single definition of a term, so long as you are clear about what you are doing. As Greg Grandin notes, Frederick Jackson Turner's frontier thesis included thirteen distinct definitions of the frontier. "Turner's genius was to embrace the unsettledness of the concept," Grandin writes, "to not try to fix the 'frontier' as any one thing."[15] In her chapter on Japanese Americans during World War II, Mae Ngai writes, "by nationalism, I mean both political support for Japan and cultural nationalism, which emphasized cultural affinities with the native country." She then acknowledges the overlap between the two categories.[16]

11. Kolleen M. Guy, *When Champagne Became French: Wine and the Making of a National Identity* (Baltimore: Johns Hopkins University Press, 2007), 2, 41–42.

12. George Orwell, "As I Please," March 24, 1944, in *George Orwell: As I Please, 1943–1946*, ed. Sonia Orwell and Ian Angus (1968; repr., Boston: David R. Godine, 2000), 113–14.

13. Marc Bloch, *The Historian's Craft: Reflections on the Nature and Uses of History and the Techniques and Methods of Those Who Write It*, trans. Peter Putnam (1953; repr., Princeton, NJ: Vintage, 1964), 176; Helena Rosenblatt, *The Lost History of Liberalism: From Ancient Rome to the Twenty-First Century* (Princeton, NJ: Princeton University Press, 2018).

14. Frederic C. Lane, "Meanings of Capitalism," *Journal of Economic History* 29 (1969): 5–12; Peter Kolchin, *A Sphinx on the American Land: The Nineteenth-Century South in Comparative Perspective* (Baton Rouge: Louisiana State University Press, 2003), 22.

15. Greg Grandin, *The End of the Myth: From the Frontier to the Border Wall in the Mind of America* (New York: Henry Holt, 2019), 116.

16. Mae M. Ngai, *Impossible Subjects: Illegal Aliens and the Making of Modern America* (Princeton, NJ: Princeton University Press, 2014), 180.

WORD CHOICE AS ANALYSIS

Edward Baptist taught me that the county in which I live— Arlington, Virginia—was named after a slave labor camp. I had known that Arlington took its name from the estate established by George Washington Parke Custis and later inherited by his son-in-law, Robert E. Lee. But the conventional term for such places—in discourse of the nineteenth century and in most histories since—is "plantation." By rejecting that period term in favor of "slave labor camp," Baptist makes readers understand the full horror that Arlington, Mount Vernon, Monticello, the Hermitage, and all the other plantations of American history were institutions designed to force labor out of captive human beings.[17] Such word choices come with costs, of course. An American "plantation" and a Nazi "Konzentrationslager" both extracted labor under brutal conditions, so connecting them with the term "slave labor camp" may help us understand the experience of enslaved workers of the 1840s, and even the self-deception practiced by their enslavers. But we should also keep in mind the differences in both operations and social meanings.[18]

Just as "one man's terrorist is another man's freedom fighter," word choice can indicate the historian's views on the legitimacy and scope of a historical event. Were the large groups of people in revolutionary Paris *mobs* or *crowds*, and if the latter, were they *les sans-culottes*, *le peuple*, *la canaille*, or *les bras-nus*?[19] Was the violence in India in 1857 the Indian Mutiny, Sepoy Mutiny, Revolt of 1857, Great Rebellion, the First War of Independence, or something else?[20] Did Executive Order 9066 authorize Japanese *internment* or Japanese American *incarceration*? (The latter emphasizes the fact that most of the people who were relocated and confined

---

17. Edward E. Baptist, *The Half Has Never Been Told: Slavery and the Making of American Capitalism* (New York: Basic Books, 2014).

18. Michael Thad Allen, *Business of Genocide* (Chapel Hill: University of North Carolina Press, 2002), 222.

19. Edward Hallett Carr, *What Is History?* (New York: Vintage Books, 1961), 28.

20. Priti Joshi, "1857; or, Can the Indian 'Mutiny' Be Fixed?," *BRANCH: Britain, Representation and Nineteenth-Century History* (blog), November 2013, http://www.branchcollective.org/?ps_articles=priti-joshi-1857-or-can-the-indian-mutiny-be-fixed.

were citizens, and "internment" refers to the confinement of enemy aliens in time of war.)[21] Be prepared to defend your answer.

PERIOD VOCABULARY OR ANACHRONISM?

Historians need to choose carefully whether to employ the vocabulary and concepts of the people they study. No combatant of 1914–18 knew they were fighting the First World War (though that term was being used by pessimists as early as 1920). So to present events from their point of view, it might be better to use terms in circulation at the time, such as the Great War or the European War.[22]

On the other hand, some historians deliberately use anachronistic language to help the reader understand the actions of people in the past. "In [an] affecting scene, the equivalent of what today would be described as a 'photo opportunity,'" writes Simon Schama, "Lafayette visited houses in the faubourg Saint-Antoine." This event took place decades before the invention of photography, and around two centuries before "photo opportunity" took on its present meaning, but the term effectively conveys Schama's claim that Lafayette was as interested in gaining favorable press as he was in actually helping the wounded heroes of the storming of the Bastille.[23] To give today's readers a sense of how nineteenth-century proslavery Southerners felt imperiled by world rivalries, Matthew Karp deploys the mid-twentieth-century terms *domino theory* and *cold war*.[24]

The decision is particularly fraught when you must decide whether to use the racial, ethnic, religious, or sexual terms—including slurs—of the period or the current ones as you write. Old

21. Cynthia Lee, "Debate over Words to Describe Japanese American Incarceration Lingers," *UCLA Newsroom*, September 15, 2015, http://newsroom.ucla.edu/stories/debate -over-words-to-describe-japanese-american-incarceration-lingers; Roger Daniels, "Words Do Matter: A Note on Inappropriate Terminology and the Incarceration of the Japanese Americans," in *Nikkei in the Pacific Northwest: Japanese Americans and Japanese Canadians in the Twentieth Century*, ed. Louis Fiset and Gail Nomura (Seattle: University of Washington Press, 2005), 183–207.

22. Stuart Lee, "The War, The Great War, The First World War," *World War I Centenary* (blog), http://ww1centenary.oucs.ox.ac.uk/memoryofwar/the-war-the-great-war-the-first -world-war/.

23. Simon Schama, *Citizens* (1989; repr., New York: Knopf, 1991), 451.

24. Matthew Karp, *This Vast Southern Empire* (Cambridge, MA: Harvard University Press, 2016), 70, 82.

terms can perpetuate stereotypes, especially about less powerful groups.[25] But they also bear history with them. George Chauncey devotes a dozen pages of *Gay New York* to a discussion of the terms used in the early twentieth century to describe men who had sex with other men. "The broad contours of lexical evolution," he writes, "reveal much about the changes in the organization of male sexual practices and identities." Those revelations are worth the cost of occasionally discomfiting his readers.[26] Kevin Boyle shared an early draft of *The Arc of Justice* with readers, who told him that "seeing 'African American' in the text jarred them out of the story," leading him to replace that term with "the now antiquated terms 'Negro' and 'colored' as well as the still common black. . . . By that choice, I mean no disrespect to the subjects of the book or to present-day readers."[27] Stephanie Jones-Rogers goes further, reproducing a powerful racial slur that appears in the transcribed interviews of former slaves, taken in the 1930s. "Making any changes to the text presented its own problems," she explains. "Such revisions would sanitize the experiences of these formerly enslaved people and make it difficult for readers to understand how they perceived what had happened to them. . . . In this book they speak in their own words."[28]

QUOTATION

Appropriate quotation is a matter of balance. Too little quotation and your work reads like an opinion piece or a fiction, not supported by research. Too much quotation and it reads like a set of notes, not a finished product that conveys your own insights and voice. It may be best to start with more and longer quotations than you think you will need, then pare them down in the revision process. Once you have assembled a paragraph with two or three

25. Bryan C. Rindfleisch, "What We Say Matters: The Power of Words in American and Indigenous Histories," *American Historian*, February 2017.

26. George Chauncey, *Gay New York: Gender, Urban Culture, and the Making of the Gay Male World, 1890–1940* (New York: Basic Books, 1994), 14.

27. Kevin Boyle, *Arc of Justice: A Saga of Race, Civil Rights, and Murder in the Jazz Age* (New York: H. Holt, 2004), author's note.

28. Stephanie E. Jones-Rogers, *They Were Her Property: White Women as Slave Owners in the American South* (New Haven, CT: Yale University Press, 2019), xx.

quotations, you will have a better sense of which one most vividly conveys a point—allowing you to cut the others—or which combination of quotations will work together if you trim each one.

Style manuals require long quotations—one hundred words or more—to be formatted as block quotations. Use these with care, since block quotations tend to disrupt the flow of your own writing, both visually and aurally. Just as a slice of fish needs to be of the highest quality to merit being served raw, a quotation has to be really good to merit being presented as an uninterrupted block. To present imperfect material in block quotation form is practically begging your reader to skip to the next paragraph, and perhaps leave the table entirely. Most scholarly quotation of textual material does not require permission from the copyright holder, but it is worth understanding the limits of fair use. The Center for Media & Social Impact offers excellent resources.[29]

The decision on whether to translate quotations from another language depends on one's audience. A journal specializing in French history may require French quotations rendered in the original, with the expectation that most readers of that journal will be able to read them. A more general journal or popular presentation might require translation.

Similarly, intended readership can inform your use of quotations from other scholars. Scholarly readers want to know how you position your argument relative to other scholars, while popular readers may not. Yet even writers of popular histories often quote scholars as a means of authority.[30] In general, historians quote other historians' arguments and findings, not their narration of events. Sometimes this feels like a missed opportunity. If another historian has written a perfectly good page-long description of the beginnings of the Panic of 1837, an event peripheral to my main topic, why must I paraphrase it or build my own from multiple sources? In practice, however, a page-long block quotation from a secondary source would be jarring to eye and ear, so I must write something that fits into my larger project.

29. "Fair Use, Free Speech & Intellectual Property," Center for Media and Social Impact, https://cmsimpact.org/program/fair-use/.

30. See, e.g., Isabel Wilkerson, *The Warmth of Other Suns: The Epic Story of America's Great Migration* (Random House, 2010), 372, 376–77.

Nontextual Information

While historians craft most of their stories with words, even a printed work can be a multimedia production, including images, captions, and quantitative information.

INTEGRATE IMAGES INTO YOUR STORY

As noted in chapter 7 images can function as vital historical evidence and enliven an article or book. Though images demand extra labor and money (for reproduction permission, image preparation, and layout), they are often worth it if they attract readers or make vivid a story or argument. Naturally, you want to select images that best suggest the themes and turning points of your narrative.

A good caption can enhance an image, identifying not only the subject but also its significance. In his story of the civil rights struggle in an Alabama county, Hasan Kwame Jeffries devotes a page to a full-length portrait of an African American man standing straight and proud in an elegant suit and vest. Jeffries could have captioned the photograph "Entrepreneur Elmore Bolling in Haynesville circa 1937." Instead, he labels it as "Entrepreneur Elmore Bolling in Haynesville circa 1937, a decade before he was murdered by whites for being too successful." The added clause chillingly connects the photograph to the title of the book: *Bloody Lowndes*.[31]

When possible, avoid inserting images into early drafts. Word processors are generally poor at handling them, and the insertion of images will swell the file size of your draft, which can get to be a problem if—as you should—you save versions at multiple stages of completion. Better to create a separate file with images, captions, and complete source information. If you use slideshow software, such as PowerPoint, to do this, you will then be prepared to create a presentation on short notice.

Think carefully before reproducing racist, sexist, or otherwise offensive images or depictions of atrocities. For some projects, such images provide crucial evidence to support analytical claims. Most

31. Hasan Kwame Jeffries, *Bloody Lowndes: Civil Rights and Black Power in Alabama's Black Belt* (New York: New York University Press, 2009), 32.

obviously, a study specifically about the evolution of racist imagery probably needs to reproduce such imagery to make its points most effectively.[32] In other cases, however, offensive imagery may be more tangential to the main story. "I see an awful lot of sexist ads," writes Mar Hicks. "And yeah, I have to talk about them, because they had a real effect. And sometimes I even have to show them. But I also have to do it responsibly. I don't play it for laughs or clicks."[33] If an offensive illustration is unnecessary, consider describing it, rather than reproducing it. Just as a good farmer will use only as much pesticide as they need to save the crop, so will a careful historian take care to use only as many offensive or stereotypical images and slurs as they need to tell their story and support their claims. If you are writing about intolerance or prejudice, you may need to fill a whole book with such material. If not, dispense the poison with an eyedropper.[34]

PUT NUMBERS IN CONTEXT

Numbers by themselves do not inform; it is the comparison of one number to the next that matters. Consider the way Daniel Walker Howe presents this finding: "According to one set of statistics, [President Andrew] Jackson removed 919 federal officials during his first year." So what? Howe continues: "this represented about 10 percent of all government employees." Ah, that sounds like a lot. But there is more: "It was more than all his predecessors had done in the previous forty years." By this point, I can understand why Jackson's actions shocked some Americans.[35]

Daniel Immerwahr notes that in 1940, nearly nineteen million people lived in US colonies. "Was that a lot?" he asks. "Not

---

32. See, e.g., Lewis Perry Curtis, *Apes and Angels: The Irishman in Victorian Caricature* (Washington, DC: Smithsonian Institution Press, 1971).

33. Mar Hicks (@histoftech), "I work on this period in history—the mid-20th century. And I see an awful lot of sexist ads. And yeah, I have to talk about them, because they had a real effect. And sometimes I even have to show them. But I also have to do it responsibly. I don't play it for laughs or clicks," Twitter, February 13, 2019, https://twitter.com/histoftech /status/1095617877917474823.

34. Susan A. Crane, "Choosing Not to Look: Representation, Repatriation, and Holocaust Atrocity Photography," *History and Theory* 47 (2008): 309–30.

35. Daniel Walker Howe, *What Hath God Wrought: The Transformation of America, 1815–1848* (New York: Oxford University Press, 2007), 333.

compared with the world-girdling British Empire, which boasted at the time a population of more than four hundred million (the great bulk of whom lived in India)." But he notes, "slightly more than one in eight (12.6 percent) of the people in the United States lived outside of the states. For perspective, consider that only about one in twelve was African American."[36] The implication is that if you think the African American experience is important to the history of the United States (and you should), you might think the same of the experience of Filipinos and others governed as colonial subjects.

Prices especially demand context; to say that something cost a dollar or a pound is, on its own, generally meaningless. For instance, the $13 million cost of the Tweed Courthouse in New York City may not surprise the twenty-first-century reader; an institutional building today is likely to cost several times that in nominal terms. Nor is it necessarily useful to try to convert a historical figure into "present-day values." Along with the problem that there are multiple, competing methods to do that, any present-day conversion will soon go out of date as your work ages.[37]

A much better tactic is to explain what else that same money could have bought in the period you are studying. To suggest how shockingly large the $13 million courthouse was in the early 1870s, David McCullough offers two comparisons: first, that the state legislature initially budgeted only $250,000; and second, that the final cost of the building was nearly twice what the United States had, a few years earlier, paid Russia for the territory of Alaska.[38] Conversely, Kate Brown tells us that in the 1950s, the Atomic Energy Commission budgeted only $200,000 for waste management at the Hanford plutonium plant. To suggest how *small* that number was, she compares it to the $1.5 million annual school budget for the workers' town of Richland, Washington.[39]

---

36. Daniel Immerwahr, *How to Hide an Empire: A Short History of the Greater United States* (New York: Vintage, 2019), 11.

37. David Hackett Fischer, *Historians' Fallacies* (New York: Harper Torchbooks, 1970), 44.

38. David McCullough, *The Great Bridge: The Epic Story of the Building of the Brooklyn Bridge* (New York: Simon & Schuster, 2012), 130.

39. Kate Brown, *Plutopia: Nuclear Families, Atomic Cities, and the Great Soviet and American Plutonium Disasters* (Oxford: Oxford University Press, 2013), 170.

A great resource for these kinds of comparisons is the website MeasuringWorth.com, founded by economic historians Lawrence Officer and Samuel Williamson, which offers various ways to contextualize prices in multiple currencies. For example, it is often useful to compare the price of a consumer good to the number of hours or days it would take an unskilled or skilled worker to earn that much. Thus, Hallie Lieberman tells us that in 1910, "the average cost of a vibrator was $16, not including special attachments." That figure means much more when she adds that "the average unskilled worker earned less than $2 per day in 1910," so that an electric vibrator would have consumed the earnings of eight days of hard work.[40] For larger investments, or to convert prices for a range of goods and services, it may be more useful to compare the cost to that of the economy responsible for the spending.[41]

Some numbers are ambiguous, and it is up to the historian to argue their meaning. Oscar Handlin gives the example of a hypothetical finding that 22 percent of the sons of unskilled laborers in Newburyport found occupations with higher status than their fathers. Depending on your prior expectations about social mobility, Handlin notes, "one could write *only* 22 percent or *fully* 22 percent with equal plausibility."[42]

SUMMARIZE DATA IN TABLES AND GRAPHS

Tables are good for displaying quantitative data, though it is generally worth asking if a graph could show the same information more clearly. For example, Christopher Wells came across a table that uses four columns and twelve rows of numbers to show differing levels of car ownership by income and place of residence. By presenting these data in a series of graphs, he makes it much easier for the reader to grasp the patterns.[43] For guidance on how to design

40. Hallie Lieberman, "Selling Sex Toys: Marketing and the Meaning of Vibrators in Early Twentieth-Century America," *Enterprise & Society* 17 (2016): 405.

41. Gregory T. Cushman, *Guano and the Opening of the Pacific World: A Global Ecological History* (New York: Cambridge University Press, 2013), xiv.

42. Oscar Handlin, *Truth in History* (Cambridge, MA: Harvard University Press, 1979), 13.

43. Christopher W. Wells, *Car Country: An Environmental History* (Seattle: University of Washington Press, 2013), 282.

a beautiful, data-rich graph, see Edward Tufte's classic, *The Visual Display of Quantitative Information.*[44]

Tables can also summarize qualitative information in a visually striking way. "The achievements of the consumer movement were extraordinary," writes Lizabeth Cohen. "With its accomplishments so taken for granted today, it is easy to forget just how impressive they were. In its heyday between 1967 and 1973, more than twenty-five major consumer and environmental regulatory laws passed, and hundreds remained under consideration." To drive the point home, she follows this passage with a table listing those regulatory laws, as well as related laws that strengthened government agencies responsible for consumer protection. The reader need not learn the details of the Fair Packaging and Labeling Act, the Flammable Fabrics Act, or the Magnuson-Moss Warranty Act; by devoting an entire page of her book to a list of such laws, Cohen impresses us with their number and range.[45]

Citation

Style manuals provide such detailed instructions for the *forms* of citation—where to put the parentheses, which titles get italics and which get quotation marks—that writers sometimes overlook the *function* of citation. In practice, historians cite sources for multiple reasons, and they divide the work between the main text and the notes. You need to consider why you are citing and devise an appropriate form that suits your needs.

WHY WE CITE

The first function of citation is to attribute a quotation or claim to a particular source, often a person. Historical research is like a courtroom trial, in which one witness after another tells what they know, or at least what they claim to know. Each account is incomplete, some may contradict others, and some will be more credible

---

44. Edward R. Tufte, *The Visual Display of Quantitative Information*, 2nd ed. (Cheshire, CT: Graphics Press, 2001).

45. Lizabeth Cohen, *A Consumers' Republic: The Politics of Mass Consumption in Postwar America* (New York: Vintage, 2003), 357–61.

than others. When it comes time for the jury to decide on the most plausible findings of fact, they will want to trace each fact back to a specific witness or witnesses. Since much of the work of history consists of weighing conflicting evidence in just this way, historians often attribute facts to witnesses directly in the main text. Take, for example, Edward Miller's account of the November 4, 1960, heckling of Lyndon and Lady Bird Johnson at Dallas's Adolphus Hotel, which cites a 1999 interview with Republican activist Joy Bell. "Bell's account of Lady Bird Johnson's demeanor during the episode differs strikingly from that in most histories," Miller writes. "Whereas the traditional narrative portrays her as shrinking behind her husband, interviews with Republicans who were present indicate a poised, resolute, and competitive woman."[46] Because he is challenging accepted understandings of this event, the attribution to Bell is too important to be left to the endnotes, though the reader will find more information there.

Other historians take a belt-and-suspenders approach, using both text and notes to match claim to the originator of that claim. Robert Post packs his history of drag racing, *High Performance*, with colorful quotations from drivers who had been interviewed by various enthusiast magazines. If he only cited the byline on the article, it might sound as though the reporter had made the statement. For clarity, then, Post credits both the driver and the reporter: "Gilmore, qtd in Fred M. H. Gregory, 'Is the Dragster Dead? Did the Funny Car Kill It?' *Car Craft*, March 1971, 16."[47]

The second function of citation is to establish the context in which a statement was made. Take, for instance, President Eisenhower's belief that segregationists were "not bad people. All they are concerned about is to see that their sweet little girls are not required to sit in school alongside some big, overgrown Negroes."[48] Had Eisenhower confined that thought to a private diary, historians might use it to explain his other actions, but they would not expect it to have influenced other people. Had he made this statement on

46. Edward H. Miller, *Nut Country: Right-Wing Dallas and the Birth of the Southern Strategy* (Chicago: University of Chicago Press, 2015), 87.

47. Robert C. Post, *High Performance: The Culture and Technology of Drag Racing, 1950–1990* (Baltimore: Johns Hopkins University Press, 1996), 365n59.

48. Earl Warren, *The Memoirs of Earl Warren* (Garden City, NY: Doubleday, 1977), 291.

national television, it would have shaped the rest of his presidency. In fact, Eisenhower made the comment privately to Chief Justice Earl Warren, shortly before the Supreme Court was to rule in the case of *Brown v. Board of Education*, and Warren resented the president's interference in a matter before the court. Because a simple footnote to Warren's memoirs will not make this clear, many historians who use the quotation take care to explain the circumstances of the conversation in their main text. Others go even further, pointing out that the statement did not become public until the publication of Warren's memoirs in 1977, years after both Warren and Eisenhower had died, a fact that furthers our understanding of how the statement did and did not shape Eisenhower's reputation.

The third job of citation, one often emphasized by style manuals, is to give researchers instructions on where to find the material cited, should they want to review it for themselves. Style manuals differ in their instructions for citations, and some cases require the scholar's judgment. For instance, *The Chicago Manual of Style* format for citations to newspaper articles does not require the name of the archive or library where one found the article. For major newspapers, which can be found in print, microfilm, or online in many places, that is no loss. But what if you are citing articles from the 1917 and 1918 editions of the *Mooseup Journal*, a newspaper so obscure it does not even appear in WorldCat? The answer, if you are a conscientious historian like Christopher Capozzola, is to write a footnote that includes precise instructions on where to find a run of the newspaper in the Connecticut State Archives.[49]

A fourth and final essential job of citation is to point the reader to other relevant scholarship. Scholars in other disciplines, notably the natural sciences, cite one another's work at much higher rates than do historians and other humanists.[50] This gives the cited scholars bragging rights when their work is evaluated by deans and granting agencies, but it clutters up the new work. By contrast, historians

49. Christopher Capozzola, *Uncle Sam Wants You: World War I and the Making of the Modern American Citizen* (New York: Oxford University Press, 2010), 226n47.

50. Patrick Dunleavy, "Poor Citation Practices Are Continuing to Harm the Humanities and Social Sciences," *Impact of Social Sciences* (blog), December 9, 2014, https://blogs.lse .ac.uk/impactofsocialsciences/2014/12/09/poor-citation-practices-humanities-and-social -sciences/.

tend to cite one another only when necessary. If, for example, I read a book that quite helpfully points me to a primary source, which I then consult directly, tradition requires me only to cite the primary source. This slims down what is likely an already long section of endnotes, but the author of that helpful book does not get a pat on the head.[51] Historians do seek to credit previous scholars for their ideas and arguments, and doing that work in the footnotes can leave a cleaner text for the reader more interested in the story.[52]

An optional fifth function of a footnote is to explain how a source supports a claim. I call this optional because in most cases this is the job of the main text; you do not want to force your reader into the footnotes or endnotes to follow your argument. However, every text is designed for multiple readers, and if you anticipate that some—but not most—will be intensely concerned with your evidence for a particular point, it may be best to explain your thinking in a "discursive footnote" that combines some of your own words with the formal citation. Political scientist Andrew Moravcsik wishes for "active citation," in which "scholars would be obliged to provide concrete evidence for controversial empirical claims, annotated to explain precisely how the source supports the textual claim."[53] That can be done, but it takes up a lot of space. For example, Camilla Townsend wrote notes so extensive (nearly a quarter of the length of the main text) that they constitute, in her words, "a parallel book."[54]

CITATION STYLES

Sadly, many footnotes fail at one or more of their tasks. For example, because historians care about *when* people wrote what they did, citation standards require footnotes to include the year in which a

51. Peter Charles Hoffer, "Reflections on Plagiarism, Part 1: A Guide for the Perplexed," *Perspectives on History*, February 2004.

52. For example, Jennifer Ritterhouse uses a footnote to explain how her use of the term "long civil rights era" compares to approaches by several other historians in *Discovering the South: One Man's Travels through a Changing America in the 1930s* (Chapel Hill: University of North Carolina Press, 2017), 297n24.

53. Andrew Moravcsik, "Active Citation: A Precondition for Replicable Qualitative Research," *PS: Political Science & Politics* 43 (2010): 29–35.

54. Camilla Townsend, *Malintzin's Choices: An Indian Woman in the Conquest of Mexico* (Albuquerque: University of New Mexico Press, 2006), 10.

document or book was first published, even if a scholar consulted a later edition. Many footnotes miss this, perhaps because authors rely too much on databases and citation software.[55] In other cases, the citation conventions can obscure sourcing. Most publishers want just one footnote per paragraph, to avoid cluttering the main text with note numbers. But if a paragraph is packed with claims based on multiple sources, this can leave the reader to guess which source supports which claim. For instance, Allen Steinberg asserts that the Weccacoe Hose Company, a volunteer fire company of the 1840s, was composed of Catholics, in a paragraph whose footnotes cite one primary source and four secondaries. Bad enough that I should have to spend the time to trace one of those sources; must I trace all five before concluding that Steinberg was mistaken on this minor point?[56] Even footnotes to single sentences can be hard to understand, since a single sentence can present multiple facts or claims.

This is an old problem. As far back as the 1690s, an intellectual complained of another writer who "piles up all his citations at the end of each article, without informing us that a particular author said one thing, and a second author another. He thus gives his reader a great deal of trouble: one must sometimes knock at five or six doors before finding someone with whom one may speak."[57] *The Bluebook: A Uniform System of Citation*—used in law reviews, legal briefs, and other legal writing—instructs writers to indicate the relationship between the claim in their text and the information to be found in the cited source, more precisely than do other forms of citation. If you want to ensure your reader can follow your claims back to the evidence, this practice is the way to do it.

Historians have also experimented with other formats. In 2003, William Thomas and Edward Ayers published "The Differences Slavery Made: A Close Analysis of Two American Communities" as an "electronic article," designed to be read on the screen rather

55. Zachary M. Schrag, "The Belmont Report Was Published in 1978, Goddammit!," *Institutional Review Blog*, June 4, 2016, http://www.institutionalreviewblog.com/2016/06/the-belmont-report-was-published-in.html.

56. Allen Steinberg, *The Transformation of Criminal Justice, Philadelphia, 1800–1880* (Chapel Hill: University of North Carolina Press, 1989), 146, 286n78.

57. Anthony Grafton, *The Footnote: A Curious History* (Cambridge, MA: Harvard University Press, 1999), 209.

than on the printed page. In lieu of traditional notes, Thomas and Ayers ended paragraphs with hyperlinks to the sources on which they relied. While this system allowed readers to compare the historians' claims to the sources far more easily than do traditional print forms, it did so at the expense of a great deal of additional labor. Moreover, the electronic article has proven harder to preserve; the "overview" that appeared in print and remains in the PDF versions of the *American Historical Review* points to a now-defunct URL.[58]

With luck, historians will continue to seek new forms of citation. Many university libraries have established institutional repositories for electronic materials that they will do their best to preserve far into the future. These can be great places for historians to deposit a more detailed set of references than their publisher can accept.[59]

Rhetorical Devices

Rhetorical devices, used carefully, can serve both storytelling and analysis, moving your reader through the story with gentle guidance rather than blunt force.

ACTIVE VERBS

Because history is the study of people and the choices they made, historians write as frequently as they can in the active voice, meaning that the subject of the sentence or clause performs the action, rather than being acted upon. By contrast, historians frown on the use of the passive voice, which often fails to explain who performed the action. "By the time the battle was over," goes one account, "100 to 120 Arabs had been killed, including women, children, and the

58. William G. Thomas and Edward L. Ayers, "An Overview: The Differences Slavery Made; A Close Analysis of Two American Communities," *American Historical Review* 108 (2003): 1299, referred readers to www.historycooperative.org/ahr/. As of 2020, that URL did not function, but a version of the article did remain online at http://www2.vcdh.virginia.edu/AHR/.

59. Zachary M. Schrag, "References for *The Great Society Subway: A History of the Washington Metro*," Mason Archival Repository Service, http://mars.gmu.edu/handle/1920/8729.

elderly." Hmm. Who killed them? Rewriting the sentence in the active voice could require identifying the killers.[60]

Yes, in some cases historians write clearly and vividly in the passive voice. Stephen Pyne, an apologist for the passive voice, offers a passage by Simon Schama, in which a crowd has seized the governor of the Bastille, the Marquis de Launay.

> His attributes of command—a sword and baton—were wrenched away from him and he was marched towards the Hotel de Ville through enormous crowds, all of whom were convinced he had been foiled in a diabolical plot to massacre the people. . . . More than once he was knocked down and badly beaten. Throughout the walk he was covered in abuse and spittle.[61]

The passive voice works here because Schama is using it to deliberate effect: telling the story from the point of view of de Launay. The marquis does not know who is wrenching, knocking, or spitting, so neither should the reader, and the confusion emphasizes the sudden powerlessness of a nobleman who, just hours before, had served as a royal official. Schama uses the passive voice to show de Launay's enforced *passivity*. It is a special case.

The key is moderation. One passive construction per paragraph is barely noticeable. But stringing together passive after passive after passive—to the point where the reader cannot find any actors—kills a story. Anthony Grafton credits his English teacher, Mr. Hyde, for his wisdom: "not that we should never use the passive voice, but never to do so without thinking."[62] And write your topic sentences in the active voice.

Pyne and others stand on firmer ground when they note that the passive voice is not the only offender. Indeed, historians need to avoid not only the passive voice but also other constructions that have the same effect. Existential phrases—those starting with "there was, there were," and so on—are technically not passive, but

---

60. Sami Adwan et al., *Side by Side: Parallel Histories of Israel-Palestine* (New York: New Press, 2012), 118. See also Geoffrey Wheatcroft, "Can They Ever Make a Deal?," *New York Review of Books*, April 5, 2012.

61. Schama, *Citizens*, 404–5, quoted in Stephen J. Pyne, *Style and Story: Literary Methods for Writing Nonfiction* (Tucson: University of Arizona Press, 2018), 72.

62. Noah Charney, "Anthony Grafton: How I Write," *Daily Beast*, July 17, 2013.

they fail to tell us who did what. And even active constructions relying on the verb "to be" tend to dull a story. Writers of scholarly history about intellectual debates engage readers by making their characters agree, argue, castigate, claim, debate, demonstrate, explain, lambaste, lament, misunderstand, proclaim, question, and rebut.[63] In a more narrative—but still scholarly—work, characters attack, endorse, fight, improvise, organize, raid, resist, seize, smuggle, strike, and vote.[64] Rather than fretting about the passive voice alone, try counting all the uses of "was" and "were" in your draft and dividing by the total word count. A ratio of one to eighty is good; one to one hundred is even better. A really strong storyteller can write whole pages without a single state-of-being verb.[65]

PEOPLE AS SUBJECTS

Too many sentences without people, or with nonhuman elements as their subjects, obscure history as severely as does overreliance on the passive voice. "Severe treatment was very common," states a Texas textbook. "Whippings, brandings, and even worse torture were all part of American slavery." Those are active-voice constructions (albeit with state-of-being verbs), but they do not tell us who whipped, who branded, who tortured.[66] What does it mean to write that capitalism led farmers to plant cash crops? Did capitalism take the form of onerous taxes that farmers had to pay in cash? Or of alluring consumer goods for which farmers eagerly sought cash? You can clear that up by stating that by writing about people and institutions, for example, the government imposed taxes, or shopkeepers demanded cash.[67] As E. P. Thompson reminds us, "we

---

63. Tai S. Edwards and Paul Kelton, "Germs, Genocides, and America's Indigenous Peoples," *Journal of American History* 107 (2020): 52–76.

64. Kornel Chang, "Independence without Liberation: Democratization as Decolonization Management in U.S.-Occupied Korea, 1945–1948," *Journal of American History* 107 (2020): 77–106.

65. Richard White, "The Writer's Studio with Richard White," *Modern American History*, April 15, 2020, 9.

66. Ellen Bresler Rockmore, "How Texas Teaches History," *New York Times*, October 21, 2015.

67. I thank Barbara Fields for insisting on this.

cannot have love without lovers, nor deference without squires and labourers."[68] So write about people and the choices they made.

METAPHORS

Always attuned to metaphors in the sources they analyze, historians sometimes deploy metaphors of their own. Perhaps most commonly, they compare one historical event to another. For instance, by titling her book *The War on Alcohol: Prohibition and the Rise of the American State*, Lisa McGirr implies a comparison to the "war on drugs" of the late twentieth century, which in turn uses a military metaphor for a law enforcement strategy.[69]

Occasionally, historians and social scientists try bolder metaphors and similes. Laurel Thatcher Ulrich asks us to imagine a 1780s community as "a breadth of checkered linen" woven from white and blue threads to create a pattern of white squares, dark blue squares, and lighter blue mixed squares. "Think of the white threads as women's activities, the blue as men's, then imagine the resulting social web. Clearly, some activities in an eighteenth-century town brought men and women together," Ulrich writes. "Others defined their separateness."[70] Sociologist Charles Tilly compares "participants in uprisings and local struggles" to "troupes of street musicians [who] drew their claim-making performances from standardized, limited repertoires," establishing a metaphor of performance that extends throughout his work on civil disorder.[71] And political scientist James C. Scott begins his critique of social engineering with what he calls "a parable": a discussion of a well-intentioned but misguided forestry scheme that produced short-term gains but long-term collapse.[72] For the rest of the book, he

68. E. P. Thompson, *The Making of the English Working Class* (1963; repr., New York: Pantheon, 1964), 9.

69. Lisa McGirr, *The War on Alcohol: Prohibition and the Rise of the American State* (New York: W. W. Norton, 2015).

70. Laurel Thatcher Ulrich, *A Midwife's Tale: The Life of Martha Ballard, Based on Her Diary, 1785–1812* (New York: Knopf, 1990).

71. Charles Tilly, *Contentious Performances* (New York: Cambridge University Press, 2008), xiii.

72. James C. Scott, *Seeing Like a State: How Certain Schemes to Improve the Human Condition Have Failed* (New Haven, CT: Yale University Press, 1999), 11–22.

suggests that human relations and processes are just as vulnerable to meddling by arrogant officials.

SIGNPOSTING

Historians use a few favorite words and phrases to draw attention to analytical claims, especially when they seek to challenge the reader's assumptions and alert them to what is new in their account. As a reader, watch for these words and phrases as signals that you should read passages with special care (for examples, see the italicized words in the following quotes). As a writer, use these expressions with equal care. They shout.

A closer look

To the purveyors of spirits, the Indians' consumption of alcohol appeared to support the Europeans' view of Native Americans as profligate and irrational. . . . A *closer look* at the ways in which the Cherokees incorporated alcohol into their tribal life, however, reveals a range of responses that suggest more than simple addiction.[73]

In fact

Most authors who have examined this incident have typically focused on the attack led by French communists, the political arm-twisting spurred on by local beverage companies, and/or parliament's exclusionary legislation aimed at Coca-Cola. . . . This article attempts to offer another perspective on the Coca-Cola affair to explain that the rejection by the French government was, *in fact*, based on underlying practical financial considerations.[74]

Rather

Despite its distant location, Alaska's largest city was not excluded from major postwar trends. *Rather*, many of the defining through lines of midcentury American history—mass migration, racial discrimination,

---

73. Izumi Ishii, *Bad Fruits of the Civilized Tree: Alcohol & the Sovereignty of the Cherokee Nation* (Lincoln: University of Nebraska Press, 2008), 13.

74. Laureen Kuo, "Another Perspective on the Coca-Cola Affair in Postwar France," *Enterprise & Society* 18 (2017): 110–11.

community formation, urban planning, and civic activism, to name a few—are present and comprise a dynamic story that until now has never been told.[75]

Reveal

Despite the limits of the archives, a regional assessment of the Spanish Caribbean during the first half of the seventeenth century *reveals* a new perspective on the English invasion. Asking not how the English succeeded in taking Jamaica but why the Spanish did not take it back *reveals* the fragmented and competitive nature of Spanish Caribbean territories as well as the ambivalent loyalties of the merchants and mariners who made their profits on the fringes of legal trade in the region.[76]

Yet

Medicare revolutionized U.S. health care. . . . *Yet* the desegregation of American hospitals is not often seen as an accomplishment of the civil rights movement, nor is Medicare often remembered as a civil rights initiative.[77]

Combinations

Historians frequently combine these expressions for extra punch. For example:

Wheatley, who is often portrayed as a lone genius, was *in fact* representative of an emerging African American antislavery critique of revolutionary republicanism. She saw herself as a member of an oppressed people *rather* than as just the pet slave of the Wheatley family or the exotic black poetess of the Atlantic world.[78]

---

75. Ian C. Hartman and David Reamer, "A 'Far North Dixie Land': Black Settlement, Discrimination, and Community in Urban Alaska," *Western Historical Quarterly* 51 (2020): 33.

76. Casey Schmitt, "Centering Spanish Jamaica: Regional Competition, Informal Trade, and the English Invasion, 1620–62," *William and Mary Quarterly* 76 (2019): 701.

77. Vanessa Burrows and Barbara Berney, "Creating Equal Health Opportunity: How the Medical Civil Rights Movement and the Johnson Administration Desegregated U.S. Hospitals," *Journal of American History* 105 (2019): 885, 886.

78. Manisha Sinha, *The Slave's Cause: A History of Abolition* (New Haven, CT: Yale University Press, 2016), 31.

QUESTIONS

Used in moderation, rhetorical questions are powerful tools for explaining the purpose of a work and its significance. As shown in chapter 13's list of exemplary thesis statements, explicit questions can powerfully explain the purpose of a work, the goal it seeks to achieve. "We have a puzzle," writes Ryan Smith. "Why, when Protestant and Roman Catholic relations were at their most troubled point in the nation's history, did denominations recast their church environments in the image of a longtime rival? Why, when the stakes seemed so high, did congregations suddenly risk placing such controversial symbols atop their own places of worship? One Presbyterian from Virginia asked simply, 'Why do we abuse the papists, and then imitate them?'"[79] With the aid of three question marks—one from a primary source—Smith has laid out his goals, explained the challenge of achieving them, and also shown that they mattered to the people of the nineteenth century.

FIRST PERSON

Historians tend to shy away from the first-person pronouns *I* and *we*. Helen Sword has found that only 40 percent of journal articles written by historians used these terms (far fewer than other fields), and that the *American Historical Review* was the only journal in her sample not to feature any first-person pronouns.[80] There is a good reason for this. In other disciplines, researchers need to insert themselves into their writing to give their drama a protagonist. "Here's a problem I faced," says the scientist in the spotlight, "and here's how I overcame it." Historians' research is often already full of compelling characters, so we serve the production best by letting them take center stage. Like puppeteers or a theater's tech crew, we dress in black to disappear into the background.

79. Ryan K. Smith, *Gothic Arches, Latin Crosses: Anti-Catholicism and American Church Designs in the Nineteenth Century* (Chapel Hill: University of North Carolina Press, 2011), 5.

80. Helen Sword, *Stylish Academic Writing* (Cambridge, MA: Harvard University Press, 2012), 39–40.

The most common exception comes when the historian wants to distinguish their work from previous accounts. "Usually we read about the *Monitor* as the story of a heroic inventor and revolutionary new warship," writes David Mindell. "I expand that story to include patrons, contractors, constructors, rivals, users, public imagery, and literary expressions."[81] This use of the first person reminds us that historical interpretation is a human activity, and it encourages us to think of Mindell's account as part of a larger conversation.

Less commonly, historians use the first person to describe their own experiences. For instance, Courtney Fullilove intersperses historical research on the collection and propagation of wheat and corn varieties with first-person "field notes" describing her own experiences of collecting seeds in the Middle East and the Caucasus. The device works in part because she uses it consistently, separating the first-person sections and placing them predictably at the end of each major part of her book.[82] It also works because Fullilove's research stories are unusually compelling, involving trips to exotic lands, not tedious hours in a library. Stories of library discoveries may be helpful for live conversations, when you are trying to interest an audience in your work. But they are less commonly worth displacing other material when you are trying to stick to a word count.

The first-person plural is especially fraught. If you are speaking of the American Revolution and assert that "we saw continued British rule as a threat to our liberty," who is "we"? Are you claiming a kinship with American rebels that you deny to American loyalists? Are you telling people of other nationalities that they should not read your work? It is generally better to speak of historical actors in the third person. Leave the first-person plural for polemics, as when Richard Rothstein uses "we" to emphasize his intended reader's place in the story, regardless of that reader's personal or family history. "*We* means all of us, the American

81. David A. Mindell, *War, Technology, and Experience aboard the USS Monitor* (Baltimore: Johns Hopkins University Press, 2000), ix.

82. Courtney Fullilove, *The Profit of the Earth: The Global Seeds of American Agriculture* (Chicago: University of Chicago Press, 2017).

community," he explains. "As American citizens, whatever routes we or our particular ancestors took to get to this point, we're all in this together now."[83]

Titles

The ideal title would achieve five goals:

- It indicates the topic of the work.
- It suggests the argument of the work.
- It piques the curiosity of a wide range of potential readers.
- It pleases the eye and ear.
- It requires just a few words.

It is impossible to do all five at once, and some titles manage to do none at all. Aim for two.

My least favorite titles are those that fail in the first goal: indicating a book's topic. Some titles are simply too vague. Rachel Hope Cleves, for instance, has noted that *Consuming Passions* is so generic that it has been used for several history books on varied topics, as well as works in archaeology and other fields.[84] Less extreme are titles that are deliberately imprecise in an effort to lure readers who may not care about the specific case study but would be interested in the overall theme. Some classic works of urban history, for instance, fail to indicate which city or cities the author has studied. While this choice indicates a claim to findings that apply beyond one case study, it can also hamper a reader who is seeking information about a specific place.

Dialectical titles

My favorite titles draw from the same dialectics that power strong historical arguments. Such titles emphasize argument and mystery, and often brevity as well, especially if the dialectic can be

---

83. Richard Rothstein, *The Color of Law: A Forgotten History of How Our Government Segregated America* (New York: Liveright, 2017), xvi.

84. Rachel Hope Cleves, (@RachelCleves) "What Is the Most Overused Title in Book History? I Want to Make a Pitch for 'Consuming Passions.' THERE ARE SO MANY BOOKS WITH THIS TITLE. WHY???" Twitter, January 17, 2020, https://twitter.com /RachelCleves/status/1214655249996242946.

expressed in just two contrasting words. Some dialectical titles are outright oxymoronic. The tension in Anne Rose's *Beloved Strangers* suggests the tensions of interfaith marriage. Carol Sheriff's *Artificial River* (about the Erie Canal) and Richard White's *Organic Machine* (about the Columbia River) both play, albeit in opposite directions, on the dual nature of waterways that people control— somewhat—with locks and dams. *Barbarian Virtues* poses a riddle: What virtues did Americans see in peoples they considered to be barbarians? *A Shopkeeper's Millennium* and *Suburban Warriors* both juxtapose a milquetoast beginning against a grandiose end. *Liberty's Exiles* contrasts positive and negative words to pose a riddle: Who would choose exile over liberty? Some titles signal a before-and-after dialectic: *Puritan to Yankee, From Front Porch to Back Seat*. Conversely, *In the Shadow of the Poorhouse* suggests the stagnation at the heart of the book.[85]

Quotation titles

Historians frequently pull short phrases from primary sources to use as titles of their works. For article and chapter titles, which need only be displayed horizontally, you can get away with a quotation of several words: "Somebody Done Nailed Us on the Cross."[86] Popular histories often feature chapter titles with evocative

85. Anne C. Rose, *Beloved Strangers: Interfaith Families in Nineteenth-Century America* (Cambridge, MA: Harvard University Press, 2001); Carol Sheriff, *The Artificial River: The Erie Canal and the Paradox of Progress, 1817–1862* (New York: Hill and Wang, 1997); Richard White, *The Organic Machine: The Remaking of the Columbia River* (New York: Macmillan, 1996); Matthew Frye Jacobson, *Barbarian Virtues: The United States Encounters Foreign Peoples at Home and Abroad, 1876–1917* (New York: Macmillan, 2001); Paul E. Johnson, *A Shopkeeper's Millennium* (New York: Hill & Wang, 1990); Lisa McGirr, *Suburban Warriors: The Origins of the New American Right* (Princeton, NJ: Princeton University Press, 2002); Maya Jasanoff, *Liberty's Exiles: American Loyalists in the Revolutionary World* (New York: Knopf, 2011); Richard L. Bushman, *From Puritan to Yankee: Character and the Social Order in Connecticut, 1690–1765* (Cambridge, MA: Harvard University Press, 1967); Beth L. Bailey, *From Front Porch to Back Seat: Courtship in Twentieth-Century America* (Baltimore: Johns Hopkins University Press, 1988); Michael B. Katz, *In the Shadow of the Poorhouse: A Social History of Welfare in America*, 2nd ed. (New York: Basic Books, 1996).

86. James C. Cobb, "'Somebody Done Nailed Us on the Cross': Federal Farm and Welfare Policy and the Civil Rights Movement in the Mississippi Delta," *Journal of American History* 77 (1990): 912–36.

quotations: "Go for the Swine with a Blithe Heart," "The Dead Salute the Gods," and "Jerry Is Counterattacking!"[87]

Book titles tend to be shorter, in order to fit on the spine of the book in letters large enough to be spotted as readers stroll through a bookstore or library, and to show up on book covers when they appear on websites and in catalogs. Thus, book titles borrowing from the Declaration of Independence use brief phrases, such as *Among the Powers of the Earth*, *The Opinions of Mankind*, *These Truths*, *Self-Evident Truths*, *Created Equal*, *Pursuits of Happiness*, and *Pursuing Happiness*, as well as the somewhat wordier *Our Lives, Our Fortunes and Our Sacred Honor*.[88] One caveat is that a good line is apt to have been used by someone else. In 1965, President Lyndon Johnson told the graduating students at Howard University that "freedom is not enough." Between 2005 and 2010, four historians published four different books, each titled *Freedom Is Not Enough*.[89]

Slogans can work well, provided they are not too long. *Free Soil, Free Labor, Free Men* and *Eight Hours for What We Will* say a lot in

87. Rick Atkinson, *An Army at Dawn: The War in North Africa, 1942–1943* (New York: Henry Holt, 2002).

88. Eliga H. Gould, *Among the Powers of the Earth* (Cambridge, MA: Harvard University Press, 2012); Richard Lentz and Karla K. Gower, *The Opinions of Mankind: Racial Issues, Press, and Propaganda in the Cold War* (Columbia: University of Missouri, 2011); Jill Lepore, *These Truths: A History of the United States* (New York: W. W. Norton, 2018); Richard D. Brown, *Self-Evident Truths: Contesting Equal Rights from the Revolution to the Civil War* (New Haven, CT: Yale University Press, 2017); Jacqueline Jones et al., *Created Equal: A Social and Political History of the United States to 1877* (New York: Longman, 2007); Jack P. Greene, *Pursuits of Happiness: The Social Development of Early Modern British Colonies and the Formation of American Culture* (Chapel Hill: University of North Carolina Press, 2004); Stanley Lebergott, *Pursuing Happiness: American Consumers in the Twentieth Century* (Princeton, NJ: Princeton University Press, 2014); Richard R. Beeman, *Our Lives, Our Fortunes and Our Sacred Honor: The Forging of American Independence, 1774–1776* (New York: Basic Books, 2013);

89. William S. Clayson, *Freedom Is Not Enough: The War on Poverty and the Civil Rights Movement in Texas* (Austin: University of Texas Press, 2010); Nancy MacLean, *Freedom Is Not Enough: The Opening of the American Workplace* (Cambridge, MA: Harvard University Press, 2008); James T. Patterson, *Freedom Is Not Enough: The Moynihan Report and America's Struggle over Black Family Life; From LBJ to Obama* (New York: Basic Books, 2010); Ronald W. Walters, *Freedom Is Not Enough: Black Voters, Black Candidates, and American Presidential Politics* (Lanham, MD: Rowman & Littlefield, 2005).

just six words.[90] Matthew Klingle's *Emerald City* takes its title from a 1982 marketing campaign for Seattle, though Klingle mercilessly notes that it can also refer to Frank Baum's "city built by conscript labor and ruled by a capricious Wizard."[91]

Some historians recycle titles from their primary sources. Sean Wilentz's 2018 book, *No Property in Man*, shares its title with an 1864 speech and pamphlet by Charles Sumner.[92] Lucy Salyer's *Laws Harsh as Tigers* comes from the title of a poem written by a Chinese immigrant on the walls of the Angel Island Immigration Station.[93] Suzanne Smith's *Dancing in the Street* and Jefferson Cowie's *Stayin' Alive* take their titles from songs analyzed in the text.[94] A variant is to slightly modify an existing title. Sarah Igo begins her book with a discussion of W. H. Auden's 1940 poem "Unknown Citizen," which she twists for her own title: *The Known Citizen*.[95]

Gerunds

Since history is the study of people and the choices they made, some historians emphasize those choices with gerunds. *Sorting Out the New South City, Electrifying America*, and *Selling Sounds* all tell us what people did. *Loving Nature, Fearing the State* tells us what they believed. Verbs of creation suit stories of technology: *Building New York's Sewers, Building the American Highway System, Inventing the Internet*. But they can also refer to the creation of ideas or institutions: *Inventing a Christian America, Creating the Corporate Soul, Becoming Mexican American*. To emphasize that

90. Eric Foner, *Free Soil, Free Labor, Free Men: The Ideology of the Republican Party before the Civil War* (New York: Oxford University Press, 1970); Roy Rosenzweig, *Eight Hours for What We Will: Workers and Leisure in an Industrial City, 1870–1920* (New York: Cambridge University Press, 1985).

91. Matthew Klingle, *Emerald City: An Environmental History of Seattle* (New Haven, CT: Yale University Press, 2009), 6–7.

92. Sean Wilentz, *No Property in Man: Slavery and Antislavery at the Nation's Founding* (Cambridge, MA: Harvard University Press, 2018), 266.

93. Lucy E. Salyer, *Laws Harsh as Tigers: Chinese Immigrants and the Shaping of Modern Immigration Law* (Chapel Hill: University of North Carolina Press, 1995).

94. Suzanne E. Smith, *Dancing in the Street: Motown and the Cultural Politics of Detroit* (Cambridge, MA: Harvard University Press, 1999); Jefferson R. Cowie, *Stayin' Alive: The 1970s and the Last Days of the Working Class* (New York: New Press, 2012).

95. Sarah E. Igo, *The Known Citizen: A History of Privacy in Modern America* (Cambridge, MA: Harvard University Press, 2018).

"bright tobacco" is a human creation, not simply a natural species, Barbara Hahn doubles her gerunds in the title and subtitle of *Making Tobacco Bright: Creating an American Commodity, 1617–1937*.[96]

Straightforward titles

A good title need not be overly clever. *The Horse in the City* is not a subtle title, but it will find readers who want to know about urban equines.[97] *The Myth of Southern Exceptionalism* is a wonderful title. You do not even need to take the book off the shelf to know its main argument.[98]

Subtitles

To find out what a book or article is really about, you often must read the subtitle. For example, "Somebody Done Nailed Us on the Cross" turns out to concern "Federal Farm and Welfare Policy and the Civil Rights Movement in the Mississippi Delta."[99] Thanks to that somewhat clunky subtitle, the article will appear in database searches for farm policy, welfare policy, civil rights, and the Mississippi Delta. Occasionally a historian will reverse the order, putting

96. Thomas W. Hanchett, *Sorting Out the New South City: Race, Class, and Urban Development in Charlotte, 1875–1975* (Chapel Hill: University of North Carolina Press, 1998); David E. Nye, *Electrifying America: Social Meanings of a New Technology, 1880–1940* (Cambridge, MA: MIT Press, 1992); David Suisman, *Selling Sounds: The Commercial Revolution in American Music* (Cambridge, MA: Harvard University Press, 2012); Brian Allen Drake, *Loving Nature, Fearing the State: Environmentalism and Antigovernment Politics before Reagan* (Seattle: University of Washington Press, 2013); Joanne Abel Goldman, *Building New York's Sewers: The Evolution of Mechanisms of Urban Development* (West Lafayette, IN: Purdue University Press, 1997); Bruce Edsall Seely, *Building the American Highway System: Engineers as Policy Makers* (Philadelphia: Temple University Press, 1987); Steven K. Green, *Inventing a Christian America: The Myth of the Religious Founding* (New York: Oxford University Press, 2015); Roland Marchand, *Creating the Corporate Soul: The Rise of Public Relations and Corporate Imagery in American Big Business* (Berkeley: University of California Press, 1998); George J. Sanchez, *Becoming Mexican American: Ethnicity, Culture, and Identity in Chicano Los Angeles, 1900–1945* (New York: Oxford University Press, 1995); Barbara M. Hahn, *Making Tobacco Bright: Creating an American Commodity, 1617–1937* (Baltimore: Johns Hopkins University Press, 2011).

97. Clay McShane and Joel Tarr, *The Horse in the City: Living Machines in the Nineteenth Century* (Baltimore: Johns Hopkins University Press, 2011).

98. Matthew D. Lassiter and Joseph Crespino, *The Myth of Southern Exceptionalism* (New York: Oxford University Press, 2009).

99. Cobb, "'Somebody Done Nailed Us on the Cross,'" 912–36.

the more specific information first. For instance, *War and Politics* would be a terrible title for a book on a relatively specific topic; no one would know what it was about. But it works as a subtitle for Kathryn Steen's *The American Synthetic Organic Chemicals Industry: War and Politics, 1910–1930*, signaling that readers who are interested in the politics of technology, or the military implications of industry, might find the book to be a useful case study.[100]

Revision

Serious writers write multiple drafts, and the more they revise, the more polished the final product. But revision takes time, and historians will often need to sacrifice polish in order to meet deadlines. A few strategies can help you make the most out of the time you have for revision.

PUTTING IT ASIDE

There is no substitute for writing a draft and then not looking at it for a while. It is hard to notice details that you see every day, whereas taking a break can help you see the draft as others will. David Herbert Donald would write two drafts of a work, then put them aside for a few weeks before trying a third draft. "I read it over, and often I say, 'Golly, how stupid I was to say this sort of thing,'" he told an interviewer, "and every now and then I'd say, 'Gee, I was pretty good on that paragraph.'"[101]

REVERSE OUTLINING

While outlines can be helpful guides as you gather your facts and ideas, they are equally valuable tools once you have written a first draft and want to check its coherence. Deriving an outline from an existing draft is a time-honored technique called "reverse

100. Kathryn Steen, *The American Synthetic Organic Chemicals Industry: War and Politics, 1910–1930* (Chapel Hill: University of North Carolina Press, 2014).

101. Judith Lee Hallock, John C. Waugh, and Drake Bush, *How Historians Work: Retelling the Past—From the Civil War to the Wider World* (Buffalo Gap, TX: State House Press, 2010), 271.

outlining": rather than starting with an outline and building into a text, starting with a completed text and crafting an outline from that.[102] One quick method of reverse outlining is to cut and paste all of your topic sentences into a separate document to see if they form a coherent narrative or argument. As noted in chapter 13 on organization, some historians write passages whose topic sentences can be strung together into a seamless summary of the longer passage. Transition words in topic sentences are particularly important. It is not enough to write a series of paragraphs, each containing insight about a particular event or sources. Words and phrases of agreement (similarly, furthermore), contrast (although, despite, however), causation (as a result, because of) tell your reader how the individual parts fit together.

If you can persuade a friend to reverse outline your draft, so much the better. You will see how well you communicated the major points. Less formally, you could ask a reader to explain your story and argument back to you.

AUDITING YOUR WORD BUDGET

Reverse outlines can also help you match your word budgets to the importance of each topic. Fiction writer Aaron Hamburger describes using reverse outlines to find the excess in his drafts. "While staring at my stories for what seemed like the hundredth time," he writes, "I decided to analyze them scene by scene, taking note of how many pages each one lasted, as well as how much of the piece was devoted to action and different characters. The math turned out to be inexorably honest. In some stories, I was embarrassed by how long I'd taken to set up my central conflict, as well as how little time I'd spent on some of the most crucial emotional moments. In other stories, I found that most of the scenes were roughly equal in length, and so cutting became as easy as an across-the-board budget cut."[103] The math is just as honest for nonfiction

102. Hardy Hoover, *Essentials for the Scientific and Technical Writer* (New York: John Wiley & Sons, 1970), 40.

103. Aaron Hamburger, "Outlining in Reverse," *Opinionator* (blog), January 21, 2013, https://opinionator.blogs.nytimes.com/2013/01/21/outlining-in-reverse/.

writing, including history. If you want your reader to pay attention to certain people, events, and themes, you need to give those people, events, and themes the most space and the most words.

WRITING FOR THE EAR

Read everything you write aloud—every word—or bribe someone into reading it to you. Rewrite anything that is hard to say or sounds repetitive. If you stumble over quotations, cut them and replace them with your own words, which are easier to declaim. "When read aloud," notes Richard White, "sentences that either lack that cadence or make no sense slap me in the face."[104]

Overlong sentences slap especially hard. I will not name names, but I once assigned a thoroughly researched and persuasive journal article whose insights, I thought, would benefit my students. Unfortunately, the author had filled the article with traps, such as a sentence—written, of course, in the passive voice—that included ninety-six words, nine commas, one set of parentheses, one unattributed quotation, and two separate footnotes. Perhaps unsurprisingly, few students read the article to the end. I suspect that had the author read the draft aloud at some point, she would have broken that beast, and others like it, into two or more sentences, making her thoughts easier to follow. The same logic demands that you check for overlong paragraphs. One hundred and twenty-five words, about five sentences, should usually suffice. If you go much longer than 250 words, have a reason.

CUTS

A work in progress is like a growing tree, sending branches in every direction that might have some sunlight. As your project matures, you need to trim some of those branches, leaving a strong central trunk that will support the weight of your main argument or narrative. Some trimming is a delight, as when you realize that rather than find an answer to the question that has been staring at you for months, you can instead delete the question. At other times,

---

104. White, "The Writer's Studio with Richard White," 2.

trimming is painful, as when a paragraph on which you labored turns out not to have a place in the final product.

"We do our research, we organize our findings, and then we engage in the ruthless editing that incorporates the relevant stack of evidence and tosses aside the rest," writes Joanne Meyerowitz, preferring a cinematic, rather than horticultural, metaphor. "Tangential themes, context, anecdotes, illustrations, and interpretive comments might not fit into the word limit, the wall space, or the fifty-minute lecture, and some of the most compelling bits gleaned from our sources might in the end stray too far from the points we hope to make. Whatever is lopped from the final product lands with a thud on the cutting room floor. It's a necessary part of the process, but for me at least, there's usually some regret."[105] If cutting your own creation is too painful, ask a friend to read the draft in search of opportunities to condense and cut. (Thanks, Steph.)

One of the glories of computers is that you never need destroy a passage that does not belong in a draft, but can instead easily move it out of the way, for the present. Switching metaphors yet again, these relocated passages can become the beginnings of future work. Writing of the "lovely paragraphs" that she had to cut from a draft, Mara Keire "keep[s] them in a file that I think of as my 'starter dough.'"[106] The process begins again.

105. Joanne Meyerowitz, "The Cutting Room Floor," *American Historian*, December 2019.

106. Mara Keire (@MaraKeire), "*whines* cutting some LOVELY paragraphs from my paper so I don't run way, way, WAY overtime," Twitter, May 30, 2019, https://twitter.com/MaraKeire/status/1134052028634816512; Mara Keire (@MaraKeire), "I Do. I Keep Them in a File That I Think of as My 'Starter Dough,'" Twitter, May 30, 2019, https://twitter.com/marakeire/status/1134229775025934336?s=12.

CHAPTER SIXTEEN

Publication

SINCE THE SIXTEENTH CENTURY, "publication" has meant the creation and distribution of a printed work. But there is an older meaning as well: the "action of making something publicly known."[1] Historians engage in publication in both senses of the word. Yes, they care deeply about typeset and printed versions of their findings: books and journal articles. But they are also broadly committed to making their findings publicly known in whatever format best suits the subject matter and the intended audience.

Often, historians publish parts of their work at several stages during a project for different reasons. Early in a project, they may seek feedback to guide future work. At a project's climax, they may publish an article or book, hoping it will endure as a polished record of their most important findings. Even then, the work of publication does not end, for they want to draw attention to the book. Similarly, historians create works in different formats for different audiences. They may target a journal article to fellow scholars, a book to general readers, and an op-ed to people who will not take the time to read the book but might benefit from a brief summary of its findings, then collaborate on a museum exhibit that retells the story using images and artifacts more than texts. All have their uses.

---

1. "Publication, n.," in *OED Online* (Oxford University Press).

Tips

- No historian is an island. Look for opportunities to work with others to test your ideas and strengthen your work.
- Peer review should be tough, fair, and encouraging.
- If you have a story to tell, tell it in more than one way.

Playing with Others

Relative to other disciplines, history is a fairly lonely pursuit. Single authorship is common, so historians can spend years working quietly on projects alone, without the constant teamwork that characterizes laboratory science or other disciplines where multiple authorship is the norm. Yet historians do work with other people, both fellow historians and outside their discipline.

Collaboration has many benefits. One is simple accuracy. As Alex Lichtenstein has argued, "All scholars make errors while conducting historical research. We mistranslate. We take poor notes in a hurry. We let working assumptions get in the way of clear-eyed knowledge. . . . But somewhere along the torturous road to publication—in a meeting with an advisor, in a dissertation defense, in a response to a conference paper, in a reader's report for a journal or for a publisher, even in a casual discussion with colleagues—another, more knowledgeable scholar usually catches these mistakes."[2] More frequently, while other scholars will not know the details of your project well enough to catch those mistakes, they can offer context and comparisons, or pose questions whose answers will make for a more compelling argument or story.

CONFERENCES

As your research progresses, it is worth keeping an eye out for conference calls for papers, since presenting at one of the conferences is an excellent way to get feedback on your work and build readers for it. Ultimately, you may be able to publish in a journal published by the association. Some scholars attend the same conference regularly

2. Alex Lichtenstein, "From the Editor's Desk: Outrages," *American Historical Review* 124 (October 2019): xv.

for years or decades, building a network of friends and colleagues from other institutions and cities. Others alternate among two or three conferences, gaining multiple perspectives on their topics. This is especially helpful if your work spans multiple subfields.

Historians around the world have developed a range of scholarly associations, and a historian's choice of affiliations can shape their scholarship for a project or throughout a career. Whether defined by geography (Southern Historical Association, Western History Association), chronology (Society for Historians of the Early American Republic), methodology (Oral History Association), subject matter (Business History Conference, Berkshire Conference on the History of Women), or some other attribute, each association creates a community of historians interested in a particular set of questions. (For a partial inventory, consult the American Historical Association's list of affiliated societies.)[3] Many of these associations are eager for new members and therefore welcoming to scholars just entering their field, at whatever stage of that scholar's career. Their annual conferences, smaller than the massive, multihotel meetings of the American Historical Association or the Organization of American Historians, can be easier venues to meet people. Student-only and local conferences can be particularly welcoming.

Large and even medium-sized conferences rarely offer opportunities for detailed feedback for a work in progress, though they may be places to meet people who will be willing to discuss a work at greater length after the conference. Small workshops, with a dozen or fewer papers, circulated in advance, can be more helpful, but they are harder to find.[4]

Any conference can be a good conference if it forces you to devote some time to your research and think about the key points. Whatever happens at the conference itself, if the deadline got you to fill in some gaps in a section of your work and to consider how to introduce the topic, you have gained something. If you meet and stay in touch with one or two people with strong shared interests, you have had a great conference.

3. "Affiliated Societies," American Historical Association, https://www.historians.org/about-aha-and-membership/affiliated-societies.

4. Linda Gordon, "The WRITER'S STUDIO with Linda Gordon," *Modern American History* 1 (March 2018): 125.

Conference formats vary, but the most common presentation format is the panel, composed of three or four presentations, followed by a comment by another scholar and questions from the audience. Scholars relentlessly mock this format, complaining of the one presenter who goes over their allotted time, and the audience members who offer comments rather than questions. (I myself fail to understand why so many people think a question is necessarily more valuable than a comment.) You can also find a great deal of advice about how to give a presentation, most of which boils down to a single instruction: rehearse your talk until you can give it in the number of minutes allotted to you, in as entertaining a fashion as possible.[5]

For purposes of a guide to historical research, it is worth emphasizing that a conference paper is a chance to get feedback on a work in progress. If you are trying to impress a potential employer or publisher, then present as polished and as seamless an argument as you can. But if you want feedback, consider posing questions to your listeners. "Does this claim persuade you?" you might ask. "Here's a perplexing primary source, or an incident. What should I make of it?" "Can you suggest other comparable stories that I should explore?" Even if you do not feel comfortable doing this in the public space of your panel, a conference should give you the chance to ask such questions of your fellow panelists before or during the conference, or during informal meetings in the hallways.

Attending conferences outside of one's discipline, or outside of academia altogether, can offer new leads and give you a sense of what questions readers might want answered, or at least new perspectives. While writing transportation history, I had wonderful encounters at the annual meetings of the Transportation Research Board, which brought together engineers, planners, and other practitioners. Even less friendly interactions can be valuable. Sarah Vogel, writing about the history of bisphenol A (BPA), was rudely interrupted by a BPA producer while presenting some of her findings. The experience, she later concluded, "helped to thicken my skin and strengthen my confidence."[6]

5. Paul N. Edwards, "How to Give an Academic Talk," n.d., http://pne.people.si.umich.edu/PDF/howtotalk.pdf.

6. Sarah A. Vogel, *Is It Safe? BPA and the Struggle to Define the Safety of Chemicals* (Berkeley: University of California Press, 2012), xx.

SOCIAL MEDIA

Scholarly conferences and journals emerged as the social media of the nineteenth century: devices that brought people together to share ideas and information, and to build relationships. Since the late twentieth century, electronic communication has supplemented these older forms. Both the tools and norms of scholarly electronic communication evolve rapidly, but some basic functions remain constant. Scholarly communication networks allow scholars to know what others are working on; to pose and answer questions; to learn about new publications, resources, and opportunities; and to make personal connections that can lead to conference panels and other forms of collaboration.

Over the years, various electronic media have come into and gone out of fashion. Prior to the popularization of the World Wide Web in the 1990s, email lists were the best tool for reaching large numbers of scholars. In the 2000s, many historians turned to blogs, whether solely authored or maintained by groups. In the 2010s, "history Twitter" increased in popularity. (I could not guess how many of the works cited in this book came to me through Twitter.) Each of these technologies has advantages and disadvantages. Choose a social media strategy that suits your larger goals.

Making connections

If you are already on a social media network, it can be relatively easy to add historians to that network. Because most Twitter users do not screen their subscribers, in a few minutes you can find and add dozens of historians to your feed, and Twitter will suggest the names of others. Just be warned that their scholarly insights can get lost amid a stream of academic nitpicking, political rants, and pictures of their pets. Worse still, some users respond to uncomfortable ideas by abusing online scholars.

Asking questions

Joining established online communities is the easiest way to become immersed in present debates, to learn about new publications and upcoming events, and to get answers to specific questions. In 1992, Richard Jensen—assisted by Wendy Plotkin and James

Mott—established H-Net, a network of email lists for historians.[7] With the popularization of blog and social media in the mid-2000s, H-Net declined in use.[8] But for the lists that are still active, it can be a great way to get a question to dozens or hundreds of specialists in your subfield.

Finding your voice

A blog post can be a happy ground in between the brief, ephemeral list message and the authoritative but ponderous journal article. Scholarly organizations, research libraries, historical societies, and simple groups of like-minded scholars host blogs on all manner of historical topics, and many welcome guest contributions. Joining a group blog with the commitment to post regularly is, of course, a greater commitment, and starting your own blog can be a greater commitment still: think hours per week. But while blogs are no substitute for peer-reviewed scholarship, they can definitely serve as a scholarly contribution, and are easily cited by others. And they may attract fewer abusive readers, thanks in part because an editorial team can delete abusive comments before they reach the writer.[9] (Unfortunately, any publication—even peer-reviewed scholarship— can inspire trolls to misogyny and other abuse.)[10]

Some historians post about their research as they go. Kenyon Zimmer posted short biographies of immigrant radicals deported by the United States during and after World War I. "If you have additional information about any of the deportees, or spot an error," he writes, "please contact me."[11] Somewhat similarly, while a graduate student at Stanford, Cameron Blevins posted the notes he took in preparation for comprehensive exams (as well as discussing his methods for preparation), a great service to others in the field.[12]

7. Richard Jensen, "Internet's Republic of Letters: H-Net for Scholars," September 3, 2000, https://web.archive.org/web/20000903084512/http://members.aol.com/danno1/whatis.html.

8. Robert B. Townsend, "Wither H-Net?," *Perspectives on History*, September 2007.

9. Jacqueline Antonovich, editor of *Nursing Clio*, correspondence with the author.

10. Emily Contois, "I Was Trolled—Here's Why I'm Turning It into a Teaching Opportunity," *Nursing Clio* (blog), July 17, 2018, https://nursingclio.org/2018/07/17/i-was-trolled -heres-why-im-turning-it-into-a-teaching-opportunity/.

11. Kenyon Zimmer, "Red Scare Deportees," *Kenyon Zimmer | Historian* (blog), http:// kenyonzimmer.com/red-scare-deportees/.

12. Cameron Blevins, "Surviving Quals, Part I: Laying the Groundwork," *Cameron Blevins* (blog), January 11, 2012, http://www.cameronblevins.org/posts/surviving

For about ten years, I maintained a blog about the regulation of human subjects research in the social sciences and humanities.[13] Every time I came across a new article, book, or other commentary, I would write up a brief summary and analysis, adding tags to mark key themes. After a few years, I could quickly compare any new material to earlier works on the topic and explain to myself and my readers the contribution of the latest work. When a journalist asked me questions, I found answers on the blog. When a journal asked me to a review a manuscript, I consulted the blog to see how the new paper compared to previous arguments. Eventually, I drew on my own blog posts for peer-reviewed articles and a book. I could have kept these notes private, but putting them online built my visibility in the field and allowed other scholars to cite my analysis.

Some historians use their Twitter accounts to address questions or misconceptions about their area of scholarship. "Online media sites like Twitter allow scholars to reach thousands of people they may never have reached in an accessible way," explains Waitman Beorn. "Academic engagement on Twitter has been called 'shallow scholarship,' but precisely the opposite is true; the very medium requires concision, structure and clarity. We are forced to address historical abuses directly, simply and publicly—not always our strong suit—but the form does not simplify the content or the message, only its delivery."[14]

COAUTHORSHIP

The ultimate form of working with others may be jointly producing scholarship. Collaboration is common in other disciplines, in public history, and in the creation of edited collections and textbooks. But it is rarer in the production of original articles and monographs.

To a degree, this is a lost opportunity. Every historian has their own set of skills and bases of knowledge, and many topics would benefit by having additional perspectives. Two or more historians

---

-quals-part-i-laying-the-groundwork/; Cameron Blevins, "Surviving Quals, Part II: The Grind," *Cameron Blevins* (blog), January 24, 2012, http://www.cameronblevins.org/posts/surviving-quals-part-ii-the-grind/.

13. Zachary Schrag, "Institutional Review Blog," http://www.institutionalreviewblog.com/.

14. Waitman Wade Beorn, "When Bad Actors Twist History, Historians Take to Twitter. That's a Good Thing," *Washington Post*, March 19, 2019.

with complementary expertise can tackle questions beyond their individual capacities. Collaboration with scholars in other fields can be even more rewarding. And working with someone enmeshed in another set of professional networks can expand your own. Coauthorship can be a relationship between peers, with scholars of complementary expertise contributing equally. Or it could be the work of a mentor—who has the needed concepts and questions but lacks time to execute the study—and a protégé who carries out the tasks and gets credit for learning on the job.[15]

Coauthorship involves potential pitfalls as well. You will need to adjust your research and writing schedule to fit another scholar's. You will need to exchange drafts and go through many rounds of writing and rewriting to get the work to sound like a coherent whole. You may feel that your coauthor is not lifting their end; indeed, and your coauthor may even agree, if they have been overwhelmed by life events. Scholars who have different ideas about the sanctity of deadlines, or different styles of communication, or different stakes in the eventual publication may not work well together. At the end of the process, you may feel you have done twice the work for half the credit.[16]

Scholars in disciplines where multiple authorship is more common have learned that it is best to negotiate authorship credit as early in the process as possible, and to manage expectations throughout. You need to agree on what you are trying to achieve with the work, and how much time and effort each of you is willing to invest. If one person cares a lot more about the project than the other, that person may feel they must complete it, even if that means doing more than their share.

Peer Review

Peer review takes two major forms: before and after publication. Prior to publication, a scholarly journal or press will seek the opinions of experts on a subject who can evaluate a work for its significance,

15. Bridget Maria Chesterton, "Historians Writing Collaboratively," *Perspectives on History*, October 2014.

16. Seth Denbo, "Whose Work Is It Really? Collaboration and the Question of Credit," *Perspectives on History*, February 2017.

quality of evidence, and persuasive arguments and interpretations, and offer suggestions for improvement. Journal reviews are often double anonymized: the reviewers do not know the name of the author, and the author does not learn the name of the reviewers. Book manuscripts are more often single anonymized: the reviewers are told the author's name, in part because they have often heard of the project before being asked to review it, so a double anonymized review would be mere pretense. If reviewers give a favorable review, they will frequently unmask themselves, either to be able to correspond directly with the author or to provide a bit of praise for the book cover and catalog.[17]

Post-publication review typically concerns major projects—books, exhibits, websites—rather than individual articles, though some articles get attention on scholarly blogs or in special sections of journals. These reviews typically bear the names of their authors and are written after it is too late for a work to be revised. In many, but by no means all, cases, this may lead a post-publication reviewer to write more gently than a manuscript reviewer.

TOUGH, FAIR, AND ENCOURAGING

While historical research and writing often involves long stretches in the company of dead people, their ultimate aim is communicating with the living. That interaction takes many forms in many stages of a project. It can be as informal as chatting with a friend or as formal as negotiating with a publisher. It can take place at the beginning of a project, during its development, and long after its publication. If you pick an important topic and tackle it well, the interaction can continue long after your own death, as future scholars grapple with your ideas and findings. If you do not find that exciting, perhaps you are not a historian.

You cannot control how future generations react to your work, but in your lifetime you have some power to shape the feedback you receive. By inviting comment in the early stage of a project, and by taking to heart the suggestions you receive, you can send the best

17.   STM Working Group on Peer Review Taxonomy, "A Standard Taxonomy for Peer Review," Version 2.0, September 29, 2020, https://osf.io/aynr5/.

version on to the next stage. There is a reason historians write such long acknowledgments sections in their books; the best works have passed through many hands.

John Staudenmaier, the longtime editor of *Technology and Culture*, asked his reviewers for comments that were tough, fair, and encouraging. I would extend that to feedback at every stage of a project, before and after publication, though perhaps tough feedback is more welcome early on, when there is still time to fix the problem. Receiving such feedback may not be pleasant, but the strongest historians are those who can hear their work criticized, acknowledge its faults, and go back to write another, better draft.

The kind of feedback you get depends greatly on your circumstances. Students are guaranteed one reader—the instructor—and possibly others, if they are in a seminar that requires peer editing, or writing a dissertation for approval by a committee. Some scholars have the resources to fly people in for a workshop on their manuscript, or social or professional connections with people willing to read drafts. Others get feedback by presenting at conferences, submitting to scholarly journals, engaging on social media, or by relying on coworkers, friends, and family members who stepped in at one point or another to read a draft or listen to a practice talk. Sometimes a really devoted friend will read an entire book manuscript, but in many cases you will get quicker and more useful advice if you break your requests down into manageable tasks. If you want comments on the structure of a story or an argument, consider asking someone to read an outline or proposal instead of an entire project.

MANUSCRIPT AND BOOK REVIEWS

Some writers expect gentle, nurturing comments like the ones they received as students. This is a mistake. The instructor's duty is to the student, and that often means pointing out just the most pressing concerns, so that the student improves without being overwhelmed. By contrast, the reviewer's duty is to the reader of the journal or the press. That can mean seizing on a manuscript's best insights and calling for the author to amplify them, or begging the editor to rush the manuscript into print so that the world will learn from it. But it can also mean pointing out every flaw in the manuscript, even if that results in the manuscript's rejection, or a demand for changes so overwhelming that the author abandons the effort. In other words, if I received a student seminar paper with eighteen significant problems, I would focus on the three most pressing issues, whose resolution would help the student grow. If I were to read the same paper as a reviewer, I would list all eighteen problems and ask that they be addressed before publication.

Thus, while there is no reason for a peer reviewer to be mean or insulting, the reviewer may have a duty to be a good bit blunter than teachers, colleagues, or friends would be. Not all manuscripts are worthy of publication, and a good reviewer will be clear enough to let the editor make that decision. A great reviewer—and I have had them— will persuade the *author* that they would be better off if their deeply flawed manuscript never got the chance to embarrass its creator.

I have two suggestions for writing blunt comments that, I hope, allow authors to accept them more readily. First, I aim not to comment about the author, whether or not I know who it is. My comments concern the work, not the person behind it. (There are exceptions, as when a press asks for a review of a book proposal and wants to know the author's reputation for doing good work.) Of course, this is precisely the opposite of the way I normally write history, in which I try to write about people and not documents. But in a peer review, gentleness may be more important than precision. Second, whenever possible, I frame my comments as questions. One could write, "this argument is incoherent!" Or one could make the same point by noting, "the manuscript makes claim x on page 8 but seems to say the opposite on page 27. Which is it?" The latter version respects the author by presuming they will be able to iron out the inconsistency, while still flagging the problem for the editor. As Barbara Young Welke has noted of the late Peggy Pascoe's grace as a manuscript reviewer, specifics amplify both praise and criticism. A good reviewer will explain as precisely as possible what is good about a manuscript and what needs work, empowering the author and editor to decide whether to invest the effort in getting the manuscript into shape.[18]

18. Barbara Young Welke, "The Art of Manuscript Reviewing: Learning from the Example of Peggy Pascoe," *Perspectives on History*, September 2011.

Editors can serve as mediators between reviewers and authors, helping authors to prioritize the comments, or even saying which they can safely ignore. The first time I received reviewer's comments on a journal submission, I was alarmed by one reviewer's suggestion of a school of theory I would need to master before proceeding. Fortunately, before I went too far, I encountered Staudenmaier at a conference. "Did *I* tell you to read that theory?" he asked. He had not told me to read it, and, to this day, I have not.

While pre-publication peer review takes place out of sight, book reviews are a form of peer review as well. One important difference is that the book reviewer is writing to a reader who—unlike the book editor—may know little or nothing about the events described in the book, so book reviews tend to devote considerable space to summarizing a book's story, rather than analyzing its approach. A second important difference is that book reviews usually come out too late for the author to fix any problems, and often when the author is seeking a new job or promotion. Reviewers therefore tend to be relatively gentle in their criticism, perhaps highlighting a few spots that could have used more attention. Experienced scholars learn to read reviews with care, seeking the real critique underneath the boilerplate praise.

Whether you are reviewing a work before or after publication, you can ask the same basic questions about its value. Obviously, the editor wants a factually accurate work, so keep an eye out for factual mistakes, however minor. Beyond that, the editor will appreciate your assessing a work's significance. Reviewers often pose the same questions about scope discussed earlier in chapter 4 on research design. Consider, for instance, the historian's choices about agency, sources, periodization, scope, and causality, as well as explicit engagement with previous scholarship.

The fairest reviews take a project on its own terms. If the project claims to include new actors in the story, ask how well it does that. If it boasts of deploying new sources, or changing periodization, or challenging existing interpretations, assess it on those terms. This need not be the only approach to a work. Perhaps the historian succeeded in their goal of presenting a story from the point of view of one group, but you can make the case that they should have offered additional points of view. But start, at least, by judging how well the historian achieved what they set out to achieve.

Print

Historians present a great deal of their work as printed texts, and for good reason. As a medium that takes readers from the beginning to the end of a text, print echoes history's flow across time. And as a medium that—if printed on decent paper—can last for centuries, print honors historians' wish that our cultures retain their memories over the long term. Scholarly historians especially value three print formats: articles, chapters, and books.

JOURNAL ARTICLES

In many disciplines—from biology to economics to law—peer-reviewed journal articles are the basic unit of disseminating scholarship. As a group, historians emphasize books, and some prolific writers rarely publish in journals. But for many historians, whether or not they also write books, the journal article is a useful tool for several reasons.

Some projects simply work best as articles. True, a great many journal articles are spin-offs from longer books or dissertations, but not all are. Undergraduates and master of arts students may be able to publish student work that would not be long enough for another format. Historians of any level of experience may want to try out a topic with an article-length work before committing to a book-length project.

Submitting to a journal often brings valuable feedback from two or more experts in one's field. And if your article is accepted and published, it will be instantly distributed to every library that subscribes, though of course this number will vary depending on the journal. In the old days, journals offered authors the chance to purchase reprints of their articles to send to friends and colleagues. These days, authors are more likely to send PDFs to interested readers who lack a subscription.

Choosing a journal is a delicate task. Journals generally ask that you not submit a manuscript to more than one journal at a time, then can take many months to give you a decision. The more prestigious the journal, the lower your chance of acceptance and the longer it may be for your article to appear, but the greater the reward at the end. I suggest reading your own footnotes and seeing which journal's articles have influenced you the most. Chances are, the editors and reviewers of that journal will be the most interested in your work.

Journal publication has its downside as well. Reviewers can be notoriously slow to read manuscripts, which gets compounded when the slowest of several reviewers determines the pace, and when the journal asks for revisions to be sent back to the reviewers. It is bad enough when it takes half a year to get acceptance; worse still to wait half a year for rejection.

BOOK CHAPTERS

Anthologies or edited volumes assemble chapters by multiple authors around a single theme. If done right, such collections can address a historical problem in greater breadth and depth than could a work by a single author. One of my favorites is *The Myth of Southern Exceptionalism*, edited by Matthew Lassiter and Joseph Crespino, with contributions by those scholars and eleven other experts in Southern, African American, and political history.[19] Some such works emerge from conferences, which offer the opportunity to exchange drafts and views with scholars whose research interests most closely align with your own. One downside of such volumes is that if a potential reader wants just one chapter, they may find it harder to find (or assign to a class) than they would had that chapter been published in a journal. As more anthologies appear both in print and in electronic databases, which allow individual chapters to be downloaded, this is something less of a concern.

BOOKS

While other disciplines emphasize journal articles as the key unit of scholarly productivity, historians cling to books. Even when historians publish in journals, they often do so as an intermediate stage on the way to the next book, adapting their articles into book chapters.

Books come in a variety of flavors, granting historians more flexibility than a single word—book—can convey. Historians distinguish

19. Matthew D. Lassiter and Joseph Crespino, eds., *The Myth of Southern Exceptionalism* (New York: Oxford University Press, 2009).

between *monographs* (specialized works based on research in primary sources) and *syntheses*, more sweeping accounts that must rely on others' scholarship. Some history books run less than two hundred pages, while others run more than eight hundred. University presses put their manuscripts through peer review, both by expert outside reviewers and by a permanent faculty board. Trade presses do not, but their editors may be able to devote more time to crafting the prose.

Regardless of these differences, all books try to explore a topic thoroughly enough to make a sustained impression on the reader and a lasting impact in our collective knowledge. As one 2010 report found, "the book continues to be the mainstay of historical publication because it allows the exposition and presentation of a solid, sustained, and closely reasoned argument that can endure into the future."[20] Paula Findlen argues that books aren't everything; "what matters is the ability to shape an important body of historical writing in whatever form it takes." Yet she acknowledges the importance of the book as a format. "A really good monograph does something that no other kind of publication does—it creates a sustained and synthetic portrait of a whole written in a single voice, allowing us to examine and learn from an author's research in gradated stages that take us through a satisfyingly interconnected portrait of a historical subject."[21] I would add that aside from the intellectual value of the format, writing a book can be deeply satisfying at a personal and symbolic level. As journals become primarily patterns on a screen, the book remains a physical object, with height and width and depth and texture and heft. And your name on the spine.

Public Engagement

Despite slurs that they have retreated from the public, historians regularly author newspaper and magazine articles, speak to reporters, maintain blogs, contribute to museum exhibits, give public

20. Diane Harley et al., "Assessing the Future Landscape of Scholarly Communication: An Exploration of Faculty Values and Needs in Seven Disciplines" (Berkeley, CA: Center for Studies in Higher Education, 2010), 396.

21. Paula Findlen, "What Counts: On Books, Articles, and Productivity," *Perspectives on History*, September 2013.

lectures, and otherwise share their findings beyond the classroom and the peer-reviewed journal. Few if any academic disciplines match their level of public engagement.[22] Some historians devote whole careers to public history, while others only occasionally emerge from their specialized studies to comment on matters of public interest. In some cases, a public appearance can lead curious listeners to the more scholarly version of one's work. More commonly, the goal is to get one's main findings across, simplifying and shortening but not distorting them.

WEBSITES AND SOCIAL MEDIA

In an age when reading increasingly means staring at a screen, historians seek ways to translate their work for the computer. Even before the introduction of the graphical browser in the 1990s, historians were seeking ways to take advantage of digital media—such as CD-ROMs—to combine text with images, sounds, and hyperlinks, forming stories and arguments beyond the confines of ink and paper. As bandwidth rose to allow a wider range of media, they turned to the World Wide Web.[23]

Websites offer important advantages over traditional print forms. They can feature color images, moving images, sound, interactive features, and masses of data, difficult or impossible to include in a print format. They can disseminate information more rapidly than can print scholarship; my colleague Lincoln Mullen's website, America's Public Bible, was reviewed in the *Journal of American History* well before it was even officially launched.[24] And if websites are open to all, they can attract thousands or even millions of

22. Max Boot, "Americans' Ignorance of History Is a National Scandal," *Washington Post*, February 21, 2019. On the day Max Boot published this rant against disengaged historians in the *Washington Post*, I conducted searches of *Washington Post* mentions of various disciplines in the previous sixty days. The *Post* had mentioned historians 304 times, compared to 87 for political scientists, 38 for sociologists, 17 for anthropologists, and 12 for criminologists. Economists earned 450 mentions.

23. Edward L. Ayers, "A New and Familiar Form of Scholarship," *William and Mary Quarterly* 76 (2019): 4–8.

24. James P. Byrd, "America's Public Bible: Biblical Quotations in U.S. Newspapers," *Journal of American History* 104 (2018): 1097–98.

visitors, compared to the hundreds of readers who might encounter a scholarly journal article or book. Sites and blogs can feature users' comments, sometimes attracting participants in historical events or people with special expertise on a topic. My own personal website of the late 1990s gained the notice of some participants in the planning of the Washington Metro, who then contacted me and helped me greatly in my research.

But everything in life involves trade-offs. A visitor's "hit" on a website may be a computer connection unseen by human eyes, or the click of an actual person who has no intention of reading what you have said. According to Blogger, my *Institutional Review Blog* attracted more than 600,000 page views, orders of magnitude over the number of people who have read my book on the history of institutional review boards. But it is the book—not the blog—that has been cited by scholars and government officials, and more readers of the book than of the blog have written to me and attended my talks. I cannot prove it, but I am confident that the book has had a much greater impact than the blog.

And it will likely last longer, for web-based scholarship has so far proven disappointingly fragile. In March 2000, scholarly organizations and presses joined forces to create the History Cooperative, an online publishing platform.[25] The site included not only scholarship that appeared in traditional print journals but also innovative digital works that, while officially published in prestigious journals, would only appear in digital form.[26] A mere ten years later, the History Cooperative closed down, taking with it the online-only content.[27] Historians and librarians are working on digital preservation strategies, and my university library has a PDF version of my blog that it will try to maintain in perpetuity. Still, scholarship on paper may outlast its digital counterpart by centuries.

25. Robert B. Townsend, "History Cooperative Continues to Grow," *Perspectives on History*, September 2002.

26. "Historicizing the City of Angels," *American Historical Review* 105 (2000): 1667.

27. Jennifer Howard, "'Journal of American History' Moves to Oxford U. Press; History Cooperative Winds Down," *Chronicle of Higher Education Blogs: PageView*, May 4, 2010, https://www.chronicle.com/blogs/pageview/journal-of-american-history-moves-to-oxford -u-press-history-cooperative-winds-down/23719.

MUSEUMS AND HISTORIC SITES

Museums and historic sites not only attract visitors who might never open a scholarly text, but they also make greater impressions than texts alone. As a professional historian, I imagine I am on the far end of the spectrum in my appreciation of textual accounts, yet some of the most meaningful experiences I have had with the past have come through visiting history museums; historic homes; former concentration camps, factories, and railyards; and other sites of memory.

These sites all make claims about the past, so it is important for scholars to help shape those messages in ways that reflect the latest understanding of events. For the most part this is the work of the public historians who staff museums and sites, producing both original scholarship and translating the work of other scholars into exhibits and tours. In addition, some historians not formally affiliated with a public history institution play important supporting roles in both establishing such institutions and shaping the messages they convey. For instance, the National Park Service spent decades carefully tending and interpreting the battlefields of the Civil War without making any comparable effort to tell the story of the Reconstruction era that followed. Thanks in part to the advocacy and scholarship of historians of the period and of the region, in 2017 President Obama established the Reconstruction Era National Monument (since redesignated as the Reconstruction Era National Historical Park) in South Carolina in order to tell the story of "the Nation's Second Founding."[28]

PRESS APPEARANCES AND OP-EDS

Speaking to reporters is a great way to get one's message out. Even in an era of dwindling newspaper readership, a single newspaper article is likely to reach many times the number of readers as

28. Gregory P. Downs and Kate Masur, "The Perfect Spot for a Reckoning with Reconstruction," *Washington Post*, October 7, 2016; Jennifer Whitmer Taylor and Page Putnam Miller, "Reconstructing Memory: The Attempt to Designate Beaufort, South Carolina, the National Park Service's First Reconstruction Unit," *Journal of the Civil War Era* 7 (2017): 39–66; Barack Obama, "Presidential Proclamation—Reconstruction Era National Historical Park," US National Park Service, January 13, 2017, https://www.nps.gov/reer/learn/proclamation.htm.

a typical scholarly work. Obviously, historians should decline to speak beyond their knowledge, but they should seize chances to answer what reporters' questions they can.

Back in the twentieth and early twenty-first centuries, authors were lucky to get a spot on one of a small number of radio interview shows. Having seen sales of my first book spike on Amazon after I appeared on *The Kojo Nnamdi Show*, I can attest that radio listeners are great readers too. In recent years, such interviewing has become democratized with the spread of podcasts, including several devoted especially to spreading the findings of historical research. Some, such as *BackStory*, are major productions. Others are just a graduate student with a USB microphone. But the format is the same, and an hour-long interview is a chance for you to present your thesis and tell a few stories. If you sell some books, so much the better.

To prepare for interviews, I suggest readying a list of talking points: key facts and claims that you hope to convey before the interview is over. In many cases, you can anticipate the questions you will be asked, especially if you have some preliminary contact with the interviewer beforehand. Or, a journalist may end an interview by asking what questions they should have asked, or simply inviting you to present any information that was not covered. If you begin an interview knowing the top points you wish to make, chances are you will find the opportunity to make them. That said, if an interviewer surprises you with a good question you had not anticipated, try to answer rather than relying on your prepared responses.

Historians have the most control when, rather than appearing in a journalist's story, they write their own magazine articles or newspaper op-eds. This may come more naturally to those who study relatively recent controversies (such as housing or immigration) that are still ongoing. But even less obvious timely topics can inform op-eds. For instance, in 2017 historians Brian Rosenwald, Nicole Hemmer, and Kathryn Cramer Brownell launched the "Made by History" section of the *Washington Post* website, promising "historical analyses to situate the events making headlines in their larger historical context."[29]

29. Brian Rosenwald and Nicole Hemmer, "Welcome to Made by History," *Washington Post*, June 26, 2017, https://www.washingtonpost.com/news/made-by-history/wp/2017/06/26/welcome-to-made-by-history/.

Some contributors offer specific advice to politicians and policy makers, but others offer more general commentary on matters of culture, science, religion, and other current affairs.

LAW AND POLICY

In addition to speaking truth to power via the press, some historians get opportunities to speak directly to legislators or courts, by testifying as experts or contributing to amicus briefs. Along with other scholars, historians express some frustration with the way their work is used, misused, or ignored by courts and policy makers.[30] As Arthur Ray has explained, "the judicial and scholarly communities employ history very differently. Scholars do not provide finality to historical interpretation. . . . Courts, on the other hand, use history to bury the past rather than to continually revisit it." Or, in the words of one Canadian justice, "litigating parties cannot await the possibility of a stable academic consensus."[31] Indeed, major court cases can get nasty, with historians on rival sides accusing each other of unethical behavior.[32] Less adversarial forums pose their own challenges. Truth and reconciliation commissions, unlike lawsuits, are designed to bring parties together, but they too can tempt historians to warp their findings into a narrative that serves a desired goal.[33] And even forums that try to provide only historical background to an issue can suffer if the surrounding politics become too rancorous.[34] Not everyone wants to know the past.

30. Tomiko Brown-Nagin, Linda Gordon, and Kenneth Mack, "Historians in Court: A Roundtable," *American Historian*, November 2017.

31. Arthur J. Ray, *Telling It to the Judge: Taking Native History to Court* (Montreal: McGill-Queen's Press, 2011), 152.

32. Katherine Jellison, "History in the Courtroom: The Sears Case in Perspective," *Public Historian* 9 (1987): 9–19; Jon Wiener, "Cancer, Chemicals and History," *Nation*, January 20, 2005.

33. Elazar Barkan, "Introduction: Historians and Historical Reconciliation," *American Historical Review* 114 (2009): 899–913.

34. Marian J. Barber, "Congressional Briefings Series to Be Revived," *Perspectives on History*, April 2012.

GRAPHIC HISTORY, MOVIES,
AND BROADWAY MUSICALS

Historical findings need not be confined to formats as stuffy as an op-ed or amicus briefs. Historians have collaborated with comics artists to produce graphic histories, the best of which are based on careful research with primary sources.[35] Laurent Dubois collaborated with Mary Caton Lingold, a doctoral candidate in English, and composer David K. Garner to make recordings based on a 1707 transcription of music by enslaved musicians in Jamaica.[36] Peter Jones used a 1948 lab report in the National Archives to recreate Senate Beer, once the sponsor of the Washington Senators baseball team.[37]

For the historian who truly wishes to shape public understanding of the past, the jackpot is mass media. Noting that Ken Burns's television documentaries have reached hundreds of millions of viewers, David Harlan writes that "his images, his particular way of seeing the past, have become part of the very texture of American cultural life. It is almost impossible for most Americans to think about the Civil War, for instance, or the history of baseball, without some refraction through the images Ken Burns has given us. . . . If we academic historians want our discipline to survive and flourish in the new media-saturated world in which we find ourselves, we will have to come to terms with Ken Burns and the kind of history he is producing."[38] This message has penetrated as far down as the middle school level, as National History Day contestants make short documentaries using some of Burns's techniques.

Feature films have an even greater impact. As Sam Wineburg— an expert on the teaching of history—has noted, quibbling about

35. Joshua Brown, review of *Battle Lines: A Graphic History of the Civil War* by Ari Kelman and Jonathan Fetter-Vorm, *American Historical Review* 123 (December 2018): 1599–1600.

36. Eric Ferreri, "A Clickable Tour of Caribbean Musical History," *Duke Today*, June 30, 2016, https://today.duke.edu/2016/06/musicalpassage.

37. Daniella Byck, "You Can Take a Sip of History, Thanks to These Local Beer Revivals," *Washingtonian* (blog), December 5, 2019, https://www.washingtonian.com/2019/12/05/you-can-take-a-sip-of-history-thanks-to-these-local-beer-revivals/.

38. David Harlan, "Ken Burns and the Coming Crisis of Academic History," *Rethinking History* 7 (June 2003): 169–70.

the content of textbooks can seem silly when "the influence of movies greatly overshadow[s] anything written in school textbooks on young people's understanding of the past."[39] Since the 1970s, historians have developed a substantial literature on movie studios' treatment of the past, and they are often willing to cut filmmakers some slack about details if the resulting film offers some larger truths about the past and, better still, awakens viewers' curiosity.[40] Unfortunately, screenwriters and producers can be reluctant to consult with historians. And even when producers seek historians' input on a script, those historians may be left dismayed by the simplifications of the final product.[41]

Some collaborations are so improbable that there is no way to plan for them. When, in 1998, Joanne Freeman defended her dissertation at the University of Virginia, she could not have imagined that seventeen years later, some of her findings would appear in the Broadway smash hit *Hamilton: An American Musical*, or that she herself would become recognizable to strangers by speaking about Hamilton on television.[42] "I heard the song titled '10 Duel Commandments,'" she recalls of her first time seeing the musical. "As it went on, I heard words from a document that I had discovered at the New-York Historical Society in the bottom of a box, and I realized the song was based on that document—and more broadly, on the chapter of my book about the Burr-Hamilton duel. I loved that

39. Sam Wineburg (@samwineburg), "Back in 2007, we found that the influence of movies greatly overshadowed anything written in school textbooks on young people's understanding of the past," Twitter, January 13, 2020, https://twitter.com/samwineburg/status/1216834700381020160.

40. Robert A. Rosenstone, ed., *Revisioning History: Film and the Construction of a New Past* (Princeton, NJ: Princeton University Press, 1995); Robert Brent Toplin and Jason Eudy, "The Historian Encounters Film: A Historiography," *OAH Magazine of History* 16 (2002): 7–12; Robert Brent Toplin, *Reel History: In Defense of Hollywood* (Lawrence: University Press of Kansas, 2002).

41. Elizabeth D. Leonard, review of *The Conspirator* by Robert Redford, *Civil War History* 58 (2012): 97–99.

42. Lauren Berg, "Historian, a UVa Alumna, Took Her Shot to Shape 'Hamilton,'" *Daily Progress*, February 18, 2017, https://www.dailyprogress.com/archives/historian-a-uva-alumna-took-her-shot-to-shape-hamilton/article_e83fb73f-0089-5520-ba84-413421c19e32.html; Joanne Barrie Freeman, "Affairs of Honor: Political Combat and Political Character in the Early Republic," PhD diss., University of Virginia, 1998.

I had something to do with the play!"[43] Few historians will have that particular experience, but any historian may. History has its eyes on you.

Letting Go

In the 1994 film *Il Postino*, a poetry-loving mail carrier copies a poem by the great Chilean poet Pablo Neruda to impress a young woman. When Neruda scolds him, the mail carrier replies, "Poetry doesn't belong to those who write it; it belongs to those who need it."[44] While I cannot endorse plagiarism, I do believe that history belongs to those who need it, and that a good work will diffuse beyond its creator's control.

Some people will misunderstand your work, some will misuse it, and many will ignore it. You yourself will probably find flaws in the work, long after it is possible to correct them. But every competent work of history is a contribution to that infinite fandom: the shared human experience.

History is for everyone.

43. Bess Connolly, "In Conversation: Joanne Freeman on Alexander Hamilton the Man and 'Hamilton' the Musical," *YaleNews*, August 11, 2016, https://news.yale.edu/2016/08/11/conversation-joanne-freeman-alexander-hamilton-man-and-hamilton-musical.

44. Michael Radford and Massimo Troisi, *Il Postino*, Cecchi Gori Group Tiger Cinematografica, Penta Film, Esterno Mediterraneo Film, 1994.

ACKNOWLEDGMENTS

FOR THE PAST quarter century I have had the honor of teaching history at Columbia University, George Washington University, Baruch College, and my longtime intellectual home, George Mason University. I am deeply grateful to every student who has worked with me to understand people and the choices they made, and I hope this book captures some of the curiosity and dedication they brought to their projects. I wrote it for them, and for all who will follow them.

I am particularly grateful to the doctoral students whose journeys taught me so much about the research process: Bill Andrews, Lindsey Bestebreurtje, Alan Brody, Justin Broubalow, Alan Capps, Ray Clark, Roger Connor, Peter Jones, Eric Gonzaba, Richard Hardesty, Mary Linhart, Jordan Patty, Jerry Prout, Gwen White, and Andrew Yarrow. Thanks also to Kelley Fincher, Jane Limprecht, Beth Wolny, and other students of my courses on research methods and writing narrative history. Teaching that last course allowed me to work with master craftsman Scott Berg, whose insights I have tried to capture in chapter 14 on storytelling. I am also grateful to everyone who sent feedback to my website, HistoryProfessor.Org, over the years.

As a teacher and researcher, I try to live up to the high standards set by my own teachers, especially Sue Ikenberry, Helen Kimmelfield, John Stilgoe, Judith Vichniac, Elizabeth Blackmar, Alan Brinkley, Howard Gillette, Ron Grele, Owen Gutfreund, Kenneth Jackson, and Herbert Sloan.

My distinguished colleagues in the George Mason University Department of History and Art History are always generous with their time and insight. I especially appreciate the help I received on this project from Joan Bristol, Benedict Carton, Michael Chang, Joe Genetin-Pilawa, Jane Hooper, Sam Huneke, Matt Karush, Cynthia Kierner, Meredith Lair, Alison Landsberg, Sam Lebovic, Abby Mullen, Lincoln Mullen, Jessica Otis, Sun-Young Park, Brian Platt, Jennifer Ritterhouse, Suzanne Smith, Peter Stearns, and Rosemarie Zagarri. I continue to draw inspiration from the life and work of the late Roy Rosenzweig. Librarian George Oberle and archivists Lynn

Eaton and Brittney Falter helped me understand research from the other side of the desk. Beyond Mason, I am grateful for suggestions and stories from Will Bachman, Christopher Capozzola, Victoria Cain, Matthew Gilmore, Sarah Jo Peterson, Rob Townsend, and Ian Watson, as well as all the historians on Twitter, whose feeds led me to many of the readings cited here. Five anonymous readers for Princeton University Press offered detailed, tough, fair, and encouraging comments in the highest tradition of peer review. Matt Avery, Natalie Baan, David Campbell, Alena Chekanov, Dayna Hagewood, Dimitri Karetnikov, Cathryn Slovensky, Kathryn Stevens, and Erin Suydam helped bring out the best in the book. My department generously funded the excellent index by Steven Moore.

I am blessed with a family that knows the value of a good question and has supported me in my seeking answers: Will Adler, Elizabeth Alexander, Judy Bickart, Thomas Emberg, Bob Fenichel, Lisa Lerman, Sam Lerman, Shoshana Lerman, David Schrag, Eleanor Schrag, Kristina Schrag, Philip Schrag, Sarah Schrag, Eve Tushnet, Mark Tushnet, and Erin Walter-Lerman. In 2020 I learned that if I am going to be confined during a global pandemic, I want to be trapped with my favorite people in the world: Leonard Schrag, Nora Schrag, and my muse, Rebecca Tushnet.

Finally, this book would not exist but for the imagination and encouragement of its editor, Peter Dougherty, who first conceived of the project and has been a constantly supportive collaborator at every stage of its creation. I hope the final product does justice to his vision.

INDEX

Acharya, Anurag, 176
acknowledgments, 201, 244; to previous
    scholarship, 94–95, 286, 287–88,
    357–58. *See also* historiography
Adams, Cecil, 44
Adams, Henry, 22, 41, 84
Adams, John Quincy, 41
Adams, Oscar, 324
Adas, Michael, 134
Adler, Mortimer, 276
agency, 12–13, 92, 388
Allen, William Sheridan, 128
All in the Family, 166–67
American Historical Association, 24, 26,
    69, 193, 252, 379
Anbinder, Tyler, 168
Anderson, Benedict, 94
Andrews, Thomas, 69, 149
Angélique, Marie-Joseph, 1
Anishanslin, Zara, 167
archives, 22–23, 52, 88, 99, 137, 184,
    186–207, 221; protocols in, 196–201,
    232, 260
Aristotle, 65
audio recordings, 165–66
Austen, Jane, 147
Aviña, Alexander, 41–42, 191
Aydin, Cemil, 89
Ayers, Edward, 88, 359–60

Bachin, Robin, 89, 92
Bailey, Thomas, 34–35
Bailyn, Bernard, 49, 60–61
Baker, Ellen, 146
Baldwin, Peter, 328
Ballard, Martha, 122, 211
Balzac, Honoré de, 147
Baptist, Edward, 339–40, 347
Barnes, Julian, 331
Bass, Gary, 17
Beard, Charles, 9, 20–21, 27
Belew, Kathleen, 110, 343

Bell, Roger, 292
Benison, Saul, 107
Benton-Cohen, Katherine, 211–12, 218
Berg, Scott, 274, 337
bibliographies, 173–74; databases for,
    178–79
Bird, Kai, 326
Black, Joel, 289–90
Blackhawk, Ned, 42
Blackmar, Betsy, 279
Black Panther Party, 294–98
Blassingame, John, 116
Blevins, Cameron, 382
Bloch, Marc, 9, 10, 28, 76
Block, Sharon, 152
Blount, Keith, 235
Boas, Franz, 211–12
Bonsall, Samuel, 158
book reviews, 388; sources for, 178–79
Boyle, Kevin, 336, 349
Bram, Christopher, 327
Brandt, Allan, 12
Bridenbaugh, Carl, 43–44
Brinkley, Alan, 218–19
Brooks, Lisa, 81–82, 149–50
Brown, Jacob, 219
Brown, Joshua, 163
Brown, Kate, 88–89, 291, 353
Brownell, Kathryn Cramer, 395
Browning, Christopher, 122, 299
buildings and places, research value of,
    169–71
Burke, Peter, 320
Burnett, L. D., 239
Burns, Jennifer, 188
Burns, Ken, 397
Burns, William, 314

Cahill, Cathleen, 217
Campbell, Joseph, 223
Canaday, Margot, 68
Cannon, John, 208–9

A NOTE ON THE TYPE

THIS BOOK has been composed in Miller, a Scotch Roman typeface designed by Matthew Carter and first released by Font Bureau in 1997. It resembles Monticello, the typeface developed for The Papers of Thomas Jefferson in the 1940s by C. H. Griffith and P. J. Conkwright and reinterpreted in digital form by Carter in 2003.

Pleasant Jefferson ("P. J.") Conkwright (1905–1986) was Typographer at Princeton University Press from 1939 to 1970. He was an acclaimed book designer and AIGA Medalist.

The ornament used throughout this book was designed by Pierre Simon Fournier (1712–1768) and was a favorite of Conkwright's, used in his design of the *Princeton University Library Chronicle*.